THE UNIVERSITY OF WINCHESTER

THE MEIJI UNIFICATION
THROUGH THE LENS OF
ISHIKAWA PREFECTURE

JAMES C. BAXTER

Published by COUNCIL ON EAST ASIAN STUDIES, HARVARD
UNIVERSITY, and distributed by HARVARD UNIVERSITY PRESS,
Cambridge (Massachusetts) and London   1994

The Council on East Asian Studies at Harvard University publishes a monograph series and, through the Fairbank Center for East Asian Research and the Reischauer Institute of Japanese Studies, administers research projects designed to further scholarly understanding of China, Japan, Korea, Vietnam, Inner Asia, and adjacent areas.

                    Library of Congress Cataloging-in-Publication Data

    Baxter, James C.
       The Meiji unification through the lens of Ishikawa prefecture /
    James C. Baxter.
           p.   cm.—(Harvard East Asian monographs ; 165)
       Includes bibliographical references and index.
       ISBN 0-674-56466-9
       1. Ishikawa-ken (Japan)—History.   I. Title.   II. Series.
    DS894.59.I838B39   1995
    952.1′54—dc20
                                                        94-38297
                                                          CIP

For my mother

and

in memory of my father

Contents

x   *Contents*

Tables

Figures

Acknowledgments

A decade in the banking industry has enhanced my understanding of debt. For me, the occasion of publication presents an opportunity to begin to repay some of the obligations I have incurred over the many years since I undertook this study. I realize that I am very fortunate to have this chance.

First among my intellectual obligees is Albert M. Craig. He gave patient, perspicacious guidance and unfailing kind encouragement, and provided a model of precise thinking and scrupulous handling of historical evidence, throughout the period when I was struggling to find this topic and compose the dissertation from which this book is descended. The late Edwin O. Reischauer helped make it possible for me to go to Kanazawa the first time, read the drafts and final version of my dissertation, and plied me with more sage advice and well targeted criticism than I could ever manage to absorb. Donald H. Shively was generous with his learning and his time, equipping me with highly serviceable bibliographic tools and pushing me to keep them sharp. Gen Itasaka raised the rewards of language acquisition far above the ordinary level with his wide-ranging, learned discussions in classes and individual tutorial sessions, and he assisted me with many problems particular to the study of Kaga and Kanazawa. Ezra F. Vogel took an interest in my progress and pressed me forward with applications of what he once aptly called his *ai no muchi,* or "affectionate whip" (purely a figure of speech in this instance), and was a constant exemplar of almost superhuman energy.

Takazawa Yūichi was a sympathetic and wise supervisor when I was very green indeed as a historian in training at the University of Kanazawa. His colleagues in the Faculty of Law and Letters, Hashimoto Tetsuya and Kobayashi Akira, shared some of their knowledge and research results with me, and permitted me to audit lectures to undergraduates. Nakano Setsuko extended invaluable aid in matters both academic and non-academic during my days in Kanazawa. In her case, especially, my debt can never be repaid. Kobayashi Akio, then a graduate student in history, led me in my first sustained attacks on the thickets of epistolary style Japanese *(sōrōbun)* and hand-written documents. The late Inoue Toshio, a noted scholar of the pre-modern peasant uprisings *(ikkō ikki)* in the Hokuriku region and an eminent presence in the history department when I was in Kanazawa, expressed an avuncular—and I suspected slightly amused—curiosity about what I was doing.

While a visiting scholar at Harvard in 1974–1975, Hiramatsu Yoshirō spent many hours reading laws on Meiji local government institutions with me, directed me to sources in legal history that I might otherwise never have found, and taught me much about the historical background. Tanaka Akira gave an illuminating series of talks on Meiji history to a group of graduate students at Harvard the next year, and asked hard questions and offered good advice to me. Kumakura Isao, in memorable evenings with a few enthusiasts in a classroom at 2 Divinity Avenue in Cambridge nearly twenty years ago, improved my now long-neglected skill at writing characters with a brush, and in the course of that taught me useful things about reading documents.

Gary D. Allinson, in 1982, did me the great favor of giving a close reading to an earlier draft of the whole manuscript of this work. If I had incorporated all his good counsel, this book would no doubt be superior to the product actually in hand, but I am better off for having tried to follow at least a few of his suggestions. M. William Steele passed along reassuring expressions of interest over two decades, beginning in conversations during our graduate student days about the events and the context that are treated in the first five chapters, and in the summer of 1992 he critiqued the next-to-last version of Chapter Six for me. Terry E. MacDougall shared some of his deep knowledge of local politics and local government when I was still working on the dissertation, and again later when we were writing related entries for the Kodansha *Encyclopedia of Japan*. James W. White and Wm. Myles Fletcher, III, lent their discerning eyes to the first draft of Chapter One, in January 1982.

This study began with digging and sifting in Kanazawa supported by a doctoral dissertation research grant from The Japan-United States Educational Commission (Fulbright Program) in 1972 and 1973. To Executive Director Natsuo Shumuta, Program Officer (later Executive Director) Caroline A. Matano Yang, Toyoko Yamaguchi, and their associates, my deeply felt thanks should be reiterated.

I have foraged in many libraries, and simply cannot do an adequate accounting of all my debts to librarians who have assisted me, but I would be egregiously remiss if I did not acknowledge the help of three, Toshiyuki Aoki of the Japanese Acquisitions and Reference Department of the Harvard-Yenching Library, Joyce Wong Kroll, formerly of the University of Virginia Library, and Key Kobayashi of the Library of Congress. I also thank Hirahata Terayasu of the Tokyo Institute for Municipal Research, for facilitating my access to the special collection of that institution.

Mitani Taichirô made time for an interview, and gave some valuable suggestions of things to read, in 1979. He set up my appointment as a visiting research scholar in the Faculty of Law of the University of Tokyo, then went off to spend a term in England, leaving me in the capable hands of Saitô Makoto, who was a gracious host. My stay in Tokyo in the academic year 1979–1980 was made possible by a grant from The Japan Foundation, and although it was not my primary purpose under that fellowship to work on the Meiji unification, inevitably, because this book was then work in process, some of my reading during that year is reflected here. I owe thanks also to The Japan Foundation for this reason.

Grants from the East Asian Research Center (now the Fairbank Center for East Asian Research) and the University of Virginia supported research during summer months in the early and middle 1970s.

Katherine Keenum, Executive Editor of the Council on East Asian Studies Publications, revived the thought of publishing this work when it had nearly been forgotten, and lent a practiced hand to the editorial process. Jay Boggis accepted the challenge of editing a manuscript replete with transliterated names and terms, and helped me tighten it up. His was no mean task for someone trained in English history who does not know Japanese, and I appreciate his assistance.

During the last stage of preparation of the manuscript, David Sensabaugh of Columbia University and Haynie Lowrey Wheeler of The Yale-

China Association were a great help to me, obtaining books and periodicals that I needed to see from the libraries at Columbia and Yale and diverting me with tales of experiences in China and Tibet.

Many friends provided shelter, sustenance, good fellowship, and good advice at various times while I was doing research. Their contributions to this work were direct and meaningful, and I could not have finished without them. I especially want Ruth Arnon Hanham, Harry Hanham, Maureen Strain Steinbruner, John Steinbruner, Martin Collcutt, Akiko Collcutt, Fowler W. Martin, Galen Fox, Carol Munnecke Fox, Don Farmer, Jane Moran Farmer, Charles N. Goldberg, and Julie Joyce Goldberg to know that they have my abiding gratitude.

Elaine Duling Baxter has given me all that one could possibly ask for of a best friend or a spouse, and I am lucky to claim her in both capacities. I have been extremely fortunate also in having parents, Jessie Catherine Apple Baxter and the late Roscoe H. Baxter, who always encouraged me to grow and to learn new things, even when that resulted in my going far away or making choices that they would not have made. I am aware that I have imposed on all of them, and that from time to time I have caused at least minor hardship with my moves and my shift from teaching to banking. I can never thank Elaine or my mother and father enough.

For the errors that remain in this book, I am to blame. The good people named above tried to save me from mistakes, and sometimes to nudge me along a different path. I confess I did not always listen as carefully as I should have or apprehend everything I was being told. Now I can only hope that my blunders are compensated for by worthwhile text surrounding them.

The Meiji Unification

Introduction

This book examines the process of nation-building in nineteenth-century Japan by describing the structure and operation of subnational entities and assessing their contributions to the making of the Meiji state. The focus is mostly on one important domain, Kaga, and on the prefecture that succeeded it, Ishikawa. Looking at policy and policymakers in Kaga from 1822 to 1871, we see that there were strong local institutions and a mentality that might well have inhibited the formation of a centralized Japan. Looking at the new system and the men who took part in it from 1871 to 1888, we observe that identification with, and integration into, a modern state occurred rapidly and rather smoothly in Ishikawa, as in most of the rest of Japan, despite separatist traditions and feelings of loyalty to the old local lords. We see also that the making of a nationally unified state was not a one-way, top-down affair, as it has often been characterized. Central-government policy makers and bureaucrats were, to be sure, the ones who shaped institutions and drew up the organization chart for subnational government. The creation of a new state in Japan required more than could be achieved by a few men in the capital, however. The political process demanded the efforts of citizens all over the nation, and many Japanese responded by working sedulously to help build a unified state.

Critics of late-nineteenth- and early-twentieth-century Japan have argued that the primary means by which the leaders obtained people's cooperation was simple coercion. Here we will see that something besides coercion was at work. The Meiji state was certainly no democracy, but it won active cooperation and voluntary compliance of people who had acquired a new sense of national identity that transcended old localisms. The case of Kaga and Ishikawa illustrates usefully how cooperation and compliance supplemented coercion, as Japan bridged the gap from fragmented polity to integrated state.

Late in 1867 and early in 1868, cataclysmic events in Japan ended over two and a half centuries of dominance by military governors (shogun) of the Tokugawa clan. On 1867/12/9 (January 3, 1868, by the Western calendar), a group of political revolutionaries proclaimed the return of ruling power to the emperor. For centuries the position of emperor had been nearly devoid of political content, but fifteen-year-old Mutsuhito embodied what was most distinctive about the island country. As the 122nd member of his family to occupy the Japanese throne, Mutsuhito stood as a symbol of the Japanese nation. The coup of January 1868 was not intended to hand actual leadership over to this youth whose reign was to be called the era of Meiji, "Enlightened Rule." Real power would be exercised by those who had engineered the overthrow of the Tokugawa. The changes in government and society that they brought about are known to history as the Meiji Restoration.

At the time they seized power, the top figures in the Restoration regime lacked a clear-cut program by which to govern. Once faced with the responsibilities of meeting the manifold domestic and foreign challenges that confronted them, the men close to the young emperor quickly realized that the model of the Tokugawa system was inadequate.

Under the Tokugawa, the shogunate *(bakufu)* and the domains *(han)* had shared power, and although its measure of power was superior, the shogunate could not directly enforce its will in the semi-autonomous domains. Financially and in their administrative and military organizations, the *han* were independent of the Tokugawa *bakufu*. Especially in the decade and a half after Perry forced open the doors of Japan, many domains manifested concern for managing their own affairs unfettered by shogunate interference, an attitude called "localism" *(kakkyo shugi)* by some historians, "a tendency to become independent" *(jiritsuka no keikō)* by others.[1] At the same time, some domains were advocating new arrangements for national policy formation that would include participation by daimyo along with elements of the court and the shogunate,[2] an alteration that would have strengthened the importance of the domains.

The desires of the *han* to pursue their own interests did not disappear overnight after the proclamation of the restoration of imperial rule. In the tenth month of 1868, Kido Takayoshi commented on this to a fellow Chōshū samurai in a letter that has become famous. "With this type of thought in which all the *han* want to elevate their own mountains higher [than the others]," Kido lamented, "it is extremely doubtful that 'unification of our imperial nation' [can be achieved]." He illustrated by drawing a picture of several mountains thrusting up alongside each other in random fashion, some high, some low. In order to stand up to the powerful nations of the world, he continued, what was needed was one edifice of state power, with the court at the apex and the core, and the *han* all fitting tightly together into the same structure. To represent his then-unrealized ideal, Kido sketched a single mountain.[3]

Other leaders of the newly formed Meiji government also saw the need to bring all of Japan under a single effective structure of control. They were determined to avert what historian John W. Hall has described as a "realistic alternative" for their time, "national disintegration, terror perhaps, or some sort of traditionalist reaction."[4]

The Meiji leaders followed what Kido in retrospect described as a two-stage plan.[5] First, early in 1869, Kido, Ōkubo Toshimichi, Itagaki Taisuke, and a few other samurai members of the new government managed to persuade the lords of the domains of Satsuma, Chōshū, Tosa, and Hizen to offer to return the registers of their territories and people to the emperor. On 6/17 of that year, the court proclaimed that it would accept the return of the *han* registers from all domains. The government on the same day named the former daimyo as chief executives of the *han*. Legally from this time the authority of the *han* governors (*chihanji*) derived from their appointment by the emperor, rather than from hereditary right, although by naming the former daimyo, the Tokyo government clearly meant to diminish the effect of the return of the *han* registers.

The second stage in the Kido plan was the elimination of the remaining vestiges of the Tokugawa system. On 1871/7/14, the government decreed the abolition of *han* and the creation of prefectures (*haihan chiken*). As the imperial rescript ordering this change explained:

> If We desire . . . to give protection and tranquility to the people at home and abroad to maintain equality with foreign nations, words must be made to mean in reality what they claim to signify, and the government of the country must center in a single authority. Some time ago

We gave our sanction to the scheme by which all the domains restored to Us their registers; We appointed *han* governors for the first time, each to perform the duties of his office. But owing to the lengthened endurance of the old system during several hundred years, there have been cases where the word only was pronounced and the reality not performed. . . . We now completely abolish the *han* and convert them into prefectures, with the object of diligently retrenching expenditure and of arriving at convenience of working, of getting rid of the unreality of names and abolishing the disease of government proceeding from multiform centers.[6]

In the rescript that George Sansom labeled "one of the most laconic announcements of a revolution ever made," the government thus acknowledged that it had not been able to control the many separate *han* administrations.[7]

In one of its most important dimensions, the problem was bureaucratic. Having inherited rather sophisticated, functionally differentiated administrative apparatuses from the domains, how could the new regime integrate these into a single effective bureaucracy? One of the most obvious steps was changing the personnel in the system. Along with the rescript abolishing the *han* went an order for the former daimyo to move to Tokyo. As the top officers of the prefectures, the Tokyo government appointed new governors, in most cases men from places outside their new jurisdictions.[8] The actuality of the government was thus brought in line with the principle adopted two years before—except in the case of the imperial family, heredity no longer determined who should hold power. Within the prefectures, it was up to the new governors to build staffs and transform them into organizations that could effectively implement new national functions.

Other dimensions of the problem facing the new government transcended the bureaucratic. To make Japan strong, the leaders needed to reorient people's attitudes toward the state and to build a sense of national identity that would go beyond old local concerns.[9] Tokyo policy makers, aiming to make their nation strong enough to stand up to the Western powers, saw gaining the support of all the Japanese people as one of their most important tasks. Within a decade of the Restoration, it came to seem that one of the best ways to win support—and to mute criticism—was to permit wider participation in government. National leaders thereupon determined to let some decision-making power devolve to the citizens, and to bring more people into the political process. At the same time, in a manner that their critics found contradictory, the central-government leaders attempted to maintain and even to strengthen their grip over the whole nation. For the most part, it was through assemblies at the prefectural and town and village levels, and through elections for those bodies, that the Tokyo authorities sought to strike the desired balance. Groping for the right formula by which to allot executive power to central and local officials, lawmakers most often arrived at the solution of increasing the supervisory powers of higher bureaucrats and delineating the hierarchy more and more precisely.

If the new subnational system had not worked at least relatively effectively and if new attitudes had not emerged, "breakdown" might have occurred.[10] It seems not unreasonable to suppose that one of the courses that breakdown might have followed would have been a return to localism, to something like the *kakkyo shugi* that had begun to emerge in the late Tokugawa period. In other developing societies, as C. E. Black has pointed out, "Some of the most dramatic pages in the history of political modernization have been concerned with the civil wars in which the struggle between centralizing, regional, and local authorities was waged."[11] How did Japan escape having such pages in her history?

Part of the credit belongs to the national leaders of the Meiji state, with their vision of "a rich country and a strong military" *(fukoku kyōhei)*. Of course historians and others have long given the Meiji oligarchs their due, but credit must also be given to the subnational system and its personnel, and to the ordinary people who took part in the new politics of late-nineteenth-century Japan. These institutions and people are easily overlooked because they operated at a low level. Another group that contributed to the integration of the Japanese state was made up of old local political leaders— daimyo and their close associates. In Ishikawa, for instance, the former Kaga daimyo continued into the 1880s to contribute their prestige and personal charisma to the cause of the very same imperial government that had forced them to give up local power. Almost certainly national unification could not have come about in Japan so quickly and relatively harmoniously without the service of all these persons or without the new subnational organization.

With the exception of the impatient Kido Takayoshi and some of his colleagues in the early-Meiji elite, nearly everyone who has considered the

transformation of Japan into a modern state has been impressed by the
rapidity with which loosely bound feudal domains were replaced by a single
national power. Other nations, even socially "advanced" ones without a recent feudal past such as Japan possessed, have not achieved so high a degree
of national integration with such dispatch. The United States in the late
eighteenth and early nineteenth centuries, and China in the twentieth, are
only two of many examples of countries in which the process of unification
took longer to complete.

Local government institutions played a key role in promoting Japan's
national integration. The basic features of Japan's modern system of local
rule evolved between 1868 and 1890. Tokyo policy makers, drawing on
both native experience and foreign models for inspiration, contributed the
legal definition of the system. They also appointed the men—prefectural
governors and their top assistants—who bore the greatest share of responsibility for implementing the system in the countryside, for outside Tokyo,
it was the prefectural and subprefectural bureaucrats who had to make the
system work. The periphery interacted with the center in the construction
of the Meiji local government system. Although the center had preponderant power in the creative process, it was through working together that
Tokyo leaders and local leaders built, by the end of the second decade of
Meiji rule, an organization that could maintain its existence and form
through its own normal functioning, independent of any outside force or
tutelage, and free of any indigenously generated radical change as well. The
Japanese had managed to bring into being a state that meets the specifica-
tions of social theorist Amitai Etzioni's useful definition of an "integrated
political community": the central government controlled the means of violence within Japan's boundaries, it could effectively allocate resources and
rewards throughout the nation through implementation of decisions made
in the capital, and it had become the dominant focus of political identification for the large majority of politically aware citizens.[12] Without effective
local institutions, it is doubtful that an integrated political community
could have come into being, or that the localism of the past could have
been overcome.

Whether the centralized structure of state power created by the Meiji leaders was good or bad is a matter of controversy. On one side is an army of

historians who argue that the Meiji system was unfair and more repressive
of the democratic tendencies of the Japanese people than it need have been,
and many other writers have further argued that the heritage of the Meiji
system seems to be habits of deference to the central government that persist even today, years after American-inspired postwar reforms have effected
a theoretical broadening of the scope of local autonomy.[13] On the other
side, scholars such as Kikegawa Hiroshi, author of masterly monographs on
the history of the local government system, maintain that the centralized
Meiji setup was appropriate to Japan in the circumstances of the late nineteenth century, that the centralized network of organs of subnational government delivered services which localities might not have provided so easily for themselves, and that this system thereby improved the quality of
people's lives.[14] The disagreement here is a variation on the controversy
over whether the central state or the local entity can provide better for the
people in both material and nonmaterial terms. The present study will not
resolve this perennial debate. What I hope it will do is to illuminate how
important the subnational system of government and people in the countryside were in Japan's modern achievement of political integration.

Before the 1980s, the lack of monographic treatment of the role of subnational government in Japan's development was a lacuna in Western writing on Japan. Kurt Steiner's contributions focussed mainly on conditions
since 1945.[15] Treatments of local government institutions in the last decades of *bakuhan* (that is, *bakufu* and *han*) rule and the formative years of
the Meiji era were sketchy and did not adequately grapple with the question
of the role of those institutions in the making of modern Japan.[16]

Recently, scholars have paid more attention to people and events and
historical forces in the countryside. Roger Bowen has written an interesting
monograph on three incidents of local opposition to the Meiji state in the
1880s, in Fukushima, Ibaraki, and Saitama prefectures.[17] Choosing to treat
only those involved in heated, sometimes violent, antigovernment activities
in 1882 and 1884, he has joined an influential postwar school of Japanese
writers who have found the deepest historical meanings to lie in what ordinary folk, not well known leaders, have done.[18] Opposition and the politics
of radical protest, and the potential those might have held for the development of democratic politics in Japan, are Bowen's chief concerns. Subnational institutions and the often undramatic ways in which people worked

with or against those institutions are not high among his interests, although he avers several times that the participants in the three "incidents of intense violence" had local self-government as one of their ideals. In the end, it seems to me, his work leaves two important questions still unsettled— whether the activists of the radical opposition were representative of vast numbers of people of similar background in localities all around Japan, and whether they understood, and desired to establish and exercise, rights of local self-government, which probably seemed quite abstract and theoretical in contrast to the particular grievances that spurred their rebellions. Evidence introduced in the following chapters suggests that while Bowen's story of opposition may be the truth about some parts of the country, it is not the whole truth about all of Japan.[19]

Neal L. Waters, in his excellent, independent-minded study of the Kawasaki region in the late Tokugawa period and the first two decades of the Meiji period, has demonstrated that much worth noting went on in an area that many had dismissed as insignificant because "nothing happened."[20] Concentrating on a subprefectural locality that was not yet a city, Waters has argued vigorously that it is a mistake to conceive of significance narrowly, as many historians of Japan have done, when examining the 1870s and 1880s, and to view only overt opposition to the authorities as having historical importance. Special merits of his work are its illumination of continuities in the leadership of an economically vibrant region from the time before the Restoration to twenty years after and its challenge of what has become a kind of orthodox view. Yet Waters devotes little space to political and administrative institutions or to people between the national level and his regional level. The present study contrasts with Waters' work in that it deals more with the prefecture, and less with town and village matters, and more with the development of the mechanism of local government, and less with horizontal organizations promoting local economic development.

Michio Umegaki gives considerable attention to the "changing central-local government relationship" in his admirable 1988 book *After the Restoration: The Beginning of Japan's Modern State*.[21] Interested in the structure and dynamic of government, Umegaki set out to account for the development of leadership and the widening of political participation in the critical decade following the proclamation of the Restoration of imperial rule, a period that he regarded as having been unduly neglected in previous studies. He succeeds in forcing a reevaluation of old images of Meiji leaders and their internal struggles to put together a workable new order that brought the periphery within the control of the central state. While he cites evidence drawn from primary materials from no fewer than twenty-two prefectures, Umegaki keeps his sights fixed on the center and on the familiar, famous figures who dominated the Restoration movement and the early Meiji government. The present monograph begins the story earlier and carries on with it a decade longer than Umegaki, and puts the focus on subnational matters from the perspective of the periphery.

In a number of long articles and one crystallized gem of twenty pages, Andrew Fraser has examined the politics and institutions of Tokushima Prefecture in the Meiji period, and in the course of his study he has elucidated many of the processes with which this book is concerned.[22] The light of history is refracted differently through different lenses, however, and readers can learn useful things from the stories and interpretations of both Tokushima and Ishikawa.

Local government was not just a policy issue at the national level in Tokyo (or Edo, as it was called before mid-1868). It was a matter that had to be worked out in the hurly-burly of particular governmental units in the countryside as well as in the capital. Personalities, groups, problems, and institutional arrangements all entered into the process that shaped state and locality. Even in the Japanese historiography on this subject, which bulks much larger than the Western corpus, there has been a tendency to stress either the nature of laws or the conflict of class interests, and to eschew dealing with the intricate particulars of this developmental dynamic. Until the 1960s, few tried to test their explanations by intensively examining local data or by exploring the relations between personalities and institutions. Recently, scholars like Ōishi Kaichirō, Haraguchi Kiyoshi, and Ariizumi Sadao have brought the writing on this subject to a new level of sophistication by combining deep knowledge of local history with thorough mastery of legal and institutional, as well as political, developments at the center.[23]

Institutions do not spring spontaneously into being. People make them. In turn, laws and institutions influence the way people act. If we try to explain institutions without reference to people's thoughts, motivations, and behavior, or to interpret people's actions, especially their political actions, without reference to institutions, our understanding will be poor. Commonplace as this point may be, it is easy to overlook the obvious, and some of the earlier studies have lost sight of it. Here, as we reexamine the history of late Tokugawa and early Meiji Japan, we must keep in mind that different forces—different personalities, different groups, different sets of problems, different sets of institutional arrangements, at both the national and local levels—were constantly in play. Furthermore these forces were not static. Their configurations and relative weights changed over time.

Especially since the late 1960s, the growth of residents' movements (*jūmin undō*) in many localities has given a fillip to interest in the broad issues of centralization and local autonomy in Japan. Environmental destruction and the outbreak of pollution-caused disease in some places have induced many citizens to feel that policy decisions made outside their communities are inimical to their best interests. New demands that decision making be decentralized, new assertions of local citizens' right to control their surroundings, have been expressed in many communities.[24] Against the background of these current developments, an investigation of the formative period of the modern local government system in Japan seems more significant than it might if everyone today were satisfied with the balance of power between center and periphery.

This study presents political development in nineteenth-century Japan through the lens of the experience of one *han,* Kaga, and the prefecture that replaced it. We follow Kaga policy under the last two daimyo, then treat the creation and modification of new prefectural and subprefectural administrative mechanisms in Ishikawa, the employment of personnel in those governmental organs, and the feelings of articulate citizens about national and local affairs.

Leaving aside for the moment why we might want to know something about the biggest *han* in the *bakuhan* system—justifications are offered below and in the first chapter—let us voice a few reasons why the prefecture is both a convenient and an instructive unit of study for anyone wishing to understand the making of a modern nation-state in Japan. The prefecture, as an intermediate level of government between the Tokyo regime and bureaucracy on the one hand and the villages and towns on the other, reflects administrative goings-on at all three levels. The prefecture can also be recommended for study because much documentary evidence is available for it. While the record may not be complete, we do have a great deal of material, including a considerable amount from the early Meiji period. Evidence like this is precisely what we need to test some of the interpretations of state-building and the local government system that have been offered by theorists and students who have concentrated on the national level. This body of evidence can be used to reevaluate past assessments, both positive and negative, of the creation of the Meiji subnational system.

Admirers of the accomplishments of Japan's nineteenth-century leaders have proposed evaluations such as these:

- The leaders of the Meiji state were not truly authoritarian, as their critics have charged they were; in establishing new institutions like popularly elected assemblies, and thereby widening the circle of participation in public affairs, the leaders acted out of the conviction that the wealth and power of Japan would be increased and everyone would benefit.

- There was no significant demand for systemic change coming from below; rather, changes were devised by higher authorities in order to improve the system. The reforms were *amakudariteki*—as if they came from heaven—and the threat of popular opposition had little influence on national leaders' decision to establish new institutions such as assemblies and to give more formal self-governing power to localities.

Those who have disapproved have offered contrasting, negative assessments:

- The history of the early Meiji period was nothing more than the record of the working out of authoritarian leaders' premeditated scheme for the establishment of "emperor-system absolutism."

- The people—the non-elite individuals and groups often ignored by historians—really wanted a larger say in the management of their own affairs. Popular demands for local autonomy could not be overlooked. Institutions that broadened political participation, such as prefectural assemblies and town and village assemblies, were concessions wrung out of reluctant authorities by the threat of massive public opposition if bodies like these had not been opened.

The material relating to Ishikawa Prefecture does not provide unambiguous support for any of these generalizations about the subnational system of the early Meiji period or those involved in its formation. There was considerable diversity from one part of the nation to another, and not only that, there was variance within this one prefecture. We find diversity in the backgrounds of those who participated in politics and administration, in how much power men of the same wealth and status in different localities might hold relative to their neighbors, and in attitudes toward the issues of the day and the myriad changes that Japan was undergoing. During the decades examined here, new representative assemblies gave the opportunity for more people than ever before to participate in government in Japan, and as voters and assembly members, most of those who were eligible took advantage of the chance. But at the same time the appointed officials of the central government were solidifying and expanding their dominance over prefectural and subprefectural affairs. By the end of the century, the formal definition of the nature and function of subnational entities had been rewritten to make those bodies "locally autonomous." At the same time, however, the volume of business delegated to such bodies by the central government had been made so large that local organs of government had to commit most of their financial resources to the delegated business and had very little left for locally initiated projects. Nearly all Japanese accepted and cooperated with the new system. Many actively collaborated in its construction. A few actively resisted and ended up being coerced into acquiescence. The picture is of sufficient complexity that characterizations of the whole system such as "emperor-system absolutism" cannot do it justice.

The case of Kaga and Ishikawa cannot be called completely typical. Nineteenth-century Japan was so diverse that any claim of typicality must be very carefully qualified. If—since—this is so, perhaps the ideal study of national unification and integration in Japan would instance many *han* and many prefectures. Yet the exposition of one example permits a concreteness that compensates for the loss of comprehensiveness that might be found in a survey, of comparable length, of many cases. I hope to have avoided the pitfalls of vagueness and overabstraction. Studies of Japanese subnational government that focus almost exclusively on institutions sometimes tumble into these traps and become "history without people" (*ningen fuzai no rekishi*). I also hope to have escaped what might be labeled the antiquarian's fallacy, that understanding is to be found simply by accumulating and lay-

ing before the reader a huge mass of material. Minute details can overload
and numb the brain at least as easily as they can spark interest.

Why pick Kaga and Ishikawa for a study like this? The position of the
area in the *bakuhan* polity before the Meiji Restoration commends it, for
one thing. Several features of Kaga might have been expected to obstruct
the transition there from government by local men to government by outsiders who were guided by a newly centralized national system. Those features draw attention as we review Meiji state-building, and they heighten
appreciation of the achievement of integration in such short order.

In the system of division of power between the Tokugawa shogunate in
Edo and the over 270 daimyo domains in the countryside, Kaga *han* occupied a special place. It was first among the domains in assessed product,
the measure by which the wealth and power of a domain were commonly
calculated. Its 1,022,700 *koku*[25] assessment was exceeded only by the
7,060,000 *koku* valuation of *bakufu* lands.[26] Kaga's own officials put the
productivity of their domain at a slightly higher figure than the official
one—in 1838 they valued the annual product at over 1,358,000 *koku*.[27]
Prestige went along with size. The Maeda, lords of Kaga, were assigned to
the *ōrōka,* or Great Corridor, first among the seven categories in the order
of precedence for attendance by daimyo on the Tokugawa shogun. For generations, heads of the Maeda clan were favored with high court ranks by the
emperor, and these, even if only honorific and not necessarily matched by
demonstrated political or military power, were unmistakable signs of high
status.[28] As such, they were sources of pride for the whole Kaga establishment, retainers as well as members of the family of the lord.

Another feature of Kaga that might have worked against its smooth integration into a centralized nation-state was its large samurai class. The
founder of the *han,* Maeda Toshiie, deserves the credit for building up a
sizable corps of loyal retainers in the late sixteenth century, when he had
been a subordinate of Oda Nobunaga and Toyotomi Hideyoshi and a status-
equal of Tokugawa Ieyasu. During the era of the Tokugawa shogunate,
successive generations of Maeda maintained a great many people of samurai
status on their large domain, and by the time of the Meiji Restoration,
there were upwards of 35,000 men, women, and children who were categorized as samurai family members.[29] This made Kaga's one of the largest

populations of samurai of any domain. Demographic data on samurai in the Tokugawa period are sparse, but estimates of the samurai populations of other big domains at the date of the Restoration have been made. Probably only the great *han* of Satsuma, with its large number of "farmer-samurai" (*gōshi*) in addition to the regular vassals who resided in the castle town of Kagoshima, had more samurai than Kaga. Satsuma samurai males numbered around 28,000. Chōshū, Satsuma's principal partner in the Meiji Restoration, had about 11,000, a number which put it near the top among the domains by samurai population.[30] Kaga had no *gōshi*, yet census-takers in 1871, when a count was ordered for the new government, enumerated over 16,000 samurai family heads—over 7,000 *shi* and over 9,000 *sotsu*.

The sheer size of the samurai class might have mattered little if most of those of that status had been disaffected with the old order and ready to reject their hereditary ties with their lord. In several domains in the waning years of Tokugawa power, numbers of samurai had done just that, leaving feudal service in order to gain the liberty to participate in nontraditional educational programs or in some cases in anti-establishment political activities. In Kaga, however, samurai had exhibited no inclination to break away from the domain during the years leading up to the Restoration. A group of pro-imperial activists who were critical of the routine of *bakuhan* policy emerged in 1864, only to be harshly suppressed by Kaga authorities, as we will see in Chapter One, but even that small coterie of imperial enthusiasts remained well within the bounds of their bonds to the Maeda.[31] Again and again in the first two decades after the Meiji Restoration, Kaga men demonstrated that they were not alienated from their old feudal lord, as they called on the Maeda for assistance or bestirred themselves to political or economic action upon the appeal of their old liege.

The point is this: Kaga had a large contingent of samurai who were still closely identified with their feudal lord in the late 1860s, and this might have produced the conditions for resistance when, in the 1870s, the social and political positions of the lord and the samurai status-group were deliberately undermined by outsiders, by men who had no traditional connection with the affairs of the Maeda domain. That widespread, tradition-oriented opposition to the new Meiji government did not spring up in Kaga and Ishikawa is intriguing. The way in which particularistic identities—bonds to lord and locality—were transcended and replaced by a national identity in Kaga is suggestive of the way in which new political loyalties were engendered all over Japan, even if local circumstances were in many ways unique.

Kaga in the 1860s was remarkable in several other respects that might have made it a difficult area to consolidate into a unified state.[32] The domain had what appeared to be adequate organs of self-government. It had, as will appear in the following chapter, made good headway on a program of strengthening itself. It was not in the throes of a crisis of leadership or bureaucratic organization that might have threatened its continued existence. Nor was its administrative structure at lower levels showing signs of imminent collapse.

Fiscally, many of Japan's domains were in dire straits in the 1860s. Not Kaga. To be sure, the big *han*'s finances were dependent on agricultural taxes to an overwhelming degree, in the typical premodern Japanese pattern. Its economic base was not adequate to meet all domanial expenditures, and for decades before the Restoration it had been practicing retrenchment and borrowing from both samurai and merchants. Still, compared with the shogunate and most other domains, the Maeda *han* was in relatively good fiscal shape on the eve of the Meiji Restoration.[33] There was thus little reason for Kaga administrators to want to give up the responsibility of managing local finances, as officials in some other domains wished to do. No Maeda retainer is on the record as expressing a desire to turn the management of affairs over to some extra-domanial authority.

In fact Kaga officials showed precisely the opposite attitude the year before the Restoration. To the British Minister Sir Harry Parkes, who paid a visit, they made clear that they wanted to continue to run their own affairs. When Parkes probed about whether Nanao might be designated as one of the five ports opened to foreign vessels, Kaga officers indicated that they believed that such a move might result in their having to share or give up responsibility for their best harbor. They were uninterested in taking such a risk.[34]

Along with the factors that might have been expected to make Kaga difficult to integrate into the new state after the overthrow of the shogunate, three more characteristics of the Maeda *han* lend it especial interest to students of nation-building: nonparticipation, nonrepresentation, and noncentrality. These features were critical in determining that Kaga under the Meiji government would not be great in the ways it had been under the Tokugawa system.

The failure of Kaga to participate in the Restoration movement, the absence of men of Kaga in the upper echelons of the central government after 1868, and the geographical remoteness of Kaga from the political and economic centers of the modernizing state combined to consign Kaga and Ishikawa to secondary importance. The biggest of the *bakuhan*-system domains became an outsider in the new Japan. Its location in *Ura Nihon*—"the backside of Japan"—is almost symbolic of its political and economic position after 1868. What happened to its major urban center is another emblem of the whole prefecture. In the mid-nineteenth century the Maeda castle town of Kanazawa had been one of the five largest cities in the land, with a population of over 100,000. After the Restoration, Kanazawa's growth lagged behind that of Tokyo, Osaka, Nagoya, Kobe, Yokohama, and many other metropolitan areas of *Omote Nihon,* the Pacific seaboard of Japan. Kanazawa languished in the late nineteenth century, and in economic development at least, the lackluster pattern of the surrounding prefecture paralleled that of its central city.

The comparative obscurity of the old Maeda territory after 1868 increases its value as an object worthy of our study. This may sound paradoxical, but it really is not. Historians and other students of Japanese political, economic, and social development—confusing notoriety for notability—have tended to neglect areas that have not been famous or important in an obvious manner. Most previous studies that have gotten past the politics and the legal changes made in the capital have devoted their attention to the outstanding exceptions. Attention has been directed to the *han* that led in the Restoration movement and their modern fate, or to the places that were the settings for dramatic confrontations between established authorities and local people opposed to those authorities. Yet the fact is that most parts of Japan were quiet, even as vast changes were occurring within them. In their very lack of notoriety, Kaga and Ishikawa are more representative of the Japanese nation than the better known and more studied exceptions.[35] This representative quality adds consequence to what might otherwise be lightly regarded as a story only incidental to the epic of the making of modern Japan.

Following the way in which the biggest domain of Tokugawa times was governed, nearly autonomously, in the last half-century of its existence, and the process by which it was unified with the rest of the country in the late nineteenth century, we can hope to arrive at a subtler understanding of Meiji Japan and nation-building than most of us have hitherto had. Acquainting ourselves with the rich spectacle of a place that has mistakenly been thought of as unspectacular, let us reimagine the great transformation of institutions, loyalties, and attitudes of nineteenth-century Japan.

ONE

The Perils of Prudence:
Kaga under Maeda Nariyasu and
Maeda Yoshiyasu

Late in 1822, Maeda Nariyasu (1811–1884) inherited the domain known commonly as Kaga, so called after the ancient province in which his family had had its headquarters for over two centuries. Nariyasu presided over this rich and important territory for nearly forty-four years, then retired and passed responsibility on to his son Yoshiyasu (1830–1874) in the fourth lunar month of 1866.[1] Yoshiyasu oversaw the transition from the *bakuhan* state, in which the Tokugawa shogunate had the greatest share of power, to the imperial state, which grew up rapidly after the overthrow of the Tokugawa. Less than two years after becoming lord of Kaga, Yoshiyasu pledged his allegiance to the emperor and severed his ties to the Tokugawa, and in the sixth month of 1869, he handed over to the emperor the Maeda clan's title to the lands and people of Kaga. The sovereign named Yoshiyasu governor of Kanazawa *han* on 1869/6/17, entrusting the former daimyo with stewardship of the area that had belonged to his family for so long, but after two more years Yoshiyasu relinquished even this last vestige of local authority. In the seventh month of 1871, in conformity with the imperial rescript abolishing the *han* as subnational administrative divisions, Yoshiyasu gave way to an outsider sent by the central government. He left Kanazawa and went to live permanently in Tokyo.

Between 1600 and 1868, no lord in Japan except the shogun had as much wealth under his control as the Maeda. At the time of the proclamation of the restoration of imperial rule and immediately thereafter, the new claimants to national authority treated the Maeda with gingerly circumspection, hoping thereby to obtain the political, military, and perhaps most of all financial support of Kaga. Kaga's size and strength perforce made its affairs an important factor in domestic political calculations in early modern Japan, and movements in Kaga politics during the era of Nariyasu and Yoshiyasu are therefore of interest to those who want to comprehend Japan's metamorphosis from a fragmented nation into a unified modern state. This chapter surveys conditions and policy in Kaga during its last half-century, and touches on the structure and traditions of the great Maeda *han*.

Factional strife muddied the stream of Kaga politics during the years of Nariyasu and Yoshiyasu, but the strong main current of Kaga political thinking and action was little changed from the previous two centuries. That main stream ran thick with particles of self-interest. Concern to hold fast to the heritage of the domain determined the major continuity in policy throughout Kaga's history. No matter who had the upper hand in the factional conflict, prudence and preservation were the guiding principles. In Nariyasu and Yoshiyasu's time, leadership alternately was exercised by conservatives, led by scions of the eight highest-ranking samurai families (*hakka*), and reformers, whose membership included middle and lower samurai as well as *hakka* men. Both strove to keep Kaga strong and independent. It was not until 1867 that Maeda Nariyasu explicitly stated his belief in the principle of domanial self-interest and self-sufficiency (*sanshū kakkyo*). Notions of self-interest and self-sufficiency were hardly new, however, having in fact swayed the minds of Kaga policy makers long before the confusion of power between pro-Tokugawa and pro-Restoration forces in 1867.

With Tokugawa Yoshinobu's resignation as shogun and the proclamation of the restoration of imperial rule, the context that gave meaning to terms and ideas changed. Cautious pursuit of local self-interest and avoidance of risk to established position did not exactly become imprudent, but the politics of prudence no longer sufficed to permit Kaga to maintain its long-standing eminence.

This was not clear at the moment of the Restoration. The course of the recent past contained little to suggest that the big *han* could not continue to look out for itself. The trend of the decades before the restoration had been divisive and toward fragmentation more often than unifying and toward integration. This makes it surprising that Kaga and other domains were eliminated within four years of the Meiji Restoration and that within a few years more the many parts of Japan were integrated into a strongly centralized state. By way of describing the baseline from which modern nation-building in Japan began, we look here at policy in the biggest domain on the eve of the Restoration.

Nariyasu's father Narinaga had no intention of surrendering the reins of power when he retired in 1822. Before passing his domain to his eleven-year-old son, Narinaga took measures to centralize local administration under his own careful supervision. In 1821, he eliminated the county-level agricultural affairs magistrates (*kaisaku bugyō*), samurai officials who had been responsible for tax and land administration since 1651. In the same year Narinaga carried out sweeping personnel changes among village-group headmen (*tomura*), who constituted the highest echelon of peasant officials, and he cut the powers of these *tomura* by giving some of their functions to lower samurai officials in the county magistrates' (*kōri bugyō*) offices.[2] Early in 1824, Narinaga set up a policy advisory council that he called the board of tutors (*kyōyukyoku*). He intended to use this body to bypass the *han* council of elders (*toshiyorishū*), which was composed of men of the eight top-ranking samurai families.[3] These changes might have strengthened the domain administratively if the man who dictated them had lived long enough to implement them. Narinaga might have been still more effective had he practiced personal economy and not depleted *han* resources by lavish spending on the expansion of his garden, the famous Kenrokuen, and on his residences.[4] But Narinaga died suddenly in midyear 1824, before his reforms could bear fruit.

　　Upon Narinaga's demise, the *han* elders assailed the board of tutors. Lacking the protection of the former daimyo, the tutors were driven from office within a year. The tutors were men of humbler social standing than their chief critics, who regarded *han* leadership as their traditional prerogative. Young Nariyasu placed his trust in the council of elders and relied especially heavily on Okumura Hidezane. Okumura was heir to a prominent family that had served the Maeda for eleven generations, one of the *hakka*, and enjoyed the comfort of an annual income of 17,000 *koku*, greater than

many small daimyo. Okumura, however, had been held in disfavor by Narinaga and had indeed been dismissed from office in 1818.

Restored to the inner circle, Okumura dominated the council of elders
until his death in 1843.[5] His years as the most powerful man in Kanazawa
were fraught with economic worries, as the inherited problems of years of
budgetary deficits were compounded by a series of bad harvests. As in the
shogunate and in several other domains, the crisis brought on by these
several lean years became the occasion for an ambitious reform effort in
Kaga, and it was Okumura who was the architect of the Kaga reforms.
Known by the era-name in which they were effected as the Tenpō reforms
(Tenpō was the name given the years 1830–1843), these Kaga measures
antedate the more famous reforms carried out in *bakufu* territories under
Mizuno Tadakuni. Okumura, the bearer of *hakka* tradition, was not one to
challenge the assumptions about society and polity that had prevailed since
the establishment of the *bakuhan* system two centuries before. Anxious to
shore up his domain in the fiscal and personnel areas in which it had once
been strong, Okumura drew inspiration from the past. He and his fellow
elders prescribed a regimen of austerity and strove to resuscitate the administrative structure that had been in place before Narinaga's alterations. Old
virtues and old offices, not radical experiments, were supposed to cure
Kaga's ills.

Kaga indebtedness had mounted to 80,773 *kan,* figured in silver, by
1830.[6] The domain leaders' first response to this situation was to exhort
people to be frugal. Inspired by old-fashioned Confucian moralism, they
issued a spate of sumptuary regulations between 1824 and 1835.[7] Aware,
from long experience, that such legislation would in actuality improve domanial finances but little, Okumura and the elders judiciously supplemented their moralizing with a program of new stipend loans imposed on
samurai retainers and with new extraordinary levies on townsmen and peasants. Samurai had been "lending" part of their feudal incomes back to the
domain since the latter part of the eighteenth century in Kaga, as had their
counterparts elsewhere in Japan. In Kaga, *han* officials raised the rates of
these enforced loans on samurai *(chigyō kariage)* in 1827 and 1834.[8] Although this helped the *han* fisc, it resulted in distress for many in the
warrior status-group, especially those with small stipends who had been
exempt from earlier stipend loan requirements. Peasants and townsmen

likewise experienced distress when the authorities ordered them to lend 6,670 *kan* of silver to the domain in 1825, and despite pressure from officials many commoners had not paid their shares by the spring of the following year. Again in 1830, 1836, and 1837, Okumura and the elders resorted to special exactions (*goyōgin* or *goyōmai*, often translated "forced loans") on commoners. The *han* demanded that peasants and townsmen pay between 900 and 1,000 *kan* a year to the exchequer from 1830 through 1841.[9]

These extraordinary levies diverted into the domain treasury wealth that commoners might have invested in enterprise or agricultural improvement, given the temperament of their times. The latter part of the Tokugawa period was not a time of stagnation. Elsewhere in Japan, commoners were bringing about great changes in regional economies and in the relations between social groups by engaging in industry outside the castle towns and the established cities and by devoting more and more effort to commercialized agriculture (and less effort to the production of grain for tax).[10] In Kaga, commerce and enterprise did not pick up the momentum that might have enabled them to break the mold of samurai control. Quite possibly the special exactions imposed by the *han* on commoners inhibited local economic development.

The special levies on both samurai and commoners did help Kaga achieve the objective of strengthening the finances and the power structure of the domain. But the habit of mind of men like Okumura precluded their imagining that economic growth might be desirable for its own sake, and it was even further outside their ken to imagine that the *han* might reap long-term benefits by promoting private savings and investment, instead of by claiming any surplus for the domain's immediate use.

For both administrative and fiscal reasons, the Okumura regime reestablished the post of agricultural affairs magistrate, redefined the duties of the county magistrate, and restored the functions of the village-group headmen. In 1833, Nariyasu reversed his father's decision of a dozen years earlier to have county magistrates manage land and tax matters as well as maintaining law and order and handling other local affairs. By 1839, eleven agricultural affairs magistrates had been appointed. As for the county magistrates, the *han* shrank their power. In 1837, after four poor harvests in five years and in the wake of popular protests against local officials and local rich men, Nariyasu and his council of elders decided to station the county magistrates in five offices in different parts of the domain, as well as in the castle town, where they had performed their duties till then. Other samurai officials were also posted in each county.[11]

These administrative changes did not result in things going smoothly. Bad weather in 1837, 1838, and 1839 left many farming families in even direr straits than the crop failures of the few years just before. Some peasants felt driven to appeal to *han* officials for relief.

The officials' response exposed the roots of the Tenpō policies. Those roots can be described as *bakuhan* traditionalist, and the officials' attitude toward the Kaga farmers recalls the dictum of Tokugawa Ieyasu that peasants should be treated so as to let them neither live nor die. Agricultural Affairs Magistrate Nagoya Hikoemon typified the hard-nosed Kaga administrator of this era. Peasants in Ishikawa County, just south of Kanazawa, appealed to him in 1838 to inspect the damage that had been wrought by a winter of heavy snows, a cold spring, and an infestation by harmful insects. They asked for exemption from taxation. Nagoya took a look and quickly decided that the situation was not nearly as bad as the peasants had claimed. Lest these or other commoners get ideas about him being soft on malingerers, he denied the peasants' appeal and jailed fifteen village leaders, including the village headman. Five of the prisoners died in confinement. In 1839 the property of all fifteen was confiscated, and the ten survivors and over a hundred members of the convicted men's families were forcibly relocated on an undeveloped tract of wasteland in another county. Having inflicted considerable misery, Nagoya came to stand as a symbol of feudal oppression in the local popular mind. Yet arguably his treatment of the peasants under his jurisdiction was not unduly harsh by the standards of the Tokugawa period. He was at least faithful to his lord, his office, and the letter of the tax laws of Kaga in the Tenpō period.[12]

The distinctive Kaga institutions of land and tax administration, revived by Okumura, worked well enough that Nariyasu and Yoshiyasu did not see fit to make further adjustments. The system kept order and delivered agricultural revenue to the domain pretty much as it was intended to do. It would not be changed until after the Meiji Restoration.

Personal indebtedness blighted Kaga society at all levels, just as *han* indebtedness stained the Maeda heritage. Okumura's council attempted to combat the problem by old means. Echoing debt cancellation measures of

1784, *han* statesmen legislated against usurious interest rates in 1837, going so far as to cancel the interest on outstanding loans and to order that
the principal on loans be repaid in installments to be renegotiated by borrowers and lenders. Separate orders extended these *han* rulings to townspeople, samurai, and peasants. As for pawned items, an 1837 order required
that they be redeemed at one-tenth the amount that had been lent with
them as collateral, without interest, by the seventh month of 1837.[13] In
this matter Okumura and the council of elders seem to have intended to be
benevolent, albeit with an ulterior motive, as they meant to strengthen the
domain by strengthening the people whom they governed. This assistance
to borrowers discouraged lenders, however, and the long-term effect of these
orders was to inhibit financial transactions that might have contributed to
local economic development.

Sale of land and pawning of land became quite common in the latter half
of the period of *han* rule in Kaga, as in other parts of Japan, and by the
1830s these practices had reached what conservatives felt were epidemic
proportions. Most disturbing were the increasing numbers of transfers of
land into the hands of town-dwellers and persons of other villages who
became absentee landlords. This flew in the face of the Kaga authorities'
social and economic ideals, and in 1837 they ordered townsman landowners
to return lands to those from whom they had obtained them. Money that
townsmen had made from land sales was confiscated. The domain government ordered villages to buy back lands that had been sold to other villages
and to allow the original owners to buy back what they had lost. These
policies hindered the concentration of lands by powerful landlords in Kaga,
but they did not help small farmers as much as the lawmakers hoped.
Within a few years, small peasants were again at the margin, and *han* income from agriculture never attained the level that samurai administrators
believed it should.[14]

Commercial policy attracted the attention of Kaga's Tenpō leaders as
another area in which the *han* needed reform. The years of Narinaga stand
out in Kaga economic history because commerce had been encouraged and
merchant associations legally recognized. More commonly in Kaga's past,
commerce had been scorned and merchant organizations discouraged. But
under Narinaga things had been different, and for a while under Nariyasu
and Okumura, Narinaga's policies stood. Trade with other parts of Japan

expanded, and more and more villages were drawn into the market economy. Official attitudes toward commerce shifted again in the early 1830s. When prices rose steeply, commerce—and Narinaga's liberal policies— seemed to conservative *han* leaders to be a problem again. Instead of blaming nature for the poor harvests that had hurt the domain and the people in the last few years, Okumura and his colleagues blamed nontraditional economic policies.[15]

In the eleventh month of 1837, *han* leaders abolished the *sanbutsukata*, an office that promoted manufacturing and commerce. Narinaga had revived this institution, which had first been established in 1778 (then closed in 1784), in order to raise money from Osaka merchants and to put that money to use in Kaga. Under the aegis of the *sanbutsukata*, Kaga merchant associations grew stronger and trade with Edo increased. But with the poor conditions of the 1830s, this office and its activities became suspect to *han* elders, and they did away with it. To counter the rise in prices, they set up a new office, the *bukkakata*. In the twelfth month of 1837, they ordered the dissolution of the merchant associations.[16]

Kaga *han* moves to control prices and commercial activity preceded *bakufu* measures along the same lines by fully four years. Like the Tenpō reforms in the shogunate, the commercial reforms in Kaga proved ineffectual in bringing about a lasting drop in prices or in increasing the prosperity of the regime and the people. Cutting spending, controlling costs, and limiting transactions by restricting merchants seemed to officials to be economically sound. Certainly these policies met the traditional standards of sagacity of Japanese officialdom. But in the 1830s and later, they were impracticable. And in the Maeda domain, unlike in Edo and other shogunal territories, the depressing effect of the Tenpō reforms was not short-lived. With rare exceptions—the famous Zeniya Gohei is one—Kaga businessmen and Kaga commercial institutions receded into obscurity for the rest of the era of *han* rule.[17]

Leaders of the Maeda government in Kanazawa justified their reform measures as being for "the greatest good of the domain" *(okuni no dairi)* and spoke of having "returned to the fundamental principles of good government and firmly established the basis for such good government."[18] Okumura and his fellow conservative reformers were motivated by their idea of the domain's self-interest. It did not occur to these well-born rulers of the largest *han* to define "the greatest good of the domain" in terms opposed to the shogunate or the *bakuhan* system. With those, they were amicably compliant. Yet two concepts animating the Kaga Tenpō reform, *han* strengthening and the preservation of the bequest of the past, contained the potential to oppose, or at least to operate without, the shogunate or the Tokugawa family. In the 1860s these principles would contribute to the development of a clearer sense of self-interest among men of Kaga.

The maladies of the Tenpō proved chronic, and Okumura's reforms provided only temporary relief. As the domain resolutely carried on debt-repayment policies begun at the end of the eighteenth century, and as those policies were made more stringent by Okumura, Kaga spent more than it took in. In 1848 alone, the deficit expressed in terms of silver came to 6,645 *kan,* equivalent to half the income of the *han* in that year.[19] Nariyasu perceived that the trend was unfavorable, and upon the death of Okumura, he sought to turn things around by giving responsibility to men whose opinions contrasted with Okumura. Leadership of Kaga in the years 1844–1854[20] fell into the hands of Chō Tsurahiro.

Like Okumura, Chō was the head of one of the "eight families," but he was not a typical Kanazawa conservative. He saw to the appointment of many men who stood out for their critical assessments of *bakuhan* shibboleths, men steeped in unorthodox ideas. To such important posts as finance magistrate *(san'yōba bugyō)* and retainer personnel magistrate *(wariba bugyō),* Nariyasu named several dozen followers of the noted Kanazawa scholar Ueda Sakunojō. Ueda had been profoundly influenced by Honda Toshiaki in 1809 when that iconoclastic proponent of new methods of strengthening Japan spent a year in the Maeda castle town.[21] By 1847, enough of Ueda's students held responsible positions that they were able to dominate *han* policymaking. They became known as "the black coat party" *(kurohaori tō)* from their customary dress.[22]

Coastal defense concerned the black coats as it had not concerned *han* policymakers for decades. Appearances of French, English, and American ships in Japanese waters in 1844, 1845, and 1846 startled Kaga bureaucrats out of the lethargy into which they had fallen.[23] In 1844, the *han* detailed a group of soldiers to Edo to study artillery techniques and cannon manufacture. Kaga began to make big guns, managing by 1847 to turn out five Western-style cannon. When a foreign vessel was sighted off the town of

Wajima on the Noto Peninsula in 1848, the Chō administration took a step that Okumura's group almost certainly would not have countenanced: They planned the mobilization of 900 farmers as soldiers to defend the domain's eastern border.[24] Little came of this plan for the next fifteen years. Still, it merits notice that the idea of making peasants into soldiers, a revolutionary idea in this age of samurai rule, got an airing by the Kanazawa black coats five years before Commodore Perry and his black ships arrived in 1853. Kaga put coastal defense installations in several places on the Noto Peninsula after 1846, manning them with samurai-status *han* soldiers, not peasants. Three months before Perry made his first landing at Uraga, Nariyasu personally inspected these facilities. No lord since *han* founder Maeda Toshiie had even set foot on Noto soil, and Nariyasu's tour was an indication of the gravity attributed by *han* leaders to coastal defense.[25] The Americans' coming heightened the sense of foreign threat. In the first month of 1854, Kanazawa leaders established a new institute for gunnery and Western military drill in the castle town.[26]

Defense policies had national implications that transcended simple domanial self-interest. Vis-à-vis the world outside Japan, the Kaga reformers of the 1840s and 1850s probably can be said to have been nationalistic. But what they had in mind for the defense of their homeland was a system of cooperation by the shogunate and the various *han*. It was not a unified system. Certainly it was not the intention of Kaga policy makers to construct an integrated national community in areas other than military defense. Nationalism need not entail a conviction that superdomanial—or more generally, superlocal—centralization is desirable.

Indeed, the black coat reformers felt the need for *han* self-sufficiency, rather than interdependence with the rest of Japan, more keenly after Perry than before. In the eighth month of 1853, they prohibited all imports and ordered that only domestically produced goods be used in Kaga.[27] They hoped to force down prices, which had intractably gone on rising, by eliminating the influence of other domains and other countries. "Imports" in their usage referred to anything made outside Kaga, and "domestically produced" meant "made in the domain." For the sake of the *han* treasury and the small landholding peasant, and for the control of commerce, Kaga leaders placed the interests of their domain ahead of the strengthening of a national market. In this they did not differ from the Tenpō leaders whom they had replaced.

While banning imports, the black coats were encouraging sales of Kaga products outside the domain, especially in the Kyoto-Osaka region. Their scruples about economic influence were one-way and did not apply to Kaga's impact on other localities. From the late 1840s they sanctioned exports of local specialty goods like paulownia and moxa.[28]

Within the domain, the black coat party promoted economic development by implementing a new land reclamation policy and by appointing commoners to a new post, in which they were supposed to facilitate production and marketing.[29] Opening new land offered small payoff, since there was little undeveloped land in Kaga; Ueda Sakonojō had observed this, and the lesson had not been lost on his pupils, though they nevertheless encouraged that reclamation be undertaken. The decision to stimulate production and marketing within the domain promised more for the future than land development, and the samurai leaders were perceptive enough to realize that the best-suited nominees for the position of facilitator were commoners. Town and village entrepreneurs (*zaigō shōnin*) were named to the new position. The new economic development policy and the facilitators helped quicken business for local merchants outside Kanazawa, who had long taken a back seat to the privileged merchants of the castle town. In contrast to the town and village entrepreneurs of regions of Japan that were more advanced economically—regions such as the Kinai or the area surrounding Edo—this inchoate capitalism of Kaga was still struggling in the mid-nineteenth century to overcome the obstacles of an unfavorable political-economic environment.

Kaga's fiscal woes resisted the nontraditional ameliorative policies of the black coats as they had the old-fashioned physic of the Tenpō conservatives. The *han* was improving its debt position, but repayments were taking a heavy toll on samurai retainers and commoners alike, and the efforts of the late 1840s and early 1850s to promote internal growth did not yield fast results.[30] Dissatisfaction brewed, as it seemed that Chō and the black coats were little more effective than Okumura and his conservative allies. Suddenly in the sixth month of 1854, Nariyasu dismissed Chō from the top-ranking bureaucratic jobs that had made possible his domination of the *han* elders.[31] The lord also discharged other officials identified with the black coat party. Nariyasu explained his action in a statement that reveals a bit of uncertainty about what constituted wise policy, but that, at the same time, is thoroughly imbued with a hoary East Asian bias against parties and factions. He conceded that some recent programs had bettered the domain, but stressed that it was not good that Chō and the black coats had come to hold a near monopoly on policy and personnel decisions, or that they operated as a party *(ittō)*. Chō had, the lord said, begun to show peculiarities *(ki no kuse),* and many of Chō's fellow-officials had evidenced eccentric beliefs *(henshin).* "If these go on growing," Nariyasu concluded, "it will become an obstacle to governance, and therefore I must dismiss [Chō and the black coats]."[32] Although the lord never specified the nature of the peculiarities or eccentric beliefs, his vague words had a mighty effect.

Conservatives in the council of elders commanded Kaga for the next several years. At the outset, after Chō's ouster, their leader was Yokoyama Takaakira, tenth-generation head of one of the eight families and heir to the princely stipend of 30,000 *koku,* who had been a member of the council since the Tenpō period.[33] Described by one prominent local historian as "an ordinary man possessed of no civil or military talent," Yokoyama depended on favored subordinates to run things for him.[34] At least some of Yokoyama's followers were reputed to be corrupt, and the consensus of students of this period is that their administration was undistinguished. For his part, perhaps in reaction to the unseemly factional squabbling that had punctuated his reign, Nariyasu seems to have entered a passive phase. Kaga politics cooled just as politics hit the boiling point in the big southwestern domains of Chōshū, Satsuma, and Tosa, and in other hot spots like Mito and Kyoto, where activists agitated for both a reorientation of foreign policy and a reordering of the basic *bakuhan* structure. In Kaga, innovative spirit is hard to discover among the policy makers of Yokoyama's day. *Han* leaders abandoned efforts to encourage non-agricultural economic activity, for example; they returned to the old emphasis on agricultural production and agricultural revenues as the basis of *han* finances.

Torpid and unimaginative as Yokoyama and his contemporaries may have been, in the management of a succession problem in the branch *han* of Daishōji in 1855–1856, they exhibited that impulse toward self-preservation and the pursuit of self-interest that inhered in nearly all the moves of Kaga leaders in the half-century before the Restoration. Ostensibly cooperating with the law and protocol of the Tokugawa shogunate, Maeda officials employed a subterfuge to ensure that title to Daishōji stayed in the family after the death of the twelfth lord of that *han,* Maeda Toshinori, in the fourth month of 1855.[35]

When Toshinori, who was Nariyasu's third son, left this world, he was only twenty-three and had neither sired nor adopted an heir. Since posthumous adoptions were prohibited and the shogunate was apt to confiscate the lands of those who died intestate, the situation demanded adroit diplomacy. Maeda officials beseeched the *bakufu* to permit Toshinori's younger brother Toshiyuki to inherit Daishōji. Perhaps in deference to the family ties, through marriage, between the Tokugawa and the Maeda, shogunal officials approved the succession of Nariyasu's fifth son, Toshiyuki. The poor young man could take no pleasure in the Tokugawa benison. He had died, at home in Kanazawa, a few days before the shogunate issued the formal notice that designated him as his late brother's heir. Maeda retainers, reluctant to approach Tokugawa officials with another special request so soon after their previous one, decided that the dictate of prudence this time was concealment. Nariyasu himself played a part, explaining to the shogun's men in Edo that Toshiyuki was ill and weak and unable to appear for the mandatory audience with the shogun. No one told Tokugawa administrators that Toshiyuki was dead. The Kaga lord asked that his seventh son Toshika be enfeoffed in his fifth son's stead. This was almost too much for *bakufu* officials, and they made the Maeda wait for over half a year before they concurred. A month after the shogunate approved Toshika's inheritance, Maeda family officials finally issued a public announcement of the death of Toshiyuki. On the twenty-eighth day of 1856, after eight months of dutiful but lifeless service as the thirteenth daimyo of Daishōji, the unfortunate Toshiyuki received a proper burial.

Yokoyama's administration bared an atavistic nature in reacting to commoners' protest movements in 1858. Poor townspeople and peasants rioted in nine places and created disturbances in several others in that year. Kaga officials brutally suppressed the uprisers and invoked ancient punishments, crucifying some, beheading others and exposing their heads. There were hints, after the commoners' leaders had been killed, that even the *han* authorities regarded some of the protesters' grievances as legitimate. But these *han* officials would not tolerate open disharmony.[36]

After the uprisings of 1858, the Kaga council of elders underwent a shakeup. Okumura Terumichi replaced Yokoyama as the principal leader. Terumichi was a nephew of Hidezane whom Hidezane's son Hidechika had adopted as he lay dying in 1844, barely a year after his redoubtable father had passed away. Terumichi has been described as a man of conservative disposition who abhorred the thought that foreign influence might color the outlook of the Maeda or their retainers.[37] Yet he recognized the need to strengthen the domain, and in order to accomplish the goal of self-strengthening he acquiesced in the return to influence of many of the black coats. By 1863, many of those reformers had resumed their old posts. No longer did they operate as a faction or dominate policy making as they had under Chō Tsurahiro. The experience of being sacked and criticized by their lord had subdued them. But they pressed successfully to implement military reforms and to open once more the offices for the encouragement of non-grain production and domestic marketing.[38]

To strengthen the *han* military, Kaga reformers in the early 1860s added Dutch studies, medicine, navigation, and depth-sounding to the curriculum of the Kanazawa military academy.[39] In 1862, they purchased a 250-ton steamship, the first of several Western ships that would carry the Maeda family crest before the Meiji Restoration. In 1865, they sent fifty young men to Nagasaki to obtain a more intensive training in Western studies than could be provided in Kanazawa.

Most remarkable among the self-strengthening measures undertaken by the black coats was the program to train peasants and townsmen as riflemen.[40] Beginning in 1863, the domain sent two or three samurai soldiers to each of twenty-two training installations around the *han*. At each site, the regular soldiers drilled fifty or sixty men who had been chosen from among non-samurai males between the ages of seventeen and thirty. All healthy commoner officials (village headmen and the like) were also required to participate in the training. Despite the effort given to organization and training, Kaga's commoner soldiery did not play a notable part in the military history of the last stage of *bakuhan* rule. This contrasts with the experience of the peasant units of Chōshū, which were vital in political and military affairs, both within the *han* and on the national stage, in the final years before the Restoration. In Kaga, apathy about national defense, preoccupation with the everyday business of making a living, and a weak sense of responsibility for the welfare of the domain as a political entity made villagers and town-dwellers a hard lot to mobilize. These commoners exhibited a short-lived enthusiasm for guns and glory, but before long their own ideas of self-interest prevailed. Training continued down to the Restoration, but absenteeism was a problem, and a first-rate fighting force did not materialize. Conceptually innovative as they were, the black coats lacked the leadership qualities they needed to motivate their commoner militiamen.

In the sphere of economic policy, the Kaga reformers of the 1860s enjoyed greater success. Because Kanazawa decision makers never set their sights beyond improving the financial standing of the *han,* however, this success was less than brilliant. Change did not occur in many segments of the local economy, nor did the idea of economic development gain a momentum of its own. The authorities continued to control the local economy for their own purposes, using their power for the benefit of the *han.* They do not seem to have dared to let the economy take its own course very far, even in those periods when they encouraged trade production by setting up a *sanbutsu kata* or some similar office, or by appointing commoner facilitators of commerce and industry in various locations around the *han.* The persistence of the policy of exacting extraordinary payments from commoners and samurai is evidence of the continuity in thinking on the part of successive groups of *han* leaders who were otherwise quite different from one another. It is true that the "loans" taken from samurai stipends and the extraordinary levies on commoners, combined with retrenchment, helped to alleviate *han* indebtedness; by Okumura Terumichi's time, the Kaga debt had been reduced to 71,783 *kan.*[41] It is also true, but no one in the Kaga leadership was canny enough to perceive, that repaying the *han* debt had a high opportunity cost. On this score, the big domain on the Japan Sea again invites invidious comparison with Chōshū. The large southwestern domain used an office called the *buikukyoku* to manage investments and to accumulate savings over a period of decades when regular expenditures—which were recorded in a completely separate set of books and handled out of separate revenues—exceeded revenues and were causing *han* debt to rise.[42] Kaga kept its creditors happy, but failed to build up significant savings or to stimulate the local economy in a noteworthy measure.

One of the steps the Kaga reformers did take to improve economic conditions in the domain was to order, in 1863, a thorough survey of the state of things. At the same time, they appointed magistrates of production *(san-butsukata bugyō)* within the finance office *(san'yōba)* to oversee the program of encouraging higher output.[43] Ten men served as magistrates of production in the remaining years of *han* rule. They were, in the words of economic historian Tabata Tsutomu, "typical lower-middle samurai," as judged by their birth-status and their stipends. (Appendix 1 shows the stratification of the Maeda retainer corps in the late Tokugawa era.) Tabata has averaged their incomes and arrived at a figure a'little over 150 *koku* per annum. Probably the status of these magistrates reflects the importance that the domain ascribed to their work—it was worth doing, but it was not all that prestigious, and it was only one of several efforts, most of them outside the realm of economic policy, that the domain was making to strengthen itself.

Out in the countryside, thirty supervisors of production affairs *(sanbutsu-kata goyō nushitsuke)* were appointed to assist the magistrates. From one to three peasant worthies in each county and from one to four townsman worthies in each town became supervisors. Every one of them was of village-group headman status or town-ward elder status.

The *han* finance office detailed the tasks of the production office and its branches in 1864. In doing so, Kaga officials articulated the notion of "the benefit of the domain" *(okuni no eki)*, a concept fundamentally the same as Okumura Hidezane's *okuni no dairi* of two decades earlier. The production office was to benefit the domain by performing three principal services: namely, expanding the output of commodities, controlling the flow of commodities and siphoning off profits for the use of the *han,* and forcing down prices. These objectives were sufficiently exciting to win the support of many middle and lower samurai and of many commoners, who came forward to help implement the *sanbutsukata* scheme for the promotion of production and marketing. Over the next several years, however, Kaga's economic reform plans got hung up on the shoals of self-contradiction. Although output was increased, too much of it was exported outside the domain, and control of the circulation of goods within the *han* was so tight that people suffered from shortages. Markets defied bureaucrats' orders, and prices kept on rising. Perhaps if economic development had been the main goal, the three services of the production office might have been successfully coordinated, and the benefit of the domain would have been a happy side-effect of the interaction. But instead the main objective was the perpetuation and strengthening of a small feudal state.

In the sixties as throughout Nariyasu's tenure as daimyo, Kaga officials had the good of the domain in the forefront of their consciousness. They construed that good narrowly. Content with their enviable position in the *bakuhan* system, they sought to remedy the ills of the domanial economy and to build up military might, but not to restructure the whole system of power that accorded primacy to the Tokugawa regime in Edo and excluded all but the hereditary followers of the Tokugawa family (the *fudai*) from participation in national decision making. For the men who dominated policy in Kanazawa, it was enough to control the biggest *han*. The ascendant virtues of the feudal ethos—loyalty and filial piety—had long since been interpreted so as to place the lord and the domain in the focal position in the samurai's value scheme. *Han* leaders redoubled the moral force of these ideals of loyalty and filial piety by rewarding obedience and punishing nonconformity, and by carefully distributing scarce official positions. Such practices inhibited most Maeda retainers from questioning the policies that Nariyasu approved.

A crisis arose in 1864 out of the newly adversarial relationship between the imperial court and its supporters, on the one hand, and the shogunate and its backers, on the other. Kaga's disposition of this crisis casts further light on the continuity in nineteenth-century *han* politics. The first half of 1864 was a particular time of troubles, and a confused changeability appears in Kaga policy. By the end of the year, however, *han* authorities reaffirmed their faith in inherited status and ideals, and rejected a vision of power that called for a restructuring of the *bakuhan* system. They also showed themselves to be averse to the risk of action. A movement to serve the emperor (*kinnō undō*) sprang up among Kaga men, challenging the supremacy of the shogunate. *Han* leaders quashed the movement, intending thereby to protect the domanial interest. By the end of 1864, Kaga dissidents no longer threatened the established order.[44]

For generations, Kaga had discouraged members of the Maeda band of retainers from fraternization with men of other *han*.[45] Applying to human relations the same bias that prompted them to try to create an economy unaffected by external forces, Kaga leaders sought to make the Maeda samurai corps more susceptible to the direction of their feudal superiors than they might have been if they had enjoyed free intercourse with critics as well as supporters of the existing system. In large measure, this attempt to foster a compliant spirit among Kaga retainers worked.

Despite the suffocating climate of opinion, a few men of Kaga dared to challenge the assumptions of the *bakuhan* system. In the early sixties, Maeda Yoshiyasu, the sickly but politically sensitive heir to the domain, lent his ear to men who wanted Kaga to change its tack in relations with the shogunate, other domains, and the emperor. Yoshiyasu troubled himself less with the burden of vested interests—interests of the *han* within the *bakuhan* system and of various social status groups—than his father. Like many Japanese of the day who were paying serious attention to politics, the heir to Kaga had come to feel that some change in the organization of decision making was necessary if Japan was to face up to foreign nations whose demands for increased communication and trade were backed by a warmaking potential obviously superior to Japan's. Yoshiyasu had also come to believe that he owed a deep commitment to the emperor.

The seeds of the pro-imperial, antiforeign movement in Kanazawa were first sown in the house of *han* elder Yokoyama Takaakira, beginning in 1860. A rear vassal who served Yokoyama, Noguchi Onokichi, returned home in that year, after a period of study in Edo, and began propagating doctrines that contained the potential to subvert the *bakuhan* framework. Noguchi inspired a number of men to become concerned about the position of the emperor in the Japanese polity, a matter to which the scholars of Mito had lately given much thought, and this stirred a new interest in politics beyond the borders of the Maeda domain. In Noguchi's circle were several highly placed samurai, men attendant upon Yoshiyasu, and a few commoners as well.[46]

Han officials tried to put a damper on the extra-domanial interests of this small coterie of imperial enthusiasts. When one of the commoners in Noguchi's group, a town doctor named Ogawa Kōzō, who had versed himself in the politics of Kyoto while studying there, presented a memorial in 1862 urging that Kaga back a new union between the imperial court and the shogunate *(kōbu gattai)*, *han* authorities not only rejected the petition, but also had Ogawa confined and manacled in his home in Tsurugi.[47]

Events the following year constrained Kaga leaders to shift their tactics. Shogun Iemochi decided to make a state visit to the old imperial capital and ordered Nariyasu and other lords to precede him there.[48] The domanial interest suddenly required men who knew something about the politics of the imperial court and other domains. Kaga bureaucrats who had confined their expertise to their own *han* and its relations with the *bakufu* turned to men like Ogawa. The doctor was pardoned, given a place in Nariyasu's retinue, provided with a small stipend, and sent to Kyoto. Several others from Kanazawa who had been aroused by the ideas of revering the emperor and expelling the barbarians *(sonnō jōi)* were also in the party that accompanied Nariyasu in 1863.

When the Kaga men reached Kyoto, they discovered that political opinion was polarized. One side, centered on the imperial court, clamored for implementation of an order to drive off the foreigners, which Emperor Kōmei had issued earlier that year. The other side, led by Tokugawa Iemochi, preferred a more moderate approach to the problem of how to deal with foreigners. The charged political atmosphere of the ancient capital shocked Kaga conservatives. Many of them came around to the pro-imperial, antiforeign position as they discussed national and international issues.

Few Kaga men became abidingly dedicated to these views, however. After Iemochi returned to Edo and Nariyasu to Kanazawa, the shogunate summoned both Nariyasu and Yoshiyasu to attend a conference of eastern daimyo. Before responding, Nariyasu called Kaga's important officials to a council in Kanazawa castle. The Maeda band decided to equivocate. They would neither commit themselves to the shogunate, as they always had done in the past, nor would they take a pro-court stance. It was determined that Nariyasu would excuse himself from the shogun's conference on grounds of a pretended illness. Yoshiyasu would go alone to Edo. Kaga would comply with the shogunate on the surface, while reserving a measure of independence and avoiding the risk of definite commitment to one side or the other.

Members of the Kaga pro-imperial party who had stayed in Kyoto succeeded in aborting this plan. By persuading two ranking court nobles to intercede with Kaga elders, the activists managed to have Yoshiyasu's trip to Edo canceled, eliminating, on this occasion, even the appearance of cooperation with the Tokugawa.

Failure to comply with the *bakufu* did not exactly constitute support for the cause of the imperial court. Nariyasu indicated this when the court called on him to return to Kyoto to pay homage to Emperor Kōmei later in 1863. Declining, the Kaga lord justified himself in a letter to the emperor:

> Your subject personally laments that although Your Majesty has repeatedly written to the shogunate urging the expulsion of barbarians, the shogunate has always postponed the date of implementing this. It is your subject's belief that the foundation of a policy of expelling the barbarians lies in bringing accord to the hearts of all the people of our land. But at present, because political orders do not go along a single path, it is impossible for the course of people's hearts to be united. Your subject feels pain in his heart day and night because of this.[49]

Nariyasu concluded by imploring the emperor to delegate to the shogunate all military matters pertaining to driving off the barbarians and, to make sure that the shogunate fulfilled its responsibility, to designate Nariyasu as the emperor's agent for remonstrating with the shogunate. Nariyasu placed himself squarely on the fence. He would serve the emperor, but on his own terms, and in a position that placed him between the court and the *bakufu*. Nothing came of his letter.

Writing to the emperor, Nariyasu marshaled several platitudes—his enunciation of the importance of accord or harmony *(wa)* and his use of the metaphor of a single path or road *(ittō)* are both hackneyed, for example—but there is no reason to regard the letter as disingenuous. A similar line of thinking led him to oppose the shogunate's plan to send a military force to punish Chōshū for its disobedience to *bakufu* policy, when word of that plan reached Kanazawa in the second month of 1864. Nariyasu wrote to a member of the shogunate's senior council defending Chōshū's actions in attempting to mediate between the court and the shogunate. As he had in his message to Emperor Kōmei, Nariyasu stressed the value of accord. This time he made clear that he believed it to be a prime necessity. The danger for Japan was external, he observed; then he asked, "If we now allow brothers to become divided against one another, with what strength do we hope to defend ourselves against foreign enemies?"[50]

Early in 1864, weary of steering between the court and the *bakufu*, Nariyasu contemplated passing the title of lord on to his son, who was already in his thirties. But because the heir associated with men who were considered radicals, men who wanted to take Kaga into the camp of the imperial court and to work against the long-accepted primacy of the shogunate, opinion among Nariyasu's senior advisers ran against turning the domain over to Yoshiyasu. It would be more politic, these conservatives felt, to wait until questions of power distribution between shogunate and court had been resolved. Yoshiyasu's succession was accordingly put off.

The high-water mark of the Kaga movement to support the emperor was reached in the fifth and sixth months of 1864. Yoshiyasu joined the Kaga contingent in Kyoto, and on the twentieth of the fifth month went to the palace for an audience with the emperor. Two weeks later Yoshiyasu expressed his *sonnō jōi* beliefs in a memorial to the *bakufu* senior council. The Kaga heir praised the extremists who had recently been pressing to drive off the barbarians and argued that all Japanese ports except Nagasaki and Hakodate should be closed to foreigners. As for the plan to send troops to punish Chōshū, still being bruited about, Yoshiyasu reminded the senior council of his father's letter of the second month and added his own opposition.[51]

Circumstances changed swiftly, beginning nine days after Yoshiyasu addressed the senior council. Chōshū soldiers based in Osaka seemed to threaten an attack of Kyoto, and on 6/24 *bakufu* officials ordered various *han*, including Kaga, to fortify strong points around the old capital. Chōshū activists scrambled to tell influential men around Kyoto more about their brand of antiforeignism and to explain why their domain should not be punished for taking an uncooperative posture toward the shogunate. Yoshiyasu was one of those who were receptive to Chōshū appeals. He sought to play a conciliatory role, sending one messenger to *bakufu* representatives in Kyoto, asking them to call off the punishment of Chōshū, and dispatching other envoys to Chōshū leaders, promising his own good offices in obtaining a withdrawal of false charges against them if they would remove their troops from the region of the capital. While Yoshiyasu was trying to avert the outbreak of open hostilities, Kaga officers in Kyoto twice refused shogunal orders to send troops to aid in the defense of Fushimi, one of the important approaches to the city.

Yoshiyasu's efforts at mediation failed. In the seventh month of 1864, Chōshū forces launched their attack. It turned out to be ill advised. Troops fighting for the shogunate thrashed the Chōshū rebels. The voices of those who had objected to a *bakufu* expedition against Chōshū were stilled. Later in the year, Kaga soldiers would join the *bakufu* force sent to southwestern Japan.

Chōshū's defeat and the fact that Yoshiyasu had associated himself with Chōshū signalled the beginning of the end of the Kanazawa loyalist movement. The Maeda heir incurred the wrath of his father and the shogun by withdrawing from Kyoto, taking a body of Kaga troops and leaving a subordinate in charge of his guard post, on 7/19, the very day Chōshū mounted its attack. Yoshiyasu, who did suffer from a chronic illness, asserted that his condition had worsened, making it impossible for him to remain on duty. This explanation satisfied no one. Nariyasu was furious when he learned that his son had left the capital, and through a messenger he lectured Yoshiyasu about the gravity of failing to stand steadfastly when he had been assigned to do so. Illness was no excuse. The *bakufu*, which was aware of Yoshiyasu's sympathies, suspected that he had left Kyoto so as not to have to fight against Chōshū or straightforwardly refuse to fight against it.

The price of engaging in anti-establishment political action was high for men of Kaga. Yoshiyasu had, on leaving Kyoto, set out on the road for Kanazawa, almost certainly in hopes of avoiding losses to his small band of loyalists. The party had stopped to rest at Kaizu, a Maeda possession on the northern shore of Lake Biwa, when men bringing instructions from Nariyasu caught up with them on 8/8. Among the daimyo's messages was one to Yoshiyasu's senior aide. This man, Matsudaira Daini, as personal attendant (*soba yōnin*) to the heir, bore responsibility for Yoshiyasu's actions in the imperial city. For abetting Yoshiyasu's pro-imperial adventurism by carrying messages to and from the Chōshū residence and the offices of the *bakufu*, Nariyasu sentenced Daini to death. He was to commit suicide on the spot. Daini carried out the lord's command without hesitation or complaint, according to the almost morbidly detailed account in the diary of Sagawa Yoshisuke. To Sagawa, Daini's vassal, had fallen the grisly task of serving as second (*kaishaku*) at the ritual disembowelment, and between the lines of his diary one can glimpse the doubts that he and the condemned man felt about Kaga feudal justice. Overtly Daini expressed no thought of disobedience or resentment. He went through with the *seppuku* with a composure that is a testimonial to the power of the samurai ideals of self-control, loyalty, and obedience.[52]

The rest of Yoshiyasu's party was permitted to return to Kanazawa. There they were brought before the domain magistrate of justice *(kujiba bugyō)*, and forty-one of them were found guilty of breaking *han* discipline while in Kyoto. In the tenth month of 1864, the magistrate pronounced sentences. Four men of relatively high samurai rank who had been close to the heir were ordered to kill themselves by cutting open their bellies. Three men were banished. Doctor Ogawa, whose birth as a commoner made thinkable a punishment less honorable than might have been meted out to a samurai of equal attainment, was beheaded. A man of rear vassal status was condemned to die by *ikidō,* the simultaneous severing of the convicted man's head and trunk, a method of execution used in Kaga but not everywhere in Japan. Four other men were sentenced to spend the rest of their lives in prison.[53] Yoshiyasu was exempted from the magistrate's proceedings, but he was placed in seclusion *(yūkyo)* as soon as he got home, and shortly thereafter, in compliance with *bakufu* wishes, he was put in domiciliary confinement *(kinshin)* as punishment for having left his guard-post in the capital without permission.

Establishmentarian officials in the domain had routed the Kaga movement to support the emperor. Talk of Nariyasu's retirement ceased for a time. The element of turbulence that had been introduced into domanial discourse by Noguchi and other advocates of the imperial cause was eliminated. Military and economic self-strengthening programs tottered along, but Kanazawa leaders shunned further involvement with the court, with other *han,* and even with the *bakufu.*

The shogun Tokugawa Iemochi pardoned Maeda Yoshiyasu in the fourth month of 1865. This act followed a lobbying campaign conducted by Nariyasu with the help of the daimyo of Hiroshima. Iemochi, no longer able to do things by his own fiat, as all his Tokugawa predecessors had been, took care to secure the emperor's agreement before lifting Yoshiyasu's confinement.

Not quite a year later, the shogun summoned Yoshiyasu to Chiyoda

Castle in Edo and informed him that Nariyasu's petition to retire had been approved. On 1866/4/4, Yoshiyasu became the fourteenth Maeda to serve as daimyo of Kaga. Nariyasu stepped aside. At Yoshiyasu's request, however, the old lord kept an eye on things and continued giving his opinions about domain policy. Healthier at fifty-five than his thirty-five-year-old son, Nariyasu would continue to influence the administration of domain and family affairs, and Maeda relations with Kanazawa samurai, on into the 1880s.

Yoshiyasu applied himself energetically to the strengthening of his domain. On 1866/8/18, he set the tone for his administration by ordering that all Kaga samurai be trained in the use of Western firearms.[54] Four months later he commanded that outmoded Japanese military ceremonial paraphernalia be discarded and needless expenditures eliminated, and he ordered his retainers to submit to him their views on reorganizing the *han* military.[55] At the beginning of the new year, he announced: "Upon careful consideration of these [collected opinions of Kaga samurai], I believe that there is no course superior to that of reorganizing our existing military system and forming rifle corps. However, this, the making of a militarized state, is an extremely serious matter, and therefore we must raise up all the strength of our three provinces (*sanshū* [Kaga, Noto, and Etchū] *zenryoku*) and spend what has to be spent, and, not being bound by past usages, we must get results."[56]

Questions of national military organization were not raised in this survey of Kaga opinion or the lord's response. What Yoshiyasu worried about was the defense posture of the domain. Over the next few months, new military training facilities were created, Kaga soldiers intensified their drill, and samurai with bureaucratic jobs were required to join the soldiers in practicing gunnery. On 1867/10/18, Yoshiyasu replaced Kaga's old-fashioned military organization with several rifle companies.[57] Four days before, Tokugawa Yoshinobu, who had succeeded Iemochi as shogun at the end of 1866, had given up the powers of government to the emperor. Tension was high throughout the land, as it was unclear who, or what kind of body, would take responsibility for managing national affairs. For several weeks an uneasy truce obtained, and there was no direct military confrontation between pro-Tokugawa and pro-imperial forces. During this time, Kaga, hedging its bets, modified its corps structure once more, forming ten rifle companies and one artillery company.[58]

The best-known historical fact about Kaga's reformed military is what the *han* did not do with it: Kaga did not send troops to Kyoto to become entangled in the struggle that culminated in the proclamation of the restoration of imperial rule on 1867/12/9. The point that needs emphasis in a study of Japanese nation-building, however, is that in the biggest domain in the land, a modern military force was being formed for the independent use of that domain on the eve of the creation of a centralizing national regime. It can be supposed that this hardly bode well for the would-be national leaders around the young Emperor Meiji.

Nor was the modernization of the *han* military the only evidence of Kaga separatism in 1867. Sir Harry Parkes, British Minister of Japan, visited the Maeda domain in the seventh month of 1867 to explore the possibility of designating Nanao as one of the five ports to be opened to foreign ships under the provisions of recent treaties. As his aide Ernest Satow later recalled, Parkes found Kaga officials unreceptive:

> What the Kaga people feared was that this would lead to [Nanao's] being taken away from them by the tycoon's government, as in former times had happened in the case of Nagasaki and Niigata. . . . The Territory of Nanao had belonged to the Maeda clan from very early times; it was the only good port in the three provinces of Kaga, Etchiu, and Noto, and could ill be spared. They would dislike to share the local administration with the [Edo] government, nor could they give it up to them altogether.[59]

Likely the Kaga officials overestimated the power of the shogunate at this time, but in being cautious and protective of Nanao, they were in tune with the dominant mood of *han* policy makers.

The announcement of the restoration of imperial rule caught Kaga leaders unready to respond. Yoshiyasu arrived in Kyoto that day, but had no part in the restoration coup d'état. The advocates of the overthrow of the *bakufu* and the creation of a new government had seized the initiative in the councils around the emperor. Tokugawa Yoshinobu, who had expected the shogunate to be replaced by a federation of lords and court in which he would hold a major share of responsibility and power, left Kyoto on 12/12 and went to his Osaka residence. The proclamation of 12/9 had not made plain how national authority would be exercised. The group around the fifteen-year-old emperor was volatile and unclear about the particulars of the course of policy once a court government had been set up. Tokugawa Yoshinobu still had the backing of many ardent partisans, quite a few of whom had followed him to Osaka, and he was widely recognized as able and experienced.

The coup of 12/9 had posed a question of allegiance. Political men had to choose between the coalition around the emperor, spearheaded by Chōshū and Satsuma, and the group that continued to support the Tokugawa. It was not congenial to Kanazawa statesmen to make a clear-cut choice, especially not in the face of such uncertainty. Within Kaga circles, the Tokugawa side was more popular than the imperial side, but there was no clear consensus. In a sense, as historian Tokuda Toshiaki has remarked, where to stand on the national power question was of secondary concern to men who were accustomed to placing the well-being of their own *han* first: "The question became, under the preponderant power of conservative upper samurai, which side should they choose for the sake of the security of their own domanial system?" [60] Yoshiyasu's first move was to extricate himself from the embarrassment of taking sides. The day Yoshinobu took Tokugawa backers to Osaka, and just three days after he himself had arrived in Kyoto, the Kaga lord reminded the court of his illness and declared that there was no need for his services in the capital anyway. [61] The next day he set out for home.

On the road, the Maeda party arrived at a formula by which to define their actions toward the competitors for national power: "If matters become extremely urgent, we will not necessarily follow the Tokugawa, but will serve the emperor and govern our own domain." The key phrase here was *kinnō kakkyo*, "serve the emperor and govern the domain" [62] The decision to take this stance was reached on 12/15 and communicated to the branch *han* of Toyama and Daishōji as well as to men in the Kanazawa government. One of the elders of Toyama *han* confided to Kaga elder Yokoyama Masakazu that he was made "extremely happy" when he heard of it. [63]

Nariyasu gave his imprimatur to the policy of concentrating on domanial self-interest when Yoshiyasu got back to the Maeda castle town. To Honda Masachika, a *hakka* head who had become one of the most influential elders

of Kaga, the former lord wrote, "On the resolve to govern our three provinces as a separate entity *(sanshū kakkyo no kakugo):* without this, nothing will work."[64]

A policy of serving the emperor and looking to the self-rule of the domain was easier to pronounce than it was to pursue. The old Maeda-Tokugawa link nearly pulled the decision to serve the emperor out of Yoshiyasu's mind, and the week beginning 1868/1/6 was blotted by a tergiversation that did not help the reputation of the big *han* or its men, at the time or later. When fighting between Tokugawa and Satsuma-Chōshū forces erupted on 1/3, Yoshinobu sent Yoshiyasu a personal appeal for military support. Upon receiving it, Yoshiyasu ordered a detachment of Kaga soldiers to march to the Kyoto-Osaka region to aid the former shogun.[65] News that the Tokugawa side had already lost the first battle in what would evolve into a sixteen-month war had not reached Kanazawa when the lord sent these troops off, and the common opinion among Kaga men at the time was that Satsuma was abusing the imperial sanction, turning the young Mutsuhito's commands to its own advantage.

Reports from Kaga officials in Kyoto, including news of the Sat-Chō victory at Toba-Fushimi on 1/4, caused Yoshiyasu to give up the idea of fighting on Yoshinobu's side. On 1/12, the Kanazawa lord sent a messenger to intercept the Kaga force on its way to the capital. Reassessing national power relationships, Yoshiyasu reverted to the decision to follow the imperial court. He wrote to the court pledging his support, also on 1/12.[66] During the next week, Kaga authorities informed all Maeda retainers of the domanial will to serve the emperor and to join the imperial armies that were being organized to overcome Tokugawa resistance.[67]

To manifest Kaga's allegiance to the imperial throne, Nariyasu journeyed to Kyoto. Substituting for his son, who was ailing again, the retired lord took 2,950 retainers with him. He arrived in the imperial city on 2/22, and was admitted to an audience with the emperor on 2/28. To symbolize their severance of bonds with the Tokugawa family, the Maeda at this time dropped the practice of using the surname Matsudaira for ceremonial purposes. The Maeda and several other daimyo lineages had borne this Tokugawa branch family name as an alternative to their own names for many generations, having been made fictive members of the shogun's clan.[68]

Maeda representatives in Kyoto petitioned the new government to assign

Kaga units to the imperial military force that was being formed to bring the region to the northeast of Kanazawa under the control of the new regime. They asked that Kaga troops be placed at the front, and they offered to undertake some of the expenses of the imperial militia.[69] The court responded on 2/23 that the composition of the vanguard had already been determined. Kaga soldiers were not immediately required, but more imperial troops and funds would be welcome in the future.[70] On 3/5, Yoshiyasu pledged to send 700,000 bales *(hyō)* of rice, over the next seven months, to help defray military expenses of the new government. The following month Maeda troops were mustered into the imperial army. By the time they returned home on 1869/3/30, over 7,200 Kaga men had taken part in the war in northeastern Japan, and 103 had given their lives in the imperial cause.

Kaga's contribution to the consolidation of imperial power in 1868 and 1869 was greater than its battlefield losses might suggest. Not only did the domain provision and pay troops—it laid out 100,000 *ryō* in military expenses and 300,000 rounds of ammunition—it also gave the court 30,000 *ryō* for administrative expenses in the pacified areas of the northeast and another 5,000 *ryō* for construction work in the imperial palace. Rice gifts from Kaga to the new government in 1868 exceeded 100,000 bales.[71]

Yet even after their decision to adhere to the coalition around the emperor, the Maeda and their top advisers did not conceive of their actions in terms of submerging themselves into a centralized nation and giving up their nearly autonomous identity. One condition that permitted them to go on oblivious of any thought of dissolution was the hands-off policy of the emperor's government. The Restoration leaders appointed their own men as governors of territories taken over from Tokugawa supporters in the war of 1868–1869, but for a while they made no move to appropriate the authority of daimyo who supported them. They left local power, including the power of taxation, in the hands of the lords and their organizations. When the emperor's officials, who had moved their operations to Tokyo (as they renamed Edo) in 1868/7, began to turn their attention to subnational administrative matters, they proceeded at a deliberate pace. Their initial move was more formal than substantive. On 1868/10/28, Tokyo policymakers ordered the *han* to reorganize their bureaucratic structures, so that all parts of the land would be under a uniform administrative system. The same law stipulated that official appointments in the *han* must be made according to men's abilities, regardless of their social status.[72]

Yoshiyasu complied with the revision of the office system and replaced the old council of elders and domain magistracies. In fact, this involved little more than changing the names in Kaga's well developed organization. Yoshiyasu ignored the part of the 10/28 law having to do with ability and status, it seems, for he made no significant personnel changes.[73] It may have chanced that ability correlated highly with hereditary status in Kanazawa, although the history of previous Kaga administrations suggests that the correlation had been irregular in the past. At any rate the top four officers in Kanazawa in 1868/12 were *hakka* family heads who had been elders, and eight of the top eleven officers were men of the highest level of samurai society whose annual stipends were 10,000 *koku* or more. In substance, in its local governance, the Maeda domain was the same in the first year and a half after the Restoration as it had been before.

Assassination may have cut off an opportunity for Kaga to come to the forefront of the Meiji leadership. Early in 1869, according to amateur historian Lieutenant General Inoue Ichiji, there was talk of a Kaga-Chōshū alliance. The key figures were Ōmura Masujirō of Chōshū, Vice-Minister of Military Affairs in the Meiji government, and Adachi Kōnosuke of Kaga, who had once been an outstanding student in the academy that Ōmura founded. Adachi was visiting Ōmura in 1869/2, with the purpose of arranging a meeting between the Meiji leader and Kaga elder Honda Masachika, when a group of disgruntled samurai—opponents of the system of universal military service which Ōmura had championed—burst in and hacked both men to death.[74] After this, talk of alliance between Chōshū and Kaga died.

The return of the *han* registers on 1869/6/17 brought Kaga more completely under the legal control of the central government. Yoshiyasu, like all other daimyo, presented to the throne the title to his lands and the people who lived on them. Everyone was to understand that these titles had been held in trust, as it were, and were now being given back to the emperor as a gesture of loyalty and unity. The emperor appointed Yoshiyasu governor *(chihanji* or *hanchiji)* of Kanazawa *han* on the same day. From this date the name Kaga was not to be used officially. The young Meiji Emperor transformed all the other old daimyo of Japan with the same stroke of his brush. No longer rulers by inheritance, the erstwhile lords became chief

administrative officers by direct imperial appointment. The Tokyo government induced daimyo to accept this change by appealing to their sense of
duty and obligation, and also by offering the new governors a salary equal
to one-tenth the annual tax revenues of their jurisdictions in the years
1864–1868. As revenues had averaged 636,876 *koku* in the Maeda territory, Yoshiyasu's stipend was set at 63,687 *koku* 6 *to*.[75] Generous treatment
of the one-time feudal barons soothed the pain that some must have felt
upon the abandonment of old usages.

Later in 1869, Yoshiyasu carried out personnel changes along with an
office reform. A few middle and lower-middle samurai—men with stipends
in the range of 200 to 500 *koku* per year—entered the inner circle of *han*
leadership.[76] The need for specialized financial expertise was probably what
pressed the Kanazawa governor to reevaluate his reliance on the well-born.
Han indebtedness had begun to climb precipitously after the Restoration,
as modernizing reforms and contributions to the new central government
were paid for.

Between 1868 and the middle of 1871, Kanazawa *han* borrowed heavily
from nongovernment creditors. Tokuda Toshiaki has calculated this debt of
the first three and a half years after the Restoration at 382,629 yen (con-
verting into the currency unit adopted in 1871, when one *ryō* was declared
to be worth one yen), a sum 12 percent greater than it had borrowed during
the twenty-four years before the Restoration.[77] Kanazawa *han* borrowings
from 1868 to 1871 were more than double those of Satsuma (Kagoshima
han) or Chōshū (Yamaguchi *han*).

The bulk of Kanazawa expenditures went to samurai in the form of stipend payments, but the *han* did provide some services. It maintained order,
for one thing; this was extremely helpful to the new central government
while the men around the emperor concentrated on defeating the Tokugawa
diehards and setting up offices to manage national affairs. *Han* administrators also performed valuable service for the new Meiji state by compiling
statistics on population, surface area, and productivity, and submitting
those to Tokyo. To enable the central authorities to evaluate the state of
local government nationwide, the imperial government on 1870/11/7 ordered *han* to report on all the changes that they had carried out. Kanazawa
officials had their report in the hands of Tokyo authorities by the next
month.[78]

The *han* did not have to remit taxes to the national treasury in the years of Yoshiyasu's governorship. Tokyo leaders did not feel strong enough to require this in the early years of their regime. In the military sphere, however, the national government imposed its control in the first month of 1870 by specifying the strength of various *han* military organizations and ordering that these forces be constituted as standing militia. For every 10,000 *koku* of regular tax revenues, a *han* was to maintain one company of soldiers. Kanazawa dissolved its rifle companies and replaced them with five infantry battalions and three artillery companies.[79] Full military integration—the creation of national armed forces that put men from various parts of Japan into the same units—would not come until after the abolition of *han* and establishment of prefectures, but this 1870 reorganization of the Kanazawa *han* militia was a major gesture of cooperation with the national government.

As the power of the men around the Meiji Emperor waxed, and they demonstrated that they could deal effectively with the multiplicity of problems that faced them, the spirit of separatism in the old Maeda domain, *sanshū kakkyo* or *kakkyo shugi,* waned. As early as 1869, when representatives of the various *han* in Tokyo debated whether Japan should keep its decentralized domanial organization (*hōkensei,* "feudalism") or, alternatively, should adopt a system of counties and prefectures (*gunkensei,* a more centralized form of subnational government), the spokesman for Kaga argued for counties and prefectures. By proposing that the counties and prefectures have hereditary governors, the Kanazawa representative hinted that his domain was loath to give up its proud heritage entirely; he seems to have had the interest of his old lord in mind. Opinion among the participants in this 1869 debate was divided, and when no consensus on the ideal form of subnational government emerged, no reforms were immediately introduced.[80] But now even men of Kaga desired stronger linkage between national and local authority.

The central government legislated the *han* out of existence on 1871/7/14. In the rescript mandating the replacement of *han* by prefectures, as we noted earlier, the emperor declared that the operations of *han* had generated "the disease of government proceeding from multiform centers." Henceforth the government would center in a single authority.[81]

Maeda Yoshiyasu and the officials in his *han* administration accepted the government's decree without any sign of resistance. Among them, if not among all men of Kanazawa, the protection of Kaga, the preservation of *han* independence, and the notion of local economic self-sufficiency no longer seemed wise. The principles that had undergirded political decision making in Kanazawa for two-and-a-half centuries no longer applied. The former lord and those who shared responsibility with him now regarded building a strong nation as the number one priority. Political prudence had a new meaning.

Men of the old Maeda band played supporting, not leading, roles in the drama of making a new Japan in the late nineteenth century. At the critical moment, before the Restoration, they had missed the opportunity to act in behalf of the imperial cause or to join the victorious coalition.

Adherence to a line of policy that had always yielded success in the past—not mere weakness or pusillanimity—explains the failure of Kaga to act or take a clear position in the conflict between the shogunate and the emperor-centered group in the period just before the proclamation of the restoration of imperial rule. Neither men at the time nor historians have generally appreciated this point. What had made and kept Kaga rich and strong within the context of the Tokugawa *bakuhan* system was caution, avoidance of risk, careful cultivation of the inheritance of the Maeda, and faithfulness to received values and ideas of good governance. Just this constellation of values—in a word, this prudence, traditionally conceived—underlay the fence-sitting and self-strengthening of Kaga in the final decades of *bakuhan* rule.

What Maeda Nariyasu and Yoshiyasu and most of the men who worked for them did not understand is that caution is not the same thing as prudence. There is risk in being overcautious. Maintaining tradition, they prevented alternative policy visions from maturing or getting a fair hearing. Such visions might have made men of Kaga more flexible and better equipped to deal with the crises of the 1860s and the challenges of making a new Japan. But the need for flexibility and innovative thinking was not evident to most of the Maeda corps in the years of Nariyasu and Yoshiyasu. In the end, the men who had hoped to conserve the Kaga heritage saw it succumb precisely because their notion of prudence was inadequate to guide them safely through the perils of changing circumstances.

TWO

A Han *Is Made a Prefecture:*
Administration in Ishikawa Prefecture,
1871–1878

After the old daimyo was gone, who ran things at the local level, and how? This chapter treats prefectural administration and finance between 1871 and 1878, formative years of subnational government throughout Japan and the period covered by the terms of office of the first two outsiders appointed as governors of the area that had been the biggest *han*. The case of Ishikawa Prefecture cannot be accounted for adequately by the interpretations of these years that have been popular among students of the Meiji era; for instance, the characterization of the early Meiji as the period of formation of "emperor system absolutism" extending to the lowest levels of society seems oversimple when one looks at the Ishikawa experience.

Men sent to Kanazawa from other parts of Japan by the central government administered Ishikawa Prefecture effectively, but they did not carry out the letter of every Tokyo decree. On the other hand, neither did they attempt to run a small independent state with procedures and institutions different from those sanctioned by Tokyo, or with a local power base of their own. In this prefecture, not all local power was subsumed to the central government during these years. Local authorities dealt with problems as they occurred, sometimes in response to central government orders, sometimes on the basis of their own reading of the local situation. The pattern does not bear the stamp of a grand design, but shows the influence of particular local conditions.

The first eleven years of the Meiji period, 1867–1878, from the Restoration to the promulgation of the so-called "Three New Laws," have long been considered the period of creation of a unified state, in terms of central government control over localities.[1] An American scholar once echoed this view by describing these years as a time when "any autonomous powers which local regions might presume to have were subsumed to the state."[2]

Notable postwar studies by Japanese historians have advanced similar interpretations and then gone a step further. University of Tokyo Professor Emeritus Ōishi Kaichirō has commented on the prefectures: "From the outset, they could not be self-governing bodies in any sense of the word. They were mere administrative organs . . . based on the rapid centralization of power which took place before mechanisms allowing for the participation of the people in government could be institutionalized."[3] Ariizumi Sadao has taken a similar line, writing that "the prefectures of that time were no more than outstations of the central government *(seifu desaki kikan)*."[4] Early in the Meiji period, many scholars have contended, the powers of the central government were extended through the prefectures down to the town and village levels, which were transformed from bodies representative of local interests into administrative organs at the tips of the tentacles of state power.[5] Many Japanese writers have agreed with the prominent student of local administration and finance Fujita Takeo that there was a comprehensive design in all that the Meiji government did, namely the establishment of "emperor system absolutism"; the centralization of power during the early Meiji was part of that design and left little room for independent action by localities.[6]

Unification and the centralization of power did not proceed at the same rate in all parts of Japan. The complex record argues against uncritical adoption of views such as Ōishi's or Fujita's. Even after the monumental imperial edict of 1871 that abolished the *han* and established the prefectures, some localities stoutly resisted the Tokyo government's efforts to centralize power. As late as 1877, the statesman Kido Takayoshi was driven to complain in his diary about one of the most flagrant cases of resistance, "While the Home Ministry has been rigorously keeping other prefectures under control, Satsuma is like an independent state. Truly this is unbearable and exasperating for the cause of imperial rule."[7] Kikegawa Hiroshi suggests that it was by no means only in Satsuma that prefectural administrators ran their jurisdictions as "small nations" in the manner of enlightened lords or governors of old and that conditions in the first decade of the Meiji era differed greatly from locality to locality according to the personality and abilities of the prefectural governor.[8]

No thoughtful student would dispute that maintaining order and establishing effective government at the local level were of paramount importance to the Meiji regime in its early years, as it attempted to stabilize its position in the new nation-state and simultaneously to institute vast political and social changes. The actual achievement of the Japanese in this era before 1878, however, has given rise to dispute, and sharply contrasting images of the nature of local government and the degree of centralization, such as Ōishi's and Kikegawa's, are apt to perplex us.

In Ishikawa Prefecture by 1878, the authority of the central government and its appointees was much stronger than it had been in 1871, but it would be going too far to term it "absolute." During these years the prefectural system was firmly established. The old *han* administrative organization was dismantled and a new structure put in its place, and no difficult obstacles hindered the replacement process. Work remained to be done, however, before the Meiji subnational system reached its full elaboration and national unification was fully achieved.

THE FIRST GOVERNOR OF ISHIKAWA PREFECTURE

A month after the abolition of domains and establishment of prefectures, the Meiji government appointed two men to the post of "chief councilor" of Kanazawa Prefecture.[9] One of the appointees, Hayashi Kōtoku, immediately asked to be relieved of this position, and the government obliged him.[10] The other man took the job. His name was Uchida Masakaze, and he hailed from Satsuma. No one was given a higher official title, and thus, as chief councilor, Uchida was in charge.

Uchida (1815–1893) was fifty-five when he was named to the Kanazawa post.[11] He had considerable experience as an administrator, but small fame, and one historian reports that prideful Kaga samurai grumbled at his coming, "What have things come to that we have to put up with this petty samurai Uchida from Satsuma?"[12] For these Kaga critics who had to live with Uchida (and for students trying to understand the early Meiji period), a more useful question would have inquired what sort of man this was, that Tokyo wanted him as prefectural governor in a time of uncertainty and change.

The second son of what might be called an "upper middle samurai" family,[13] Uchida had won recognition from Satsuma leaders in 1862. Summoned to Edo by Shimazu Hisamitsu, the father of the lord and the effective head of the domain, Uchida managed to smuggle weapons into the shogunal capital for use by the Satsuma contingent there. Officials of the shogun questioned Uchida about allegations that he had committed an illegal act, but the cargo had already been unloaded, and the investigators were unable to back their suspicions with evidence.[14]

By 1863 Uchida was an assistant *(soeyaku)* in the Satsuma establishment in Edo and had succeeded his heirless elder brother as head of their family. When Shimazu Hisamitsu went to Kyoto in 1863/3 to discuss the implementation of the policy of expelling the barbarians with leading daimyo Hitotsubashi (later Tokugawa) Yoshinobu, Matsudaira Shungaku, Date Muneki, and Yamanouchi Yōdō, Uchida was ordered to go along.[15] It is unlikely that Uchida Masakaze was in Hisamitsu's closest circle of advisers, for when Hisamitsu gave up the consultations after only a few days and returned to his castle town of Kagoshima, Uchida was not in his retinue. Instead, Uchida went to Osaka, where the *han* assigned him to its business affairs office as magistrate. This was a respectably responsible, if not a glamorous, post in the *han* exchequer.[16] Only seventeen days later, Uchida returned to Kyoto to the Satsuma residence, where he rose to the position of financial affairs officer *(kattegakari)*. In 1865, he had first the status of *sobayaku,* then *sobayōnin,* both translatable as "personal attendant" of the lord. A decade later, after he retired from service in the Meiji government, Uchida would go home to Kagoshima as an official in the Shimazu household, and we might guess from this that even before the Restoration, he had a rather close relationship with Hisamitsu or with the daimyo Tadayoshi.

In the tumultuous Restoration year 1867, Uchida moved from financial affairs to military responsibilities, becoming magistrate of supply *(ō konida bugyō)* for his domain. After the proclamation of the Restoration, Satsuma relieved him of this charge, and he stayed in Kyoto for much of 1868, while Saigō Takamori and other Satsuma military men played prominent roles in the war against *bakufu* diehards in the Northeast. Evidently it was not because he was out of favor that Uchida had remained in the capital, for in 1868/9, he was called to Edo and made responsible for business in the military affairs office *(gunmukan)*. With this appointment, he became an official of the new central government.

When the *han* reformed their systems of administration and official titles in response to a central government order,[17] Satsuma made Uchida *sansei,* which was the third-highest position in the new system of *han* offices.[18] He was assigned to Tokyo as the domain representative *(kōginin)* from Satsuma. In this capacity he sat as a member of the policy deliberative body known as the Kōgisho (later renamed the Shūgiin) which opened 1869/3/7. In 1870 Uchida became an official of the council of state *(dajōkan)*. At the same time the emperor bestowed court rank on him, granting him the fifth rank, junior grade.[19] He was still working in the central government when he was tapped as governor of what was then called Kanazawa Prefecture.[20] Uchida's activities and accomplishments in office in Tokyo are nowhere recorded in detail, but one story that has survived casts him in the part of an old-fashioned political hard-liner. After the assassination of Vice-Minister of Civil Affairs Hirosawa Saneomi in 1871, according to this account, Uchida argued for the imposition of martial law. He was opposed in debate by Kuroda Kiyotaka and others, and he lost.[21]

More important than Uchida's defeat in this instance is the fact that he was in a position to participate in such a debate in 1871. His contumelious Kaga critics should have noted that "this petty samurai from Satsuma" was a mature bureaucrat, accustomed to responsibility and seasoned in the important affairs of his home domain and the new Meiji government. He may not have been nationally famous, but he was not a nobody.

THE PRO-SATSUMA FACTION IN KANAZAWA

It is commonly believed that Uchida was sent to Kanazawa in response to the wishes of an activist group there.[22] Since 1869, some Kaga samurai had had close contacts with Satsuma. In that year, Kanazawa *han* had ordered two young samurai, Kuga Yoshinao and Yoneyama Michio, to make a tour of observation of other provinces of Japan and gather information for refer-

ence as the Kanazawa government carried out various changes. The pair had
gone to Kyoto and consulted Iwashita Masahira, a Satsuma samurai who
headed the Kyoto office of the council of state, and Komatsu Tatewaki,
formerly an elder of Satsuma and also an important man in the Restoration
movement and the new government. Iwashita and Komatsu advised Kuga
and Yoneyama to go to Western Japan, and at the end of 1869, the Kaga
observers boarded a steamship owned by Okayama *han* and sailed to Nagasaki.[23] After a brief stay there, Kuga and Yoneyama made their way to
Kagoshima. In the Satsuma town, the Kanazawa men became friendly with
the Restoration hero Saigō Takamori and his lieutenant and friend Kirino
Toshiaki. Kuga and Yoneyama were deeply impressed by the state of military preparedness in Satsuma, in terms both of materiel—Satsuma had built
up an impressive stock of Western-style weapons—and of samurai spirit.
Already in 1869, Satsuma men harbored a desire to enhance national prestige on the Asian continent.[24]

So enthusiastic were Kuga and Yoneyama about what they had learned
in Kagoshima that they began working on a plan to institute changes in
Kanazawa on the Satsuma model. Leaving Kagoshima early in 1870, they
intended to present the plan to Kanazawa decision makers as soon as possible. Most of the details of their plan have been forgotten, but the first step
in their proposal reminds us that men of Kaga still regarded their lord
favorably and expected that the Maeda would continue to have a major role
in local affairs in the future: Kuga and Yoneyama suggested sending Maeda
Toshitsugu, Yoshiyasu's heir, to study in Kagoshima, accompanied by some
ten outstanding young men of the Kaga *bushi* class.[25]

Before they got back to Kanazawa, the young information-gatherers
stopped in Osaka, where they met a powerful Kanazawa official named Kitagawa Inosaku. Kitagawa dashed cold water on their hopes of persuading
han leaders of their reform plan. Disgusted, Kuga submitted a notice (*dappan todoke*) that he was leaving the *han* and withdrawing his name from the
rolls of Kanazawa *bushi*. Activist samurai of other domains had made this
move fairly often in the years leading up to the Restoration, in order to
gain freedom to act independently on their anti-establishment convictions.
But not samurai of Kaga—there virtually no one handed in such a resignation of status. Kuga's alienation from the *han* turned out to be of short
duration. A Kagoshima samurai friend intervened to calm his ruffled feel-

ings and mediate with Kanazawa authorities to withdraw the resignation notice.[26] Shortly thereafter, in 1870/7, Kuga was granted official permission to return to Nagasaki. He went again to Kagoshima late that year, evidently in hopes of meeting Restoration government leader Iwakura Tomomi, who was there to talk with Shimazu Hisamitsu. Kuga did not get access to Iwakura, but he did meet Kirino Toshiaki in the Satsuma town, and they discussed political affairs. Kuga decided to go to Tokyo. Early in 1871, he left Kagoshima, and two months before the proclamation of the abolition of *han* and creation of prefectures, he reached the new imperial capital.

When *haihan chiken* was announced, Kuga at once got together with other Kanazawa men in Tokyo, including Sugimura Hiromasa and Obata Zōji. They secured an interview with Itagaki Taisuke, who was then a councilor of state. The Kanazawa men reported in depth on the state of their home prefecture, and lobbied with Itagaki for the appointment of a man from Satsuma as governor. Uchida Masakaze's selection for the Kanazawa post is often said to be the result of this meeting.[27]

Nearly any notable man of Satsuma would have satisfied the desires of Kanazawa partisans, so long as he proved familiar with recent reforms in Kagoshima and able to promote similar reforms in Kanazawa. Many Satsuma samurai would have had personal connections with the powerful Satsuma men in the central government. Kanazawa men, who were unrepresented in the upper reaches of the new central government,[28] might well have found great appeal in the prospect of plugging into the Satsuma network of contacts, for the sake of advancing both policy ideas and their own careers. From the point of view of the central government, also, a man from Satsuma would have been a natural choice to be the first appointee as chief officer of what had been the biggest *han*. A man from Chōshū might have done as well. For the new Tokyo regime, the important thing was that the top Kanazawa executive be known to be reliable and loyal to central authority and that he be capable of winning respect in an area with a reputation for haughtiness.[29]

No documentary evidence exists that would prove that Kuga and his associates asked for Uchida by name when they talked to Itagaki about a governor, but even if they had not been acquainted with each other before, it is clear that these men were in touch almost immediately after Uchida was named chief councilor. Uchida appointed Kuga to an official post in the prefectural bureaucracy just a week after he himself had been designated to take the top spot in Kanazawa; he stationed Kuga in Tokyo to handle prefectural business there.[30] Uchida employed Sugimura on 1871/9/25, and four weeks later raised him to provisional chief councilor, the highest ranking officer named by the new governor. Yoneyama Michio also was in the handful of top prefectural officials in Uchida's first days, being named to a post on 1871/9/27.[31] Many Kanazawa men would take places in the new prefectural officialdom, but these admirers of Satsuma are remarkable for the early dates of their appointments and their high ranks. Whether they had a long-standing personal link with Uchida or not, their association with Kagoshima must have been helpful to them.

SHIFTING PREFECTURAL BOUNDARIES

The new chief councilor reached Kanazawa in the ninth month of 1871, a month after Maeda Yoshiyasu had departed for Tokyo as ordered by the central government. Uchida set up office in what had recently been used as the *han* office building, the former residence of the Chō family in Naga-machi, a section of town in which many samurai had long made their homes.[32] The new chief administrator at once encountered a welter of problems, some endemic in the process of structural change in government, some peculiar to the traditions and factional rivalries of Kanazawa.

One source of confusion for early Meiji local administrators was shifting boundaries. Redefinitions of administrative districts were nothing new in Japan, but the scale of change in 1871 was unprecedented. Just before the abolition of the *han*, there were three urban prefectures (*fu*), one city (*shi*), forty-one rural prefectures (*ken*), and 265 *han*. With the annulling of *han* and creation of prefectures, there were three urban prefectures and 302 rural prefectures. Amalgamations reduced the number of rural prefectures to seventy-two by the end of 1871, as the national government sought subnational simplicity and ease of management.[33] The area under Uchida's control typified the expansions and contractions being experienced all around Japan. By the second month of 1872, seven *han* and two areas that had been administered by shogunal agents before the Restoration had been incorporated into Ishikawa Prefecture. Four years later part of three more former *han* were added.[34] Not until May 9, 1883, were Ishikawa Prefecture boundaries set where they remain today. Subprefectural administrative districts, too, were redefined many times, as we shall see. Uchida and his contemporaries could hardly have escaped being hampered by these repeated changes in the populace and the subprefectural local officials to whom they had to give direction and leadership.

Kanazawa Prefecture at the time of Uchida's appointment consisted of most of the ancient province of Kaga—all of Ishikawa County and Kahoku County—as well as most of Noto Province and most of the Etchū Province counties of Tonami, Imizu, and Niikawa. Daishōji Prefecture encompassed Enuma County and most of Nomi County in Kaga. Before the end of 1871, Daishōji was merged into Kanazawa Prefecture, and Noto and Imizu County in Etchū were separated from it; Nanao Prefecture was created from Noto and some contiguous areas, and the other parts of Etchū Province that had been in Kanazawa Prefecture were united with Nei County to form Niikawa Prefecture. This left just the old Kaga Province in Uchida's jurisdiction.

Uchida's responsibility grew the next year when Nanao Prefecture was done away with and Noto was put together with Kaga again. In the eleventh month of 1872, part of the foothills around Mt. Haku were added to Uchida's jurisdiction. No more boundary redefinitions took place during the first governor's term, but several more occurred in succeeding years. In April 1876, all of Etchū Province became part of Ishikawa Prefecture (as Kanazawa had been renamed), and all seven counties of Echizen Province were added four months later.

For nearly five years after this 1876 amalgamation, Ishikawa was the largest prefecture, in population, in the land. Its territory took in most of four ancient provinces. Superordinate size was not a permanent feature of the prefecture that replaced the largest *han,* however. In 1881, the government established Fukui Prefecture, placing the Echizen counties under a new prefectural administration, and in 1883, the present boundaries of the region were set when the government put the Etchū areas into a new prefecture, Toyama, reducing Ishikawa a final time.[35]

The numerous changes in the administrative map annoyed some critical observers of the Meiji government. A society of Kōchi men complained in 1877 in a memorial to the emperor: "The country has been divided up into prefectures, and various offices have been established in connection therewith, but they are so frequently changed, one [ancient] province being divided into two or three counties, or several being amalgamated into one prefecture, that the greatest inconvenience is occasioned. The government is, in fact, always endeavoring to decrease the little power possessed by the local authorities, and to concentrate it wholly in its own hands."[36]

Another perspective on the impact of boundary redefinitions and other administrative changes is indicated by the figures in Appendix 2. In the first four years after *haihan chiken*, about the only thing that remained relatively constant in the area around Kanazawa was the number of ex-samurai.[37] The size of the population, the number of counties, towns, wards, villages, and administrative districts *(ku)*, not to mention the number of ancient provinces, all went up and down erratically.[38] This fluctuation almost surely gave headaches to early Meiji governors and their assistants.

BUILDING A PREFECTURAL BUREAUCRACY

The central government appointed only the top two or three officials of a prefecture. Filling the positions below those offices was one of the duties of the governor and his principal assistant.[39]

Uchida's first task when he got to Kanazawa in 1871/9 was to build a prefectural bureaucracy that was loyal to the new state and responsive to his leadership. One of his main objectives was the subordination of Maeda family influence to that of the Tokyo regime. It might not be possible to extinguish feelings of loyalty to the old lord completely, but it was essential to construct an official apparatus that operated on different grounds.

Immediately after the imperial edict had proclaimed the end of *han* and the beginning of prefectures, the central government issued a directive providing for an orderly transition to prefectural administration: "Regarding the present abolition of *han* and establishment of prefectures, until there are further instructions, *han* officials from chief councilor on down shall carry on their duties as before."[40] In Kanazawa, *han* officials did not remain long in their old jobs, despite this order. By the end of 1871, it appears that the upper levels of the prefectural bureaucracy had been filled by new appointees.[41] Turnover was rapid at lower levels, as well. Prefectural archives contain the names of 504 men who served in prefectural posts before 1872/2, and of this 504, only 73 (14.5 percent) were named to positions in the prefecture after 1872/2.[42] (See Table 1.)

TABLE 1   *Turnover in the Bureaucracy in the Early Meiji Period*

Office	Number of Men Who Served in This Post in Kanazawa Han, 1869–71	Number of Kanazawa Han Officials Who Became Ishikawa Prefecture Officials	Percent of Kanazawa Han Officials Who Became Ishikawa Prefecture Officials
Chief councilor	6	1	16.7
Provisional chief councilor	10	1	10.0
Shōsanji	7	0	0.0
Gon shōsanji	4	1	25.0
Kanazawa kenchō shusshi	1	0	0.0
Shōsanji shiho	8	1	12.5
Daizoku	47	13	27.7
Gon daizoku	39	8	20.5
Shōzoku	118	23	19.5
Gon shōzoku	156	10	1.0
Shisei	76	11	14.5
Chōshō	32	4	12.5
TOTAL	504	73	14.5

Source: Compiled from *Ishikawa ken shiryō, kan* 68–69, *furoku,* (*Kyū Kanazawa ken*) *kan'in rireki* 1, 2, *IKSR,* vol. 5, pp. 441–615.

Elsewhere in Japan, some early governors responded to the challenge of creating a new officialdom by importing large numbers of staff members from their homes and from other parts of the nation. In several prefectures, such as Iwate, Saga, Shizuoka, Aomori, and Akita,[43] the old *han* apparatus was swept away entirely and all officers were replaced. Wholesale replacement of locals with outsiders certainly served as a continuing reminder, in those places where this occurred, that a new power ruled the land. Uchida did not make a clean sweep of *han* officials in the old Maeda castle town, but he did make a great many changes, installing new men, most of them young samurai who had had no part in Kaga decision making before the Restoration.[44] The appointment of Kuga Yoshinao as a middle-ranking official *(gon daizoku)* and the elevation of Sugimura Hiromasa, for a brief time, to the number-two position in the prefectural hierarchy, show that Uchida was willing to use local talent that had not been recognized under the

Maeda. Of the men who had occupied the highest posts in Maeda Yoshi-yasu's *han* administration, only one, Obata Zōji, became an official under Uchida Masakaze, and in Obata's case it was over a year before he was made a grade nine official of the prefecture.[45]

Hakka men who had become Kanazawa *han* councilors after the Restoration, as well as men who had held other *han* posts with considerable power and responsibility, left official service for good soon after the abolition of the *han*.[46] These retirements deprived the new prefecture of some experienced administrators, and they may also have been costly for Kanazawa men with political ambitions. One of the *han* officers who stepped down when the prefecture was set up, Yasui Akichika, had close relationships with the important Meiji statesmen Sanjō Sanetomi and Kido Takayoshi. He had established those connections in 1868–1869 when he worked in the new government in Tokyo as an official recommended by the *han*.[47] Conceivably the connections might have been exploited, if Yasui had stayed in office in Kanazawa, to give local men leverage against Uchida and other outsiders in local affairs. But like many high-ranking samurai, Yasui quit local government service and moved to Tokyo.[48]

Uchida's strategy for building a new officialdom in Kanazawa called for heavy reliance on local men, including some who had been exposed by travel or study to new currents of thought flowing in Japan. As we have seen, Kuga and Yoneyama had been students of comparative administration; others, among them Sugimura and Ōtsuka Shirō, had studied modern military techniques at the Fushimi military school, and at least one, Hasegawa Jun'ya, had studied in Nagasaki.[49] Sugimura, Ōtsuka, and Hasegawa moved from positions in the *han* military to responsible civilian posts in the new prefecture, exemplifying a fairly common career pattern for early Meiji subnational officials. The extent to which the governor from Satsuma assigned prominent roles in his administration to men from Kanazawa is suggested by the fact that eighteen of the top twenty-five men in Ishikawa Prefecture in Uchida's day were former Kaga samurai. Youth was the rule, even in the upper echelons of prefectural officialdom—eleven of these eighteen Kanazawa men were born after 1840, and when Uchida arrived on the scene, the average age of these eighteen men was thirty-two.[50] Over the three and a half years of Uchida's tenure in Kanazawa, three quarters of his appointees to office were local men.

Some other governors also hired many locals. Historians Ōshima Mitsuko and Haraguchi Kiyoshi have noted that in prefectures that succeeded big *han*, governors tended to have staffs dominated by men born in those *han*. It was in the prefectures in areas formerly governed by small *han* that Meiji governors employed mostly men from other parts of Japan.[51] This pattern may have emerged because the pool of available talent was larger in the former big *han* with their large samurai populations, since levels of education and administrative experience were higher among men of samurai status than among men of other backgrounds at this time. In several southwestern prefectures that had played major roles in the Restoration—Saga, Kōchi, and Yamaguchi—the governors named local men to more than four out of every five posts in the prefectural office, almost certainly in recognition of the importance of those areas to the new government in Tokyo.[52] Governors like Uchida Masakaze probably calculated that using local men to effect changes could make those changes more palatable to the populace. Almost certainly Uchida intended to domesticate the prefectural structure, to make it seem familiar at the same time as new and different. By getting former Kaga samurai committed to the success of the prefecture, he could ease the transition to the new form and the new substance of Meiji rule. Having these men participate in the operation of the prefecture was a good way to elicit their support. The governor was acutely aware of the special problems posed by the large number of ex-samurai in Kanazawa, as he showed when he petitioned the central government for permission to move the prefectural capital in 1871/12. Uchida reported that some seventy or eighty percent of the former samurai in town did nothing but collect their stipends, and he made clear that this was a source of difficulty.[53] Although prefectural employment could be given to no more than a handful of Kaga's nearly 17,000 ex-samurai family heads, the placement of some local men in the prefectural bureaucracy tied Kaga men to the new system, both symbolically and through personal networks. Whatever potential there might have been for the rise of localism and anticentral regime, anti-Uchida feeling was thereby diminished.

THREATS OF DISORDER AND OTHER PROBLEMS

The problems of changing boundaries and personnel were common to many prefectures. Complicating these for Uchida were a number of problems peculiar to Kanazawa, beginning with unruliness and obstructionism on the part of many men who were unhappy with the changes that were occurring. In the last few months of 1871, several reforms underscored the point that real power now lay outside Kanazawa. On 1871/10/10, the venerable local office of *mura kimoiri* (village headman) was abolished, and newly appointed district officers, *kuchō* and *fukukuchō,* became the responsible administrators at the subprefectural level. These officers were appointed by the governor and paid out of local levies *(minpi).*[54] On 12/5, Kiriyama Junkō, who had been provisional chief councilor in his native Ōgaki Prefecture (today part of Gifu Prefecture), was named by the central government as provisional chief councilor of Kanazawa Prefecture.[55] His appointment meant that the two highest officials in the prefecture were outsiders, and the number two man was not even from one of the great southwestern *han* that had led in the Restoration.

A vague feeling that disorder threatened had prevailed in Kanazawa from the time the *han* was abolished, and this was intensified two months after Uchida arrived, when two officials of the new prefecture were murdered. The slain men were victims of a vendetta that had its roots in the period between the proclamation of the restoration of imperial rule and the creation of prefectures. The murderers were followers of Kanazawa *han* councilor Honda Masachika, a *hakka* leader who identified with the aims of the Restoration and was instrumental in starting Kanazawa on the path of Meiji reform. Honda had been assassinated on 1869/8/6 by reactionaries who opposed the changes he championed, and although his killers had been captured and executed, some of their accomplices (or at least close associates) had escaped with lighter sentences or acquittals. This was unacceptable to Honda family vassals, and when two of the men who had been connected with Honda's assassins became officers in the new prefectural bureaucracy, it became too much to bear. Fifteen former Honda retainers hatched a revenge plot. On 1871/11/23, they struck down Okano Teigorō, one of the prefectural officials, and another man; a day later, they ambushed Taga Kenzaburō, the other prefectural bureaucrat, and killed him.[56]

As soon as they had accomplished their mission, the avengers of Honda Masachika turned themselves in. They bore written statements of their objectives, which they had prepared before going out after their targets. Under the Ministry of Justice regulations of the day, they were brought to trial in Kanazawa, with the proceedings conducted by officials of the prefecture, in 1872/3. Twelve men who had once served the principal *hakka* house of Honda were sentenced to death. In recognition of their loyalty to their slain master, they were permitted the privilege of carrying out their own executions by self-disembowelment (*jisai*).[57]

Not only prefectural officials Okano and Taga, but also several central government officials had fallen at the hands of assassins in the early years of Meiji, and the Council of State finally acted to ban vendettas in its Notification Number 37 of February 7, 1873. It ordered that "appropriate punishments be meted out to any who, mired in old customs, wantonly stab persons to death."[58] This notification testifies to the authorities' awareness of this problem of public safety—officials of the new state at the national level and in the prefectures could hardly have escaped being concerned. Bureaucrats' sense of the precariousness of public order might well have been heightened by observing how easily Okano and Taga had been cut down in Kanazawa.

A disturbance known as "the uprising of the straw raincoats"—named after a garment that peasants commonly donned, along with large sedge hats, to mask their identities when they took part in disruptive or rebellious actions—threatened the order of the Kanazawa region at about the same time as the plot to avenge Honda Masachika was coming to fruition.[59] Some 8,000 peasants in Daishōji Prefecture mounted a protest movement in the eleventh month of 1871 after the authorities had imposed additional taxes in an effort to bring prefectural finances out of the red. Led by a villager named Niiya Riyomon, the farmers demanded abolition of the village-group headman (*tomura*) institution and the investigation of certain officials whom they felt to be corrupt. More importantly, as Kanazawa historian Takazawa Yūichi has emphasized, the protestors put together a bill of grievances in which they insisted upon "treatment according to the regulations of the imperial court." In doing so, these Daishōji peasants explicitly endorsed the ideals of the Restoration; the regulations that they had in mind were expressed in the Oath of Five Articles of 1868, in which the emperor had seemed to promise Japanese subjects an opportunity to participate in deliberations over policy. Takazawa and others who have analyzed this Daishōji event of 1871 have seen it as exemplary of the "improvement of conditions" type of uprising (*yonaoshi ikki*) that occurred frequently in the latter part of the Tokugawa era and in the early years of Meiji rule.

Peasant protestors and rioters were not acting out of revolutionary class consciousness, but out of moral outrage at the bungling of particular officials in a particular case. In the Daishōji case, some of the demands of the uprisers were met. The extra levies were decreased, and within a month of the disturbance, the foundering Daishōji Prefecture was subsumed into Kanazawa Prefecture. As had often happened when peasants challenged the authorities in the period of rule by shogunate and domains, the leader of the straw raincoats was jailed even as the legitimacy of his cause was being acknowledged, and he died in prison the following year.[60] This Daishōji disturbance turned out to be isolated, but prefectural authorities at the time had no way of knowing that it would be. Concern about keeping the peace in the countryside had to be added to their worries about maintaining order among the samurai in town.

Late in 1871, Uchida Masakaze decided to appeal to the central government to move the prefectural office away from Kanazawa. Most local historians have seen this as a response to samurai resistance to his leadership in the old Maeda castle town.[61] Uchida complained to Tokyo in 1871/12 that many former samurai (*shizoku* and *sotsu*) were concentrated in the city, living off their stipends, and that around 70 or 80 percent of these had no employment. By that estimate, something between 11,000 and 13,500 men of these statuses—not counting members of their families—were without regular work, a circumstance that gave rise to social problems and that must have produced much personal anxiety as well. Uchida faulted the ex-retainers of the Maeda for self-indulgence, then commented on the potentially corrosive effect that bad behavior by samurai might have on the whole of society: "If old extravagant habits are not rinsed away, it will be extremely difficult to change the direction in which the ignorant people (*gumin*) are tending." He recommended that the prefectural office be moved to the town of Mikawa, and the area under his administration be renamed Mikawa Prefecture.[62]

Part of Uchida's proposal was accepted. The Council of State ordered the move in a terse directive of 1872/2/2: "The name of Kanazawa Prefecture is changed to Ishikawa Prefecture. The prefectural office is established at Mikawa (formerly the village of Motoyoshi)."[63] Five days later, the Ishikawa Prefectural Office issued the official explanation of the move of the prefectural capital. It stressed geographic reasons for the switch, observing that

Kanazawa had been well located to administer Kaga, Etchū, and Noto when all three of those provinces had been under the same authorities, but Kanazawa was not centrally located in the jurisdiction that had been created in 1871/11. Mikawa was in the center of the new prefecture, and it was convenient for the transmission of official notices, for communications in all directions, and for traffic with the various ports. The name Ishikawa was taken from the county (*kōri* or *gun*) in which Mikawa was located.

Insofar as the transfer to Mikawa was motivated by a desire to ensure stability, the shift was a failure. Both samurai and townsmen in Kanazawa were shocked by the move, and their dissatisfaction was vented in a series of outbursts of streetfighting and violence. There was even a plot to attack Uchida's residence, but it was thwarted.[64]

PRINCIPLES OF SUBNATIONAL GOVERNMENT

The prefectural office tried to shore up a sense of order among the people by publishing "General Considerations on Prefectural Government" (*kenchi gairon*) in 1872/5. Uchida and his aides intended this document to educate the citizens, to win sympathy for what officials were doing, and to elicit a cooperative spirit for change. The authors of these "General Considerations" espoused many liberal beliefs at the same time as they put forward their agenda for institution-building:

> Why do nations have governments? Governments go to the root of unifying and combining the people of the nation (*okuchō*) and of preserving the rights and possessions (*kenchi shiyū*) of subjects (*shinmin*). Therefore, the subjects do not exist for the sake of the government, but rather the government exists for the sake of the people (*kokumin*). . . . Given that the prefectural office is a part of the government, it is unnecessary to argue the point that the people of the jurisdiction (*kannai no jinmin*) do not exist for this government, but rather the prefectural office is there for the people of the prefecture. For this reason, in contacts between the prefectural office and the people, and also in contacts of the people with each other, both officials and people shall perform their allotted duties (*honbun*). Since the prefectural officials have been established to institute and protect the rules (*kisoku*) on rights (*kenri*) and duties (*gimu*) in order to bring about an increase in well-being (*kōfuku*), these officials have the right to administer government orders on behalf of the people, and the

duty to protect the people. In respectful obedience to the imperial oath [of five articles], we must choose men of talent as officials. As for the people in the prefecture, they have the duty to respect the restraints [of the law] and the right to receive the protection of the prefectural office. In the increase of well-being based on these rights and duties, the officials of the prefecture and the people must meet in assembly on friendly terms *(kenkan to jinmin to shitashiku kaigi sezaru o ezu)*. This is universal justice *(tenchi no kōdō)*. Having said this, however, to make it effective, we must pay careful attention to time and our purposes. Today is the time, and enlightenment and renovation are our purposes. In the remote villages the conservative moral fiber *(korō kōki)* has loosened and been cast aside, and consequently we must build schools to reorient every kind of human emotion and custom in the direction of enlightenment. These schools, taking locality and customs relating to human emotions into account, will teach about the form of government brought about by the Restoration and will foster the moral order. For dealing with the changes in conditions since the Restoration and the areas of enlightenment and civilization *(kaika bunmei)*, for the dissemination of knowledge about laws and ordinances from the imperial oath on, and for the spread of news on everyday affairs and the like, nothing could equal these district *(ku)* schools. As knowledge is developed, we hope in succession to create assemblies, to encourage thrift and diligence, to open the way to an increase in well-being, to make financial sources *(zaihon)* prosper, and to become the basis for a peaceful people *(anmin)*. Not to err in this order of things and to do their work in a cooperative manner—these are the credo of the officials of this prefecture.[65]

When this statement was published, Uchida and Kiriyama gave prefectural officials a special admonition to adhere to its principles and a reminder that unless every official, not just the governor, did his job properly, the prefecture could not succeed.[66]

These "General Considerations" are eloquent testimony to the high aims of the prefectural bureaucrats of the time. They show that the reformistic ethos, or at least the reformistic discourse, of the 1870s had penetrated down to the level of prefectural officials, affecting even men of conservative bent like Uchida Masakaze.

Their elevated tone and content notwithstanding, the "General Considerations" had a nugatory impact on the political atmosphere of Ishikawa Prefecture. Uchida felt that further expostulation was required, and finally in the seventh month of 1872, he addressed an appeal for order to the people of Kanazawa. "The recent unprecedented violence is the work of beasts, not of men," the governor wrote. He allowed, at least rhetorically, that it was possible that the trouble stemmed from his own mediocrity and stupidity *(yōgu)*. He requested that citizens report any parties to violence to the authorities.[67]

Uchida's public entreaty got results in a way that the "General Considerations" had not. Over 500 men joined together to form a police auxiliary. Upon obtaining the sanction of prefectural authorities, they dedicated themselves to restoring order to Kanazawa. Several officials were among the members of this auxiliary, and they contributed a part of their salaries to a fund out of which those who actually went on patrol were paid. At the time they organized, the volunteer constables articulated a philosophy of public service in a statement that exhibits a mix of national consciousness and local interest, a combination that marks many of the activities of politically aware men in Kanazawa in the early years of Meiji:

> At the present time, it is the purpose of our league to serve the nation. If any parties carrying out acts of violence should appear, we desire to offer our own lives [to restore order]. In the normal conduct of affairs, however, it is our purpose to pay close attention in every district *(ku)*, to observe any disturbances, and to assist the police. Our major objectives are to protect life and to make safety and liberty attainable in all things, with honor as our principle. Therefore, as soon as there is any disturbance of the peace within the town or elsewhere, we will reason [with the disorderly elements], we will remonstrate [with them], and without applying undue force we will settle such matters peacefully.[68]

Eking out the small prefectural police force of seventy-two, the members of this auxiliary walked the streets of Kanazawa and assisted district officials with their duties for two months. They disbanded in 1872/9. The prefecture, reporting to the Ministry of Finance, gave honorable mention to those who had contributed funds to support this auxiliary.[69]

Growth in physical dimensions provided the excuse to return the prefectural office to the only major city in the region. Ishikawa Prefecture absorbed the Noto peninsula on 1872/9/25, when Nanao Prefecture was abolished. It took in more territory when the foothills around Mount Haku were separated from Asuwa Prefecture and placed within the jurisdiction of Ishikawa on 1872/11/17. Although the governor never moved to Mikawa, even after his petition to change the location of the prefectural office had been approved, the alterations of the first year after the switch from *han* to prefecture had precipitated a rapid decline in the fortunes of Kanazawa. Many former samurai residents of the city emigrated to rural areas or to other cities. Commoners' businesses suffered, and the number of households in the city decreased.[70] The population of Kanazawa dropped from 123,453 at the time of *haihan chiken* to around 100,000 a year later.[71] The transfer of the prefectural office to Mikawa may have speeded the decline of the old castle town by fanning social unrest rather than calming it, and it is likely that the government recognized this. On January 14, 1873 (two weeks after they had adopted the Western calendar), the government reestablished Kanazawa as the capital of Ishikawa Prefecture.[72]

Within the expanded prefecture, Kanazawa was centrally located. The government noted this in its announcement that Kanazawa was once again the prefectural capital. All but the most austere of prefectural bureaucrats must have been pleased by this development, for, even reduced in size, the one-time castle town had more human resources, more amenities, and more diversions than any other town in the prefecture.[73] Moreover, successful administration of the prefecture was closely dependent on the effective governance of its biggest population center, and this was expedited when prefectural authorities were on the spot.

BUREAUCRATIC POLITICS UNDER UCHIDA

Once the prefectural office had been brought back to Kanazawa, things settled down. This time the prefecture set up in the former *han* bureau of repairs *(eishū kyoku)* on the boulevard called Hirosakadōri, near the location of the prefectural office today. The calmer atmosphere may be partly attributable to the fact that the central government looked more powerful and more secure with every day that passed. The prefectural apparatus likewise gained simply by virtue of endurance. Uchida himself helped by projecting an image of competence, an image that had been burnished by the dignity of his public appeal for order and by his promotion to a higher bureaucratic rank, provisional governor *(gon rei)*, on 1872/9/5. Uchida also seems to have managed his subordinates in the prefectural bureaucracy with considerable skill.

Building on the core of pro-Satsuma men like Kuga and Sugimura, Uchida encouraged the growth of a faction that supported him. An aide of his who had also come to Kanazawa from Satsuma, Tsutsui Ei, discerned a "righteous party" *(seigitō)* and a "scoundrels party" *(kanbutsutō)* among prefectural officials early in 1872. Uchida's backers, as Tsutsui saw it, belonged to the former category. The other group he excoriated:

> The scoundrels party repeatedly does what it wants, and daily does harm to the nation. . . . The scoundrels take no account of the nation. They are covetous of public funds *(kankin)*, and moreover they do not concern themselves with the advantage or disadvantage of the people. They take bribes, and without discriminating right or wrong, forthwith give official sanctions.[74]

Uchida's aide from Kagoshima did not scruple to name names in his assessment, which made its way to the central government in Tokyo, He called for an inspection *(gokensa)* of the tax supervisor and the criminal law supervisor, and he listed Naitō Sei, Takahashi Shōhei, Yamada Sasuke, and Terao Takutarō as members of the scoundrels party. These four men had formerly served in the Kanazawa *han* government, and had stayed in their positions after the creation of the prefecture. Tsutsui identified two other former Maeda retainers, Sekizawa Fusakiyo and Hirano Hikonojō, as ringleaders of the scoundrels in retirement.[75]

The righteous party boasted more members—maybe Tsutsui intended to show that the governor had more supporters than resisters. Among the fourteen that Tsutsui catalogued were Sugimura Hiromasa, Yoneyama Michio, Hasegawa Jun'ya, Ōtsuka Shirō, and other new men whom Uchida had brought into government service. The governor placed these righteous party members in upper- and middle-level positions *(daizoku* and *chūzoku,* usually)*, and most of them stayed in office throughout Uchida's time in Kanazawa. Many of these men became active in the first important political society formed in Ishikawa Prefecture after the Restoration, the Chūkokusha, and through this organization, they became linked with the early people's rights movement. But even while, as members of their political society, they sometimes disagreed with policies of the central government, as prefectural officials, righteous party members cooperated with the governor who had been sent to Kanazawa by that central government.

The factions that Tsutsui described could be traced back to the final years of *han* rule, although he seems not to have realized this. The key difference between the factions probably lay not in their propensity to take bribes or work hard or be idle, but in their extralocal orientations. After the Restoration, Kanazawa men had split into rival camps over the question of who was best suited to lead the new state. One group looked to Chōshū, the other thought more highly of Satsuma. The former was led by Han Councilor Honda Masachika and Naitō Sei, while the latter included young Kuga Yoshinao and Yoneyama Michio. After the establishment of the prefecture and the appointment of a Kagoshima man as governor, the Satsuma-oriented group was more amenable to Uchida's direction than the pro-Chōshū faction. It was the Chōshū-aligned group that had the more impressive connections to the Restoration movement—Honda, Naitō, and their associates were regarded as the successors of the coterie of Kaga loyalists that had been ruthlessly suppressed in 1864—but these pro-Chōshū holdovers from the Maeda administration had short careers as prefectural officials. Unable or unwilling to ingratiate themselves with Uchida, they received no promotions or new appointments to office in the Ishikawa prefectural bureaucracy after 1872/2.[76]

Once the "scoundrels" were out of office, the field was open for the dominance of the pro-Satsuma party. The product of the resulting cooperation between bureaucrats and governor was local stability. Those resisters of Uchida's authority who had made his first months uneasy were beaten. Some dissatisfactions remained, but they were directed at the national government. Between late 1872 and Uchida's retirement, there were no serious challenges to the authority of the prefecture or its high officials. Perhaps in recognition of Uchida's administrative success, the government advanced him to the full rank of governor *(kami,* or *kenrei)* in December 1873.

ADMINISTRATION AND FINANCE IN THE NEW PREFECTURE

During Uchida Masakaze's tenure in office, order was achieved in the countryside as well as in the city—between the incident of the "straw raincoats" and 1875, not a single instance of a peasant uprising is recorded in Ishikawa Prefecture[77]—and just as importantly, an administrative framework was erected and operating procedures were regularized. Tokyo was never out of the minds of prefectural officials. Reports and inquiries flowed steadily from the prefecture to ministries and agencies of the central government. On occasion, Uchida and his aides were impelled by their reading of local circumstances to contradict central government policy. In such instances, they reported their actions and the reasons behind them to the appropriate national officers and asked for approval, and the central authorities, anxious to reinforce their representatives in the countryside, usually went along. Uchida succeeded in bringing the area under his jurisdiction into the national structure of decision making and administration to a greater degree than it had been during Yoshiyasu's days as daimyo and governor. That, of course, is exactly what central government leaders had intended should happen with the establishment of prefectures. But Uchida was not a robot, able to act only at the remote-control command of Tokyo, and his achievement would not have been possible without the help of the many local men who joined to make the new prefectural regime.

An investigation of the fiscal practices of a successful prefectural administration will add to our still-fragmentary image of how Japan built a modern integrated state. Documents similar to budgets survive, and constitute a guide to what Uchida and his assistants were able to do in Ishikawa Prefecture. Data from those documents has been arranged in Appendixes 3 and 4.

Government spending in Ishikawa was colossal, when compared to the assessed product of the prefecture. Outlays administered by the prefecture came to 93 percent of assessed product in the fiscal year beginning 1871/10, and to over 76 percent in the following year. Even though the assessed product, which was an agriculture-based estimate, was not precisely the same as the gross prefectural product, in Ishikawa as in other rural areas of Japan at this time, agricultural output was overwhelmingly the most important part of the gross domestic product. The actual weight of government spending was probably only marginally less than these figures suggest.[78]

The greatest concern of the prefecture in the early years was the payment of the former daimyo and samurai. How rice and money payments were disbursed to those ex-warriors is not clear, but a good many clerks must have been kept busy with the bookkeeping. The budget figures leave no doubt that the whole operation was a terrible burden. This was the case all over Japan, but it was true a fortiori in Ishikawa Prefecture. Confronted year after year with financial statistics that proved that the system of annual payments to the old feudal class was draining too great a portion of the nation's scarce resources, the central government was compelled to reevaluate the importance of paying off the members of the recently displaced ruling class. Over the objections of many influential men both inside and outside the government, the dominant leaders of the Meiji state finally decided to do away with that system entirely. In 1876, the last payments in this program were made.

While the stipend system was in place, payments to the Maeda and their former retainers siphoned off a substantial portion of Ishikawa Prefecture's funds. Table 2 summarizes how prefectural spending was allocated in the fiscal year that began 1871/10. Stipends for ex-samurai and ex-governors took over three-quarters of the total. In the following fiscal year, 91.7 percent of spending in Ishikawa Prefecture went to hereditary stipends. Perhaps no other part of Japan besides Kagoshima had so high a concentration of ex-samurai; including family members, the former daimyo, *shizoku,* and *sotsu* composed about 14 percent of the population of Ishikawa Prefecture in 1871–1872, and about 8 percent in 1873 (after a territorial expansion and a change in the definition of *shizoku*).[79] A report submitted by the prefecture to the minister of finance in October 1874 estimated tax income at around 370,000 *koku* and stipend payments at around 300,000 *koku.*[80] In 1875, over 91 percent of prefectural outlays went to samurai. Until the stipend system was abolished, only a small fraction of prefectural revenues could be put toward government services and projects. Ishikawa fared worse than most prefectures in this regard; national figures indicate that about one-third of government revenues derived from land tax went to pay stipends, whereas in Ishikawa the proportion was three-quarters to nine-tenths.[81] A large number of samurai had once been a source of strength for the Maeda. It had become an albatross around the necks of the Meiji administrators who inherited the Maeda jurisdiction. Taxes on stipends were collected from 1874 at graduated rates from 2 to 35 percent, but they brought only a small portion of Ishikawa stipends back into government coffers.

Another legacy of the old *han* that required the attention of early prefectural administrators was the local military organization. Through the second month of 1872, the maintenance of those units cost the prefecture

TABLE 2   *Expenditures of Ishikawa Prefecture, 1871/10–1872/9*

	Amount in Yen	*Percent of Total*
Stipends paid to Kanazawa ex-samurai	1,015,908	58.3
Stipends paid to Daishōji ex-samurai	70,531	4.0
Ex-governors' stipends	241,967	13.9
Military expenses	172,110	9.9
School expenditures	37,860	2.2
Officials' salaries	20,229	1.2
Miscellaneous other	185,140	10.6
TOTAL	1,743,745	100.1 [a]

Source: Appendix 3 (data from *IKSR*, vol. 4, pp. 264–266).

Note: [a] Percentages have been rounded to the nearest tenth of 1 percent; the total is actually 100.0.

¥94,800, and another ¥74,950 had to be laid out to send troops to various corps area headquarters at the order of the central government. After stipends, military spending was the largest item in the first prefectural budget, at 9.9 percent of the total. With the creation of a national army in 1872, *han* military units were dissolved, and Ishikawa Prefecture was spared further direct spending on defense.

Education was a priority of the prefecture in the budget of 1871–1872, though schools got much less from the prefecture than the ex-samurai or the military did. School expenditures for that year were estimated at nearly ¥38,000. That Ishikawa authorities had high hopes for schools is evident from the "General Considerations on Prefectural Government" quoted above. The system of funding education changed in 1872, and school expenditures do not show up in prefectural budgets after that, but the prefecture continued to promote schools.

In the eighth month of 1872 the Ministry of Education promulgated the epoch-making Regulations for Education (*gakusei*), putting into law the policy of promoting universal primary education. According to these regulations, the nation was to be divided into eight university districts; Ishikawa Prefecture was to be in the third district.[82] The following February the regulations were amended, and Ishikawa was put into the second of seven university districts.[83] Ishikawa was subdivided into five middle school districts, with an average population of 133,989. The Regulations for Education called for 210 primary schools in each middle school district, but in the early years of implementation the number fell far short. One source records that there were 145 primary school districts within all five of the middle school districts in Ishikawa Prefecture in 1873.[84] This was only 13.8 percent of the number that should have been established according to the regulations. In Kanazawa, there were ten primary school districts in 1873; by the Ministry of Education formula there should have been over a hundred.[85]

The prefecture performed five major functions in education after the introduction of the 1872 regulations: It directly operated a normal school and a middle school; it defined district boundaries; it designated district superintendents (*gakku torishimari*); it issued regulations pertaining to education (most of which emanated from the Ministry of Education or were inspired by it); and it channeled funds from the central government to the school districts.[86] The Regulations for Education provided that educational funding should come out of local expenditures and not out of central government tax revenues, but the Ministry of Education quickly recognized that it could not enforce this policy and that it would have to provide funds to aid localities.[87] In June 1873, national aid to primary education (*shōgaku itaku kin*) was set at ¥90 per 10,000 population, to be distributed to prefectures and combined with private donations (*jinmin no kifukin*) to support the schools.[88] Ishikawa Prefecture should have received a little more than ¥6,000 in direct aid from the Ministry of Education in both 1873 and 1874. The prefecture decreed in May 1873 that insufficiencies in school funds should be made up by the levying of local exactions, though officials did not specify how and at what rate those were to be collected.[89]

Uchida, Kiriyama, and Sugimura set the pattern for private contributions to education, giving ¥100 each in 1872/11. Their public-spirited example was followed by prefectural councilor Kumano, who gave ¥30, and by many others, both former samurai and commoners, who made donations in varying amounts. Some members of the *hakka* and other high-ranking samurai families pledged to give a fixed proportion of their stipends, usually a thirtieth or a fortieth, to schools.[90] An inheritance from the old Kaga academies provided one more source of funds for education in Ishikawa Prefecture. Books that had been the property of *han* schools, some of them rare old books, were sold in March 1873, and the proceeds were put toward the purchase of new textbooks.[91]

The law empowered the governor to appoint school district superintendents within his prefecture. If he chose to, the governor could name the administrative district chiefs (*kochō* and *risei*) to this educational management position.[92] In Ishikawa, Uchida kept the school district superintendents and the administrative chiefs distinct. Two prefectural directives of 1873 provided for appointment of school district superintendents, and another directive required administrative district chiefs to discuss the establishment of primary schools with school district superintendents.[93] Prefectural records do not contain the names of the school district superintendents, but the mere fact that the governor put different men in charge of schools must have diminished the possibility that administrative chiefs might consolidate power over many facets of life in their districts. It would have been in Uchida's self-interest to place men who were loyal to him in the school management posts, rather than men who followed or were closely sympathetic with the district chiefs. It seems that this is what happened, for administrative district chiefs saw the school superintendents as allies of the governor, even after Uchida's retirement, and they objected to the inclusion of the school officials in a proposed prefectural assembly when there was talk of establishing such a body in 1875.[94]

Building and maintaining a bureaucracy uses up resources, whether that bureaucracy turns out to be an efficient administrative machine or an incompetent bumbledom. In Ishikawa, where officials can be credited with having contributed to the making of a modern state, bureaucrats' salaries and "regular" (*jōhi*) expenditures were the next biggest items after payments for stipends, the military, and schools in the 1871–1872 budget figures. By 1874, salaries and operating expenditures were the largest items in the reported budget.[95] Governor Uchida, bemoaning the insufficiency of resources available to the prefecture, attempted in August 1873 to reduce expenditures by demoting nearly all prefectural administrators one step on the ladder of officialdom. This move did not achieve its desired end. Expenditures on salaries in 1874 were the same as they had been the year before.

Regular expenditures of the prefecture included officials' expenses on travel, wages of low-level employees, equipment and materials used in the prefectural office, and the like.[96] Because of the relative heaviness of these regular expenditures, perhaps, extra levies had to be imposed to supplement prefectural revenues, in order to pay subprefectural officials and operating costs.

Religious intolerance lay another burden on Uchida's administration. As is well known, the Meiji leadership was not initially disposed to grant religious liberty, and the state renewed the old proscription of Christianity in one of its first decrees after proclaiming the restoration of imperial rule.[97] A year later some villagers in Kyushu caused a sensation when they openly professed themselves to be Christians, having maintained their faith secretly through centuries of repression. The state responded by arresting some 3,700 people. It was decided to parcel these lawbreakers out among several *han* for detention, and in 1869/11, Kanazawa *han* received charge of 510 persons who were guilty of Catholicism.[98] The Maeda authorities housed the prisoners in what had been a bathhouse less than a mile from Kanazawa castle. For over three-and-a-half years, until the Meiji government yielded to pressure from Western governments and lifted the ban on Christianity in March 1873, these "believers in heterodoxy" stayed in Kanazawa.[99] Ishikawa Prefecture spent between ¥6,300 and ¥7,700 a year to keep these internees, roughly the same amount per capita as was spent on criminal prisoners. When the Kyushu Catholics were at last freed and permitted to return to their homes, Kanazawa financial officers must have been as pleased as the devoutest Buddhists and worshipers of the native deities to see them go.

No government can long survive unless it establishes and keeps public order. This, like other goods, does not often come free; certainly in early Meiji Japan, it did not. Public order was another object of the prefectural authorities' use of limited revenues. Police and prison expenditures rose from less than 1 percent of prefectural outlays in 1871–1873 to 19.8 percent in 1874.[100] The percentage for 1874 is biassed upwards by its omission of the large outlays for stipends of ex-samurai. Nevertheless, a significant fraction of the funds available to the prefecture for business other than the support of the old feudal class was tied up in maintaining law and order and providing for incarcerated criminals and vagrants and their guards and caretakers. Had not volunteers come forward to pay for the police auxiliary, the proportion would have been even larger in 1872.

Relief and welfare concerned Uchida and his successors to some extent, but caring for the poor and the victims of disaster never took precedence over other prefectural business. Expenditures for these were quickly reduced, from ¥7,000 in the fiscal year beginning 1871/10 to ¥650 in fiscal year 1873.[101] Officials resorted to calling for private contributions for relief and welfare as well as for education. The pattern of donations shows that certain privileged citizens were moved by a spirit of noblesse oblige. Yokoyama Masakazu, the one-time elder of Kaga, pledged in 1873 to give one-tenth of his annual stipend to help rebuild part of the imperial palace that had been destroyed by fire and to ease the suffering of the poor; his contribution to the poor came to ¥22.[102] Other former samurai gave lesser sums in the same year. Small district chief Kasamatsu Ken promised to give 85 percent of his official salary to poor relief. Most donations to the poor, unlike Yokoyama's or Kasamatsu's, seem to have followed a fire, flood, or typhoon, and this ad hoc charity was not regular or generous enough to fill all needs for aid. Collections in affected localities were as common a source of relief as prefectural loans or individual private contributions.

PROCEDURAL CHANGE AND A CHANGE IN THE CHIEF OFFICER

Despite the fiscal constraints that limited its delivery of services and its carrying out of construction projects, the prefecture had a broad enough range of responsibilities that administrators came to fear foundering in a sea of paperwork. In mid-1873, Councilor Kiriyama proposed to Uchida a strategy for simplifying administration. Unless his plan was adopted, he implied, the people's trust might be lost:

> In issuing orders to the people we must respect first things first, and it is imperative that we not lose the people's trust even the slightest bit. However, although we are presently achieving success in carrying out business in an orderly way, the number of official documents that we receive has reached around 4,000 per month, and it is extremely difficult to deal uniformly with these. From this complexity arise inadvertent delays and cases of interference in trifles, and we must not fail to perceive that the true essence of the locality is being lost. Therefore, let us distinguish matters according to their seriousness into those which are covered by previous regulations and those which are not covered by precedents. Let us separate matters requiring earnest discussion from those which only need acknowledgment.[103]

Uchida accepted this advice. Thereafter business was divided into two categories, that needing the decision of the governor and that which could be
settled by the decision of a prefectural department chief. This simplification
anticipated a notification handed down to all prefectures by the Council of
State in November 1875, establishing a similar classification of business
into that which governors themselves could take care of and that which had
to be submitted to a central government ministry before it could be acted
upon.[104] When they streamlined routine bureaucratic procedures in Ishikawa in 1873, Uchida and Kiriyama acted to meet exigencies in their particular jurisdiction, not to respond to some Tokyo directive. Rationalization
did not always depend on orders from the center.

After three-and-a-half years in Kanazawa, Uchida Masakaze asked the
home ministry to replace him. In March 1875, his request was granted. He
spent some months in Tokyo, then returned home to Kagoshima in the
company of Shimazu Hisamitsu in March 1876. Years later, Uchida wrote
that at the time of his retirement from Kanazawa, he found himself in
agreement with the views of Hisamitsu, who had since 1871 made a habit
of opposing most of the reform measures of the central government. Hisamitsu, the onetime de facto ruler of Satsuma, had been against the abolition
of *han*, and had supported those administrators who had made Satsuma
"like an independent state" in the early Meiji years. He had opposed the
commutation of samurai stipends. Perhaps in 1875 Uchida did hold extremely conservative opinions similar to the Shimazu family head. Certainly, he was compatible with Hisamitsu, and shortly after returning to
Kagoshima, he was named an official in the Shimazu household administration. The onetime personal attendant took the position of steward (*karei*),
the top job in the household of his former lords, and remained in that post
for eight years. Later he joined the board of directors of the Fifteenth National Peers Bank.[105]

In spite of the conservatism that he avowed later on, which must have
caused him to chafe at some of Tokyo's directives during his term in the
governor's chair, Uchida managed things in Kanazawa in such a way as to
help bring Japan together as a strong, unified state. Much of the time, he
had conducted his business according to the principles that he had made
public in his "General Considerations" and his appeal for order in 1872.
Those principles were, for their day, more liberal than conservative. But

probably more important to Uchida than abstract principles was the practi-- cal task at hand, the business of putting together an organization for subnational administration that worked. In this, he served the Meiji regime well.

Kiriyama Junkō succeeded Uchida as chief officer. He was the only man to rise to the governor's chair in Kanazawa from within the Ishikawa prefectural bureaucracy during the seventy-seven years of operation of the Meiji system, before popular election of governors was introduced under the 1947 constitution. Born a samurai of the small Ōgaki domain in 1832, Kiriyama had been nominated for service in the new Tokyo government in 1868 when the *han* were asked to send good men to staff new offices. After a year as a financial affairs officer of the central government, he returned to his old domain to become provisional chief councilor, making him one of the most powerful officials after the governor. Ōgaki was absorbed into Gifu Prefecture in 1871/11, and within a few days the central government picked Kiriyama for further service and sent him to Kanazawa as deputy councilor *(gon sanji)*. He was thus inserted as the number-two man in Uchida Masakaze's prefectural office, ahead of Kanazawa-born Sugimura Hiromasa. A year later the government promoted Kiriyama to councilor *(sanji)*. Administrative detail was his forte, and as Uchida's aide he became known as a good nuts-and-bolts man.[106]

Unlike his predecessor, Kiriyama did not have *han*-clique connections with powerful figures in the central government. Moreover he was relatively young, forty-five, when he took over as governor in 1875. But he was, like Uchida, an experienced administrator. He knew his territory intimately from his years as councilor. Undoubtedly his appointment had his former chief's approval. As co-signer of the 1872 "General Considerations on Prefectural Government," he was on the record as committed to the spirit and the national objectives of the state leaders in Tokyo. In no respect was the choice of Kiriyama as governor an adventurous move. Home Minister Ōkubo could be confident that he knew what kind of man he was naming. Ōkubo showed his confidence in Kiriyama in April and August 1876 when the home ministry added the territory of two eliminated prefectures, Niikawa and Tsuruga, to the Kanazawa jurisdiction.

A man from Chōshū who had been sent to Kanazawa by the ministry of finance in 1872/1 became Kiriyama's principal assistant and served in that capacity for the governor's entire term. Uchida had named this man, Ku-

mano Kurō, to a position just below Kiriyama in 1872/4. Kumano moved
up a grade on the bureaucratic scale when Kiriyama took the top spot.
Together this pair handled personnel matters and relations with political
activists quite differently from Uchida. They were much more inclined toward conflict and confrontation, as their dispute with fractious subprefectural officials in the summer of 1875, which is treated in Chapter Four,
illustrates. Within six months of Kiriyama's promotion to governor, all
forty-three chiefs of large districts, the major subdivisions of the prefecture,
were changed. Kiriyama and Kumano could abide neither the pro-Satsuma
party among prefectural officials nor the Kanazawa political society, which
many of Uchida's appointees had joined. When presented with a challenge
to their authority, Kiriyama and Kumano swiftly took advantage of their
powers over inferior officials and asserted their own supremacy.[107]

ADMINISTRATION AND FINANCE UNDER GOVERNOR KIRIYAMA

Regulations did not distinguish between national taxes and prefectural taxes
in the early 1870s. In September 1875, the Council of State decreed that
from that time on, there would be such a distinction, and it clarified the
powers of the central government and the governor in dealing with collections and disbursements of taxes. National taxes were to be collected by the
Ministry of Finance and put into the national exchequer. Prefectural taxes
were to be collected by prefectures and put into the prefectural purse for
use within the jurisdiction. The governor was to investigate methods of
collection and disbursement of the subnational levies and then to obtain the
approval of two ministries, finance and home, for the plan of implementation that he devised.[108] This 1875 law made the bulk of the taxes fall due
to the national government, and it strengthened the power of the Tokyo
bureaucracy to define categories and determine rates of subnational exactions, as well.

The land tax went into the national treasury. Not much was left to the
prefectures. When Ishikawa established prefectural taxes in February of the
following year, these amounted to little more than license fees for various
businesses. Those who had to pay prefectural taxes were listed: restaurateurs, confectioners, innkeepers, hot springs innkeepers, bathhouse opera-
tors, mineral bath keepers, hairdressers, photographers, sellers of cosmetics,

toy merchants, tobacconists, pawnbrokers, and dealers in old books.[109] No one engaged in a modern manufacturing or marketing venture paid prefectural taxes, except photographers. This may have been because no new-style enterprises could be found in Ishikawa at this time, but just as likely it was because the governor and his administration wanted to promote more investment in modern businesses and thought that exemption from prefectural taxes might be a useful incentive.

In 1875, various prefectural taxes had raised ¥14,628 for Ishikawa, an amount less than half of I percent of the assessed product of the prefecture.[110] By comparison, the national land tax took more than 35 percent of the assessed product.[111] Yet it was out of these paltry revenues, out of this one-half of I percent of prefectural product, that the prefecture had to pay for sluiceways, bridges, encouragement of enterprise, hospitals, and industrial expositions. The national fisc provided nothing for these; there was no more. In addition, the prefecture had to draw on these limited resources to pay part of its police expenses and the cost of tax collection itself.

Ishikawa laid out an amount nearly equal three-fifths of the assessed product of the prefecture in 1875. Ninety-nine percent of the ¥1,747,880 spent by the prefecture that year were provided by the national government. Once again hereditary stipend payments appeared in Ishikawa's accounts. Over nine-tenths of total expenditures were allotted to former samurai.

Two years later (no figures for 1876 are available), under new regulations on prefectural taxes, Ishikawa spent ¥42,565 out of prefectural taxes and another ¥9,148 out of excise taxes.[112] We can be fairly sure that revenues were equal, or nearly equal, to disbursements. Together prefectural taxes and the additional prefectural levies came to less than 2 percent of the assessed product of Ishikawa in 1877. The national land tax at this time was taking about 30 percent of the assessed product of the prefecture.[113]

Total prefectural spending by Ishikawa in 1877 was ¥1,244,539, the equivalent of about two-fifths of the assessed product. Again, nearly all of the funds came from the national treasury. Stipends of the old Kaga samurai appear in the prefectural budget for the last time in this year, and account for nearly 88 percent of all outlays. Administrative costs—salaries, office operating costs, and the like—took another 8 percent. That left just over 4 percent of prefectural resources, less than 2 percent of the assessed product of the prefecture, for schools, police, roads, hospitals, encouragement of enterprise, and other services provided by the prefecture (services which included, for the first time, the hygienic examination of licensed prostitutes).[114]

The millstone of payments to samurai was cast aside at last in 1878. In that year, Ishikawa spent less than one-fifth of what it had the year before.[115] More of the prefecture's resources could be allocated to other uses. Kiriyama and Kumano put much of the available funds into administrative expenditures. They raised outlays for salaries and almost all other categories of bureaucratic costs. Across the board, they spent about 30 percent more on administration of the prefecture in 1878 than they had in 1877. Routine expenditures *(jōhi)* in 1878 came to ¥122,060, of which about 30 percent was covered by prefectural taxes.[116]

The important point to be drawn from all these figures on spending is that Ishikawa Prefecture under Kiriyama, as under Uchida, spent most of its budget on maintenance of the bureaucratic system and on continuing to provide previously established services. Under neither of the first two governors did Ishikawa put much toward improvement of the economic infrastructure. Moreover the prefectural government invested only a token amount (0.15 percent of the assessed product of the jurisdiction) in human capital, contributing less than ¥5,000 toward school expenses in 1877, for example.

The probable, if obvious, explanation for the pattern of use of funds in Ishikawa is poverty. The national government provided the funds to liquidate the system of stipends to former samurai and to pay the routine costs of administration, but there was nothing left out of national exchequer contributions that the governors might have applied to projects of their own invention. Local resources for the prefecture, tapped through the system of prefectural taxes, were not abundant enough to provide Kiriyama's administration with the funds required for improving services, instead of simply maintaining them. Kiriyama might have been happy to spend more, at least in some areas, had more been available. He was inclined to promote the cause of education, which prompted his admirers to dub him "the education governor."[117] From the time that he was councilor of Ishikawa, Kiriyama showed great interest in the prefectural normal school and its attached primary school. In September 1875, he transferred responsibility for the Kanazawa medical school, the forerunner of today's well regarded medical faculty of the University of Kanazawa, to the prefecture. The following year he encouraged the opening of branch medical training centers in Toyama and Fukui. At the middle school level, he helped with the establishment of an agricultural training school and an English school in 1876.[118] If unrestricted by a small prefectural tax base, Kiriyama quite possibly would have done more. As it was, he had to promote education more by verbal encouragement than by the distribution of official monies. He applied most of Ishikawa's scarce fiscal resources to other delegated business.

THE POWER AND PRESTIGE OF THE GOVERNORSHIP

The position of prefectural governor was by no means a powerless one, even if men like Kiriyama had little latitude for exercising their own judgment about prefectural spending. Governors had considerable scope for independent decision making in matters of personnel and, until implementation of the Three New Laws of 1878, in subprefectural organization. Kiriyama demonstrated his power in those areas by naming new large district chiefs in 1876 (see Chapter Four). In effect, his moves anticipated the changes of the 1878 system, which strengthened governors' hands in their subprefectural dealings.

The powers of Kiriyama and his fellow governors were sufficient to elevate the prestige of their office, and one scholar has written that by the second decade of Meiji people had come to feel toward governors as they used to feel toward great daimyo.[119] It would be an exaggeration to say that Kiriyama Junkō was held in such awe in Kanazawa, but it is not too much to say that his administration reinforced the governorship. Besides getting rid of dissident officials in 1875 and carrying out the reorganization of 1876, Kiriyama effectively managed the expansion that made Ishikawa the largest prefecture in the nation in both territory and population from 1876 to 1881. The very fact that the central government nearly trebled the size of the prefecture during his administration almost certainly further heightened the prestige of both Kiriyama himself and the governor's chair in Kanazawa.

After a little more than three years at the top of the Ishikawa bureaucratic pyramid, Kiriyama was given the dignity of a new title. On May 15, 1878, he was promoted from provisional governor (*gonrei*) to governor (*kenrei*).[120] Ironically, only one day before this, a plot hatched within his jurisdiction had reached fruition in the assassination of the home minister in Tokyo. Kiriyama was not punished or in any public way blamed for this act of terror, but the news of the murder, when it reached Kanazawa on May 16, must have embarrassed him, for as governor, he was responsible for maintaining law and order in Ishikawa.[121]

EMPEROR, GOVERNOR, AND FORMER DAIMYO—SYMBOLISM AND NATIONAL INTEGRATION

Nine days after the assassination of Home Minister Ōkubo Toshimichi, the emperor announced that he intended to travel to the Hokurikudō and Tō-kaidō regions, and to inspect living conditions and material progress there.[122] This would be the Meiji Emperor's third tour within his realm; in 1872, he had visited western Japan, stopping in several towns that had been important centers of imperial loyalism before the Restoration, and in 1876, he had visited northeastern Japan, the Tōhoku region.[123] These trips had had satisfying results. For his part, the emperor had gained direct knowledge of the life of his subjects—much more than most of his seques-tered predecessors on the throne. As for the state, leaders believed that the central government had profited from the spontaneous outpouring of rever-ence of the Japanese people toward their sovereign. This was as the planners of the tours had wished. The memorial suggesting an imperial tour in 1878 had originated in the army ministry, and the political uses of the emperor's travels were clear to nearly everyone.[124] By focusing attention on the head of the state, the emperor and his advisers were able to bring about an increase in popular loyalty to the national government.[125]

Tokyo leaders, when they planned the Hokurikudō-Tōkaidō tour, were acutely aware that their leadership was not popular among all of the nation's subjects, particularly among many ex-samurai. The home of the assassins of the most powerful member of the government was especially suspect as a hotbed of antigovernment feeling. Perhaps for that reason, as well as be-cause it was the principal city of the Hokurikudō, Kanazawa was made one of the main stops on the 1878 tour. Japan's symbol-system had a living person at its center, the latest in "the line unbroken for ages eternal." Meiji policy makers calculated that a personal appearance by the emperor would strengthen the hold of the national government on an area in which people's loyalty was in doubt.[126]

Accompanied by Minister of the Right Iwakura Tomomi, Councilor of

State Ōkuma Shigenobu, Councilor of State and Minister of Industry Inoue Kaoru, Minister of the Imperial Household Tokudaiji Sanenori, and 794 other attendants, the emperor departed from Tokyo on August 30, 1878.[127] The entourage was the biggest to go with the emperor on any of his travels. Seventy-two days would be spent away from the capital. All along the route, local authorities laid elaborate preparations for the imperial visitation. The prefectural governors were the official hosts within their jurisdictions. Likely all of them did as Kiriyama Junkō, who crammed statistics and other information on his prefecture in anticipation of having to respond to the august inquiries of the ruler.[128] In return for their efforts, the governors could hope, if all went well, that some of the monarch's charisma might rub off on them, conferring greater authority in future dealings with the populace.

The entrance of the imperial party into Ishikawa was delayed by heavy rain. When the procession reached Itoigawa in Niigata Prefecture, just across the boundary with Ishikawa, Iwakura Tomomi passed the word that the tour would halt for a while. Both people and draft animals needed to rest. When the emperor arrived in Itoigawa, Kiriyama was there, ready to escort the monarch across the border and through Ishikawa Prefecture. When everyone was settled, Kiriyama called to ask after His Majesty's health, and was received in audience. After only one day of rest, the huge party moved on, passing into the biggest prefecture on September 28. Governor Kiriyama and his deputy, Chief Secretary Kumano Kurō, formally welcomed the emperor at Oyashirazu.[129]

The authorities took extraordinary precautions to ensure the emperor's safety in Ishikawa. In September, Kawaji Toshiyoshi, the highest-ranking police officer in the land and the head of security for this tour, had ordered the detention of eighteen former samurai of Kanazawa who were alleged to be extremists. Kawaji saw also to the transfer and replacement of some of the soldiers stationed in Kanazawa prior to the sovereign's arrival.[130] He had a personal motive, beyond his usual sense of duty, for executing his mission carefully: He had been among several Meiji leaders identified by Ōkubo's Ishikawa-born murderers as deserving to be killed.[131]

The emperor arrived in Kanazawa on the afternoon of October 2. Crowds of people lined the streets to get a glimpse of his party. Kawaji's constables held them in check. Policemen patrolled every street and alley of the city.

Maeda Nariyasu was among the select few who actually greeted the emperor personally in Kanazawa. The former daimyo sent His Highness a gift of Kanazawa confectioneries—still much prized today—and was granted an audience. Upon the departure of the tour party after three days in Kanazawa, it was Nariyasu who saw the emperor off, riding with him as far as Nonoichi, some fifteen kilometers from the old castle town.[132] Nariyasu's respectful behavior in Kanazawa on this occasion, in view of those whom he himself had ruled, underscored once more for the populace that Japan's political system really had changed. The former lord not only acquiesced in, but positively endorsed, the new regime.

The planners of the imperial schedule in Kanazawa had arranged to have the monarch see a combination of the old and the new. He made the rounds of the prefectural office, the normal school, the women's school, the Kanazawa Judicial Court, the exhibition hall in Kenroku Garden in which nearly 4,000 local products were arrayed, the famous Kenroku Garden itself, the Seisonkaku villa, the hospital, the garrison, the prefectural middle school, and the brassworks run by Hasegawa Jun'ya and Ōtsuka Shirō. The Meiji Emperor was an alert tourist, often asking questions of his hosts.

The sovereign did more in Kanazawa than just learn about local affairs. He used the opportunity to distribute gifts and rewards, singling out men who had served him in some capacity. He made a memorial offering at a shrine in honor of those Kanazawa men who had died fighting for the government in the Restoration War of 1868 and in the rebellions of Saga and Satsuma. He received in audience an ex-samurai named Togashi Takaaki who had been blinded in action as he fought on the government side against the rebels led by Saigō Takamori the previous year. To Togashi, a paragon of loyalism, the emperor presented a roll of *habutae* silk and fifty yen. Others recognized with smaller gifts included soldiers stationed in Kanazawa, prefectural officials, judges, subprefectural officials, teachers in the normal school and the medical college, and people who had lived eighty or more years. In all, the emperor bestowed a little over ¥1670 during his twelve days in Ishikawa Prefecture. He showed his respect for local tradition by giving two rolls of red and white *habutae* silk to the shrine that commemorated Kaga's founder, Maeda Toshiie.[133]

The imperial entourage left Kanazawa on October 5 and travelled southwestward through the prefecture. The emperor demonstrated his concern for the welfare of the common people by contributing money for the relief of victims of recent earthquake, fire, and flood disasters in the counties of Shimo Niikawa, Nei, and Nyū.[134] On his last night in Ishikawa, October 8, he entertained Kiriyama and Kumano at a banquet in Imajō. As a sign of his appreciation of the governor's efforts on his behalf, he made Kiriyama a present of the sake cup that he used that evening.[135]

The antibureaucratic historian Irokawa Daikichi has written that the imperial tours inspired the common people almost not at all. The crowds that turned out along procession routes were often composed mostly of primary school pupils, Irokawa says, while the reaction of ordinary folk was, in effect, "It won't do to let anything get in the way of the farmwork. We can't be running out to greet [the emperor]. Leave us alone." It was only officials and the socially prominent who came into contact with the royal personage, or who benefited from his favor, during the tours, Irokawa avers. If the tours succeeded in anything, the historian concludes, it was in winning over more of the upper crust to the side of the government against the people's rights movement.[136] Other sources, notably the Imperial Household Agency's *Annals of the Meiji Emperor,* contradict Irokawa, telling of peasants gathering in crowds along the emperor's path. A contemporary American observer tells of common people "gather[ing] up the soil on which the imperial feet had stepped, believing that earth thus consecrated would cure diseases."[137] Common citizens of one city greeted their monarch by staging a kind of parade, massing outside his lodging place one evening, lighting the area with huge lanterns that they carried. The same night, "lanterns hung from the eaves of every house in the city, expressing the people's welcome."[138]

As to the type of people who were admitted into imperial audience, Irokawa seems to be correct. Whether he draws the correct inference about people's attitudes is problematic. It is not easy to prove a causal connection between the emperor's tours and popular behavior after the tours. About all that can be stated with confidence is that during these visitations, no disloyal sentiment was expressed anywhere in the sovereign's proximity. In the case of Ishikawa Prefecture, after the emperor's visit, there was hardly any antigovernment activity for three years. Power in the prefecture was transferred without incident to a new governor. The circumstantial evidence from Ishikawa offers little support for Irokawa's argument. Probably Irokawa, with his focus on the common people, diverts attention from the most important aspect of the trip, anyway. It must not be overlooked that the emperor reinforced the sense of service to the nation of those with whom he did come in contact, the leaders in the countryside. His rewards boosted morale among officials and soldiers. It is a near certainty that after meeting the ruler men like Kiriyama and Kumano felt an even stronger personal stake in the welfare of the young state than before. But among the general public, as well as the local elite, the imperial tours heightened awareness of the state and positive feelings toward the man on the throne. Clearly the tours did the central government no harm, and likely they did a great deal of good, in promoting the cause of loyalty to the integrated nation-state that had been taking shape since 1868.

With the conclusion of the emperor's visit to Ishikawa, Kiriyama's major acts in the prefecture were completed. The former Ōgaki *han* samurai stayed on in Kanazawa until his request to retire was granted on February 24, 1879. During his three years and eleven months as chief administrator, he had made changes in personnel and in the structure of subprefectural organization that had strengthened the power of his office. He had taken these steps to increase the effectiveness of his own administration, not just to strengthen the centrally directed bureaucracy. The adjustments he made were not all ordered by Tokyo. His performance of his duties, like Uchida's before him, kept him in tune with the authorities in the capital, but Kiriyama was not merely a minor instrumentalist in an orchestra conducted by Ōkubo or someone else in Tokyo. The story of his years in Kanazawa does not resemble a part in a master symphonic score building toward a climax of "emperor system absolutism," or toward any other certain, predetermined conclusion. Rather this story stands as testimony to the uncertainties of the critical first Meiji decade to which Michio Umegaki has drawn our attention, uncertainties of the actors both in Tokyo and in the countryside, and uncertainties as to how the changing central-local dynamic would turn out.[139]

Both of the first two outsiders who administered Ishikawa Prefecture adapted very well in the face of uncertainty. Their own strong performance on the job increased the central government's power over the localities. But they did not bring the subnational administrative system to its final form. Further changes needed to be made. The process of national unification and integration continued.

THREE

Subprefectural Government in the New Prefecture, 1871–1878

Villages had been the most important source of economic support for the feudal governments of Tokugawa times, and after the Restoration the new government had no immediate alternative to depending on agricultural taxes. No other available resource was as rich as the villages. Yet for a time, the Meiji leaders hardly tapped the localities. Other problems facing them at the national level consumed nearly all the energies and all the political and financial resources that they could muster. For a while after the proclamation of the return of imperial rule, other than some name-changes little was attempted in local administration and taxation below the level of the prefecture or *han*. Taxes, for example, continued to be paid as before. In the *han*, that meant that they were mostly remitted in kind to the *han*, and not to the central government. But it quickly became evident to some statesmen that in order to insure survival of the new state, the *han* and prefectures had to be more tightly integrated. It likewise became clear that local administration and finance at the lowest levels had to be transformed. The goal of central government policy toward towns and villages became— to use twentieth-century terms—mobilization of people and resources for national purposes. The Meiji state needed to control the localities to a greater extent than the Tokugawa *bakufu* had.

There were three major phases of local government institution-building in the Meiji Emperor's reign:

1871–1878. Following the Household Registration Law of 1871, the government had the prefectures divided into large and small districts. These districts replaced traditional town and village organs as the units of local administration, and their chiefs became the principal local officers and liaisons with the state.

1878–1888. With the promulgation of the codes known as the Three New Laws in 1878, irregularities were eliminated and the system made uniform for the whole nation. Elected assemblies at the prefectural and subprefectural levels were introduced. The government revived the old counties, towns, and villages as units of government and scrapped the large and small administrative districts. New local tax laws were put into effect.

1888–1890. New laws on the organization of cities, towns, and villages outfitted Japan with a "modern," that is to say European-style, set of subnational institutions in 1888. The set was completed, on paper, in 1890, with new laws on prefectures and counties.

A more complex periodization scheme would be required to account for the considerable regional variation in Japan, especially in the first of these phases. Broadly viewed, however, these were the stages in the efforts of the Meiji leaders to grasp the local community, to mobilize its energies for national purposes, and to regularize the handling of local affairs under the central direction of the Home Ministry.

This chapter describes the first of these three periods. Subprefectural government in Ishikawa Prefecture between 1871 and 1878 broke centuries-old patterns of organization of the Maeda domain. Annexations of neighboring prefectures between 1871 and 1876 made Ishikawa the most populous prefecture in the land. The new authorities, represented in Kanazawa by Governors Uchida and Kiriyama, carefully built a local base that could be used to strengthen central control of the big prefecture. Ishikawa prefectural authorities followed Tokyo's guidelines in establishing a large and small district system, beginning in 1871, but the governors modified that system as they gained experience and perceived ways in which Tokyo directives seemed inapplicable to conditions in their jurisdiction. Changes in the Ishikawa system in 1876 anticipated changes that were adopted nationally in 1878 and 1880.

VILLAGES UNDER THE RULE OF SHOGUNATE AND DOMAINS

Before we can appreciate the changes wrought in the localities between 1871 and 1878, we need to flesh out our image of local administration and finance at the time of the Restoration. Here, for the sake of simplicity, we will concentrate our attention on village organization. Two facts justify this focus. One is that most of Japan, like most of Kaga, was rural. The other is that in urban areas, the hierarchy of governance and the procedures utilized by the rulers were basically similar to those of rural areas.[1] A writer looking at Kaga has still another justification for not treating pre-Restoration administration in the one city in that *han,* namely that James L. McClain has already done the job extremely well in his book *Kanazawa: A Seventeenth-Century Japanese Castle Town* and in a perceptive article on the Meiji transition in Kanazawa.[2]

The smallest unit of communal organization for administrative and tax purposes during the era of *bakuhan* rule was the *mura.* The word *mura* is usually rendered into English as "village," but before the Restoration, it referred to a hamlet, or what today is called an *aza* or *ku,* rather than to the collection of hamlets that is officially designated a *mura* in post–World War II Japan. From the point of view of *han* and *bakufu* bureaucrats, the village, and not the individual villager, was the important object of administration. The village was the entity responsible for remitting taxes. It provided its own (non-samurai) officials, who served both the feudal authorities above and the villagers below.

From the point of view of its peasant residents, the village was a collective body, with common property and common business in which they shared. The noted legal historian Nakada Kaoru believed an analytical category from German jurisprudence to be useful in understanding the Japanese village. He characterized the traditional village as a *realler Gesamtperson,* and emphasized the collective nature of the village as a juridical person that represented its members in their entirety, but did not have a separate legal existence apart from the people who constituted it, such as a modern corporation has.[3] Any land possessed by the village was the common possession of all members of the village, and any debt or litigation entered into by the village was the common debt or litigation of all the villagers. If village land was sold, it was sold in the name of the village as a single body. If, however, a resident wished to use the village land in a manner that did not require alienating it—for example, if he wished to gather firewood and brush from the commons—he could exercise in his own right his share of the general possessory right of the village, and there was no need for the community as a whole to act.

The hierarchy of administration of villages in the Kaga domain is shown schematically in Figure 1. The head of the village in Kaga was called *kimoiri* (literally, "liver roast," so called, perhaps, because doing the job well required so much effort that the officeholder felt a burning sensation—heartburn, perhaps—inside). The *kimoiri* was elected by the landholders of the village from among families holding land worth two or more *koku*.[4] In practice, the villagers nearly always chose one of the two largest landholders in the village, but the position was not strictly hereditary. The peasants' selection had to be confirmed by the agricultural affairs magistrate (a samurai appointee of the *han,* mentioned in Chapter One and also below). In instances when the villagers could not agree upon a headman, the head of the group of villages *(tomura,* to be described below) to which the village belonged, would designate a headman. If the *tomura* found no one in the village suitable to fill the post, either the *kimoiri* of a neighboring village would be called upon to perform the duties of leadership of the headless village, or a man from another village who was not already a headman would be invited to become *kimoiri* of the village that had none. In a Kaga village, the *kimoiri,* assisted by a few other men, determined how much agricultural tax individual villagers should pay, and collected and delivered the tax-grain to the *han* authorities after the harvest. The headman served as the principal channel of communication between the ruler and the populace. At village assemblies *(mura yoriai),* he read official regulations and notices, and expressions of the lord's will, to the mostly unlettered farmers. Occasionally he reported on the people's living conditions and moods to the samurai officials. The headman kept the records of the village's business, and affixed his seal to documents of transactions involving members of the village. If noncriminal disputes arose in the village, it was the *kimoiri* who bore responsibility for seeing them resolved peaceably, and he often acted as conciliator or mediator between the opposing parties. Finally the headman was supposed to provide a moral role-model for peasants, to be an

FIGURE I   *The Hierarchy of* Han *Rule Over Villages: Kaga in the Early*
            Nineteenth Century

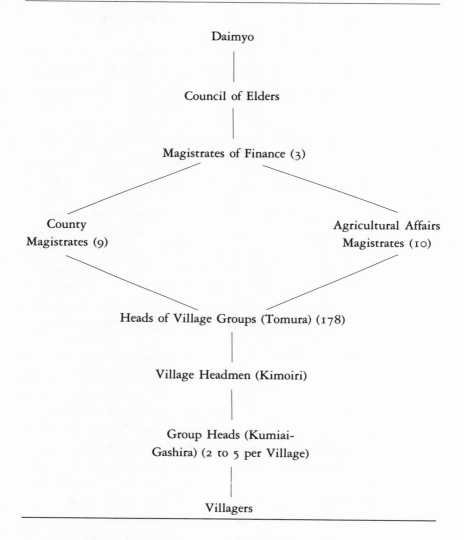

Daimyo

Council of Elders

Magistrates of Finance (3)

County
Magistrates (9)

Agricultural Affairs
Magistrates (10)

Heads of Village Groups (Tomura) (178)

Village Headmen (Kimoiri)

Group Heads (Kumiai-
Gashira) (2 to 5 per Village)

Villagers

Sources: Wakabayashi, *KNSK,* vol.2, pp. 919–927, appendixes 2, 3; *Ishikawa ken no rekishi,* vol.1
p. 147.

upright father-figure who could reinforce on the spot the remote patriarchal authority of the daimyo himself.[5]

In Kaga, "group heads" *(kumiaigashira)* assisted the *kimoiri*. The group heads were several men chosen from among those villagers who could write and calculate, and their principal function was to represent their fellow peasants in planning for the well-being of the community. At the same time as they helped him, the group heads were to supervise the headman and ensure that he not commit any improprieties. The *kimoiri* and the *kumiaigashira* were, in the customary law of the *bakuhan* age, qualified to act as organs of the village and as representatives of it.[6]

Villagers met in an assembly *(mura yoriai)* when a matter important to the whole community arose, in Kaga as in other parts of Japan. Each family head was to attend or be represented by proxy at meetings of the assembly, but in fact the privilege of speaking was restricted to landholding peasants. The assembly was a forum in which at least some villagers had an opportunity to express themselves, and in matters pertaining exclusively to the village, to make rules for themselves. Not all assembly time was given to discussion. Peasants sometimes had to listen to the headman read the proclamations, exhortations, and instructions of their social and political superiors. On occasion the village assembly discussed the apportionment of the land tax. The *han* delegated the task of making assessments on individual villagers, and when it took up matters of land taxation, the assembly was acting as the lowest level of *han* administration, rather than as an autonomous body. But villagers in assembly did exercise a measure of local autonomy in deciding community expenditures and the assessments to be made on villagers in order to defray the costs of such undertakings. They also clearly acted as a self-governing body when they determined, for instance, village regulations that set bounds on the behavior of inhabitants.

Moving up the ladder of Kaga administration, the next step above the village was the group of villages *(tomura,* literally "ten villages," but usually several tens of *mura).* These groups had been systematically organized in the mid-seventeenth century. At their head was a peasant official, usually a man from a locally notable, wealthy, powerful family. His office came to be known by the same word as the group of villages, *tomura,* and it corresponded to the post called *ōjōya* in other regions of Japan. The *tomura* was charged by the *han* with responsibility for administrative and tax affairs of the villages in his group. Appointed by the domain, the *tomura* was the lowest-ranking bureaucrat in the *han* organization. He was a *han* official who was of peasant status, and he was not a representative of the peasants like the elected *kimoiri*. The duties of the village-group headman included transmitting orders and instructions from the county magistrate (*kōri bugyō*) or the agricultural affairs magistrate (*kaisaku bugyō*) to the village headmen, and exercising general administrative, police, and judicial functions for the group of villages. Most important, it was the village-group headman who had to see that the villages paid their taxes.[7]

Between the *tomura* and the domain's financial office in Kanazawa were the county magistrate and the agricultural affairs magistrate. Appointees to these offices were chosen from among the middle-ranking samurai (*heishi*) of the Maeda family's band of retainers.[8] The powers and responsibilities of these two kinds of magistrates extended over approximately one county (*kōri*).

County magistrates were to take care of general affairs—personnel questions, public construction, and judicial decisions in nonfelonious criminal cases. During parts of the period of *han* rule, as noted in Chapter One, the county magistrates managed tax matters for their districts, but they did not do so during the three decades prior to the Meiji Restoration. After 1839, there were three county magistrates for Kaga Province, four for Noto Province, four for the counties of Tonami and Imizu, and two for Niikawa.[9]

Agricultural affairs magistrates served in a position that was peculiar to Kaga. Maeda Toshitsune had created this office in 1651 to play a role in his successful effort to regularize the administration of the agricultural tax system and stabilize the power relations between peasants and fief-holding samurai.[10] Thereafter, except during two brief periods when the lord expanded the purview of the county magistrates and temporarily abolished the office of agricultural affairs magistrate, these samurai bureaucrats handled all business related to land tax, land reclamation, and agricultural improvement, and adjudicated disputes involving land.[11] In the last years of *han* rule, there were ten incumbents of the agricultural affairs post, each entitled to three low-ranking samurai (*ashigaru*) assistants and to whatever other staff help might be found necessary. Both the county magistrates and the agricultural affairs magistrates were accountable to the domain's financial affairs magistrates (*san'yōba bugyō*), whose office was in the castle town.

SUBPREFECTURAL GOVERNMENT AFTER 1871

Between 1867/11 and 1871, some of the local offices of the territory administered by Maeda Yoshiyasu were renamed, but changes were mostly cosmetic. *Tomura* became *gōchō* and then *risei,* all the while continuing to perform the same functions as before the Restoration. Not until after the abolition of the *han* were important alterations made in the local administration of this area of Japan.

In the fourth month of 1871, the national government promulgated a law that mandated organizational change within the *han* and the prefectures. The main point of the new Household Registration Law was to create conditions for taking a unitary census for the entire nation. Following the model of the Kyoto census, which had in turn been inspired by Chōshū household registration regulations, this 1871 law called for all persons to be counted, regardless of their social status. This was a departure from past practice, in which only commoners were counted regularly, and samurai and those with religious vocations were counted separately, when they were counted at all. The house (*yashiki* or *kaoku*) was made the unit of registry in the 1871 law, and once it had been determined who was the head (*koshu*) of the household (*ie*), he or she both became the legal representative of that household and received full responsibility for and power over its affairs. It was up to the head of the household to report to higher authorities on several matters: the number of people in his or her household; household members' names, ages, occupations, and relationship to the head; household members' religious affiliations; and any changes in the household's composition resulting from marriage, adoption, or the creation of a branch family. Being legally answerable for their family members—bearing the weight of collective responsibility—household heads were induced to cooperate with the new registry system. Some historians have seen in this 1871 law the creation of an organ of state power, in the person of the household head, extending to every Japanese subject.[12]

To carry out this new Household Registration Law, the government ordered that districts (*ku*) be established, each encompassing about 500 households. These new districts were independent from the existing towns and villages whose inhabitants were to be counted in the census, although it was legal for a village or town head to become a census officer. Each district was to have at least one "chief" *(kuchō)* and one assistant "chief" *(fuku kuchō)*. Perhaps these men should be called registrars, for their function, under the registration law, was to keep an accurate census of the households, population, births, and deaths within their districts, as well as emigration from and immigration into those districts. Beyond the keeping of these records, the officers of the new districts had no powers and no responsibilities. The immediate purpose, for the national government, was to gain exact knowledge of the number and distribution of Japanese subjects. Without that knowledge it was difficult to mobilize the nation's resources to create a strong state. The Meiji leaders had reached the point at which they felt they had to address questions of subprefectural and subdomanial organization.

In the city of Kanazawa, implementation of the Household Registration Law commenced in 1871/8, shortly after the abolition of the *han*. Seven districts were set up, and a chief, an assistant chief, and a tax inquiry officer *(sozei shirabeyaku)* were appointed for each district.[13] In the rest of the prefecture, the old counties were abandoned as anything but geographical names, and new administrative districts were set up in 1872/2.[14] Thereafter, reorganizations of the local administrative system occurred with bewildering frequency. During 1872, for instance, Ishikawa Prefecture first adopted the designations large district *(daiku)* and small district *(shōku)* to refer to its administrative districts, then renamed the chiefs and their assistants, then replaced the term *daiku* with *ku* for the large districts and the term *shōku* with *bangumi* for the small districts, and finally revamped the local office system, placing a district chief *(kochō)* in charge of each large district and an assistant district chief *(fuku kochō)* in charge of each small district.[15] Basically, the prefecture retained the system of large and small districts, with each large district containing six or seven small districts within it. By the end of 1872, the eight old counties of Ishikawa Prefecture had been reapportioned into forty-four large districts.[16] When the prefecture reported its statistics for the next year, there were forty-three large districts and 233 small districts.[17] At the town or village level, from November 1873, there were 586 men called *kochō* and 1,647 men called *fuku kochō* assisting the large and small district chiefs, who had once again been renamed, this time *kuchō* and *fuku kuchō*.[18] For the sake of comparison, it can be noted that there were 150 prefectural officials in Ishikawa at this time.

The names by which the large and small district chiefs were known changed several times between 1871 and 1879, but their method of selection did not. They were appointed, not elected. The government judged that the old village headmen had often abused their power. To eliminate an unwanted inheritance, the Council of State abolished the old offices of village headman and village-group headman on 1872/4/9.[19] The state did not prohibit the appointment of former headmen as district chiefs, but it made plain that a break with the past was desirable. The choice of new district chiefs was to be up to officials who reported to the central government.

Ishikawa residents accepted all the changes of the Household Registration Law and local district definitions without resistance. It does not appear that the state had to coerce them at all to get them to cooperate with the new system—collective responsibility was nothing new, and the drawing and redrawing of boundaries and changing of names of officials probably seemed rather remote to most people, not very important to their daily lives. There was no protest against the elimination of local election of headmen in the big prefecture, either.

From the time the old positions of village headman and village-group headman were eliminated, all matters relating to the land and people in the large and small districts were in the hands of the officials appointed under the Household Registration Law. The districts became general administrative districts, not just units of census-taking. The old towns and villages, conversely, ceased to exist as administrative entities and became no more than bearers of expenditures for delegated duties. The Ministry of Finance took another slap at the old village headmen on 1872/10/1. Acknowledging that the headmen had often acted improperly, the ministry sought to forestall a recurrence of corruption by providing that the new district chiefs must follow strictly the regulations of their office and that salary payments to those chiefs must be investigated and reported to the central authorities.[20]

Changes in the law did not eliminate all continuity with the Tokugawa period system. At first, the kind of man chosen to staff the new system was not very different from the former headman-type. In some places the local personnel after 1871 were not only, in Robert Spaulding's phrase, "generically indistinguishable from their Tokugawa predecessors,"[21] they were the very same men. Village headmen and village-group headmen were often employed as district officials.[22] On the continuity with pre-Restoration leaders and values, Neil Waters has written discerningly, showing that in the Kawasaki region, an area with few ex-samurai residents, local leaders were able to maintain their authority into the Meiji era and that "they proved capable of manipulating the administrative apparatus to alter the effects of some of the early Meiji reforms," particularly in areas that affected local economic interest.[23] Ōishi Kaichirō found that men of village-headman background often became subprefectural officers in Fukushima, which did have many former samurai; Ariizumi Sadao noted the same thing in Yamanashi, another area with few ex-warriors; and Gary Allinson observed a similar continuity in the Kariya area, which had former samurai as well as commoners among its residents.[24] In Ishikawa Prefecture, according to one student of the old *tomura* system, "to the posts of district chief and assistant district chief, many *tomura* and descendants of *tomura* were appointed."[25] The *tomura* scholar does not name names or provide other evidence in support of his assertion, and it seems that a comprehensive roster of the names and social backgrounds of all the district chiefs and assistant district chiefs of Ishikawa does not exist. Nevertheless, writers on several localities in the prefecture remark on the continuities in local personnel from the *han* period to the Meiji period. In the villages that today are part of the city of Hakui, for example, the community's official history avers that "among those appointed as large and small district chiefs, members of the class that had formerly been *tomura* and village officials were numerous." Again, in Suzu and Fugeshi Counties, two of the four large district chiefs had surnames that were the same as *tomura*. It seems possible that they hailed from families that had been local officials since the seventeenth century.[26] In Nomi County, the eleventh-generation head of a *tomura* family became a *kochō*.[27]

Not all appointees as district chiefs were of peasant-official background. Former samurai also served. Among the men who formed the upper half of the prefectural bureaucracy between 1886 and 1884, eight of seventy-one had served as appointed chiefs or assistant chiefs in large or small districts between 1872 and 1875. Two of those eight were former samurai.[28] While some *tomura* families registered as *shizoku* after 1872, these two former district officials appear not to have come from the village-group headman class.[29] One had been a *han* soldier, and the other was from a branch of the illustrious Chō family. The city of Kanazawa had at least four, and possibly more, ex-samurai among its seven district chiefs, as of 1873; Yoshida On'ichirō, Hayashi Kenzō, Nagao Sukenobu, and Tsuda Kinzō were all former Maeda retainers. Hasegawa Jun'ya, another Kaga samurai and one-time *han* soldier—and future mayor of the city—became, in August 1873, the first to fill a new post, a kind of super-district-chief's position in Kanazawa. These ex-samurai working in local government in their home town all had been political activists in the early years of prefectural rule, joining with others of similar class background in debating and submitting petitions on the issues of the day. The five named here had all served as prefectural officials under Uchida before becoming Kanazawa district chiefs.[30]

Early in 1875, the prefecture was redistricted. A list of Kanazawa district chiefs at the time reveals that both the system and the personnel had changed a good deal. In place of the seven large districts into which it had been divided in 1872, Kanazawa in 1875 had eleven districts. Not a single man who had been a district chief in 1873 appears on the lists of 1875 chiefs. In both years, there were seventy-three assistants to the district chiefs. Among those men, also, there was a great deal of turnover.[31] Later the same year, all forty-three district chiefs in Ishikawa Prefecture became embroiled in a controversy with Governor Kiriyama Junkō. Only seven of the forty-three chiefs' names are available, and of those seven, four can be definitely identified as *shizoku.*[32] We might guess that the other thirty-nine district chiefs were also *shizoku,* since they were all associated with the Chūkokusha, the Ishikawa political society that was dominated by ex-samurai. At the end of August 1875, the Ishikawa district chiefs quit, en bloc, and Kiriyama was able to replace them as chiefs with men of his own choosing.

The above account suggests that subprefectural government in the early Meiji years was not the exclusive preserve of the old peasant and townsman officials and their descendants. Both former commoner worthies and former samurai served as chiefs and assistant chiefs in the large and small districts. At the district level, as at the prefectural level, the pattern of bureaucratic appointment probably reflected the desire of the governor and his highest-ranking subordinates to co-opt as many of the recognized leaders of their jurisdiction as possible. In a prefecture with a large ex-samurai population, that meant employing many ex-samurai at the grass-roots level of local government as well as in the prefectural office.

After the abolition of the old village headmen and their urban counterparts in 1872, the district chiefs and their assistants came to hold "control over all matters relating to the land and people in their respective jurisdictions."[33] Because the governor had the power to appoint these chiefs, it might be supposed that the prefectural office called all the shots in the subprefectural units. This was not the case. The assistants one step down from the small district chiefs, many have pointed out, were the consanguineous or functional descendants of the traditional village headmen. These assistants at the town and village levels were considered by law to be the general representatives *(sōdai)*, or deputies, of their towns and villages, and they apparently acted as a check against the chiefs' "control over all matters." Called *kochō* after 1873, these representatives could conclude contracts in the name of the towns or villages, and this power constituted a measure of local autonomy.

On the other hand, it must be noted that there was little scope for independent action on the part of towns and villages. With the passage of time, the *kochō* came to function more and more as government officials and less and less as representatives of the people of their communities. The load of delegated business grew heavier. As if to recognize this, a Council of State Notice declared in March 1874 that the status of these subprefectural officials should be considered the same as that of bureaucrats in the national administrative organization.[34] Ishikawa Prefecture enacted Provisional Regulations on Districts on November 1876, tightening the grip of higher officials on the localities. One writer commented after examining these regulations that "we must not fail to note that towns and villages at that time were not at all locally autonomous bodies."[35] Even the village-level *kochō* were appointed by high prefectural authorities, according to these 1876 rules, and a historian of the city of Nanao writes that the *kochō*'s principal duty was to convey the wishes of his superior to the people below.[36]

The 1876 regulations made clear that in Ishikawa the large district chiefs *(kuchō)*, small district chiefs *(fuku kuchō)*, and the *kochō* were regular officials. Ranks and salaries were stipulated. The tone and institutional implications of the forty-eight-article Provisional Regulations on Districts are evident in the description of the large district chief:

> One per large district. Junior twelfth grade. Salary ¥20 per month. The large district chief shall have general control over his district, and shall observe the laws and regulations of the state. He shall be charged with the duties of reporting to superior authorities and transmitting [laws and regulations] to the people. Through official orders and public proclamations, he shall see that the laws and regulations of the state are universally observed. All matters of business that must be paid for out of local levies (*minpi*) in the large district, including roads, schools, encouragement of enterprise, and granaries for relief, are the responsibility of the chief. When a citizen makes a request or an inquiry for which there is an established precedent, it can be handled by the *kochō*. However, in cases when the request or inquiry is out of the ordinary, the large district chief must be consulted. The chief must devote himself to making accurate assessments of the numbers of households and of people, to encouraging enterprise and fostering education, and to promoting the peace and prosperity of the people of his district, and he must see that nothing about the condition of the people is kept from the attention of the ruler.

Small district chiefs were assigned the thirteenth official grade and ¥15 a month by these same Provisional Regulations, and *kochō* got supplementary grade one and ¥10 a month. The hierarchical chain of command was made clear in a clause reading: "The promotion and dismissal of district chiefs and lower officials is [subject to] the order of the prefectural office. The large district chief may, however, inspect and report on the diligence of *kochō* and lower officials."[37] For his part, the *kochō* was required to cooperate with the district chief in encouraging enterprise and school attendance. To some local officials, so strong a measure of central authority was unwelcome. Ishikawa Prefecture large district chiefs had petitioned the Home Minister in August 1875 during their dispute with Governor Kiriyama, indicating that they were not happy with their designation as regular government bureaucrats. They argued that the fact that they were paid out of district monies (*kuhi*) differentiated them from central and prefectural government officials.[38] Nothing came of their petition.

An official rationale accompanied the Ishikawa regulations of 1876. It stressed that the district offices were established for the convenience of the people, and that there should be a clear separation of duties between the prefecture and the districts.[39] But the main thrust of the reform was toward greater centralized bureaucratic control. The appointment and supervision provisions of these provisional rules strengthened the power of the governor and his chief aide, both of whom were Tokyo appointees.

Before issuing these provisional regulations, the Ishikawa authorities had requested the Home Minister's permission to redistrict the prefecture once more, on the grounds that the system then in use lacked consistency, having been set up right after the abolition of the *han* in what then had been the three prefectures of Kanazawa, Nanao, and Niikawa.[40] The Home Minister approved, and on November 1, 1876, Ishikawa Prefecture revised its district boundaries. The new large districts were coterminous with the *han*-period counties, with a couple of exceptions. The prefecture thus anticipated a major feature of the first of the Three New Laws of 1878, the revival of the county as an administrative unit. In the Ishikawa archives, the first large district is defined simply as Enuma County, the second large district as Nomi County, and so on.[41] The three provinces of Kaga, Noto, and Etchū were divided in 1876 into thirteen large districts, each with a chief and an assistant chief. The large districts were subdivided into between ten and thirty small districts, each with a chief assisted by an unspecified number of assistants at the old town and village level.

Statistics that permit comparisons of Ishikawa districts before and after the 1876 reform are available only for the two ancient provinces of Kaga and Noto, but these indicate the extent of change: The number of large districts and large district chiefs was reduced from forty-three to eight, and that of small districts and small district chiefs from 233 to 131.[42] How many town- and village-level officials there were after the reform is unclear. There had been over 580 men with the title *kochō* and over 1,600 with the title *fuku kochō* before the reform.[43] The new system called for one *fuku kochō* for every 50 to 200 households. Thus there should have been between 683 and 2,732 *fuku kochō* in Kaga and Noto, figuring from the number of households. The average population of a large district in Ishikawa Prefecture (all three old provinces) on November 1, 1876, was 103,530. The average small district population was 5,493.[44] (For the correspondence between the new large districts and the old counties, along with population statistics compiled by large and small district officials, see Appendix 5.)

The changes in subprefectural organization in Ishikawa enabled the governor and his central government superiors to tighten their grip on the localities. While the responsibilities of large district chiefs were enlarged in proportion to the increase in size of their jurisdictions, the fact that there were fewer of these chiefs meant that they could be more easily monitored by the Tokyo authorities and their direct appointees. The same principle obtained in the case of the reduced number of small district chiefs. So far as personnel management was concerned, central control was enhanced, not diminished, by the 1876 reforms. For Governor Kiriyama and Councilor Kumano, this was important. Their 1875 battle with the forty-three large district chiefs had been unpleasant. With fewer chiefs to keep track of, Kiriyama and Kumano could rest easier, knowing that the odds of an embarrassing repetition of conflict had been considerably lengthened.

The benefit of Ishikawa's 1876 reforms might not have been only to the government. Possibly the localities gained from more effective administration. The record is not extensive enough to enable us to be sure. In the letter of the law, at least, a change of October 1876 raised the stature of urban districts, towns, and villages all over Japan.[45] The Tokyo government, in regulations pertaining to common property and public works, recognized these local entities as having juridical personality.[46] When dealing with public loans, property, and construction matters, the urban districts, towns, and villages were considered legal persons. Communities at this level were not made units of local self-government by these regulations, but they were vested with legal competence to manage certain of their affairs. This legislation can be viewed as a prelude to the 1878 law that elevated urban districts, towns, and villages to the status of regular administrative bodies and gave them some self-governing powers.

The Financing of Subprefectural Government

Once new subprefectural offices had been established, and both commoners and samurai appointed to staff them, how did the community pay for the work they supervised? Local government had to be paid for, and salaries for the officials who worked at this level had to be provided, regardless of whether it was the state or the people that benefited most. The record of local government finances in the early Meiji years indicates that a good portion of local expenditures was for business delegated by the central and prefectural authorities. The revenues that the central government derived from the land tax were virtually all committed to other purposes and could not be allocated to financing of local activities. The burden fell on the localities themselves.

Immediately after the adoption of large and small districts as administrative units, a type of local tax called *minpi* (literally, "people's expenditure") was introduced.[47] This was a levy collected by the districts to pay for services that the locality itself was responsible for, or for services provided from above that central government or prefectural funds only partly covered.

In August 1874, while Uchida Masakaze was still governor, Ishikawa Prefecture systematized the collection of these local exactions. Prefectural officials and district officials held a meeting that was called a "prefectural assembly" (*kenkai*), at which they adopted a Plan for the Assessment of Local Tax. This plan specified not only rates for such levies, but how different services would be provided out of funds drawn from different tax bases. Construction of irrigation reservoirs and water gates, for example, would be paid for out of taxes on all the land under cultivation in the community, but not lots on which houses stood. Schools would be provided for by household taxes. Salaries of large and small district officials, and all their office expenditures, would be covered by taxes on both land and households. *Minpi* were bound up with the regular expenditures of the locality by this plan, and the majority of services were to be paid for with monies raised by the exactions on households.[48] *Minpi* added significantly to the taxpayers' burden. One of the foremost students of local government finance in Japan, Fujita Takeo, has estimated that *minpi* took between 7 and 15 percent of farm families' incomes between 1874 and 1877.[49] That was a lot, coming on top of the national land tax and prefectural levies, which took more than a third of the same families' income in those years.[50] These taxes weighed more heavily on families with lower incomes than those who were more affluent. Well-to-do folk had more left over after taking care of their tax obligations. Most people in nineteenth-century Japan, of course, had very modest incomes.

In 1874, the Council of State ordered prefectures to submit details of *minpi* collections. On September 20, Kiriyama Junkō, as deputy for Uchida, sent Ishikawa's report to the first minister of the state, Sanjō Sanetomi.

Figures for Kaga and Noto were kept separate. Table 3 shows the major categories of *minpi* spending in that year. Kiriyama submitted to Sanjō details of outlays for twenty-four different items.[51]

One of the most remarkable things about the 1874 Ishikawa *minpi* is that they exceeded prefectural expenditures by 40 percent, if samurai stipend payments are left out of the calculation. By far the largest portion of these local exactions went to pay salaries of subprefectural officials. Less than a quarter of the amount that went for officials' salaries was allocated to school expenditures, which were the next largest area of *minpi*. When office expenses and the like are included, the cost of maintaining the local bureaucracy dwarfs the expenditures on education and other services even more. In Kaga, salaries, office expenses, travel on official business, mailing, and associated expenses took 60.7 percent of *minpi;* in Noto these took 80 percent.[52]

Minpi for schools were not impressively large. They amounted to less than 11 percent for the whole prefecture. While schools did receive some funds from the Ministry of Education and some private contributions, it is almost inconceivable that publicly supported schools could have had much in the way of equipment and materials. More likely education proceeded

TABLE 3   Minpi *in Ishikawa and Its Two Provinces, 1874*

	Ishikawa Prefecture		Kaga Province		Noto Province	
	Amount in Yen	Percent of Total	Amount in Yen	Percent of Total	Amount in Yen	Percent of Total
Officials' salaries	38,861	46.4	27,846	44.4	11,015	52.4
School expenditures	9,166	10.9	7,460	11.9	1,706	8.1
Roads and bridges	5,899	7.0	5,698	9.1	201	1.0
Office costs	5,002	6.0	3,598	5.7	1,404	6.7
Other	24,793	29.6	18,114	28.9	6,679	31.8
TOTAL	83,721	100.0	62,716	100.0	21,005	100.0

Source: Constructed from data in *IKSR, kan 42, seido bu, shokusei,* Meiji 7-*nen,* vol.3, pp. 488–489; also see *IKGS,* vol.1, pp. 144–145, and *NSS,* p. 576.

Note: Percent total of Ishikawa Prefecture *minpi* appears not to equal 100.0 because of rounding to tenths of a percent; actual total is 100.0.

under spartan conditions. Attendance fees, a few sen a month per student, could hardly have affected this very much.

Roads, bridges, and dikes had to be maintained by localities in early Meiji Japan. The central government did not provide funds for such facilities. Ishikawa Prefecture and its localities did not wholly neglect these prosaic but critical elements of the economic infrastructure, but it is obvious from the paltry sums spent that no construction was going on in Noto and that little worth note could have been done in Kaga. Two years after the first railway in Japan was laid down on the Pacific Seaboard side of Honshu (between Shinagawa and Yokohama), the absence of activity in road and bridge building—technologically simpler, and cheaper, than the construction and running of a railway—might be a good index of the economic sluggishness of the big prefecture beside the Japan Sea. It would have been a great strain to raise more public funds through *minpi* exactions just to build more roads and bridges. Railroads, which required more knowhow and more capital than it was feasible for Ishikawa to raise, were out of the question as an object of Ishikawa people's spending.

The national land tax reform *(chiso kaisei)* of 1873 increased the bureaucratic bite of *minpi* yet again. Expenditures associated with this change were not included in the 1874 Ishikawa report on local exactions, but a later Ministry of Finance report presents the costs to the government *(kanpi)* and costs to localities *(minpi)* for administering the land tax reform from its beginning to its end, from 1873 through 1880.[53] The government paid only 15 percent of what it cost (¥291,000) to carry out the reform in Kaga and Noto, while the localities in those two old provinces paid 85 percent (¥1.7 million).[54] Nationwide the cost of administering the land tax reform was approximately ¥37.1 million, of which ¥29.1 million, or 78.5 percent, was drawn from *minpi*.[55] In Ishikawa in 1874, the cost of the land tax reform was far higher, surely, than the figure for land title inquiry that appears in the report on *minpi*. Salaries and wages of the officials involved, including some staff hired especially to work on land tax and not on any other local business, added even more to the cost of the reform.

Land tax reform aside, there was little left out of the local tax collections after the expenses of the local bureaucracy, schools, and public works maintenance had been taken care of. The remaining amount—23 percent of *minpi*—went for salaries of Shintō priests, fire prevention, guards, prisons, water and sewage, flood prevention, family registry, and hour-bells. These might as well have been the routine expenditures of a local community in traditional Japan. There was no modernizing vision here, just a desire to continue the kinds of services that people were accustomed to. These outlays served to maintain, rather than improve, the community.

Regional differences in development were exacerbated by the pattern of *minpi* spending. Noto, relatively poor to begin with, allocated just 8 percent of its local levies to education and 1 percent to construction of economic infrastructure. In Kaga, 12 percent and 17 percent of *minpi* were put toward these. One scholar has applied to Noto the saw "poverty breeds poverty," and it does seem that the failure, or inability, of Noto communities to invest in education and social overhead capital got that province into a vicious cycle from which, it might be argued, it has yet to recover fully.[56]

Delegated business strained Ishikawa's limited fiscal resources. This is indicated by the 1876 statistical tables for the prefecture, which permit us to compare *minpi* with government expenditure *(kanpi)* in the area of police expenditures. Regrettably, since forms of government data-collection changed frequently in the early Meiji period, there are no other reports on Ishikawa Prefecture *minpi* similar to that of September 1874, on the basis of which we might construct a time series. Still, the figures on spending for police suggest that localities paid much for delegated business. It was the Home Ministry and the prefectural police office that decided how many police there should be, where police stations and police boxes should be located, what the duties of a patrolman were, what procedures the police should follow, and the like. But it was the localities that bore most of the cost. Against the central government's expenditure of ¥16,950 in Ishikawa Prefecture in 1876, localities paid ¥21,255, or 56 percent of total police expenditures.[57]

In 1878, *minpi* was 4.7 times larger than prefectural expenditures. Some of these local levies of 1878 were spent in the changeover to the system of the Three New Laws, but the great bulk of them was laid out before the new local government system was implemented.[58] Prefectural taxes in 1878 came to barely over 4 percent of local levies.

The scale of *minpi* spending in 1878 was almost incomparably larger than it had been four years earlier, ¥1.5 million versus ¥83,721, a difference that is not accounted for merely by the geographic expansion of the prefecture. More was being required of the localities. Outlays for construction were up in 1878 over 1874, although not by huge amounts. Expenses for schools increased to 17 percent of *minpi,* up from 11 percent. That some emphasis was being placed on education is clear when we note that the amount put toward schools in 1878 was twenty-eight times what it had been in the two provinces of Kaga and Noto in 1874. Some new categories of local expenditure had emerged in the mid-seventies: encouragement of enterprise, police expenditures, public health. Looking into the items on which *minpi* were spent, we discover that 29 percent went for roads, bridges, and dikes, and of that, 80 percent was for facilities that benefited particular towns or villages and was therefore paid for only by those towns and villages. Perhaps local communities were able to exercise some control over what they were spending their local taxes for. On the other hand, police expenditures, if we add in those for and by particular towns and villages, consumed 4 percent of local exactions, and communities had little control over how this money was spent.

"People's expenditures" were paid from funds raised in addition to the regular land tax, which already amounted to approximately 40 percent of the annual crop. Governor Uchida himself considered the regular land tax to be an excessively heavy burden on the people of his prefecture, and the additional requirement to pay *minpi* was felt keenly by the taxpayer.[59] *Minpi* were at the root of clashes that broke out between the *kuchō* and the *kochō,* on one side, and the people, on the other.[60] Some subprefectural officials felt themselves in an impossible dilemma, trapped between their sense of obligation to support the system and their sense of compassion for the many families for whom paying the local levies was a hardship. Appeals to the prefecture for a reduction in *minpi* issued from the brushes of such humanitarian local bureaucrats, but to no avail.[61] Reductions were not forthcoming, and out of their irritation with the way local expenditures were managed, many taxpayers conceived a growing resentment against the whole system of local government.

Ōkubo Toshimichi, the most powerful man in the central government, noted the widespread dissatisfaction with the post-1872 local government structure. The fact that the system had evolved on a trial-and-error basis meant that although local organization and procedures of operation had been regularized prefecture by prefecture, there was, from the central government's viewpoint, not enough coherence or unity in the whole system. Ōkubo determined to make the system more uniform. So that citizens would not blame the central government for all that even the lowest subprefectural officials did on the job, he planned to give localities more control over their own affairs. As we shall see in Chapter Five, his plans were partially realized in the system of the Three New Laws after 1878. Subnational assemblies were set up, elections were introduced for members of these assemblies and for town and village administrators, and other revisions in the law broadened the scope of local decision making—in theory. But the changes inspired by Ōkubo would not add up to local autonomy for towns and villages, and the legal mechanisms for supervision and control of the localities would be strengthened after 1878.

In Ishikawa, the institutional framework in 1878 was not at all what it had been in Kaga *han* in 1871. Local administrators had effectively, if unwittingly, readied the ground for the system of the Three New Laws. By 1878, localities in Ishikawa had been made integral parts of a national administrative system, with large and small districts the units of administration below the prefecture. Officials of both large and small districts were appointees of the governor. Personnel changes had been made, as the first two governors had employed both ex-samurai and commoners in subprefectural administrative positions. While many of the first appointees seem to have been the same men who had managed local affairs under *han* rule, or men from the same families, by the end of the first Meiji decade new blood had been infused into the system.

Good numbers of men were ready not just to accept changes passively, but to work for the new state at the local or prefectural level. The rest of the citizenry of Ishikawa was satisfied to comply with the new structures, along with the new obligations and the new freedoms, of the Meiji state. It had become routine for central and prefectural authorities to pass along a great deal of business to subprefectural units, and to require the localities to bear the financial burden through *minpi* exactions. All these changes caused some friction between authorities and citizens, but in Ishikawa this friction never kindled a major blaze. Overt protest was rare, and it was not directed at the system. Subprefectural units of government in 1878 were working much as the governor and his Home Ministry superiors wished.

FOUR

Hopes for National Influence and Their Frustration: Politics in Ishikawa Prefecture, 1872–1878

In the early days of prefectural government, many men in Uchida Masa-kaze's jurisdiction were casting about for ways to participate in the affairs of the new Japan. They fixed their attention on the national stage, for the most part, and it was to national policy issues that they addressed them-selves in the memorials and petitions that document their activities. From our considerable historical distance, we can see with preternatural clarity that political activists in Kanazawa were out of the loop of early Meiji national policy making. Up close, with all the distractions and distortions of contemporaneity, they could not see that. What they saw clearly was that the political situation of the nation was in flux. Systemic changes and personnel changes seemed almost daily occurrences. Many men around Ja-pan who were not direct participants in central government decision making had become politically engaged; many expressed themselves; not a few con-ceived ambitions to gain a voice in national affairs. Although out of power, they imagined that they might influence its exercise, or even that they might vault to responsible positions in the government. The political activi-ties and pronouncements of Kanazawa men at this time, and their ambitions and opinions, were important locally because they set a tone and left examples for later activists. They have also a larger significance, in that they reflect the consciousness of an important segment of the whole society of early Meiji Japan. They illuminate, for our better understanding, the thinking of those who cared about the critical issues of the day and wanted to contribute to a resolution of the problems of the polity, but who happened to be out of power.

While national affairs occupied them for most of the years of Uchida and his successor Kiriyama, Ishikawa men got into one of their biggest disagreements over a local matter, the question of the composition of a prefectural assembly. Their debate casts light on an area about which historians have disputed, that is, how people in the Japanese countryside perceived citizens' roles in local government in that era. The historiographical conflict has pitted those who assert that popular demand for participation in local government was low, and that the system provided opportunities that the people had not sought,[1] against those who argue that only the demands of citizens led a reluctant government to adopt laws providing for a greater popular role in local government, and that even then the government was careful to structure the system so that real autonomy was impossible and power remained concentrated at the center.[2]

This chapter concentrates on politics in Kanazawa and the surrounding prefecture from 1872 through 1878. It begins with a petition submitted in the early days of the governorship of Uchida, and ends with a homicide—a political assassination by Ishikawa men that had a large impact on the central government—near the end of Governor Kiriyama's time in office.

EARLY EXPRESSIONS OF CONCERN FOR THE NATION

Nearly all the Ishikawa men who became involved in politics in the early Meiji period were of the samurai class. Many of the activists who signed memorials and participated in the political societies of this time also served as officials in the prefectural bureaucracy. For men of their family background, government service was a natural career choice.

Former retainers of the Maeda like Sugimura Hiromasa, Kuga Yoshinao, Yoneyama Michio, Hasegawa Jun'ya, and Ōtsuka Shirō demonstrated a positive identification with the new political order in Japan by taking positions in the new prefectural administration. Through their close cooperation with Uchida Masakaze, they evidenced their willingness to accept outside direction of local affairs. To these men of Kanazawa, local self-government was not an issue. These men felt local pride, compounded with elements of regret and shame that their *han* had not participated in the Restoration, but they had no desire to maintain the integrity of their old domain as something apart from or special within the Meiji state.

The orientation toward national questions is already apparent in one of the earliest recorded expressions of opinion in Ishikawa Prefecture, a petition of the fifth month of 1872. Worried that the defense capabilities of the new Meiji regime were inadequate to the foreign challenge, Sugimura and some associates in prefectural officialdom joined with other ex-soldiers such as Shimada Ichirō and submitted a proposal to Ishikawa Prefecture. They adumbrated a plan that would have assigned them a meaningful function in the new state: "All the people should be soldiers. We should model ourselves on the British and French examples, recruit volunteers, and build a barracks. Drilling with modern weapons and practicing modern military tactics, in time of emergency we would be ready to augment the small force of the corps area garrison."[3] The petitioners acknowledged that there were no public funds that could be diverted to the undertaking that they proposed. They therefore offered to have the officers of their military organization make a deposit in the Kawase Gaisha, a Kanazawa banking institution, sufficient that the interest would cover their operation. This gesture paralleled that of the backers of the police auxiliary set up in Kanazawa in the same year, but in this instance, the object of concern was the nation, and the subscribers could expect nothing in the way of local return, such as contributors to the police auxiliary might have looked for. Still they offered both money and voluntary service. In the end, Uchida and his deputy Kiriyama rejected the Ishikawa men's plan—in part because they could not be certain that hotheaded elements of the old *han* military would not enlist and pervert the admirable stated purpose of the volunteer militia.[4]

As might have been expected of a group enthralled by the Satsuma spirit and the charisma of Saigō Takamori, Sugimura, Kuga, and their friends were extremely sensitive about what they perceived to be the national honor. They needed little prodding to espouse the cause of continental adventure, if that were a way to defend Japan's honor. One grand opportunity to defend Japan seemed to come their way in 1873. In August of that year, while many of Japan's top leaders were on a diplomatic mission in Europe, the policy makers who had stayed at home reached a secret decision to send Saigō to Korea. Officials of that neighboring kingdom had scorned Japan's announcement of the Meiji Restoration, objecting in particular to the Japanese use of the title "emperor" to refer to someone other than the Chinese ruler, whose suzerainty the Koreans continued to recognize. The Koreans had also made insulting insinuations about Japan's importation of Western civilization. In 1872, the leaders of the peninsular kingdom went so far as to cut off regular negotiations with the Japanese at Pusan. Japanese indignation grew, and by the summer of 1873 it had reached so high a point that Saigō was able to prevail in debate within the stay-at-home government. He expected that he might be executed or assassinated in Korea. His own loss of life would be worthwhile, however, for it would give Japan the *casus belli* for a war that he and his followers believed necessary. A victorious conflict would benefit Japan by making its position more secure vis-à-vis other nations, especially Russia, and by providing an outlet for unrest among former samurai at home.[5]

Two months after the secret government decision was taken, Sugimura and a group of his followers drafted a petition for submission to Tokyo authorities. Again the men of Ishikawa requested to take up arms, this time as the vanguard of a thousand-man force to Korea. Before their petition could be submitted, the decision to send Saigō to Korea was reversed by a stronger group in the central government centered on Iwakura Tomomi, Ōkubo Toshimichi, and Kido Takayoshi, who had come back from abroad.[6] Reform at home was established as the first priority. A military expedition to Korea was ruled out as too expensive and too risky. Shortly thereafter Saigō Takamori, Itagaki Taisuke, Soejima Taneomi, Etō Shinpei and Gotō Shōjirō quit their offices in the Tokyo government and went back to their homes.

The October 1873 petition of Sugimura and his associates was never read by central government leaders, but the opening phrases are a strikingly direct statement of the desire to make up for lost opportunities and the sense of shame that underlay nearly all actions of Kanazawa political men in the early Meiji period:

> Because we have no talents and are without ability, even though the
> nation has undergone a great change since 1868, we have been unable
> during that time to achieve anything of merit. Our first aim is to repay
> our debt for the immeasurable benevolence of the nation. Our second aim
> is to fulfill our duty to cooperate with all the people of the nation.[7]

Also noteworthy in this document is a brief recitation of Sugimura's role in
the reformed Kaga military just before its dissolution in 1870. The writers'
local pride in that force composed of both samurai and commoners is clear,
as is their belief that such a military body might play a role in Japan's
defense needs of 1873. The defeat of the proposal to send Japanese soldiers
to Korea was a grave disappointment to Kanazawa's would-be volunteers.

Half a year later, Sugimura joined with no fewer than 2,000 other Ishikawa men in petitioning Army Vice-Minister Saigō Tsugumichi. This time
the supplicants asked to be made the vanguard of an expeditionary force to
China.[8] They were stimulated by the central authorities' decision to send
troops to Taiwan, ostensibly to punish the natives of that island for crimes
against Ryukyuans and Japanese. In 1871, fifty-four Ryukyu inhabitants
had been slaughtered after being shipwrecked on Taiwan, and two years
later, four people from Oda (now part of Okayama) Prefecture were attacked
and robbed after being cast ashore. The Meiji authorities sent Soejima Taneomi to China as Special Envoy and Minister Plenipotentiary in 1873, but
Ch'ing leaders refused to take responsibility or to make restitution. After
an interval, Tokyo decided to try to turn the situation to their advantage,
by using China as an outlet for dissatisfied samurai. Ōkubo and Iwakura,
who had staunchly opposed sending troops to Korea, changed their minds
about the utility of a vent for samurai frustrations when their former col-
league Etō Shinpei led a rebellion of ex-warriors in Saga in 1874; in Satsuma, too, the atmosphere among old samurai was growing more and more
volatile.[9] Kanazawa men also evidenced high martial spirit in their April
1873 petition.

Perhaps because it became easier for them to define their own political
identity when they contrasted their new state to the outside world, and
because the definition could become sharper as other nations opposed or
threatened Japan, these Kanazawa patriots were seriously concerned about
how Japan looked abroad. Having read in a newspaper a report that the
American minister to Japan had persuaded the Japanese government to call

off the expedition to Taiwan, Sugimura and others wrote to the Left Chamber of the Council of State on April 25, 1974. "If Japan now changes its decision and stops this undertaking," they predicted, "internally it will give rise to apprehensions on the part of the people, and externally it will invite the scornful laughter of all foreign nations." [10] They insisted that the expedition must go on.

In this same entreaty, the Kanazawa writers referred to central government officials as *yūshi* ("office holders"). The phrase implies a perception of politics as an affair carried on, and contended over, by those who are in power and those who are out; this is a view that may not seem brightly fresh, but that differs from the view of affairs of state that was orthodox for centuries before the Restoration. Probably it was not coincidental that the same diction had been used in January 1874 by Itagaki and others who banded into the Aikokusha in their proposal that a representative body be established. Itagaki and his associates had berated the *yūshi* for monopolizing power and failing to take the wishes of the people into consideration, [11] and *yūshi sensei* ("despotism of the office holders") became one of the catch phrases of the popular rights movement in its attacks on the government. The phrase would often reappear in antigovernment statements by Kanazawa men in the early Meiji.

If there was any opposition within Ishikawa to the bellicose stance assumed by Sugimura's group, it was mute. Shimada Ichirō, who was scathingly critical of prefectural officials because of what he regarded as their unseemly taste for pleasures and luxuries, signed his name to the petitions of 1873 and 1874, along with many of the men he criticized. That the will of Kanazawa men was united apparently mattered little. Their energetic expressions of their opinions elicited no response from the central government. In fact, the Tokyo authorities decided to act exactly contrary to advice like that from Ishikawa, and to call off the expedition to Taiwan, but their change of mind came too late to stop Saigō Tsugumichi, whom they had placed in command of the Japanese force. On May 2, 1874, Saigō left Nagasaki for Taiwan with some 3,600 troops. Within a short time the Japanese gained control of the island, setting the stage for the negotiations between Ōkubo Toshimichi and the Chinese which resulted in an indemnity and clear title to the Ryukyus for Japan. But Ishikawa men played no role in any of this, neither in the decision making nor in battle. To them it seemed that another great opportunity to recover honor had been lost, that their will to serve had been ignored.

While the Korean crisis of 1873 was still boiling, Sugimura and Kuga left their positions in the prefectural administration. Sugimura resigned as provisional councilor (*gon sanji*) on August 29, 1873, and Kuga quit as *chūzoku* on September 15.[12] Why these two left office when they did is unclear.[13] Most of their political confederates in the Ishikawa prefectural administration stayed in office for another two years or so, even though all of these men had been dropped a rung on the ladder in a wholesale down-shifting of bureaucratic ranks in late summer 1873. Political associates of Sugimura and Kuga such as Kojima Hikojiro, Inagaki Yoshikata, Obata Zōji, Yoneyama Michio, Katō Kō, Ōtsuka Shirō, and Shiba Kiichi, as well as Kuga himself, all had their ranks lowered on August 17. So did other Ishikawa officials, excepting only Uchida, his deputy Kiriyama, and Sugimura. On August 19, Uchida issued a statement explaining that the demotions were necessitated by budgetary stringencies.[14] Most prefectural officials seem to have accepted this explanation at face value, and reconciled themselves to lower pay.[15] But Sugimura and Kuga, leaders of the pro-Satsuma faction, quit their posts, and the pay cut and lower prestige of a lower title may have figured in at least Kuga's decision to resign.

Unburdened of official obligations, Sugimura and Kuga could express their sentiments on pressing issues openly and without restraint. It would have been difficult for them to take the stances they did in the petitions of October 1873 and April 1874 if they had remained in their relatively high prefectural positions. They became free also to travel when and where they wanted, and after the disappointment over being excluded from the Taiwan expedition, the first place they wanted to go was Kagoshima. In June 1874, they made the passage to Satsuma.[16] Their hero Saigō Takamori was there, having returned after quitting the government. The visitors from Kanazawa renewed their old contact with Kirino Toshiaki, who spent a good deal of time with them, detailing Saigō's ideas on continental policy. Kirino took into his home as a boarder a nineteen-year-old named Chō Tsurahide who had made the trip from Kanazawa with Sugimura and Kuga. Chō was a relative of Chō Tsurahiro, the one-time leader of Kaga *han,* but his imprint on history had nothing to do with his family; four years after staying with Kirino, he would become one of the assassins of Ōkubo Toshimichi, who

122 Hopes for National Influence, 1872–1878

had once been close to, but later became the rival of, Kirino's patron and friend Saigō.

After a month in Kagoshima, Sugimura and Kuga returned home. Their esteem for Saigō undiminished, they promoted the image of the great Satsuma military leader. Nearly everyone in Ishikawa who cared about politics came to revere Saigō. Yet Sugimura, Kuga, and other leaders of Kanazawa activists were attuned to other modes of political expression besides Saigō's. Once their hopes to play an important part in some military adventure had been dashed, they changed. Their focus continued to be on the national scene, but they tried a new approach.

THE CHŪKOKUSHA: THE FIRST POLITICAL SOCIETY IN ISHIKAWA PREFECTURE

In December 1874, these men united to form a political society similar to the Risshisha, which had been founded in Kōchi eight months earlier by Itagaki Taisuke, Kataoka Kenkichi, and others. Ishikawa men called their new organization the Chūkokusha, and the name itself signals a difference in orientation between Kanazawa and Kōchi. Itagaki's group had named themselves the Risshisha, "Society to Establish One's Moral Will," after the title of a translation of Samuel Smiles' *Self-Help*.[17] Confucius, not some Western thinker, inspired Sugimura and his fellow-activists. The Kanazawa men called themselves the Chūkokusha, "Society for Loyal Advice," drawing a phrase from the *Analects*. ("The Master said, 'Advise [friends] loyally and lead them skillfully.' ")[18] The notion of loyalty conveyed by the first character of the society's name, *chū*, is redolent with Japanese tradition, having been one of the key virtues of the warrior. *Risshi* was a new idea, associated with the progressive West, while *chūkoku* was a familiar old notion sanctioned in the Oriental Classics. The names of their organizations suggest contrasts in attitude between Kanazawa men and Kōchi men that are worth remembering and pondering, yet these contrasts should not be allowed to obscure the fact that on many questions, the positions of the Chūkokusha ended up quite close to those of the Risshisha.

The formal inaugural meeting of the Chūkokusha took place in January 1875, a month after the date of the prospectus (*shuisho*) of the group.[19] Over a thousand men joined the new society. Nearly all, if not all, of them, were former retainers of the Maeda.[20] The preponderance of ex-*bushi* in political affairs was of course the rule in Japan at the time. The Risshisha was also made up almost exclusively, if not exclusively, of *shizoku*. Owing to the class and educational background of the participants, the 1870s, during which the Chūkokusha and Risshisha flourished, has been labelled the phase of "upper class people's rights" in one common interpretation of the political history of Meiji.[21] The samurai bent of the Chūkokusha was underscored by its announcement, at the time of its founding, of a branch society that had the ostensible objective of promoting the sciences, agriculture, technology, and the economy to benefit the nation, but which was, in reality, an assistance association for former *bushi* who were having trouble adjusting to changing economic conditions.[22] In this, too, the Chūkokusha paralleled its Kōchi predecessor, which took the providing of relief to needy ex-samurai as an important objective from the start.[23]

The prospectus of the Chūkokusha has never received the analytical scrutiny that has been given the founding document of the Risshisha, no doubt because the members of the Kanazawa society never gained fame as did Itagaki and Kataoka and other associates of theirs. However, as a clear statement of the fundamental political beliefs of a sensitive and sophisticated group of men whose aspirations for influence did not at the time seem vain, the Kanazawa prospectus deserves inspection.[24]

Several passages of the Chūkokusha prospectus bear a fairly close resemblance to parts of the Risshisha. Likely the authors of the Kanazawa document had read what their Kōchi counterparts adopted in April 1874; possibly they had a copy in hand as they wrote. Unlike the Risshisha writers, however, Chūkokusha writers employed a Sinified parallel prose that gives their prospectus a slightly archaic flavor. This style was probably chosen deliberately, not only because it allowed the drafters to exhibit their skill at what Fowler calls "elegant variation," but also because it was well suited to the explication of an unfamiliar political philosophy. The parallel phrases often clarify one another. The style, reminiscent of philosophical writing of an earlier age, probably speeded the domestication of new ideas inspired by the West among men whose education had contained strong doses of the Confucian classics.

The first section of the Kanazawa document contains an explicit repudiation of the notion that there are or should be class distinctions in the state:

"We are all alike; we are the people of Imperial Japan. Without distinction as to noble or base, revered or despised, we equally possess certain rights."[25] This statement seems to deny any claim to special status by members of the new political society, regardless of their samurai background.

Other statements in the prospectus might be interpreted as contradicting the profession of equality. One phrase might be understood as either "Fortunately like-minded friends such as you hitherto were samurai," or "Fortunately like-minded friends such as you have long been literate men," and the ambiguity of the wording might betray ambivalence in the thinking of the Chūkokusha organizers. It may be that members of this Kanazawa society held an exclusive attitude toward non-samurai, such as Professor Tōyama Shigeki detected among the Risshisha men of Kōchi.[26] Still, they did profess belief in equality, and in their critique of prevailing conditions, it was political cleavages, not social ones, that were their chief object of derision: "There are some whose irresponsible words and actions do harm to the nation. There are still some who do not do their duty as citizens. There are still some who do not exercise their rights as citizens. There are some who fail to observe the proper order of executing laws. There are destitute people who have not yet achieved their due. How deplorable this is."[27]

A striking feature of the Chūkokusha document is its total concentration on national needs and national identification. Local benefits, local needs, local growth, local political autonomy are not mentioned. The first section does contain the assertion that members of the new society, as sons of Kanazawa *han*, have warm natures (*jōgi moto yori atsushi*), and thus "especially desire to endeavor together and endure together to accomplish [their] duties as citizens of the nation." The Kōchi group had made the same claim in almost precisely the same words. Apart from this appeal to local consciousness, the prospectus is devoid of references that might place it. The principles it sets forth could apply to any part of Japan, or indeed to nearly any state of the nineteenth century; even the names Ishikawa and Kanazawa do not recur.

The society's four main tenets were advanced in the middle four sections of the foundation document:

1. Revere the imperial line, and repay your debt to the nation.
2. Make your intentions proper, and make your actions pure.

3. Make your faith [in the nation] sincere, and value your honor.

4. Exercise your rights, and accomplish your duties.

The first and third of these deal with responsibilities and duties of good Japanese subjects. The explanation following the first statement strongly associates the imperial institution with the national and racial identity of Japanese. The gloss begins with the litany of the unbroken line: "First of all, our imperial family has no peer among all the nations of all the ages in its long continuity, one family through 123 generations [sic] and 2534 years." It goes on to aver that the flesh and blood of all Japanese subjects are bathed in the same stream, and that truly within Japan the subjects are all of one family and all men are brothers. The section elaborating the first principle concludes, "We must revere and preserve the fundamental character of the nation, and diligently repay our debt to the nation." The comment on the third principle cautions that the nation will decline if faith and honor are taken lightly and not cultivated.

The second and fourth principles of the Chūkokusha have to do with rights and duties and their definitions. The gloss on the second claims that "now the citizens at large know that they have rights to liberty and independence" *(fuki jishu no kenri),* but sees a special leadership role for Chūkokusha members in demonstrating to the people how to realize these rights. The comment on the fourth precept of the society is nearly twice as long as any of the others:

We citizens of Japan are all equal, and all have certain rights and duties. Having independence, we cultivate life, and making business prosper, we increase welfare. This is our proper part as citizens, and it cannot be taken away by authority or overpowered by wealth or rank. Those who would cultivate these rights and duties depend on the protection of the government, but if the government goes beyond its proper realm of authority and becomes despotic and capricious, rights will be extinguished and the balance between rights and duties will be lost. The sphere of energy of the nation will be diminished. When the nation has vigor, then the state will be wealthy and powerful, and the well-being of the people will increase. This vigor can only be successfully achieved when the energy of each one of the people is collected and combined together. Therefore, if the energy of one citizen is lost, the nation suffers by losing that much energy. If the energy of ten million is lost, how can wealth and power be maintained and how can the well-being of the people be achieved? Thus each of us bears responsibility in this nation. At present, however, there are some people who have a plethora of duties and a dearth of rights. The peasants, for instance, are in this condition. There are others who do not fulfill their duties yet have some rights. Samurai and merchants are examples. As we all are equally brothers in the same family, is it not of great concern that those who have thus lost the balance between rights and duties thereby harm the vigor of the entire people? We in the Chūkokusha desire, by means of what we have, compensating for our weaknesses, to do our duty and to maintain our rights, and to fulfill our individual responsibilities and to promote the vigor of the nation. That is, again, to do our proper part as citizens.

This passage has a stirring hortatory quality, yet for all the talk of Japanese citizens' rights and duties, those key notions are left undefined. The expression of worry that the government might exceed its proper powers is not matched by a proposal of a method for countering despotism. The observations that certain people, who are identified in traditional class terms, suffer from an imbalance of rights and obligations, likewise are not accompanied by any concrete suggestion of how to rectify the situation.

On the subject of recourse against capricious authorities and unbalanced institutional arrangements, the vagueness of the Chūkokusha prospectus contrasts with the proposal for a national assembly *(tenka no minkai)* that is repeated three times in the Risshisha's foundation statement. In both the Kōchi and the Kanazawa documents, concepts such as freedom and independence are used without being defined, but the Risshisha's espousal of the idea of a national assembly implies a more fully developed conception of the role of citizens in government, and of the respective dimensions of government authority and citizens' rights, than the Chūkokusha's iteration of the need for cooperation in fulfilling responsibilities.

Judging by its foundation document, the first political society in Ishikawa Prefecture appears to have been nationalistic, yet suspicious of the national government that threatened to gain too much power over the citizens; assertive of citizen's rights, yet unready or unwilling to advocate a popular assembly; and cognizant of the power of ideas of freedom and independence and of rights and duties, yet vague as to the exact meaning of these concepts. Framers of the prospectus focussed on the affairs of the nation and overlooked any connection that might have been found between the "right to independence" *(jishu no kenri)* and the form of local government. Indeed, if Chūkokusha members had seen any link between this "right to independence" and the idea of local autonomy, they might have made a conscious decision not to express it. While acutely aware of their local heritage and hopeful of vindicating the honor of their home region, they wished above all else to prove themselves as responsible participants in national affairs. They may have feared that the mere mention of local power would cast doubt on their sincerity in identifying the imperial line and the nation as their first concerns.

One more contrast with the prospectus of the Risshisha is worth mention. Itagaki and his Kōchi associates were so wrapped up in the study of Western models that they inserted four references to Europe and America in their foundation paper, and they offered some explicit comparisons of the West and Japan. One of these notes that "in European languages government officials are called 'public servants' "; this leads into a direct attack on contemporary Japanese officials. The Chūkokusha prospectus contains a favorable comment on Western nations' unity *(gasshū)*, but this is not followed by an attack on Japanese officials, nor is there anything else that might be considered a direct condemnation of the Meiji government. In sum, both the Risshisha and the Chūkokusha were animated by conceptions of freedom and independence that were novel in the Japan of 1874. The Kanazawa political organization, though, was more moderate and less inclined to endorse Western models than the Kōchi group was.

Initially the Chūkokusha seems to have been conceived as a debating society and as an organ for disseminating information about official orders and proclamations, news, and memorials to the government. Although it was provided that after discussion within the society, "loyal expostulations" *(chūkan)* might be addressed to the government,[28] little was said that might have indicated that members of the organization would soon become involved in the movement for "people's rights."

Two branch societies launched simultaneously with the Chūkokusha indicate, by their aims, that Kanazawa political activists were interested in education and the economy, as well as politics. The Meigisha (Hall of Clarifying Moral Principles) was an adult education institute, aimed at lifting the level of learning of people who had no higher than a primary education. Graduates of the Meigisha's program were to be made members of the Chūkokusha. The other branch society, the Kaigyōsha (Society for Establishing

Business), was a mechanism for promoting economic advance. This organization was to be capitalized at ¥75,000, to be raised by selling 3,000 shares to members of the parent society at ¥25 per share. The ambitious aspirations of its members were set down in the Kaigyōsha's Outline of Plans for Enterprise, which itemizes total anticipated expenditures of ¥60,000 in ten categories.[29] The range of manufacturing and marketing ventures in which the Kaigyōsha planned to invest is impressive: tea, silk and cotton weaving, bronze and nickel wares, herring and salmon farming, fish nets, *tatami* mats, nails, glazes, pottery, glass dishes, lamps, bottles, processed salts, Hokkaidō development, and publishing. Permission was to be sought to build a Western-style sailing ship at Nanao, at a cost of ¥20,000 for use in shipping products turned out by the enterprises of the society.

This Society for Establishing Business never got off the ground. In the most comprehensive history of the Kanazawa business community since the time of the Meiji Restoration, this branch of the Chūkokusha rates nary a single mention.[30] Political as well as economic reasons may have predetermined the unhappy fate of the Kaigyōsha, for its parent society experienced both internal dissension and external disapproval from its early days.[31] Whatever the cause of the Kaigyōsha's lack of success, the failure had both economic and political significance for Ishikawa Prefecture. Several of the proposed businesses of the society were to have been operated within the prefecture; all were to have been run to benefit men from Ishikawa. Chūkokusha members eschewed thinking of local autonomy as a political objective, but they did mean to promote the economic development of the prefecture, through the activities of the Kaigyōsha. In effect they were localizing the "rich nation" part of the popular Meiji slogan "rich nation, strong military" (*fukoku kyōhei*), just as some of them had tried two-and-a-half years earlier to localize the "strong military" phrase when they asked for approval to form a local militia.

When the Kaigyōsha failed, the advancement of the local economy was left up to individual and smaller corporate enterprises. The pace of development was slower than in some other parts of Japan and slower than it might have been if there had been a strong and purposeful local organization to spur it forward. The failure of the Kaigyōsha had an indirect political effect as well. Success would have given the Chūkokusha a strong economic base for its political activities, a lever to use against the central government, which Chūkokusha members saw as threatening to go beyond its proper limits.

Shortly after its inaugural meeting, the Chūkokusha sent two men to Osaka to take part in a conference. Itagaki Taisuke had taken the initiative in calling this February 1875 meeting of men from political societies from all over Japan. Kuga Yoshinao and Shimada Ichirō were the delegates from Kanazawa, and finding themselves in agreement with the principles adopted by this convention, they made the Chūkokusha a member of the new national organization that was formed there, the Aikokusha (Society of Patriots).[32]

The Aikokusha put love of country and loyalty to the emperor above all else, but enunciated also the belief that "the right to liberty [should] be extended" and that the societies belonging to the Aikokusha must "labor for the good of all the people."[33] Heavy stress was laid on communication among the participating societies. Exchange of information on the state of the nation and on political questions was to be regularized through conventions to be held in Tokyo every February and August, and through several meetings per month of delegates from the constituent societies.

Back in Kanazawa, the reports of Kuga and Shimada evoked enthusiastic response. When the Aikokusha held the first of its projected meetings in Tokyo, no fewer than seven men from the Chūkokusha presented themselves. Article II of the Aikokusha constitution had provided only that "two or three members from each society of each prefecture" should assemble for discussions.[34]

The Aikokusha was not a very robust body, in spite of the high emotional energy of some of its members. In March, Itagaki accepted an invitation to rejoin the government, and his national political society began to wither.[35] The Aikokusha had already made an impact on political life in Ishikawa Prefecture, however, by greatly stimulating thought about rights and duties and about the question of popular assemblies. Chūkokusha members had come into contact with other "liberals" and had assimilated principles that would soon set them in conflict with the authorities who had been sent by Tokyo to govern their prefecture. Association with the Aikokusha had not resulted in the emergence of any great national leaders or thinkers from Ishikawa, but it had raised the level of consciousness there and transmitted new ideas about political philosophy, political organization, and the urgent issues of the day.

CONFLICT WITH HIGH PREFECTURAL AUTHORITY AND AMONG ISHIKAWA MEN

A change in the occupant of the governor's chair hurt the Chūkokusha. Governor Uchida had been favorably disposed toward the society; after all, many of its members had cooperated very nicely with him. When Uchida retired in March 1875, Kiriyama Junkō was promoted from councilor *(sanji)* to provisional governor *(gon rei)*. This rise from the ranks of the prefectural bureaucracy, never repeated in prewar Ishikawa history, meant that the new chief administrator was already well known in Kanazawa. Kiriyama had a reputation as a capable but colorless administrator and also as an opponent of Sugimura Hiromasa, with whom he had clashed before Sugimura left office. Elevated to provisional councilor to be Kiriyama's top assistant was Kumano Kurō, a native of Chōshū who remembered that the pro-Satsuma party in Kanazawa had hounded pro-Chōshū men out of the Ishikawa prefectural bureaucracy a few years earlier. Together the two new highest officials constituted a formidable force hostile to the Chūkokusha. Within a short time, several members of the political society had resigned or been removed from prefectural official duties.[36] Soon their organization itself was in eclipse.

Just as destructive of the Chūkokusha as pressure from Kiriyama and Kumano were internal conflicts that came to a peak in June 1875. The issue was local popular assemblies *(chihō minkai)*. The struggle shows that there was at least some interest in the question of the form of local government in Ishikawa, and that there were men who wanted to increase the say of local citizens in determining policy. But lack of unity among the local political activists undermined these positions and contributed to the demise of the Chūkokusha. The battle over assemblies was fought on two fronts, one between Chūkokusha members and high prefectural administrators, and the other between the Chūkokusha mainstream and factions that had split from it. In the end no popular assembly was held by Ishikawa Prefecture, and one historian has labelled the affair the Dannoura—that is, the Waterloo—of the Chūkokusha.[37]

In May 1875, the Council of State issued to the prefecture a notice informing the highest officers that a Prefectural Governors Conference would open in Tokyo on June 20, 1875. This meeting had first been called a year earlier, then postponed.[38] Some central government leaders thought of the Prefectural Governors Conference as the prototype of a lower house of a national assembly, while they regarded the recently created Genrōin as a proto-upper house.[39]

The same day as the announcement of the Prefectural Governors Conference, another notice set the principal items on the agenda for that meeting: roads, dikes, and bridges, and local tax expenditure; local police; local popular assemblies; and methods of poor relief.[40] Two weeks later, another topic, methods of building and maintaining schools, was added.[41] Before going to Tokyo, governors were to have assemblies called in each of the districts *(ku)* in their jurisdictions, so that popular opinion *(minron)* on these matters might be aired. After the district assemblies had been held, there were to be prefectural assemblies *(kenkai)* to discuss the issues and opinions. At the Prefectural Governors Conference, governors would present the views that emerged from the local assemblies, as well as their own opinions.[42]

In Ishikawa, the question of popular assemblies, particularly a prefectural assembly, generated a heated debate. Governor Kiriyama and Provisional Councilor Kumano planned to convene, for five days beginning June 1, a prefectural assembly composed of district chiefs, middle school district directors, and prefectural officials who would be designated by the governor.[43] Many district chiefs, happening to be members of the Chūkokusha, found this plan unpalatable. Kiriyama and Kumano had already made clear their dislike of the political society, and these district chiefs anticipated that the deck would be stacked against them in a prefectural assembly composed partly of the governor's appointees. The Chūkokusha men doubted that their opinions would have a chance to prevail.

All forty-three district chiefs of Ishikawa Prefecture convened their own three-day meeting in Kanazawa, beginning May 19. In a hurry to form their own united front against Kiriyama and Kumano, the chiefs ignored the instruction that they hold district assemblies. They reached a consensus

on each of the four areas that had been listed in the Council of State Notification of May 5, and they submitted a report on their decisions to Kumano.[44] The governor had already gone to Tokyo on business and was not
scheduled to return until after the conference. The district chiefs claimed in
their report that their discussions had the effect of making opinion in the
prefecture unanimous, and that they represented the views of all the people
of the prefecture.[45] They were untroubled by the thought that they had
forgone a chance to back up their claims by actually holding district assemblies and listening to the people of their jurisdictions. Nor did they see a
need for Ishikawa to call the proposed prefectural assembly, once they had
set down their opinions in their report to Kumano. It did not occur to the
district chiefs to mount an articulate attack turning on the question of the
composition of the assembly. They might have bargained, promising to
cooperate if the prefectural assembly were made more truly representative.
They did not. It may be that they were so absorbed in the adversarial
relationship with Kiriyama and Kumano that they overlooked ways they
could obtain local representative institutions. It may be also that they simply did not understand representative government as a constitutional principle worth fighting for.

In response to the district chiefs' report, Kumano declared that since
assemblies had not been held in the districts, as required by the Council of
State before the prefectural assembly could open, the opinions and proposals
of the district chiefs could not be considered. When the district chiefs stuck
obstinately to their position and still did not call assemblies in their separate districts, Kumano put off the opening of a prefectural assembly indefi-
nitely. He announced that the report of the district chiefs did not represent
public opinion *(yoron)* and that it was not the sort of thing Kiriyama could
use at the Prefectural Governors Conference.[46]

The district chiefs decided at this juncture to submit their views directly
to the central government. A delegation led by Nakamura Shunjirō went to
Tokyo and managed, after persuading Sanjō Saneomi to intercede in their
behalf, to get the Genrōin to accept a petition outlining the district chiefs'
position in the conflict with Kumano.[47] Perhaps to establish at the outset
that they were no revolutionary malcontents, these Chūkokusha petitioners
endorsed the developments that had taken place in the Japanese polity over
the last several years. In their submission, they singled out the abolition of

han and creation of prefectures as one of the most notable of these developments, and they evinced a positive attitude toward further change:

> For more than 2,500 years since the founding of our nation, we were accustomed to a despotic form of government. . . . Since the Restoration, however, the debates of the central government have determined future national policies after broadly considering circumstances throughout the world. To make Japan powerful and rich and able to stand up to foreign nations, traditional government practices that are inappropriate to the conditions of the present day have been reformed. Among the greatest reforms was the abolition of the domains and the creation of prefectures. But now we have come to the great revolutionary change of [establishing] constitutional government. We submit that, in these times of change, to achieve good results in administration, the welfare of the common people is more important than any other matter.

Nakamura and his fellow petitioners explained how they had convened a meeting of district chiefs and reached unanimity, and went on to claim that their opinions were those of some 700,000 people of Ishikawa Prefecture. Then they described the district chiefs' own conception of their official duties:

> In keeping with the enlightened decrees of the sage emperor, we will energetically assist with the myriad sectors of national policy, and with raising the standard of the people. If we wish to uphold the intentions of the emperor, and to exercise our duties as citizens, what could be of greater benefit to the nation than for us to carry through the orders of the court and transmit the feelings of the people? We must explain the will of the emperor and government to the people, and we must report the feelings of the people to the emperor and government. This is the job which we district officials have been appointed to do.

The Ishikawa chiefs concluded by appealing to the leaders in Tokyo to ratify their views:

> We have recorded the results of popular discussions and present these to the Genrōin separately. We hope that this will be put before the Prefectural Governors Conference.

Without commenting on its contents, the Genrōin agreed to pass the Ishikawa group's petition on to the governors. Upon learning that their submission would be seen by the governors, Nakamura and his companions returned to Kanazawa. They did not wait to see what action the assembled governors might take. They believed that they had justified the district chiefs' noncooperation with the prefectural assembly plans of Kiriyama and Kumano and that they had won their battle against higher officialdom. They were mistaken.

Even before the district chiefs had presented their petition to the Genröin, events transpired at home to undermine their cause. Within the prefecture, a second type of opposition to the district chiefs appeared, lending strength to Kumano's position. This new opposition coalesced around Shimada Ichirō and some other men who had only recently been involved in Chūkokusha activities alongside Nakamura and his group. Shimada and 220 others, including many assistant district chiefs *(fuku kuchō)*, other low-level local officials, and some influential citizens, signed a statement that charged the district chiefs with having improperly appropriated for themselves the role of representatives of the people.[48] In the view of the 221 signatories of this statement, the district chiefs had not only contravened prefectural directives issued by the governor and his deputy, by causing the cancellation of the prefectural assembly, they had also gone contrary to the people's interests. The district chiefs' obstruction of prefectural orders, they wrote, "of course must not be permitted by the government, but further it is not what the people want."[49] The new group presented their document to Kumano on June 6.

Such a negative assessment of the obstreperous Chūkokusha-affiliated district chiefs was most welcome to Provisional Councilor Kumano. No doubt he realized that should any blame be assigned for the failure of Ishikawa Prefecture to hold a prefectural assembly, this petition of the assistant district chiefs and their allies supported his own position. On the basis of this document, he drew up a new report that cast the district chiefs as the villains, and sent it to Kiriyama. Kumano's new report arrived in Tokyo after the Nakamura group's petition had reached the Prefectural Governors Conference. Kiriyama was surprised and annoyed to learn that, contrary to the assertions of the district chiefs, considerable difference of opinion existed within his jurisdiction.

Only nine days after submitting their statement to Kumano, Shimada Ichirō, the educator and former prefectural official Katō Kō, and several other signers of the critique of the district chiefs communicated directly with the men whom they had criticized. They deplored the fact that there was a wide gap between the district chiefs and the assistant district chiefs and that the document submitted by the district chiefs to the Genrōin was not based on actual expressions of the people's desires. They called the positions taken by the district chiefs "arbitrary decisions on top of arbitrary decisions." They declared that holding a prefectural assembly was "a great event for which the people must be consulted," and that it was extremely regrettable that things had reached the point of the assembly's being called off. These critics of the district chiefs stated their own willingness to work within the system and to cooperate with government orders: "we do not wish to go against the government notice summoning the prefectural governors." [50]

At the Prefectural Governors Conference, no notice was taken of this conflict in Ishikawa. Though the issue of popular assemblies in general was debated at length, neither the Nakamura group's petition nor Kumano's second report seems to have come up. For his part, Kiriyama determined to investigate the contending parties when he returned to his jurisdiction. Back in Kanazawa, the prefectural assembly was postponed—as it turned out, for the duration of Kiriyama's nearly four years in office. Failure to hold a prefectural assembly before the Prefectural Governors Conference was not unique to Ishikawa; in fact, Kido Takayoshi observed at the conference that seven prefectures had established prefectural assemblies, and one urban and twenty-two rural prefectures had held assemblies of district chiefs, while two urban and seventeen rural prefectures had not held such assemblies. [51] This left a sizable number of prefectures with no assemblies at all, and only a few with prefectural assemblies. Still, Ishikawa Prefecture stands out as a case where an assembly was planned, then called off because of a disagreement between the authorities and members of a political society.

The conference of governors concluded on July 17, 1875. Kiriyama Junkō, on his return to Kanazawa later that month, decided to begin reasserting his gubernatorial authority by publishing his views of popular rights. In his "Comment on the Distinction between the Spirit and External Forms in Discussing People's Rights," he attacked proponents of "liberty and people's rights" for failing to understand what constitutional government really was. [52] He began by accusing the advocates of people's rights of deliberately misinterpreting the emperor's intention, stated in the rescript

of April 14, 1875, gradually to establish a constitutional form of government.[53] Since the Restoration, the governor remarked, Japan had modeled
many institutions and practices after America and Europe and had opened
up the road to the protection of people's rights, discarding in the process
old practices of oppression and servility. In 1874 and 1875, the emperor
had made clear his will to hold assemblies so that the people might be
educated in civic responsibility step by step. Constitutional government
could not be instituted in one fell swoop, Kiriyama believed; it must be
achieved incrementally. In the meantime, it was the people's duty toward
the government to recognize their own nature and capabilities, and to observe the laws of the nation.

The right to make the constitution is held jointly by the ruler and the
subjects, Kiriyama declared. Since it is impossible for the ruler to hear the
views of all the people, representatives are selected and made to form deliberative bodies, which are invested with the right to make laws. On behalf
of the people, the ruler and these deliberative bodies establish the constitution and decide on policies of state. Kiriyama contended that there was a
proper sequence that should be followed in the establishment of assemblies
of the people's representatives. The government, he believed, had recognized this and had made popular assemblies one of the main topics of the
recently concluded conference of governors. The governors had agreed that
district and prefectural assemblies should be started, with district chiefs
(*kuchō*) and small district chiefs (*kochō*) as their members. Small district
assemblies might be the best mechanism for dealing with local problems.
It was necessary, however, that there be basic uniformity in the selection
and procedures of such deliberative bodies all over the nation. The plan to
take district chiefs and small district chiefs and make them the members of
local assemblies had been submitted to the Genrōin, the Ishikawa governor
noted, but before it could be considered final it had to be approved by the
emperor. Until regulations regarding their operation were promulgated, the
opening of small district assemblies should be put off. Only when assemblies had been established from the small-district level through the national
level, and only when those assemblies demonstrated their responsibility,
would it be possible to say that Japan had changed to a constitutional form
of government.

Kiriyama insisted that to demand to participate in national affairs without passing through the proper sequence of institutional development, and to oppose the government and its orders, would be to misapprehend the imperial rescript of April 14, 1875. The people have the right to participate in affairs through representatives who are delegated to debate issues in assemblies, he acknowledged, but to go beyond that is not the concern of the people. He was willing to recognize the principle underlying the various levels of local assemblies—he acknowledged the right of the people to participate in the governance of the nation. But Kiriyama worried that this might lead to a tyranny of the people *(minjin senken)*, and he tried to distinguish between popular participation, of which he approved, and popular sovereignty, of which he did not.

Contemporary views on people's rights fell into two categories, as he saw it. One type of thinking appreciated the spirit of people's rights; the other, only the external forms. Those who understand the spirit perceive the most pressing needs as exercising their natural freedom and independence in the proper sequence in the development of Japanese political institutions, performing their duties as citizens, and achieving a climate of independence. In contrast, those who appreciate only external forms pay no heed to the proper developmental sequence or to proper conduct, but incite the ignorant with glib talk, tend to confuse people's rights with the tyranny of the people, and fail to do their duty to the state. Out of this dichotomy of views arises a split between civilization and barbarity, and this leads inevitably to a contravention of the emperor's will. Proponents of "people's rights" misconstrue this important point, Kiriyama believed, but he was hopeful that a genuinely constitutional form of government might be achieved in Japan in the future, if the self-styled "people's rights" advocates would correct their misunderstanding and comprehend the true spirit of people's rights. This, he concluded, was what the emperor had desired when he ordered the gradual construction of a constitutional form of government.

In articulating these gradualist sentiments on constitutional development, Kiriyama aligned himself with Kido Takayoshi and Ōkubo Toshimichi.[54] He was arguing as much against people's rights advocates outside Ishikawa Prefecture as he was against members of the Chūkokusha. Yet that he addressed the issues in the manner he did probably reflects his awareness that Kanazawa men were connected to a nationwide movement for popular rights. It is possible that some Chūkokusha members used radical rhetoric in demanding assemblies and a constitution immediately; even if they did not, it is understandable that Kiriyama might have associated the opinions of the Kanazawa political society with radical views being expressed elsewhere in Japan.

The Ishikawa governor was not at all opposed to a constitution, so long as the people, when they exercised their rights through their representatives, kept in line with the emperor's intentions.[55] He took it as axiomatic that good government could only be achieved when the emperor's will was followed. Popular sovereignty and democracy—"the tyranny of the people"—were neither necessary elements of constitutionalism nor consistent with his notion of the emperor's will.

Stressing the primacy of the emperor's will, Kiriyama made an enormous qualification of "rights" and left the door open to absolute rule by the hereditary monarch or his chosen agents, with popular participation amounting to little more than window dressing. On the other hand, he was, like Kido and Ōkubo, advocating the establishment of a constitutional system. He was hardly an old-fashioned conservative who would exclude the people from any role in government. His anxiety about the danger of the "tyranny of the people," while excited by monarchist loyalty, echoed a fear that had been shared even by the Founding Fathers in the United States of America, when they sought to compose a constitution that would provide for balanced government and ensure against the excesses of democracy, that is, against the tyranny of the majority.[56] Gradualist views like Kiriyama's later received the endorsement of Western observers of Japan. Not only the German legal scholars like Gneist and his students Roesler and Mosse approved of Japan's gradual approach to constitutionalism, but Ulysses S. Grant and Herbert Spencer also recommended a slow, steady course that would be consistent with past Japanese experience.[57] Seen in context, the second governor of Ishikawa does not appear "absolutist" or hidebound, although he may not have been very progressive.

Having aired his theoretical views and his criticisms of extreme advocates of people's rights, Kiriyama took little time to investigate the conflict that had ended in the scuttling of the Ishikawa prefectural assembly. Quickly deciding who deserved punishment, he fired Nakamura Shunjirō from the office of district chief on August 4.

Anticipating this move, the other district chiefs had already appealed to the Osaka Higher Court for a judgment upholding Nakamura's good name. They believed that the governor had slandered their leader. While the case was pending, the district chiefs pressed Tokyo to change the system that allowed higher officials to decide on the promotions, demotions, or dismissals of lower officials without being required to make clear the reasons for these moves. Resentment of what was perceived to be arbitrary administration reached a peak on August 30, 1875. The rest of the Ishikawa district chiefs resigned en masse that day. To Home Minister Ōkubo they submitted a memorial expressing regrets about having served in the system as it was then constituted and proposing major changes:[58]

> Councilor Kumano looks into dismissals and transfers in the General Affairs Section [of the Prefectural Office] and says in his instructions, "The promotion and demotion of officials of *hanninkan* rank and lower is within the power of the governor. He is not required to explain [his actions]." Yet, although district officials do have the duties of regular members of the government bureaucracy *(juntō)*, since in fact their salaries are paid with district monies *(kuhi)*, they are not like other government officials. At times district officials receive requests from the people and act as their representatives, but this cannot be said to be beyond their powers *(kenri gai)*. Presently in this prefecture [officials are] promoted, demoted, placed in office, or dismissed according to the wishes of higher officials *(kanson tokushi)*. If one has objections and asks for an explanation, higher officials claim raison d'etat *(kōken)* and do not include [any other reasons]. This must be recognized as oppression. Looking back at our own careers, we were all selected by officials and employed. We were wrong to take posts on those terms. We implore you to examine closely conditions in Ishikawa Prefecture, to consider the failures in its administration, and *until such time as a publicly elected popular assembly* (kōsen minkai) *shall be opened, to order the public election of district officials* (kuri kōsen). If the people of the prefecture are allowed to expand the scope of their discussions, and are enabled better to perform their duties as citizens, what could be more fortunate?

In proposing the election of district officials, these resigning district chiefs came close to taking a stand for local control over local affairs. But they did not pursue the point or even enunciate it very clearly. Their argument was obscured by being put forward in the context of a conflict with Kiriyama and Kumano. Once out of office, the former district heads did not effectively propagandize their cause. There is no record of their case being argued before the public whose interests they claimed to want to advance. Despite their membership in an organization that was part of the early people's rights movement and despite their belated espousal of the principle of popular election of local officials, the Chūkokusha-affiliated district chiefs never managed to give a satisfactory answer to the charge of Katō Kō and his group that they did not consult the people as required by the government directives preparatory to the Prefectural Governors Conference. Seeking a remedy for what they believed were arbitrary actions of high prefectural authorities, they contented themselves with appealing in writing to a still higher authority, Ōkubo, and with withdrawing from service in the prefectural organization that they condemned. They made their case in terms that were too particularistic to be enduringly influential, and then they backed away from a struggle.

The departing officials' petition to the home minister did not detail what popularly elected assemblies should be created or how members of those assemblies should be selected. They made no suggestions regarding the nature and functions, and the legal competence, of local assemblies. The language of their petition contains no hints that they consciously recognized local autonomy—in any measure—as an important issue. There are criticisms of the top authorities in Ishikawa Prefecture in this document, along with a belief in citizens' participation in government. But an unambiguous, explicit demand for an elected assembly with significant powers over local affairs is absent. After Kiriyama's "Comment" blasting those who would have established assemblies quickly without passing deliberately through a series of preparatory stages, the petitioners' requests seem mild. The Ishikawa district chiefs were much less radical than Kiriyama's unnamed targets. The tone of their petition is not demanding. Even though they expressed an earnest desire to have publicly elected popular assemblies, they did not try to organize popular support for such bodies. Their actions provide little that later historians might point to as evidence of grassroots demand for local control.

With the resignation of the district chiefs and the firing of other Chūkokusha members from the prefectural bureaucracy, the political society ceased to be an important factor in local affairs. It did linger on in existence for a few more years, and it continued to be a source of identity for some of its members. Kuga Yoshinao, for instance, in 1877 still considered it personally significant that he was an officer of the Chūkokusha.[59] Further, although Sugimura Hiromasa retired from active political life and went to live in Nanao, people continued to approach him as leader of the Chūkokusha until the late seventies. But the vitality of the society had been snuffed out by late 1875. The Osaka Higher Court dealt one more heavy blow in August that year, when it dismissed the suit brought by the district chiefs on behalf of Nakamura Shunjirō. The issue had in actuality already been decided. Effective dissent was up to others, not members of the Chūkokusha.

DISCONTENTED FORMER SAMURAI—THE KANAZAWA SHISHI

Because there was no antigovernment uprising of ex-samurai in Kaga such as occurred in Saga, Chōshū, and Satsuma, many people suppose that there were no discontented former warriors in the old Maeda domain. This is wrong. A group opposed to central government policy and also dissatisfied with the tactics of the Chūkokusha did emerge in Kanazawa in early 1875. It grew more and more strident in its criticisms of Tokyo leaders, and it also flailed away at Kanazawa luminaries like Sugimura.

The outstanding personality among the Kanazawa malcontents was the hot-blooded ex-soldier Shimada Ichirō. The possessor of a fierce countenance and an awkward hand, Shimada was one of those people who transform the flow of events into a maelstrom merely by setting foot in the stream.[60] He was an extremist and a believer in direct action. Born the eldest son of a low-ranking Kaga samurai (*ashigaru*), Shimada Kanesuke, in 1848, Ichirō had studied gunnery as a youth in the *han* institute for Western military training. He served with the Kanazawa contingent in the war against the Tokugawa diehards in northeastern Japan in 1868, was wounded, and returned to Kanazawa, where he rose in the *han* military to the rank of captain. The dissolution of the domain military units forced a change in his life; he went to Tokyo to study French military science in the well-known Saitō school. In the capital Shimada became a frequent caller on his fellow Kanazawan Kuga Yoshinao. They were joined by others, including Chō Tsurahide, for discussions of Korea, the Saga rebellion, and the expedition to Taiwan. Having sided with Saigō Takamori on the Korean issue, Shimada grew more and more dissatisfied with government policy. He decided that he was too old, at age twenty-six, to continue studying; he should involve himself totally in state affairs.[61] He became convinced of the inefficacy of the memorials that he and his associates were submitting to the government on questions of national policy. By the autumn of 1874, he later stated, "I realized that there was no alternative course but to use force and fell the evil men around the emperor."[62] At the time he did nothing drastic. Instead he went home and took up with the men who would presently form the Chūkokusha.

Like his friend Kuga, Shimada became one of the officers of the Chūkokusha when it organized, and in February 1875, he represented the society at the founding convention of the Aikokusha.[63] In a way his inclusion among the Chūkokusha delegates to Osaka was an anomaly, for he had provoked controversy and acted as a divisive force in Kanazawa political circles from the moment of his return from Tokyo. Just before the Chūkokusha was launched, for instance, he and eleven others impugned the courage of the Kanazawa activists who had petitioned to serve as the front rank of an expeditionary force to Taiwan:

1. More than 2,000 of you appealed to serve as the vanguard of a military expedition to China. Now you have settled into harmony [with government policy]. What has become of your will to volunteer? What are your aims?
2. At this moment there are no more than ten men with a will to give their lives immediately. If there should be an emergency, is this enough? Have you not firm wills? Or is it that you have them, but lacking a plan for preserving them, cannot act to bring them together because there was no virtue *(toku)* in your volunteering as the vanguard?[64]

These same memorialists whom Shimada's group attacked were at that very moment putting together plans for the first Kanazawa political society. Shimada was not content with expressions of willingness to serve if called upon. He wanted action.

Shimada's notion of virtue was not confined solely to questions of the will to act in the public political arena. Personal morality also concerned him. Idealistic, inflexible, and heedless of his own welfare, Shimada in many aspects of his behavior and thought was a typical *shishi,* or "man of high purpose"; his character closely fits the personality-model that Professor Marius Jansen masterfully limned in writing about Sakamoto Ryōma.[65] But unlike the heroes of the Restoration movement who were "roisterer[s] given

to wine and women," Shimada appears to have been a puritanical *shishi*. He may not have practiced austerities—nowhere is he described as abstemious—but he was intolerant of men who did not keep their indulgence in physical pleasures within certain bounds. His strait-laced sensibilities were offended by the behavior of some prefectural officials who happened also to be members of the group that organized the Chūkokusha. Several of these sons of Kaga had begun to affect a self-important style, wearing silvered swords and swaggering about during working hours, and parading their status in the entertainment sections of Kanazawa in the off hours. In another public blast, this time in an open letter, Shimada charged that such men had become accustomed to extravagances and addicted to the pleasure quarters, and had lost their sense of limit on carnal excesses.[66]

Undaunted by, or unconcerned about, any ill-feeling that his attacks on the courage and morality of Chūkokusha members might have provoked, Shimada approached leaders of the society early in 1875, seeking assistance for another attempt to replicate Satsuma in Kanazawa. He wished to establish a private academy like the Shigakkō which Saigō Takamori had set up in 1874 at Shiroyama in Kagoshima. At first Sugimura Hiromasa encouraged Shimada and seemed to promise financial support, but in the end no money was produced. No private academy was built in Kanazawa.[67] Shimada and around four hundred men who shared his ideas and admired his personality thereupon distanced themselves from the Chūkokusha mainstream. Vituperating the leaders of the society, they set up their own headquarters in a small temple in another part of town. They became known after the name of that temple as the Sankōji faction.

Shimada's desire to set up a private academy in Kanazawa is one more example of the continuing magnetic force of Satsuma and Saigō on political men in other parts of Japan. The attraction began, after 1874, to pull some activists in a new direction. Wanting to influence national policy, but blocked from the regular channels of power, men like Shimada came to see their differences with the Meiji government as irreconcilable, and their best hope for correcting the situation in armed rebellion. Others who were drawn to the example of Saigō, such as Sugimura Hiromasa, also grew more implacable in their opposition to government policies, yet did not go so far as to advocate violent direct action against the Tokyo leadership. It was volatile men like Shimada who would threaten the stability and order of the young Meiji state.

THE SATSUMA CONNECTION—TALKS WITH KIRINO TOSHIAKI

Conditions and moods in Satsuma became popular topics among Ishikawa
men again in 1874 and 1875. Sugimura and Kuga had visited Kagoshima
in June 1874, and later that year Nakamura Shunjirō and Ishikawa Kurō
made the journey south. Nakamura and Ishikawa committed the record of
their discussions in Kagoshima to paper, and the document that they produced, which was then circulated in their home town, survives to lend a
more obvious historical significance to their trip than to many of the activities of Kanazawa men of their era.[68] Their record affords insight into both
the thinking of Saigō and the consciousness of Ishikawa activists. As he had
been on earlier occasions, Kirino was the Satsuma connection for the men
from Kanazawa.

Asked for details of the conflict within the Meiji government over Korea,
Kirino discoursed on the long-range objectives and the underlying principles of his positions. Frequently quoting Saigō Takamori, he indicated that
the great man's views were consonant with his own. The ultimate goal was
grandiose: Kirino wanted no less than to build a foundation for a Japanese
incursion into Europe and America.[69] Immediately, the insolence of Korea
provided an excellent opportunity for Japan to assert its military strength
and gain a foothold on the continent, which could quickly be extended to
China and Manchuria.[70] Kirino recounted the plan to send Saigō—and, in
his version, himself—as envoys to Korea, "to offer ourselves to the court of
Japan, to lose our lives in that land, and thereby to stimulate Japan to
adopt a great and wise policy for the future," and he inveighed against
those in power in Tokyo, calling them "children, pleasure-seeking and in-
dolent, who look after themselves but are forgetful of the nation."[71] The
Kagoshima leader counselled his callers from Kanazawa to be sure to pick
the proper time and place to act on their hopes to contribute to the nation:

> When the affairs of the realm keep their proper pace, when the time
> comes, when both nature and man permit, we may exert our strength
> and offer ourselves up with the deepest feelings of loyalty and sincerity,
> and performing the duties which must be done, we will achieve success.
> But if the time does not come and nature and man do not permit and
> the proper pace is lacking, though we act out of patriotism, we will not
> be doing what must be done, . . . and will not achieve success.[72]

Kirino, very concerned about the dangers of bad timing, asked rhetorically, "What use to the nation is it to work and die for nothing?," and commented, "You must realize that the present government is not worth saving. To want to preserve and restore it is to be unable to throw off feelings of love for those little girls [in the government], and this must be labelled 'womanly and childish love,' or 'excessive solicitousness.' " [73]

Pleading his antigovernment case in a very different tone from the advocates of parliamentarism such as Itagaki, Kirino asked the Kanazawa men of spirit to join him and Saigō in a future action. The rebellious nature of what he had in mind could not be mistaken.

> Cease your thoughts of preserving and restoring the government, make the scale of [your ambitions] greater, calmly and deliberately cultivate a heroic spirit. You will see that the government, adding error to error day in and day out, will in the end lose the favor of heaven and invite trouble for itself. When there is no controlling its collapse, that will be the time, that will be the day when nature and man permit, that will be the circumstance in which we must not fail to do our duty as citizens, with the true feelings of Japanese subjects. Then we must brace ourselves, vent [our feelings], and do what is mete. This is what I implore you, and it is Saigō's view as well. Think over the state of things, and if you agree with us, tell your friends. Wait for the day in the future when it is opportune, then join with us. [74]

In his answer to his visitors' last question, Kirino reinforced his criticism of the Tokyo authorities. [75] The words of Nakamura Shunjirō and Ishikawa Kurō are themselves worth quoting, as they reveal unequivocally the sense of shame over past inactivity and the desire to compensate which gnawed at Kanazawa ex-samurai:

> You and Mr. Saigō have worked hard and accomplished many worthwhile things over the years. It is thus well and good for you now to retire to your homes and patiently await the opportunity [to execute your plans]. By contrast, we have been able to accomplish nothing during the period of great changes in the nation from 1868 to the present. Lacking a part to play as subjects or duties as citizens, we are unable to content ourselves with merely being passive all the time. Therefore when we see your desire to overthrow the government, [for us] to look on in silence seems all the more to be to lose the proper order of subjects and citizens. What do you suggest that we should do? [76]

Kirino answered that he recognized the urgency of the feelings of the Kanazawa men, and that these were the sentiments of men of determination. For the time being, nonetheless, there was nothing to do but wait. "If we rush heedlessly to do things and press to build merit, we will most certainly lose in [some] rash action."[77] The present Tokyo leaders would, by their inability to negotiate treaties on equal terms with the Western powers, threaten the national polity *(kokutai),* and when they did the people of the nation would be unable to sit idly by. "When the time comes for the treaties to be revised, the people will rise up and sweep out the little girls at court. Then Japan will face the other nations, exert its national power, and decide the defeat or victory of its opponents." At the psychological moment when the people rose up, Saigō and he would rouse all the people of Kagoshima to act. Kanazawa men should do likewise. Kirino looked forward to the day "when we shall meet amidst soldiers and horses."[78]

This appeal made a deep impression in Kanazawa, especially on Shimada Ichirō and his circle. Chō Tsurahide, already disposed to identify with the opinions and ambitions of the Saigō clique because of their earlier hospitality to him, went again to Kagoshima in 1874, and did not return until October 1876.[79] Kirino's anti-government stance probably seemed more and more attractive to Kanazawa men in the months after Uchida retired and Kiriyama and Kumano took over the top posts in the prefectural government. Nakamura himself did not take Kirino's advice to have nothing to do with the government, at least not so literally as to resign from his official position. He continued to serve as a district chief through much of 1875, as we have seen, until the governor fired him. Possibly contact with the dissatisfied samurai in Satsuma did contribute to Nakamura's sense of resolve in his battle with prefectural authorities in 1875, even though his tactics were different from those urged by Kirino. Ishikawa Kurō later became a propagandist for the raising of troops to join samurai rebellions in Saga and Kagoshima, though he proved less willing than Shimada, Chō, and some others to follow through on such plans.

In March 1875, a formal ceremony was held to commemorate the founding of the Chūkokusha, and Shimada and a hundred of his followers sought admission to the hall, although they had already split with the mainstream of the society. Sugimura and the mainstream leaders tried to keep the Shimada faction out. There followed one of the most dramatic confrontations in the annals of Ishikawa history, a veritable *mie* scene for actors in a kabuki play.[80]

Shimada demanded to know why the society's leaders were barring his group, when their sincere concern for the nation was in no wise inferior to that of the regular Chūkokusha members. Sugimura replied that although Shimada's followers and the regulars had the same aspirations *(kokorozashi)*, there was a difference in the depth (lit., "thickness"—*kōhaku*) of their feelings. Shimada responded wrathfully. By *kōhaku*, did Sugimura mean "red and white" (also pronounced *kōhaku*)? As he spoke, Shimada uncovered the sleeve of his white undergarment with his left hand, and reached into a nearby brazier and grasped a glowing red coal with his right. He glared around the room. Friends and foes alike were stunned into silence by this demoniacal demonstration of physical bravery and indifference to pain.

Somehow, Inagaki Yoshikata, then a young prefectural official and a member of the Chūkokusha, succeeded in guiding Shimada out of the meeting hall and pacifying him.[81] Apparently unhurt by the hot charcoal, Shimada agreed to lead his group out of the hall, and to let Inagaki, who was himself in disagreement with the tactics and leadership of Sugimura Hiromasa and Hasegawa Jun'ya, mediate between Shimada's radical wing and the moderate mainstream. They would seek agreement on common stands and a common course of action.

Inagaki's mediation failed. The Sugimura-Hasegawa majority, calling Shimada an "advocate of violence" *(wanryoku ronsha)*, refused to enter into negotiations with him. Even the patient Inagaki, after cultivating friendly relations with Shimada for a short time, fell out with him, and the two exchanged epithets. The Sankōji faction went into political quarantine.[82]

Shimada's virulence helped lay the Chūkokusha low in June 1875, although other forces were also at work. Shimada played a prominent role in the conflict over local assemblies which led to the departure from office of many of the political society's members, as we have noted. Nevertheless, despite his experiences of opposition to the Chūkokusha and against all reason, Shimada clung to the hope that he might win the society's 2,000-odd members over to his views.

The passionate ex-soldier's best-remembered attempt to raise support among the moderates took the form of an open letter, dated August 8,

1875, addressed to members of the Chūkokusha. Characteristically not troubling to couch his message in politic language, he restated his belief that Japan was in great danger and needed true men of determination who were ready to give up their lives for the nation. Of this type, he remarked, he found fewer than a hundred in the Chūkokusha. Those men, though few in numbers, might become the core of a group that would join with the four hundred members of his Sankōji faction "to serve in a national crisis" (*kokka kankyū no jū ni ōzu beshi*). What was lacking in the spirit of the Chūkokusha members was moral force (*toku*), he wrote, and this lack of *toku* could be attributed to the infrequency of meetings of the society, to the fact that the society did not respond to popular feelings, and to the failure to achieve internal accord among the more than two thousand members, despite their nominal unity. Putting out of mind the disastrous history of his relations with the Chūkokusha, Shimada now appealed for unity: "Until we accomplish something truly meritorious, there are no distinctions of leaders and followers. I fervently hope that working together we can construct an excellent program, and that all in the Chūkokusha will gain moral force. Keeping this in mind, not only will we not be inferior to the men of determination of Satsuma and Tosa, we will be preeminent throughout the nation." [83]

His sense of urgency about the situation of the nation was balanced in Shimada's thought by an intense awareness of the prestige traditionally enjoyed by Kaga and by a desire to revivify it. He shared the regret over the lack of recent accomplishments that Nakamura and Ishikawa had lamented to Kirino, and he challenged Chūkokusha members to show some mettle. At the same time he was proud of his Kaga heritage, and tried to exploit it with a reference to the size and character of the old Maeda retainer corps. "Several tens of men of spirit is not enough in a time of emergency. Among the more than 20,000 samurai [of Kaga], there are many with wills of iron and stone." It was mainly, he said, because they did not put enough stress on unity, because they had not reached policies that all members supported, that these strong-willed men had failed.

The Chūkokusha, in the words of one historian, regarded Shimada's proposal as they would have an offer of food from an enemy. [84] No one answered Shimada's invitation to work together.

Rejected in their attempt to gain broad support for their ideas, Shimada and other discontented ex-samurai of Ishikawa Prefecture began to plan other ways to influence the state of the nation. Ironically—for many of Shimada's confrères were policemen, professionally bound to keep the peace[85]—the method they chose was violent. These believers in direct action began to look for an opportune moment, just as Kirino had suggested.

Until 1877, the configuration of circumstances held them in check. Shimada tried to rally fellow malcontents to the cause of rebellion against the government when Maebara Issei revolted in Hagi in October 1876, but only a hundred Kanazawa bravoes were willing to take up arms, and Shimada gave up the thought of trying to join Maebara.[86] It took the great Saigō's uprising in Kagoshima in February 1877 to stir Kanazawa men to serious anti-government plotting. Chō Tsurahide came up with one of the first plans. He proposed to join forces with dissatisfied samurai of the northeastern part of Japan, from Shōnai (around Tsuruoka in Yamagata Prefecture). Shōnai had been the domain of a hereditary daimyo, and out of Tokugawa loyalist sentiment had resisted the new government in the war following the Restoration. Chō had contacts in that area whom he had gotten to know in Kagoshima, and he was confident that Shōnai men, like his own circle of Kaga men, would fight on Saigō's side against the government.[87]

Kaga chauvinism was responsible for aborting Chō's plan. Before trying the idea out on his Shōnai friends, Chō decided to inform Shimada and make certain he had the support he counted on in Kanazawa. Shimada was incensed at the thought of men of powerful Kaga allying themselves with a little, weak area such as Shōnai. Without Shimada's backing, Chō had to seek another means of helping his Kagoshima friends.[88]

Next, Chō, Shimada, Murai Teruaki, Shioya Saburō, Sawada Takanori, Itaga Yoshitoshi, and Kakida Masatsugu made a pact to put together a military force to link up with Saigō. To raise money for the venture, Murai, Shioya, and Sawada concocted a scheme to rob a district office, but they dropped the plan just before it was scheduled to be put into effect.[89]

In March 1877, Shimada and Chō made another attempt to organize rebel troops. They debated strategy with several other dissatisfied Kanazawa men—Mizukoshi Masanori, whose house was the meeting place for the group, Ishikawa Kurō, Sawaguchi Kiichi, and others. Ishikawa, who had contributed a great deal to the atmosphere of hero worship of Saigō by circulating *Tōin sendan,* turned out to be less ardent for the Kagoshima cause than the others. He argued against raising the flag of rebellion. The rest of the group disagreed. As a first step toward aiding Saigō, they dispatched Mizukoshi and Sawaguchi to Kyoto to reconnoiter government activities there. Mizukoshi had been a page to Maeda Toshitsugu, heir of the last daimyo of Kaga, and the plan was for him to pretend to be in Kyoto in order to visit Toshitsugu. The ruse did not work. Mizukoshi and Sawaguchi arrived in the old imperial capital on March 11 and immediately fell under police suspicion. Early the next morning, before they could carry out their mission, constables took them into custody.[90]

Again in April 1877, Shimada and Chō called on Ishikawa Kurō to seek his cooperation in raising troops to fight with Saigō Takamori. According to Ishikawa's reconstruction a year later of his own thought process on this occasion, "I believed Saigō Takamori to be without peer among Japanese subjects. I also thought the error of the government to be immeasurable. Nevertheless, from the outset I argued that to resist the imperial family was to commit treason. This was certainly to go in the wrong direction."[91] The dilemma posed by loyalty to the emperor, on the one hand, and concern over the "wrongs" of the Tokyo government, on the other, was not easily resolved, even for an admirer of Saigō. For many, rebellion seemed to be justified because the government was acting in a way contrary to the "true" interests of the emperor, but Ishikawa Kurō's case shows that not all critics of the government could accept the rebels' reasoning.

The central government briefly tried to take advantage of old feudal loyalty, as well as loyalty to the emperor, to drum up reinforcements for the army in the fight against Saigō, and this experiment further complicated the picture for the discontented samurai of Kanazawa. In June 1875, after early efforts at recruiting for the Imperial Army in Ishikawa Prefecture had yielded disappointing results,[92] Maeda Toshitsugu sent his household steward, Murai Kō, to Kanazawa to help raise troops. Toshitsugu, who had succeeded to the headship of the Maeda family upon Yoshiyasu's death in 1874, felt angry or embarrassed that his family's old retainers had not answered the government's summons. Toshitsugu and his grandfather Nariyasu addressed their former vassals in a letter: "Much of our old domain is in Ishikawa Prefecture, and the masses of samurai differ in many ways from those in other prefectures. However, we do not hear that the masses of samurai have responded to the government call for recruits differently from those in other prefectures. As this is our ancestors' old fief we cannot sit quietly and do nothing. From now on, we urge the stouthearted to serve the wishes of the court, to do their duty as citizens, to set His Majesty's mind at ease, and to ensure that there be no stain on the honor of our ancestors. Nothing could be happier for us." [93]

Responding to their former liege, 1,200 men in Ishikawa turned out to join the government army. So successful was the call from the Maeda that Minister of the Right Iwakura Tomomi became alarmed. If an appeal by the old lord could evoke such an enthusiastic response where the government's own call had not, might there not be a danger of a resurgence of feudal sentiment, and might it not be antinational? Iwakura had Maejima Hisoka, then a Home Ministry official, write to Kumano Kurō in Kanazawa to call off the recruiting effort that used Toshitsugu and Nariyasu's summons.

Although Iwakura and Maejima never knew it, their move had the side-effect of putting an end to another of Shimada Ichirō's plots. [94] Shimada had imagined that he and others who actually sided with the rebels might join the government force, then, on reaching Kyoto while en route to battle Saigō, turn coat to strike at the government. He had tried to get the cooperation of Sugimura Hiromasa and other Chūkokusha figures, but had been coldly rebuffed. [95] Joining Shimada would have been going against the will of the Maeda family as well as against the government in Tokyo. Few were willing to go so far. [96] Some who were approached by Chō and Shimada gave *taigi meibun*, "the highest duty of all," as their reason for refusing. [97]

THE ASSASSINATION OF ŌKUBO TOSHIMICHI

None of the attempts by discontented ex-samurai of Kanazawa to assemble a band of soldiers to join Saigō bore fruit. News reached Kanazawa that government forces had surrounded the Satsuma rebels in Kumamoto in April, but still Shimada could get no more than a few volunteers. Finally he adopted a new tack. As he later explained, "We wished to raise troops and join Saigō, but our strength was insufficient, and we could not. Therefore we decided to kill Councilor of State Ōkubo and others." [98] If the Kanazawa *shishi* could not fight the government in open battle, they would become executioners by stealth, and do away with evil leaders. Having arrived at this strategy, Shimada wanted to go to Kyoto, where the government was quartered during the Satsuma rebellion. Because that city was under martial law, however, his chances of succeeding were extremely slim, and he put off acting.[99] In September 1877, Saigō's forces were defeated, and when the outcome of the conflict could no longer be doubted, the great military leader of the Restoration died by his own sword. The loss of their hero and role-model did not demoralize Shimada's party into giving up their fight. In effect, they just added revenge to their list of motives. To Shimada's group, homicidal direct action seemed not at all futile or quixotic.

Looking back with hindsight, many historians, including those of the Saigō-worshiping ultranationalistic Amur River Society who wrote on these events nearly half a century later, have belittled the meaning of the assassination of Ōkubo. Once the Satsuma rebellion had been quelled, their argument goes, the government was secure. The course of Japanese history would have been drastically altered had the rebellion been successful in 1877, but the murder of a government minister a year later was insignificant.[100]

This argument depends on unverifiable assumptions about the nature of Saigō's rebellion and about what might have happened but did not. Without attempting to refute the argument, we can note a couple of points that it overlooks. First, Ōkubo was the most powerful man in the government, and even though we cannot be sure what difference his continued presence would have made in the months and years after May 14, 1878, it violates common sense to maintain that it would have made no difference at all.[101] Second, the assassination of Ōkubo manifested the dissatisfaction of some former samurai in a part of Japan that by this time, after years of Uchida and Kiriyama's stewardship, was coming to be thought of as a good example of untroubled compliance with the Meiji government. Murder was the distorted extreme expression of hopes that had been continually frustrated, desires to affect national policy and to make an honorable impact on history. As evidence of anti-government feeling in a part of Japan that had been quiet for some years, the successful plot to kill Ōkubo merits our notice.

Kuga Yoshinao was one of the first to be told of the new strategy of assassination. As he later testified, Shimada and Chō had hit upon the idea of killing government leaders well before Saigō's final defeat. Kuga recalled that he had come down to Kanazawa between March and May 1877 and that Shimada and Chō called on him to discuss national affairs on April 20 or 21. Blaming Kido Takayoshi and Ōkubo Toshimichi for the demise of Etō Shinpei and Maebara Issei, and for the almost hopeless plight of Saigō Takamori, Shimada and Chō had already determined to strike Kido and Ōkubo down. They wanted Kuga, who was well known as a prose stylist, to provide them with a felicitously phrased composition that would set out their reasoning and justify their violence. "In the past," they told Kuga, "there have been instances of evil ministers being eliminated, but because the assassins did not inform others of their thinking, what they had in their minds ended up being unclear." They would avoid that mistake. Kuga turned the earnest plotters down, citing his membership in the Chūkokusha and that organization's opposition to violent direct action. Shimada and Chō refused to take no for an answer, but kept pressing, and after a few days and another interview, Kuga agreed to lend his brush to the conspiracy. He was convinced, he told a court in 1878, that Shimada and Chō's intentions were "very different from those of hot-blooded rowdies who lightly resort to violence." Kuga claimed that he made clear to the two that he would have nothing to do with their actions other than writing the paper which they had requested. He drafted the document and gave it to them.[102]

Before Shimada and Chō could bring off their operation, one of their primary targets, Kido, succumbed on May 26, 1877, to an illness that had debilitated him for years. Hindered because during the Satsuma rebellion the state was under martial law, the Kanazawa swordsmen saw Saigō die and the winter pass before their chance to get at Ōkubo came. In November 1877, Chō renewed contact with Kuga, who had gone back to Tokyo, and the following spring Shimada also went to the capital. Acting with unwonted caution, Shimada destroyed the statement of the plotters' aims before leaving Kanazawa, having decided that it would be too risky to carry it on his person as he traveled.[103] In Tokyo, Shimada called on Kuga and asked him to write a new *zankanjō,* or statement detailing reasons for carrying out an assassination. He handed over a draft that he and Chō had prepared, and asked Kuga to elaborate it. Kuga complied, finishing the document in late April 1878.[104]

Unlike a military uprising, an assassination plot needed only a small number of persons to be successful. Shimada and Chō had enrolled Sugimura Hiromasa's younger brother Bun'ichi, Wakida Kōichi, Sugimoto Otogiku, Asai Hisaatsu, and Matsuda Katsuyuki as members of the cabal. All but Asai, whose place of registry was Shimane Prefecture, were from Ishikawa. In Tokyo, these determined men avoided police attention while carefully noting the habits of the home minister. When they assembled on May 7 or 8, they knew that Ōkubo called at the palace every fifth day, on dates ending in four and nine, and that he left his residence at eight in the morning and passed through Kioi-chō in Kōjimachi-ku in Tokyo.[105] They chose May 14 as the date for the powerful minister's death. They would kill him on his way to his regular audience with the emperor.

On May 13, Shimada entrusted two copies of the *zankanjō* to Kimura Chiei, a former Kaga samurai then living in Tokyo, who, though not involved in the plot, was a childhood friend of his.[106] Shimada asked Kimura to deliver the document to the influential newspapers *Chōya Shinbun* and *Kinji Hyōron*.[107] At the end of the copy for the *Kinji Hyōron,* Chō and Shimada appended a note requesting that their statement be forwarded also to the *Nichinichi* and *Yūbin Hōchi* newspapers.[108]

Early the morning of the fourteenth, under a threatening sky, Shimada, Chō, Wakida, Sugimoto, Sugimura, and Asai hid themselves in the tall grasses alongside the wall of the mansion on Kioizaka occupied by the nobleman Mibu Motonaga. For some time, it was quiet. There was no traffic on the road next to the mansion, which lay on the route that Ōkubo Toshimichi rode to the palace. Shortly after eight o'clock, the home minister's carriage drew near. The hidden men leaped from behind their cover and hacked at the legs of the horses, bringing the vehicle to a stop. Wakida killed the driver with a thrust to the chest. Ōkubo struggled to get out of the passenger's compartment, but before he could get his feet on the ground, the swords of Shimada and his men found their mark. Ōkubo, says an account that purports to be based on an interview with Shimada when he was in jail afterwards, looked Shimada in the eyes with a terrible, fearsome expression, then without uttering a word took seven or eight steps and fell dead.[109]

Dropping their weapons at the scene of their crime, the assassins went to turn themselves in. Their surrender was premeditated. They marched to the main gate of the Imperial Household Ministry and proudly announced to the guards what they had just done. They handed over a copy of their *zankanjō.*[110] They themselves would offer no more armed resistance to the Meiji government. They were confident that others would be inspired by their brave and honorable example and that pure and good men of the land would rise up and force the government to change its wayward nature. This expectation, revealing of the assassins' mentality and their personality type, proved to be false. They could have had no doubt that by surrendering to the authorities they were accepting death sentences. But they depended on the impact of one act of unsullied will, and their explanation of the reasons for it, to cause a sea change in national politics. As to the details of what might happen after their violent deed of May 14, 1878, they seem to have devoted very little thought. Their meticulous planning went only as far as the publication of their *zankanjō.*

THE ZANKANJŌ

The plan of these men of determination went awry in a critical way when their carefully drafted statement of justification went unpublished. Kimura had mailed the two copies that had been left in his hands to the newspapers, but the editors had lacked the temerity to print the document in its entirety. One, the *Chōya Shinbun,* ran an article saying that it had received a copy of the assassins' statement in the mail, and quoted the five major charges. But that paper gave no space to the details of the Shimada group's reasoning, and observing that the murderers' bill of grievances was "not something that can be recorded casually," it immediately turned its copy of the *zankanjō* over to the police.[111] The authorities regarded even the scanty notice given by the *Chōya* as a "disturbance of the peace" (*kokuan no bōgai*), and ordered the paper to halt publication temporarily.[112] The authorities prevented wide distribution of the offensive issue of the *Chōya;* a government order to stop delivery was telegraphed to Osaka, and not a single copy of the *zankanjō* extract was made available in that city.[113] Had their statement of self-vindication been widely read, the assassins' example might have impressed large numbers of discontented ex-samurai in just the way they hoped. In the event, it was suppressed, and did not see the light of day until decades later.

Six men had drawn swords at Kioizaka, and ninety-nine others were implicated in the crime in one way or another.[114] They were the violent fringe among former samurai of Ishikawa Prefecture.[115] They were not the only ex-warriors who were disconnected, however. There were many others around Kanazawa who shared some of the same dissatisfactions, though they had no use for Shimada and Chō and their drastic tactics. The list of criticisms of Ōkubo in the *zankanjō* articulates some of the perceptions and feelings of these other men, as well as the motives of the murderers themselves. The document can be taken as one more expression of the will to influence national politics that had informed most of the public acts of Ishikawa men in the early Meiji period—the most desperate expression, to be sure, but different from other statements less in substance than in detail and in association with a bloody deed. A passionate nationalism and a deep concern for the state of affairs at the national level suffused the *zankanjō*, and it was these feelings that bound together contradictory or ill-matched grievances. The sentiments set down by Kuga were representative of an important mode of political thinking in the 1870s, even if Shimada's group was unrepresentative in its resort to direct action.

The opening line of the assassins' manifesto appealed to all, from the highest to the lowest, in the nation: "We most humbly address His Majesty the Emperor and report to the more than 30,000,000 people in Japan." [116] Upon examination of the current situation, they remarked, they observed that government regulations and laws accorded with neither the will of the emperor nor the public opinion of the Japanese people; "rather they are decisions arrived at by a mere few important officials without full and careful consideration." Government leaders were abusing their offices and thinking only of their own good, the *zankanjō* charged, and continued:

> We enumerate [these officials'] crimes as follows. First, they have hindered the expression of public opinion and have repressed the people's rights, and have made government a private affair. Second, with their arbitrary issue of laws and regulations, with backdoor dealings and public undertakings, they have willfully expanded their own power. Third, promoting construction that is not urgent, they place a priority on useless ornamentation and squander the national wealth. Fourth, they alienate patriotic, loyal men; they are suspicious of patriots as hostile elements; and thereby they give rise to internal disturbances. Fifth, erring in their course in foreign relations, they impair Japan's national prestige. [117]

The conspirators from Kanazawa identified with the late rebels of Satsuma, whom they called "the men of determination and the patriots of the nation (*tenka shishi yūkokusha*)." They saw the rebels' defeat as disastrous:

"While men such as Saigō and Kirino were alive, there were constraints on the evil officials, and they could not go to extremes of corruption. Now, however, because they [Saigō and Kirino] have died, there is nothing to make the evil officials think twice. They do violence as they please."

Ōkubo was by no means the only minister who deserved to be struck down, in the Shimada party's view, although he ranked with Iwakura Tomomi and the late Kido Takayoshi as the worst. But Ōkuma Shigenobu, Itō Hirobumi, Kuroda Kiyotaka, and Kawaji Toshiyoshi "must not be spared," and in addition there were Sanjō Sanetomi and others whom the assassins dismissed contemptuously: "This gang of nonentities (*toshō no yakara*) is not worth counting."[118] In the *zankanjō*, the Ishikawa *shishi* explained how they had decided to eliminate either Kido or Ōkubo, and described Kido's natural death as an instance of "divine retribution" (*myōchū*) for his "monstrous evil" (*taikan*). They stated their belief that "when the nation sees what we have done, [people] will be certain to rise up in sympathy and inherit the spirit which we leave behind," and deliver "Iwakura Tomomi and the rest of the band" to the same fate as Ōkubo's.[119] "With our deaths," said Shimada and his fellow conspirators,

> we serve the nation. We revise the politics of the future. The prosperity of our nation lies in the enlightened understanding of His Majesty the Emperor and in the public opinion of the people of Japan. We desire that the despotism of those in office be replaced according to the imperial rescript of April 1875, based on the Oath of Five Articles sworn at the time of the Meiji Restoration, that a popular assembly be created immediately and public opinion be adopted [in making policy], and thereby, that the vigor of the imperial line, the eternal [prosperity] of the nation, and the peace of the people be attained.[120]

To the Kanazawa malcontents, Saigō's views and popular opinion were identical. In this very important sense, the exaltation of the memory of Saigō and Kirino in the *zankanjō* represented something other than an item in an announcement of a feudal-style vendetta. Shimada's group believed that the government had betrayed the promises of the Oath of Five Articles—particularly the promise to establish assemblies widely and to decide all matters by public discussion.[121] In the minds of men like Shimada, this betrayal was demonstrated equally by the failure to establish a national assembly and by the obstruction of the policies supported by men like Saigō, Etō, and Maebara, who were the greatest patriots and the truest representatives of popular opinion. The government had moved step by step away from the ideals stated in the Oath of 1868, replacing the chamber of *han* representatives with the Shūgiin (House of Representatives), and the Shūgiin in turn with the Sain (Left Chamber), and the Sain in turn with the Genrōin. These bodies were less and less representative, and by 1878, the *zankanjō* maintained, the Genrōin did not even conduct pro forma discussions of the petitions submitted to it by citizens, but merely collected those petitions in silence. Public opinion had been shut out of the decision-making process, and government leaders had taken to defending themselves with the argument that "the standard of civilization of the Japanese is not sufficiently high to have popular assemblies."[122] The "evil officials" who had robbed the people of their rights, not Saigō, Etō, and Maebara, were the real rebels in Japan *(kokuzoku)*.[123]

The Ishikawa party had other sources of discontent. The *zankanjō* instanced laws regulating newspapers (1875), a mining deal involving Inoue Kaoru, and Kuroda Kiyotaka's unpunished drunken murder of his wife to show the irresponsibility of the early Meiji leadership. Less specifically, the statement asserted that bribery and collusion with private interests were nearly universal among government officials.

On economic issues, Shimada's group had little to say. They charged the government with wasting money on nonessentials, but they did not analyze where public money should be spent. One waste, they implied, was the government's copying the external features of Europe and America while failing to appreciate that the internal essence of European and American prosperity was an aggressive, expansive, martial spirit,[124] but the *zankanjō* did not elaborate.

The document of justification prepared by Ōkubo's assassins did not directly treat issues of local government. There was general criticism of the excessive issue and revision of laws, and an attack on some opponents of the Shimada group back at home: "Officials of our prefecture of Ishikawa show off their power and indulge in corruption in the most extreme ways." But there was no explicit discussion of the form of local government or participation in local government, matters that were of great interest to the home minister whom the conspirators thought so evil.

Contrary to their confident expectations when the murderers turned themselves in to the Imperial Guard, their manifesto went unpublished, and masses of brave men did not rise up to finish the job of ridding the government of evil officials. What did happen was a testimony to the rapid institutional development of the Meiji regime. Shimada, Chō, Wakida, Sugimoto, Sugimura, and Asai were immediately handed over to the national police, which began a thorough investigation of the Kioizaka incident, taking oral depositions from the principals, and, as names were mentioned, arresting and collecting evidence on others implicated in the case. On May 17, the Supreme Court (Daishin'in) appointed a special panel of inquiry, headed by Tamano Seiri, who later was to be Japan's Chief Justice.[125]

Shimada and the others got what appears to have been a fair trial. Tamano submitted recommendations for sentences to the Ministry of Justice on July 5. He prefaced these with the opinion of the special tribunal that the six who had carried out the assassination should be treated according to the usual provisions of the law. It was the finding of the court that the accused should not stand trial for the crime of high treason *(kokujihan)*.[126] This decision alone gave the trial of Ōkubo's assassins singular importance in Japanese legal history; the prosecutors had pressed hard, on behalf of the government, for the charge of high treason, and in denying this, the court asserted its independence and proved that it was not an automatic rubber stamp for the judgments of the government.

On July 25, 1878, the Ministry of Justice gave its sanction to the recommendations of the special court. Two days later the judges passed sentence on twenty-eight defendants. The six assassins were condemned to die that same day. They were taken to Ichigaya Prison, and at 11:30, they were beheaded. Four of the remaining defendants were sentenced to life imprisonment, and thirteen to terms ranging from a hundred days to fifteen years. One man was acquitted *(menzai),* and four people were found innocent *(muzai).* All but two of the guilty parties were from Kanazawa. All had been samurai. The court ordered all of them stripped of their status as *shizoku.*[127]

With the trial and punishment of Shimada, Chō, and their co-conspirators, samurai discontent in Ishikawa was crushed. The men who had taken direct action assured themselves of a unique place in the modern history of Ishikawa Prefecture, a position symbolized by their cenotaph at the foot of Nodayama, the huge cemetery outside Kanazawa. A set of six monument stones commemorating the assassins of Ōkubo Toshimichi is enclosed by a low iron-and-stone fence. One gatepost carries the inscription, "erected in 1928." Into the other is chiseled the name of the organization that erected the monument, Meiji Shishi Keisan Kai, "Society to Honor the Men of Determination of Meiji." Fifty years after the Kioizaka incident, the murderers were remembered with respect as Kanazawa's *shishi*.[128]

Apart from their fundamental difference over the role of violence in political opposition, the moderates of the Chūkokusha mainstream and the extremists of Shimada's Sankōji faction shared many positions. Both took national issues as their first concern. They tried again and again to exert some influence on national policy formation. They gave only secondary attention to questions of the form of local government or local policies. Neither contributed to any sustained movement to influence local government. They did not question the basic structure of the national or local government, only personnel and policies. In the abstract, both advocated representative, fair, and effective government. In many ways, the moderates and extremists of Ishikawa were similar, and both contributed to the integration of their home area into the centralized Meiji state.

Almost in spite of themselves, these men had great impact on local affairs, as bureaucrats and as participants in controversies like that over a prefectural assembly. In accepting new structures of central and prefectural government, in staffing prefectural and subprefectural offices, in working with Governor Uchida (and, less harmoniously, with Governor Kiriyama), the political activists of Ishikawa provided significant assistance to those who were working to establish a stable regime in Meiji Japan. In the end, their hopes for national influence were frustrated. But their thinking and their actions inevitably constituted an important legacy. Orientation toward the center was a key element in that bequest. Local pride and the hope to retrieve lost honor, too, were passed on to later activists in the prefecture. Separatism, or a strong, articulated desire for local autonomy, did not number among the basic underpinnings of Ishikawa men's thinking in the early Meiji, and did not become part of their legacy to later times.

FIVE

National Integration Completed:
Ishikawa Prefecture in the Decade of the
Three New Laws

Four days before the execution of Shimada Ichirō and his five accomplices in murder, the government promulgated new regulations on local government. These rules soon came to be called the Three New Laws (sanshinpō). They might be regarded as Ōkubo Toshimichi's posthumous answer to his critics. Ōkubo had been instrumental in drafting them, and he had piloted them through the channels of government decision making in early 1878.[1]

The Three New Laws laid the legal foundation for a system of local government, uniform for all Japan, that endured for a decade. The new system replaced a motley array of prefectural and subprefectural structures and put an end to trial-and-error procedures. In theory, and in some measure in practice, the new arrangements allowed a greater measure of participation by citizens in government than had been permitted in the first Meiji decade. It was this feature that constituted Ōkubo's response to what his detractors called his "dictatorship." The new laws created prefectural assemblies and redefined rural divisions, urban districts, towns, and villages. The assemblies and the reconfigured local entities provided new forums for citizens' expression of political sentiment.

Ever since their promulgation, there has been disagreement about the essential character of the Three New Laws. Nearly a century after the laws took effect, the noted historian Ōkubo Toshiaki, grandson of the redoubtable Meiji statesman, accentuated the positive side of the system. Stressing the opening of government to citizen participation, Ōkubo wrote that the Three New Laws "changed the policy of centralized bureaucratic rule which had prevailed from the early years of Meiji to a policy of locally autonomous administration."[2] Another recent historian, Ōishi Kaichirō, well known as an authority on Meiji local government and as a critic of the central regime's policies, has argued that the Three New Laws were intended primarily as a countermeasure to the growth of peasant unrest and the people's rights movement. Ōishi did not put his case in categorical terms, however; he conceded that these laws "had an epochal meaning as the cornerstone of the system of local autonomy in Japan."[3] Other students have denied that the 1878 system constituted a meaningful step toward local self-rule. Legal historian Yamanaka Einosuke, for example, has maintained, on the basis of his analysis of Ōkubo's original proposal for reforms, that the primary aim was to placate popular resistance to the central government. Surveying local institutions and politics after 1878, Yamanaka concludes that the principal significance of the system lay in the strengthening of centralized bureaucratic control, rather than in the slight expansion of de jure local self-government.[4]

Ōkubo Toshiaki, Ōishi, and Yamanaka all can find evidence on which to build their cases, for the fact is that the Three New Laws had both democratic and authoritarian aspects. Ōkubo Toshimichi's 1878 plan had advocated a difficult-to-achieve exact division of power between prefectural governors and heads of counties and cities (*gunshichō*) on the one hand, and the independent local residents on the other. The system of the Three New Laws attempted to recognize the "dual nature" of local government and to organize responsibility and power so that localities and their officers would function both as organs of central government and as organs of independent local entities.[5] A balance between the two natures was probably impossible to strike. Almost inevitably, when the system was implemented by real people with real interests, conflicts emerged, and the delicate balance of the theory was destroyed.

Ishikawa, the largest and most populous prefecture in Japan when the Three New Laws were promulgated, is not famous as a scene of anti-government political agitation in the late 1870s and 1880s, which were years charged with confrontations of the authorities by activists who made much of local as well as national concerns. Fukushima, Saitama, Kōchi, and a few other prefectures where there were emotional and sometimes bloody clashes stand out in the collective memory of Japanese who give attention to center-periphery relations. Ishikawa does not. Yet Ishikawa provides excellent illustrations of the tensions in the Three New Laws system. In 1882, for instance, a severe struggle broke out between the third governor and the prefectural assembly, and one of the issues was local control over local affairs. In the end in Ishikawa, as elsewhere in Japan, the institutional setup of the Three New Laws permitted central, or centrally appointed, authorities to prevail.

This chapter takes up the institutional changes in the decade of the Three New Laws and shows how Tokyo was strengthened and the advocates of local power were squelched. The assessment presented here leans in the same direction as Ōishi's or Yamanaka's. But those historians have gone on to link their observation that the central regime was strengthened with a larger interpretation that an absolutist phase in Japan's history was unfolding. On this important point, the argument here is different. Apart from the problematic nature of the stage theory of history upon which Yamanaka and Ōishi predicate their work, their notion of Meiji absolutism seems derived from, on the one hand, a reading of the laws that does not adequately account for the ordinary dynamic of push and pull between people and institutions, and on the other, a presumption that all center-strengthening measures in this period, including the institution of new forms of local government, were unilaterally imposed from above (that is, from the center) and did not also involve compliance and voluntary cooperation from below (from the periphery).[6]

Leaving questions of politics, and of coercion versus compliance, for the next chapter, here let us look at the organization and operation of the local system in the second Meiji decade. Both the prefectural and the subprefectural levels are treated in this chapter. The two levels were intertwined in the reasoning of policy makers after Ōkubo, to whom the problem seemed, even more clearly than in the first ten years after the Restoration, a question of how to increase central control while at the same time widening the role to be played by localities and their officers. Systemic changes were calculated to strengthen the central government vis-à-vis the prefectures and the subprefectural units of government. Subnational officials were required to spend more time and energy on delegated business than on local initiatives. Revenue sources that had been available to local entities were tapped by the national government.

So far as once-puissant Kaga was concerned, the Three New Laws period brought about the completion of the process of national integration. By the mid-1880s such opposition to the young Meiji state as there had been in the 1870s and early '80s had either been routed or given way to cooperative attitudes that made centralization easier to achieve. Ishikawa came to function as part of the integrated state mechanism. Those citizens who participated in administration and politics, as bureaucrats and as elected members of assemblies or as town and village chiefs, contributed to the smooth running of the whole Meiji machine.

THE SYSTEM OF THE THREE NEW LAWS

Japan at the beginning of 1878 had no single system of local administration below the prefectural level. Various schemes had been worked out by different prefectures to implement the Law on Household Registration of 1871. Moreover, no devolution of responsibility had been made by the central government, with the result that the Tokyo authorities were held responsible for "even the most trivial blunders of the village head."[7] The need for a comprehensive reform of this non-unitary system was pressing, and it was desirable to introduce uniformity as subprefectural units were reorganized. During the first half of 1878, policy makers devoted much thought and discussion to the question of local government. Ōkubo Toshimichi initiated the debate in a memorial submitted to the throne on March 11, and later the issue of local government organization was mooted in the second Prefectural Governors Conference and in the Genrōin. These deliberations finally bore fruit in three decrees of the Council of State, promulgated on July 22, 1878, which changed the governance of prefectures as well as of governmental entities below the prefectures. Council of State Decree Number 17 was the Law Governing the Organization of Counties, Urban Districts, Towns, and Villages; Number 18 was the Prefectural Assembly Regulations; and Number 19 was the Local Tax Regulations.[8] Another regulation adopted two years later, the Urban Ward, Town, and Village Assembly Law, is commonly regarded by historians as completing the system of the Three New Laws.

Kikegawa Hiroshi has periodized institutional development in the decade of the Three New Laws, discerning three phases. Until 1880, the trend was toward the expansion of the powers of the prefectural assemblies, but then in 1881 and 1882, revisions of the laws limited those powers and provided for stricter supervision of the assemblies. In 1884, national control of the subprefectural organs of government was considerably tightened. The position of town or village chief, which had been elective according to a provision of the first of the Three New Laws, became appointive. And at the prefectural level, assembly actions were limited even further in 1884.[9]

Nearly all actions by the Tokyo government in the decade after 1878 were conditioned by the authorities' desire to economize. Suppressing the Satsuma rebellion of 1877 and commuting the old samurai stipends had forced the state to make extraordinarily large outlays of money and had stimulated runaway inflation. The government seemed incapable of restoring financial order until 1881, when the resolutely severe Matsukata Masayoshi took the reins of economic policy. The operation of the Three New Laws system subsequently was deeply influenced by Matsukata's deflationary measures. Along with his controversial policy of selling off government-operated industries to private entrepreneurs at a fraction of the original investment, Minister of Finance Matsukata practiced retrenchment. One of the techniques by which he achieved a reduction in state spending was the delegation to localities of certain expenses that had previously been borne by the nation.[10]

In effect, the Three New Laws system provided a way to get localities to shoulder more of the administrative and fiscal burdens of the emerging integrated state. To see this process and its effects, let us take up, in the order of their issue, the Three New Laws and the most important modifications of them as they were put into practice.

COUNTIES, URBAN DISTRICTS, TOWNS, AND VILLAGES

COUNTIES AND URBAN DISTRICTS. The first of the new laws of 1878 restored the county, *gun,* as an administrative district. In many parts of the land, as in Ishikawa, the *gun*—or *kōri,* as the same character was usually pronounced at the time—had been a unit of samurai administration during the Tokugawa period, but since the enforcement of the Household Registration Law of 1871, it had become merely a geographic name without governmental function. The real administrative districts from 1872 were the large districts *(daiku)* and small districts *(shōku).*

Ishikawa Prefecture had anticipated the first of the Three New Laws by making the county into an administrative district in 1876, although it continued to use the name *daiku* rather than *gun.* Under the 1878 law, Ishikawa discontinued the use of numbers to identify the biggest subprefectural districts. The First Large District became Enuma County, the Second Large District Nomi County, and so on, reviving old place names. Kanazawa became the only urban district *(ku)* in the prefecture.

The 1878 law provided for the appointment of a head official, or chief, for each county or urban district. The prefectural governor was given power to appoint. The county and district chiefs received the eighth official rank on the table of officers of the Meiji state, and they were paid salaries up to eighty yen per month, depending upon the circumstances of their jurisdiction. An administrative ordinance issued three days after the publication of the Three New Laws specified the primary responsibilities of the county and district chiefs: They were to carry out the laws, orders, and policies of the central government and the prefectural governor, to report on their actions to the governor, and to supervise the chiefs of towns and villages.[11] The job description is short and its terms general, but it required the chiefs to be at least as attentive to their bureaucratic superiors as to the common folk who lived in their counties or districts.

Ishikawa Prefecture implemented the new law on December 9, 1878.[12] Seventeen offices were set up to administer twenty counties—in three cases the authorities decided that a single office was adequate to serve two counties. With the creation of counties and the urban district, branch offices of the prefectural government no longer seemed necessary. On December 20, 1878, Ishikawa Prefecture abolished the branch offices it had established in Toyama and Fukui.[13] The major administrative subdivisions became Kanazawa and eighteen counties, which are charted in Appendix 6.

Governor Kiriyama made his first appointments as county and urban district chiefs on December 17, 1878. Judging by the eight of his choices whose names are known, he selected cautiously.[14] By law, all of the chiefs had to be men from the prefecture; some in the Tokyo government believed that the chiefs should be well regarded landowning men of the particular county or district that they were to serve.[15] Kiriyama, by selecting several ex-samurai from Kanazawa, disregarded the view that the best chiefs would be men with roots in the locality. What Kiriyama evidently valued more was bureaucratic experience. Immediately prior to becoming county or urban district chiefs, four had been chiefs of large administrative districts in Ishikawa; two had been officers of Ishikawa Prefecture; and one had been a home ministry official assigned to Kagoshima Prefecture. For the former district chiefs, Kiriyama's action of 1878 changed their official rank and the name by which they were called, but not their duties. The governor did move these ex-district-chiefs to new jurisdictions. As chief of Kanazawa Urban District, Kiriyama named Ōnogi Katsumasa, previously secretary of Kanazawa large district *(kushoki)*. Born into an upper samurai family of Kaga, Ōnogi had in his youth been a close companion of Maeda Yoshiyasu, and he had become one of the few Kaga men to take part in pro-imperial activities in the years before the Restoration. In 1864, he had incurred the wrath of the conservative leaders of the domain, and they had stripped him of his samurai status and banished him to Noto Island. After the Restoration, Ōnogi's youthful activism was viewed in a different light, and he was pardoned. He became acquainted with Kiriyama in 1872, when they worked together on the project to build a shrine in memory of the founder of the Kaga domain, Maeda Toshiie.[16] Ōnogi and at least four of the six county chiefs whom we can identify had begun their careers as civilian or military officials in Kaga before the abolition of *han* and establishment of prefectures. One, Nakagawa Tadayoshi, Nomi County chief, had been fairly high-ranking, but had resigned his post when Uchida Masakaze arrived in Kanazawa.[17] All five county chiefs for whom we have career records were born into samurai families. At the time they were appointed county or urban district chiefs, these men were not as young as the officials to whom Uchida had entrusted many responsible posts when he had begun constructing the prefectural administration. The average age of Ōnogi and the five county chiefs in 1878 was slightly over forty-five; Uchida's top eighteen appointees from Kaga had averaged thirty-two years old in 1871.[18] Predictably, none of Kiriyama's nominees as county or district head was associated with the Chūkokusha or the Sankōji faction. Kiriyama's successors, it is interesting to note, appear to have found his prejudice against early Meiji activists from the prefecture to be impolitic. Within a few years, prominent members of the Chūkokusha like Katō Kō, Sugimura Hiromasa, Inagaki Yoshikata, and Ōtsuka Shirō all had been appointed county or urban district chiefs as later governors sought to involve respected local leaders in their administrations.

Of course, the new law did not require county chiefs or the Kanazawa urban district chief to do all the business of their jurisdictions without assistance. Secretaries or clerks *(shoki)* were appointed to staff the county and urban district offices. In 1880, there were 276 secretaries serving under eighteen county and district chiefs. The most populous county, Tonami, had twenty-three secretaries looking after the affairs of its 190,000 people. Nei County, with around 67,500 inhabitants, had twelve secretaries. Kanazawa and the other counties of the prefecture fell between the extremes of Tonami and Nei in numbers of clerks. On the average, the ratio of secretaries to population was about 1:6,000.[19] Secretaries were appointed by the governor after they had been nominated by the county chiefs or the Kanazawa district chief.[20]

Salaries of the chiefs and secretaries of counties and urban districts were paid out of local taxes. It was up to the governor to set these salaries in accordance with the needs and the resources of the locality.[21] Seventeen county chiefs in Ishikawa Prefecture in 1880 were paid an average of ¥45 per month, and the chief of Kanazawa urban district was paid ¥70, even though by law all these chiefs held the same rank, the equivalent of the eighth official grade.[22] Secretaries ranged from rank-equivalent to grade ten through rank-equivalent to grade seventeen, and their salaries from ¥25 to less than ¥10 per month.[23] In all, ¥46,696 was laid out for the salaries of county and urban district administrators in Ishikawa Prefecture in 1880.

Curiously, in the bureaucratic parlance of the day, the chiefs and secretaries of counties and urban districts were referred to as "people's officials" *(minri)*, in contradistinction to "government officials" *(kan'in)* at the prefectural level. Neither prefectural bureaucrats nor county or urban district officials were elected by the people; both types were appointed by the governor. The only obvious difference between them was that prefectural bureaucrats were paid out of monies disbursed by the national exchequer to the prefectures, while the officials of counties and urban districts were paid out of local taxes collected by the prefectures.

TOWNS AND VILLAGES AND THEIR CHIEFS. Besides establishing counties and urban districts, the Law Governing the Organization of Counties, Towns, and Villages raised the status of towns and villages as administrative units. The small districts, which had been created to administer Japan under the Household Registration Law of 1871 and subsequent legislation, and which had been superior to towns, villages, and urban wards, were abandoned at the same time as the large districts.

Between 1871 and 1878, little regard had been given to customary definitions of communal units, and in defining large and small districts, "natural" communities had been split or had been thrown together with other communities of a quite dissimilar character. This had led in some instances to confusion, dissatisfaction, and inefficient administration. Leaders such as Ōkubo desired to remedy this by promoting, where practicable, a return to old town and village boundaries, in defining the lowest-level administrative entities. The advantage of these boundaries was that they had been accepted for generations. The numbers used to designate subprefectural administrative divisions in the early 1870s were dropped. Old place names were taken up as official designations of towns and villages as well as counties.

In the minds of institution builders in Tokyo, the new towns and villages were endowed with a "dual nature" *(niyō no seishitsu)*. A town or village under the new law was to be a unit of self-government, and at the same time it was to be part of the state administrative apparatus. Ōkubo Toshimichi, in his March 1878 memorial, emphasized the former aspect, and spoke of towns and villages as "independent districts of local citizens' society" *(jūmin shakai dokuritsu no ku)*. To reinforce the idea that their jurisdictions were self-governing units, Ōkubo sought to draw a clear distinction between the officials of towns and villages and other government bureaucrats. The distinction was embodied in an explanation of the draft of the new law that was distributed to the participants in the Prefectural Governors Conference in April 1878: "Prefectures and counties are now made administrative districts *(gyōsei no kukaku)*; towns and villages are to be regarded as natural communities *(shizen no ichi buraku)*. Chiefs of towns and villages are of the people, not of the bureaucracy. They are the representatives (*sōdai*) of the towns and villages. We intend to delegate to these chiefs responsibility for the affairs of the towns and villages which they represent, and not to put curbs on them."[24]

In the event, the phrase referring to the town and village chiefs as "representatives" of their communities—it was Ōkubo's choice of words—was too radical for the members of the Genrōin, who had to pass the proposed legislation before it became law. The governors had raised no objections to it at their conference, but when the Genrōin acted on enforcement regulations for the law on local organization, the idea that chiefs were representatives was eliminated. Town and village chiefs became functionaries (*rijisha*), but not, in law, representatives (*sōdai*) of their communities.[25] The Genrōin did not eliminate Ōkubo's conception of towns and villages as self-governing units, but in making this change in the description of the local chiefs it placed stress on the other aspect of the "dual nature" of these communities, namely, their function as administrative units of the state.

So far as the boundaries and names of towns and villages under the new law were concerned, Tokyo leaders certainly had no intention of mandating a complete return to Tokugawa-period boundaries and definitions of communities. Some rationalization of local administration was intended. Where the populations of "natural" towns or villages were small, several such communities might be placed within the jurisdiction of a single town or village office and of a single chief, just as two or more counties might be joined for administrative purposes. The aim of the policy-makers was to eliminate the worst features of the small-district system and to create local governmental units with which residents might identify more closely than they had with the small districts.

In the first Meiji decade, small district chiefs had gotten into more and more difficulties with residents of their districts, usually over taxes. One of the objectives of local government reform in 1878, therefore, was to reduce the friction in relations between citizens and local officials. To give reality to the principle that chiefs of towns and villages were of the people, the logical step was to make these new posts elective. Small district chiefs between 1871 and 1878 had of course been appointed. The Law Governing the Organization of Counties, Urban Districts, Towns, and Villages itself did not specify how the chiefs were to be selected or appointed; it simply stated that chiefs *(kochō)* should be placed in towns and villages. A home ministry notification of August 1878 clarified the point,declaring that town or village chiefs should be elected when possible.[26]

Ishikawa Prefecture adopted rules for the popular election of town and village chiefs on December 17, 1878.[27] Particulars of this election law are unknown, but it is improbable that they were more liberal than a revision of August 1879, which extended the voting privilege to male residents who were above the age of twenty, paid land tax, were not bankrupt, and had not been imprisoned on a criminal sentence for a term exceeding one year.[28] Women were not mentioned in the August 1879 election rules, but they did not have the suffrage, even in cases when they were recognized as heads of households.[29] The attitude of Ishikawa lawmakers toward women was probably implied by the company assigned them in an article of a March 1878 regulation: "Female heads of households and those who have served criminal sentences may not participate in these elections."[30]

Eligibility to be elected chief of a town or village was restricted to male residents twenty-five and over who were not already officials and who met the other qualifications of voters. Although in principle there was to be one chief elected in each town or village, in practice there were cases in which a single chief was selected for several towns, wards, or villages. The chiefs of urban districts and counties were responsible for announcing and administering the elections of town and village chiefs, and the governor had the power of oversight. The term of office of a town or village chief was set at four years.[31]

By making the town or village chief the elected choice of the tax-paying male residents of the locality, the government involved communities in their own governance to a greater extent than they had been before. Elected chiefs were something more than just administrative organs in the service of higher authorities, even if the law refrained from making these chiefs "representatives" of their communities. This feature of the early Three New Laws system was changed in 1884 when election of chiefs was scrapped in favor of appointment, but for several years, the method of selecting chiefs of towns and villages was what Ishikawa district chiefs in 1875, in their fight with Governor Kiriyama, had said it should be.

Ishikawa Prefecture set the location of town and village offices on December 17, 1878, the same day on which it issued regulations on the popular election of town and village chiefs.[32] Not every town and village became the seat of an office. At the time of promulgation of the Three New Laws, there were 5,685 villages *(mura)* and 1,142 towns and wards of urban areas *(machi)* in the big prefecture. There were far fewer offices *(kochō yakuba)*— 1,504.[33] The urban district of Kanazawa can be cited to show how localities were grouped for administrative purposes: There were 537 *machi* (wards), but only eighty-two *kochō yakuba* (ward offices) in the city, which had a population at the time of just over 108,000.[34] In fact there was much variation among the counties in the ratio of town and village offices to towns, wards, and villages. Nei County had one office for every 15.7 towns, wards, and villages, and five other counties had ratios of one to ten or more. At the other extreme, in the counties in Echizen, the mean ratio was 1:1.8. The size of the population for which a town or village chief was responsible varied similarly, with the extremes being fewer than 400 (in Sakai County and the combined county of Nanjō-Imadachi) and more than 4,400 (in Nei County).[35]

A simple instance of how the organization of towns and villages under the Three New Laws system contrasted with the large and small district organization before 1878 is the case of Nanao, the port on the Toyama Bay side of the Noto Peninsula. In 1876, the area that corresponds to the present city of Nanao was nearly all in the Third Small District of the Seventh Large District of Ishikawa Prefecture, under one small district office.[36] With the implementation of the Law Governing the Organization of Counties, Urban Districts, Towns, and Villages, four offices were set up in the area of Nanao, and four chiefs were selected. Each office, and each chief, had jurisdiction over five or six wards.[37]

The new law did not define town and village officials as prefectural officials, even though they were paid out of local taxes collected by the prefecture. It was up to tax-paying males in a community to elect a chief; it was not up to them to define what the chief's job should be. The Council of State enumerated the duties of town and village chiefs in a notice on the prefectural bureaucracy published three days after the promulgation of the Three New Laws.[38] Chiefs were charged with a great deal that can only be deemed delegated business—tasks assigned to them by higher authorities, in addition to responsibilities arising from their positions as functionaries of their own towns and villages. Among such duties of chiefs that primarily served the state were collection and remittance to the government of the national land tax and other taxes; maintenance of the household registry; handling of conscription inquiries; notarizing of deeds of sale and pawn tickets on land, buildings, and ships; management of the cadastre of land titles; notifying the police of sicknesses or unnatural deaths of, or accidents involving, orphans or travelers; reporting to higher authorities those who were in distress after a natural disaster; reporting the names of citizens who might be commended by the state for some demonstration of virtue; and reporting to superior authorities on the state of waterways, roads, dikes, bridges, and the like. Chiefs did have some duties that might be regarded as primarily benefiting the locality and its citizens: encouraging school attendance by young children; keeping an up-to-date register of the seals (*in'ei*) of people of the town or village; preserving and protecting the account books of the town or village; and seeing to maintenance and repairs of those town or village facilities that were supported by local levies (*kōgihi*) other than prefectural taxes (*chihōzei*). But the foremost obligations of the town and village chiefs were to the state. To remove any doubt about local chiefs' responsibility to take care of delegated business, the 1878 notice stipulated, "In addition, business that is ordered by the prefectural governor, the county chief, or the urban district chief must be done according to those orders."

The multiplicity of delegated tasks assigned to town and village chiefs did not stop Ishikawa Prefecture from reaffirming, on December 17, 1878, the dual nature theme, which by then would have been familiar to all Japanese who paid any heed to subnational affairs: "The character of the office of town or village chief has two aspects, that of administrator of state business, and that of functionary of the town or village itself."[39]

It is difficult to determine what changes in local leadership came about as a result of the introduction of popular elections of town and village heads. The records of the prefecture and the histories of the prefecture, cities, towns, and counties are uniformly unhelpful. One village chief in Ishikawa Prefecture between 1878 and 1884 is known to us by name: Ishiguro Toshinaga of Nomi County, the eleventh-generation head of a family that had hereditarily provided village-group headmen in the centuries of *han* rule.[40] Elected chief of sixteen villages in 1881, he apparently was atypical among the town and village heads of his day. The best monograph on the Kaga village-group system observed that "very few men of old village-group headman families became town or village chiefs" after 1878.[41] Surely nearly all town or village chiefs outside the old castle towns must have been of commoner backgrounds. Few ex-samurai, even in Kanazawa, met the tax-paying qualification to serve as town or village chiefs. It is probably safe to assume that the men elected as town and village chiefs were mostly of well-to-do landowning families, if not of the old village-headman class.[42] Members of this class of commoner landholders were becoming increasingly involved in politics in the late 1870s and early 1880s, not only at the local level but also in the new prefectural assemblies and in the national political party movement.[43]

In the early 1880s, as Matsukata's deflationary policies took effect and hit the rentier class particularly hard, taxes and government fiscal policies became critical issues to men in the countryside. The party movement was radicalized under the influence of landholding commoners who had joined the former samurai founders in the parties. For the new breed of party members, moral suasion, which had been preferred by men like Itagaki Taisuke and Ōkuma Shigenobu as a means of pressuring the government into making changes, was too mild. In many prefectures, including, briefly, Ishikawa, young activists came to command center stage in prefectural assemblies in the early 1880s, and they fought bitterly against the ruling bureaucracy and its spending policies. At the subprefectural level, also, dissatisfactions with central government directives found a theater of expression in the new town and village assemblies.

Tokyo authorities reacted to the changes in the political climate. In 1881 the government finally responded to repeated demands that a popularly elected national assembly be established. A rescript announced that a national diet would be convened, not immediately, as many had urged, but in 1890. With respect to governance in the countryside, several moves by the government between 1881 and 1884 aimed at tightening central control. Central authorities responded to prefectural assemblies' attacks on governors and government spending by strengthening the powers of the governor and the home minister, by creating a new standing committee in each prefectural assembly (in the expectation that this body would cooperate with the governor more readily than the whole assembly), and by prohibiting members of one prefectural assembly from joining forces in common cause with members of another.

Turning its attention to problems at the subprefectural level, the Tokyo government in 1884 ordered major reforms affecting both assemblies and town and village chiefs. The reform of May 7, 1884, drastically reduced the number of town and village chiefs and made the position of chief an appointive one. From this time until the "local autonomy system" was implemented after 1888, the governor of a prefecture chose one man from among three to five nominees for each town or village chief's post. The nominees were put forward by their communities through an election, but the final word was the governor's.[44] Before the reform, 408 men had been serving as town and village chiefs in the two ancient provinces of Kaga and Noto (which after the establishment of Toyama Prefecture in 1883, comprised the whole of Ishikawa Prefecture). After the 1884 change, there were just 160 town and village chiefs in this area.[45] The nationwide impact of the reform is suggested by some figures cited by Kikegawa: in 1882, 3,833 former samurai and 29,924 commoners held office as town and village chiefs; in 1887, those numbers had been reduced to 3,521 and 7,489 respectively.[46] Slightly more than two-thirds of the posts for town or village chief had been eliminated, and only a quarter as many commoners were serving in the latter year as in the former.

In theory, the number of towns and villages administered by a single chief was not to exceed five, and the number of families was not to be greater than 500. In practice, more than half of the town and village chiefs in Japan after the 1884 reform had more than five towns and/or villages and more than 500 families within their jurisdictions. In the area around Nanao, for example, the districts presided over by town and village chiefs were from two to five times as large as the ideal prescribed by the law.[47]

The fourth Ishikawa governor, Iwamura Takatoshi, almost surely used his power of appointment to place men who supported his own policies. He had been in office in Ishikawa for over a year by the time of the reform, long enough to have gained knowledge of local men. It is highly unlikely that he—by repute an authoritarian, a man who amused himself by making his subordinates bark like dogs[48]—would have appointed anyone identified as his opponent. Once again we are handicapped in analyzing the impact of a change in the system, because no roster of town and village chiefs for 1884 survives. From a list of all Ishikawa Prefectural Assembly members of the Meiji period, however, we can identify six men who were named town and village chiefs in 1884; all had sat in the prefectural assembly since the fourth governor had come to Kanazawa.[49] Four of these appointees were from Nomi County, the others from Ishikawa and Kahoku counties. All were of commoner status. Five had been raised in farming families, and the sixth had been adopted into a family of apothecaries.[50] That they had been elected to the prefectural assembly obviously marks these men as local notables, yet we must not overlook the fact that they had not been chiefs at the time of the reform. No doubt the governor knew them. He appointed them at a time when the total number of town and village chiefs was being reduced to less than two-fifths of what it had been. Effectively, the governor picked them to replace someone else, or even to replace two or three pre-reform chiefs. If the pattern of these men's appointments was a common one, the changes in personnel among town and village chiefs must indeed have strengthened the position of the centrally appointed governors, just as the reform intended.

The governor's role in town and village affairs was thus enlarged by the 1884 change, and the town and village chiefs were absorbed into officialdom. The chiefs were removed yet one step further from Ōkubo Toshimichi's idea of "representatives of the towns and villages." Election of local administrators was reintroduced into Japan with the adoption of the "local autonomy system" in 1888, but even after that, chiefs were held in check by a firm hierarchy of superintendence. The reform of 1884 was a critical move in the erection of this structure of superintendence.

TOWN AND VILLAGE ASSEMBLIES IN THE THREE NEW LAWS SYSTEM. In 1878, the Enforcement Regulations for the Three New Laws raised the possibility of town and village assemblies (*chōson kaigi*) being opened, though these Enforcement Regulations did not mandate that localities must create such bodies.[51] Deliberative councils at this level would be empowered to act on local matters, so long as they could provide means of paying for their actions through local levies (*kōgihi*), which were distinct from the local tax (*chihōzei*) determined by the third of the Three New Laws.

Actually, Ishikawa Prefecture had begun laying the groundwork for such town and village assemblies even before Ōkubo had submitted his memorial proposing changes at the local level. The Ishikawa plan for restructuring town and village government was embodied in the Provisional Regulations on Towns and Villages issued in March 1878. The prefecture called for the establishment of consultative meetings (kaidō kyōgi) in the towns and villages (chōson). Ishikawa officials apparently were already preparing to make towns and villages the basic units of administration below the large districts; small districts were not even mentioned in these March 1878 regulations. The new consultative meetings were to discuss five important areas of local business: education, encouragement of enterprise, granaries for emergency relief and poor relief, accumulation of funds for education, and town and village expenditures.[52]

Governor Kiriyama associated these regulations with the imperial rescripts of 1874 and 1875, which had, as he put it, "looked forward to the gradual progress of the people."[53] In his promulgation message to the people of the prefecture, he discoursed on the need for local assemblies: "As the world progresses, matters in which the people have intercourse also become many and various, and there is frequently public business that calls for consultation, yet it would be troublesome for all the people to meet together directly on each such occasion. It is plain that the best solution is to elect delegates and to charge them with carrying out consultations on such matters." In the absence of national legislation providing for town and village meetings, the prefecture "temporarily" established its own regulations "to facilitate the organization of consultation . . . and hoping gradually to fulfill the true spirit of a popular assembly."[54]

The mere fact that such town and village meetings were established in Ishikawa Prefecture in 1878 is notable, although details of the implementation of these regulations remain obscure. It was two years before town and village assemblies (chōsonkai) were provided for nationwide by the Law on Urban District, Town, and Village Assemblies of April 8, 1880. Kiriyama's administration seems to have been in the van in this area of local institution-building. But if they had caught some of the liberal fever of the early Meiji period, Kiriyama and his aides were not delirious. They did not go so far as to give the new town and village meetings decision-making power. In Ishikawa, these assemblies were to be consultative, and their actions not binding on administrators.

The prefecture broadened the scope of local assembly deliberations in a new set of rules issued in March 1879. From that time, town and village assemblies were to convene for not more than three days, about twice a year, to discuss (1) local rates to be paid by households toward town or village expenditures *(kyōgihi)* and (2) rates to be paid by households toward the household tax component *(kosūwari)* of the local tax *(chihōzei)*. To be a member of one of these councils, according to the revised regulations, one had to be a male property owner who had resided in the town or village for a minimum of one year. The assemblies became slightly more powerful than their consultative predecessors, yet they were severely limited by two provisions in the new rules: Town or village chiefs had to give their approval to assembly decisions before implementing them, and assembly actions pertaining to commonly held property had to be sanctioned by three levels of officials—town or village chief, county or urban district chief, and prefectural governor—before becoming effective.[55]

Kanazawa held an election in 1879 to choose representatives to a federated assembly for its wards. Twenty-four representatives convened in September that year for a month-long session—quite a bit longer than the March regulations had prescribed—during which they discussed assemblies, education, hour-bells, inoculations, fire prevention, and emergency and poor relief.[56] We do not know whether any of this assembly's actions received the requisite approval of the appropriate higher authorities and was put into effect. What is clear is that the members of this federated council believed in the usefulness of a body like theirs. The speaker of the assembly addressed a petition to Governor Chisaka calling for the rapid establishment of a regular city assembly.[57]

Even though we lack specific information on the activities of Ishikawa town and village assemblies under the March 1879 regulations, we can guess something of the nature of electoral politics in the city of Kanazawa by looking at the list of members of the federated assembly.[58] Three members were former Kaga samurai who had been prominent leaders of the Chūkokusha: Obata Zōji, Yoneyama Michio, and Sugimoto Seishun. Nearly all of the remaining twenty-one assemblymen had surnames that appear in the register of retainers of the Maeda family at the end of the period of *han* rule.[59] Assembly member Watase Seirei had inherited a stipend of 230 *koku* as a Kaga samurai, and even after the Restoration was closely associated with the Maeda house; after fighting in the war of 1868, he had become a *han* and prefectural official, then spent some years as an attendant in the Maeda household in Tokyo.[60] Elsewhere in Japan, this was a time when the most remarkable phenomenon on the political stage was the entry of commoners by election to the new assemblies. In the old castle town of Kanazawa, connection with the Kaga upper class tradition probably conferred an advantage to men like Watase, even in elective politics. It is also imaginable that the charisma of Saigō Takamori was still at work—voters could not have forgotten that Obata and Yoneyama had been key figures in the pro-Satsuma faction in Ishikawa Prefecture in the years just after the Restoration.

The central government finally acted to provide local deliberative bodies nationwide on April 18, 1880, more than two years after Ishikawa Prefecture had established such bodies. The Law on Urban District, Town, and Village Assemblies created assemblies on one model all over the nation, and with this April 1880 law the basic structure of local government under the Three New Laws was completed. The new law superseded previous local regulations on subprefectural assemblies and raised the legal status of these bodies from mere consultative organs to decision-making ones.[61] The authorities, especially the governor, were given powers of oversight and sanction that impelled the town and village councils to be cautious. If the county chief or urban district chief considered some action of an assembly within his jurisdiction to be improper, he could suspend execution and put the matter before the governor. The governor could delay the implementation of any assembly legislation that he regarded unlawful. The governor had the power to dissolve a city, town, or village assembly. Nothing in the law prevented the governor from making decisions affecting the locality when the assembly was not in session.[62] The role of town and village assemblies under the 1880 law might be aptly described with the phrase that Robert E. Ward used in speaking of post-World War II village assemblies: "They discussed and they approved."[63] They did not have a wide arena in which to exercise their own initiative.

Kanazawa revised its assembly regulations after the ten-article national law on local assemblies was promulgated.[64] The first of thirty-seven articles declared that the Kanazawa council would "confer and decide upon" matters pertaining to public business of the city, in particular matters of budget, revenues, and disbursements, and publicly owned properties. In the 1880 regulations, as before, the city assembly was required to take care of a tax levied by the prefecture, namely the household tax; the assembly had to determine the amount that each ward of the city should pay.

The Kanazawa rules went further than the national law in providing for executive superintendence of assembly actions. Article V stated simply, "Decisions of the assembly must receive the approval of the urban district chief." No qualifying phrase like "in cases when the chief considers an assembly action unlawful" appears. The framers of the Kanazawa regulations had no qualms about administrative supremacy. Like the Tokyo policy makers, the authors of the Kanazawa rules believed that there should be local popular input into the decision-making process. That was what the city assembly was for. But in the end, executive authority should be strongest. Article VII also required that assembly decisions be approved by the urban district chief before they could be implemented.

Even at the lowest grass-roots level, the franchise and eligibility to be elected to an assembly seat were restricted. To vote, one had to be a male head of a household, above the age of twenty, resident in the city, sane, solvent, and law-abiding to the extent of not having spent one or more of the last seven years in prison. To be elected to the assembly, one had to meet the qualifications to vote, to have been registered in the city for at least one year, and not to have resigned a city assembly seat within the four preceding years. Nor were these limitations on the electorate and on the pool of eligible candidates the only things that kept the Kanazawa council from being truly popular in the sense of representing all the people.

The system of elections provided for by these 1880 regulations was indirect. Before the assembly was chosen, election committee members had to be selected, in a ratio of about one per hundred households. It was the election committee members who met and actually chose the assemblymen; this was done in each of seven electoral districts.[65] From three to five seats in the assembly were allotted to each electoral district, so that each assemblyman represented, on average, just over 3,600 inhabitants—but only a handful of voters. In all there were thirty seats in the council.

Probably the members of most town and village assemblies around Japan during the Three New Laws period represented fewer inhabitants than the councilmen of Kanazawa. In Ishikawa Prefecture, only the big city left evidence of implementation of the law on local assemblies, and we cannot say how representative other localities' councils were.

Across the nation, the subprefectural assemblies failed to work out as Tokyo leaders had anticipated. Assembly members and town and village chiefs came into conflict, and "abuses of all kinds developed." [66] Finally on May 7, 1884, the government promulgated a comprehensive revision of the Law on Urban District, Town, and Village Assemblies. Home Minister Yamagata Aritomo sent an explanation to all prefectural governors three weeks later: The 1880 law had been too broad and vague in making "public business of urban districts, towns, and villages" the purview of the assemblies, and to correct this, the revised law narrowed the local councils' scope to "matters which must be paid for with the monies of urban districts, towns, or villages." [67] The revised law made the urban district, town, or village chief the president of the assembly; the original law had had no provision regarding the presidency. Yamagata accounted for the change: "The reason for making the urban district chief or the town or village chief, who is a functionary, the president of the assembly is that in urban district, town, or village affairs, nearly everything must be done as a single unitary body, with no separation between the chief and the assembly members." He argued further that it went against Japanese tradition for the president of a local council to be someone other than the local chief; here he alluded to the village assembly *(yoriai)* of pre-Restoration days, which had been led by the village headman.

The 1884 revision took the power to originate bills away from local assemblies. That power henceforward would be vested in the urban district, town, or village chief alone, because the practice of allowing assembly members to introduce bills had produced conflicting results, and, in Yamagata's words, "inevitably led to abuses." Other provisions of the 1884 revised law, and of the home minister's explication, reveal that Yamagata was wary of entrusting local citizens with what he thought to be too much power. The executive authority of the chiefs vis-à-vis the councils was strengthened, as was the hierarchy of oversight of assembly decisions by prefectural and national officials. Under the 1880 law, several urban district wards, towns, or villages could join at their own initiative to create an association *(rengō kuchōson kai)* or an irrigation association *(suiri dokō kai)*, and they could define their own boundaries when they did so. The revised law provided that only the governor had the power to create such associations. All these changes of 1884 combined with the reduction in the number of town and village chiefs and the conversion of the post of chief from elective to appointive and yielded a local government structure that Tokyo leaders found more pliable and less likely to produce "abuses." This phase of the Three New Laws period had an undeniably authoritarian tenor.

THE PREFECTURAL ASSEMBLY

The second of the Three New Laws established representative assemblies in all of the prefectures. This was an epoch-making move on the part of the Tokyo government. Elected councils would meet annually in each prefecture to discuss the prefectural budget and local tax matters. Some prefectures had already inaugurated their own deliberative bodies, but often appointed officials, rather than popularly chosen representatives, served as members, and the sessions were called on an irregular basis. Under the new law, the people's representatives in prefectural government became the yeast that caused the brew of politics to ferment. Not infrequently the taste of the end product confounded the expectations of central government brewers. After some years, prefectural assemblymen quieted down to a routine of cooperation with the authorities, but by that time legislative bodies had been created at the lower town and village levels and had been promised for the national level. The prefectural assemblies had given the people a new voice in government and had pioneered for both grass-roots assemblies and the first successful non-Western elected national legislature.

The Prefectural Assembly Regulations, composed of thirty-five articles, were a watershed, but they were crafted to minimize politically or socially revolutionary consequences.[68] Elections were provided for, but the electorate was carefully limited. Suffrage was extended only to males twenty-five and over who had their domiciles in the county or urban district in which they would be voting and who paid land tax of five yen or more. The tax-paying requirement meant, in the case of Ishikawa, that the privilege of voting for the prefectural assembly was more exclusive than that for recently instituted consultative bodies at the subprefectural level. The usual categories were expressly excluded from the franchise: lunatics and idiots, persons sentenced to a year or more of imprisonment at hard labor, and bankrupts who had not met their obligations. To be eligible for election to the prefectural assembly, one had to meet the qualifications of a voter and in addition to have paid ten yen or more in land tax and to have lived more than three years in the prefecture. Officials and teachers were prohibited from standing for or accepting election to the prefectural assembly.

The first *Statistical Annual of the Empire of Japan* gives figures for 1880 that reveal how few were allowed to participate in the new electoral system. In all thirty-nine prefectures, 1,513,308 men had the vote, and 867,192 met the qualifications to be elected. Those numbers were 4.27 percent and 2.45 percent, respectively, of the whole population. The situation in Ishikawa, the prefecture with the biggest population, was typical: Of 1,833,778 inhabitants, 31,423 (4.44 percent) could vote, and 48,835 (2.66 percent) could be elected.[69] Some of the more conservative leaders of the Meiji state had tried to keep the electorate even smaller, arguing in the Genrōin that only those who paid at least ¥10 annually in land taxes should be enfranchised, but the opinion of the participants in the second Prefectural Governors Conference was that suffrage should be extended to men who paid ¥5 or more, and the governors' view prevailed.[70]

Not only was the electorate restricted, but other provisions of the Law on Prefectural Assemblies patently were intended to constrict the activities of those bodies and maintain the power of centrally appointed officials without diminution. An assembly could not debate and pass upon a wide variety of issues, nor could it legislate. What it could do was to "consult upon the budget of the expenditures to be defrayed out of local taxes (*chihōzei*), and upon the means of raising local taxes," and "consult upon matters relating to the prefecture on the request of the governor."

The role of the governor in the prefectural assembly was a large one, and the supervisory powers of the governor and the home minister were great. Only the governor, the law specified, could initiate bills for the assembly's consideration; members could not introduce their own bills. Resolutions of the assembly had to win the approval of the governor before going into effect. If the assembly made a decision the governor deemed unworthy, the governor was required to report his reasoning to the home minister and request guidance. The governor had the power to open and close the assembly. If the regular session, which was to convene in March and to meet for no longer than thirty days, was not sufficient to complete the business at hand, the governor could prolong the session and inform the home minister of his action. The governor could also summon an extraordinary session of the assembly, if he thought it necessary; again, he had to report his action and his reasons to the home minister. If he felt that the debate in the assembly was disturbing the peace or was contrary to the laws and regulations of the nation, the governor had the power to prorogue the assembly and ask for instructions from the home minister. The home minister possessed the power to dissolve the assembly.

The new prefectural deliberative institution did have some powers. Prefectural budgets and local tax matters had to be submitted to the assembly, and the members soon learned that they could make things difficult for the governor, and sometimes force him to modify his proposals, by refusing to go along with his budget and tax bills. Also, although it was not as potent a political weapon as the ability to legislate at their own initiative would have been, members did have the power to petition the central government on matters affecting the interest of the prefecture. To utilize this power, the speaker of the assembly had to allow a motion, and a majority of the members' votes had to be obtained. The Ishikawa Prefectural Assembly attempted to take advantage of this provision of the law in May 1882, when the members passed a motion to petition the home minister, asking for the dismissal of Governor Chisaka Takamasa.[71]

The results of early prefectural assembly elections reveal much about the distribution of power in the new system. The law stated that up to five assemblymen should be elected by each county or urban district, depending upon its size. Ishikawa Prefecture held its first assembly election in April 1879, choosing sixty-nine members; only the Tokyo and Hyōgo prefectural assemblies were larger. In the big Hokuriku prefecture, the distribution by district or county ranged between two and five seats: Kanazawa had four seats; Enuma, two; Nomi, three; Ishikawa, four; Kahoku, three; Hagui, three; Kashima, three; Fugeshi, three; Suzu, two; Tonami, five; Imizu, five; Nei, three; Kami Niikawa, five; Shimo Niikawa, four; Nanjō, two; Imadachi, three; Nyū, three; Asuwa, three; Yoshida, two; Ōno, three; and Sakai, four.[72] In terms of the ratio of residents to assemblymen, representation in Ishikawa was not as good as in most other prefectures. In 1880, in all of Japan, the mean number of citizens represented by each assembly member was 18,416; in Ishikawa Prefecture, the number was 26,576.[73] After the partition of 1881, which carved Fukui Prefecture out of Ishikawa, the gap between Ishikawa and the national average grew even larger, as the following table shows:

Prefecture	Population per assembly seat
Ishikawa	28,833 (highest in Japan)
Kagoshima	27,453
Kumamoto	23,652
Fukui	16,048
Tokyo	12,886
Kyoto	9,178
Iwate	9,038 (lowest in Japan)
National mean	17,907

Source: *Nihon teikoku tōkei nenkan,* vol. 2 (1883).

The first prefectural assembly election in Ishikawa, in April 1879, was a confused affair. Some men were elected in more than one district. Others declined to take the seats for which they had been chosen. Katō Kō, locally renowned as a Chūkokusha stalwart and then as a leader of the opposition to the forty-three recalcitrant district chiefs in 1875, instanced the former phenomenon. Elected in both Kanazawa and Kahoku, he chose to represent the latter constituency. Popular with assemblymen, as with voters, and respected for his learning—son of a scholar in the Kaga *han* academy and himself once an instructor in that school, he had studied also in Nagasaki and Tokyo—he was picked by the representatives as their first speaker. Hasegawa Jun'ya obtained more votes than any other candidate in Kanazawa, but he had not campaigned for election and refused to join the assembly.

Voter turnout for this first prefectural assembly election was low. It was reported that the local intelligentsia felt that the powers of the new assembly were vague and unimpressive.[74] Because the law had tied the franchise to payment of land tax, wealthy commoners—landlords in particular—were the dominant element of the electorate. In the first election, nevertheless, quite a few former samurai were sent to the Ishikawa Prefectural Assembly. Surely this reflected their prominence in political affairs both before and after the Restoration, before new local issues began to be generated by the prefectural assembly itself.

Very few were privileged to participate in the electoral process in the

decade of the Three New Laws. The system had been deliberately designed
to be limited. Ōkubo, other members of the high councils of government
in Tokyo, and the prefectural governors had not desired a democratic voting
setup, and they had not created one. Ishikawa Prefecture illustrates this
nicely. Another important feature of the electoral system of this time is also
evidenced in the big Hokuriku prefecture: There were wide disparities
among the voting districts, resulting in large differences in the weight of
single votes, depending on where they were cast. Ratios of inhabitants to
assemblymen ranged from 1:18,627 to 1:36,550; ratios of voters to assemblymen ranged from 1:87 to 1:2,489.[75] There was a sizable gap between
the districts with the highest proportion of the population able to vote and
the lowest. Ishikawa ranked thirty-third among the forty prefectures in
1881, with 4.18 percent meeting franchise requirements; Shiga Prefecture
was first with 8.26 percent eligible to vote, and Tokyo Prefecture last with
1.36 percent. But the range within Ishikawa was slightly greater than that
between Shiga and Tokyo: Nomi's 7.59 percent dwarfed Kanazawa's 0.32
percent.[76] All voters and all prospective assembly members were landholders, but the political potential of a man who paid five yen in land tax in,
say, Kami Niikawa County was almost double that of his counterpart in
nearby Nei County, and that of a Kanazawa voter was vastly greater. These
political demographics have not been much analyzed. The common historical interpretations of the second Meiji decade usually stress that the landlords emerged to political importance and imply that all landlords in all
parts of Japan had common class interests.[77] Prefectural assembly members
may have had some common interests, notably holding the line against
taxes, but the record shows that they certainly did not agree with one another all the time. The differences among their constituencies, and among
the support structures they had to build or manipulate to be elected, might
account for their disagreements with each other in chamber.

The Financing of Prefectural and Subprefectural Government

The third of the Three New Laws laid down uniform rules for the collection
of taxes at the prefectural and subprefectural levels. In the first decade after
the Meiji Restoration, Tokyo leaders told the Prefectural Governors Confer-

ence in April 1878 that the national government had not had time to deal with every problem that demanded reform.[78] Thus decisions about the assessment and collection of local levies *(minpi)* had been left up to the prefectures. As a result, sundry schemes for making these exactions had evolved. Neighboring prefectures differed in the names and categories that they used in their tax laws, and also in the rates. The absence of coherence in the system almost inevitably gave rise to difficulties. As a government working paper put it, "This is not the way to perpetuity."[79] It was time for national action.

After passing the Governors Conference and the Genrōin, new local tax regulations were promulgated as a simple-looking set of seven articles.[80] The former local levies *(minpi)* and prefectural taxes *(fukenzei)* were to be replaced by new "local taxes" *(chihōzei)*. Article I established three categories of local taxes: (1) taxes on land amounting to no more than one-fifth of the national land tax, (2) business taxes and miscellaneous taxes, and (3) household taxes. Specific limits on these categories of taxes were to be clarified by separate regulations.

As for what the new local taxes were to be used for, in contrast to the many categories of expenses that appeared in the Ishikawa *minpi* reports of 1874 and 1878,[81] the new law set forth twelve categories of expenditures that were to be covered. The list is suggestive of the central government's strategy of getting subnational units of government to pay for services on which national policymakers had placed priority, and over which localities could exercise little discretion:

1. Police expenditures.
2. Construction and maintenance of riparian works, bridges, and roads.
3. Expenses of the prefectural assembly.
4. Expenses for preventing epidemics.
5. Expenses for prefectural schools and aid to primary schools.
6. Construction and maintenance of county or urban district office buildings.
7. Salaries, travel expenses, and office expenses of county and urban district officials.
8. Expenditures for hospitals and orphanages.
9. Expenditures for port officials and shipwrecks.

10. Costs of disseminating proclamations or regulations not applying to other prefectures.

11. Expenditures for the encouragement of business.

12. Salaries and office expenditures of town and village officials.

Article III of the regulations commented on what was left over: "Those expenditures that affect only a particular town or village, or a particular urban district, are left to the discussion of the people of that town, village, or urban district. Such expenditures are outside the limits of the things that must be defrayed by local taxes."[82] This meant that localities had to raise their own funds, by making new exactions on their residents, for any projects of their own devising, or for facilities like schools for which the *chihōzei* revenues were inadequate. What had been the major component of local levies before 1878, the household taxes (*kosūwari*), had now been appropriated for prefectural, county, and urban district expenditures.

The other articles of the local tax law of 1878 redefined the fiscal year as July 1 through June 30, replacing the calendar year, and spelled out the roles of the governor, the prefectural assembly, and the home and finance ministers in dealing with expenditures paid out of local tax revenues. By February of every year, the governor was to draft both a budget of the regular expenditures that had to be paid out of local taxes and an estimate of local tax revenues. These documents were to be forwarded to the prefectural assembly at its regular session in March; the second of the Three New Laws had made consulting on the local taxes the principal function of the assembly. When the delegates had passed the budget and the estimate of revenues—the law did not anticipate assembly disapproval—the governor had to send both sets of figures to the home and finance ministers. The new law allowed a prefecture to raise emergency levies in the event of a natural disaster, so long as the prefectural assembly approved and the measure was reported to the home and finance ministers.

Recent local precedent should determine rates of collection of the local taxes on land and households, the government declared.[83] This policy left some leeway for localities to apply their own discretion. In the case of Kanazawa, it led to the adoption of a complex but apparently progressive formula for determining tax rates, with eleven classes of households based on the value of an average *tsubo* (3.305 square meters) of land, recognizing differences in land values from one neighborhood to another.[84] Late in 1880, the government raised the ceiling on the land-based local tax. That had been set at one-fifth the national land tax rate in 1878; recognizing the need for an increase in local revenues, the lawmakers reset it at one-third the national rate.[85]

Rates for business taxes (*eigyōzei*) and miscellaneous taxes (*zasshuzei*) were specified in a Council of State decree at the end of 1878.[86] Business taxes were of three types, differentiated, it would seem, by the potential profitability of various lines of enterprise. Companies (*kaisha*), pawnbrokers, money changers, wholesalers, and the like were assessed up to ¥15 in local taxes; brokers, middlemen, restaurateurs, gardeners, bathhouse keepers, and the like, up to ¥10; and retailers, ¥5 or less. Miscellaneous taxes hit those in the amusement industry harder than just about any other group of taxpayers. Among those assessed were theaters, licensed brothels, restaurants, houses of assignation (*machiaijaya*, places where a man could meet female or male entertainers), bathhouses, hair stylists (except barbers who clipped in the Western fashion), actors, and those involved in Japanese wrestling (*sumō*) exhibitions. These various enterprises or individuals paid local taxes at rates running from 50 sen a year through 5 percent of their income to half their national tax assessment. Theaters might pay up to ¥150, actors up to ¥60.

The list of miscellaneous taxes is a reminder of the cultural richness of Japan when its leaders launched it upon the course of "modernization." For a man, although not for a woman, the nation offered a profusion of entertainments and amenities, so long as one had a little money. More soberly, the amusement industry constituted a sizable reservoir for local entities to tap, especially in towns like Kanazawa which boasted a complete inventory of pleasures. Before the laws of 1878, levies on the amusement industry had not been systematically assessed and collected. Thereafter, taxes on entertainment, as well as other kinds of business taxes, became as important to prefectural finances as the household tax. In prefectures with rapidly expanding economies they became even more important.[87]

Various enforcement regulations and supplements to the law on local taxes circumscribed the powers of the prefectural assembly to control spending out of those taxes. An appendix to the government notice that categorized and limited business and miscellaneous taxes, for example, warned that "in the event that an assembly should eliminate or make excessive cuts in the amount of required payments, the home minister shall enter into the records a budget based on the amounts spent in the previous fiscal year, and shall authorize immediate enforcement." This same appendix identified seven of the twelve categories of expenditures to be covered by local taxes as "required expenditures."[88] The scope for local decision making about what to do with local taxes was thus narrowed, and central government priorities reinforced. At the prefectural and county levels, required expenditures and delegated business outweighed discretionary expenditures and locally originated business.

Perceiving that the greatest beneficiary of the changes of 1878 was the central government and feeling pressed by national and prefectural tax demands, prefectural assemblymen in the 1880s began to voice their opposition to the tax plans presented by governors. Ishikawa assembly members confronted their governor in 1882, and a disagreement over local taxes was one of the key issues. Despite the emergence of opposition in the new forum provided by the prefectural assemblies, however, the authorities continued to get their way in matters of local finance, as well as national finance. Assemblymen sought cuts in local taxes, but local taxes rose steadily through the decade.

SOURCES OF FUNDS. Subnational entities drew sustenance from four types of funding during the decade of the Three New Laws. The national treasury provided funds of two types, "official expenditures" *(kanpi)* and "supplementary funds" *(hojokin).* The prefectures imposed local taxes *(chihōzei)* on residents. And towns and villages raised additional local levies *(kyōgihi).* The monies from the national exchequer went for some of the regular operating costs of prefectures. The local taxes were used to pay other prefectural expenses and some of the costs of subprefectural government. The impositions of towns and villages supported services and facilities that benefited only the residents of those localities.

After 1880, pursuant to Council of State Decree Number 48, the proportion of funds provided by the national treasury dropped, while that of local tax collections rose. In keeping with its retrenchment effort, the central government ceased paying for public works and for building and repairs of offices, prisons, and the like. National aid for schools also stopped. Prefectures and municipalities, if they wanted to maintain or expand such facilities, had to take over fiscal responsibility. Matsukata's policies brought on a deflation, particularly devastating to people who paid rents or who had to repay loans and interest. In this severe environment, national taxes did not decline and local taxes went up, making it a tough time for taxpayers.

The worst crunch of deflation and retrenchment was over by 1885. After that, national government outlays to subnational units rose again, so that by the end of the decade, the total amount of these outlays was almost exactly what it had been at the beginning. These trends appear in figures published in the *Statistical Annual of the Empire of Japan,* which made its first appearance in 1881. The numbers, as the title connotes, were for the whole nation. The central government's contribution to the total revenues of subnational units declined from 20 percent in 1880 to less than 15 percent in 1882, then gradually recovered to around 20 percent for the years 1886–1888. The amounts given to Ishikawa, and the percentages of total prefectural spending that those amounts covered, over the years 1880–1890, can be seen in Appendix 7. These national funds were not unrestricted grants, but were earmarked for particular expenditures of the prefectures, including salaries of prefectural bureaucrats and police expenditures. Decisions about the use of these funds were up to the governors and the bureaucracy; neither prefectural assembly members nor town and village officials had any say about "official expenditures" or "supplementary funds."

Not all prefectures were the same. The central government contributed more to the support of some than of others. The biggest prefectures and those with important trading centers received the most favorable treatment, in terms of national treasury funds for regular prefectural expenditures. Ishikawa, Tokyo, and Hyōgo received considerably more than less populous prefectures such as Mie or Gifu, which had neither ports nor large cities. Ishikawa did not long enjoy this most-favored-prefecture treatment, because Fukui Prefecture split off from it in 1881 and Toyama Prefecture in 1883, but the national government continued to reward size and commercial or strategic value in making disbursements to prefectures for the remainder of the decade.

Prefectural taxes went up and stayed up over the course of the decade. Between 1879 and 1882, nationwide, they rose by just over 27 percent, to ¥16.9 million, and they edged upward by nearly 5 percent more by 1887, to ¥17.8 million. As a percentage of all revenues available to prefectures and other localities, these local taxes increased to over 44 percent in 1887 from under 35 percent in 1880.

Town and village levies rose by 17.5 percent from 1880 through 1882. Then these localities reduced their rates, and by 1887, town and village levies stood at less than 80 percent of their 1880 level. Conceivably, the town and village councils, which determined these rates, decided that the national and prefectural tax burdens were so heavy that taxpayers needed some relief.

USES OF FUNDS. The majority of local outlays went for things over which prefectures and municipalities had little control. The central government, as it solidified national power, used the subnational entities. Subnational units spent most of their financial resources and time on assignments from Tokyo. Local spending was heavily committed to things like police and officials' salaries. As noted earlier, Tokyo cut its contributions to prefectures sharply in 1881, and public works, schools, and public building and repairs were thereafter the responsibility of the localities. Ishikawa Prefecture pumped up its spending to more than make up the difference in national spending. Prefectures could increase spending somewhat after the 1880 amendment of local tax regulations permitted them to increase the rates they could collect on land, from one-fifth of the national land tax amount to one-third.

The most prominent items on the list of the prefecture's expenditures were police, administration of counties and the urban district, administration of towns and villages, education, and prisons. Typically, more than two-thirds of all outlays went for these five items. The bulk of this spending went to pay salaries. Appendix 8 shows how prefectural tax revenues were allocated in Ishikawa over the years 1880 through 1890.

Police cost the prefecture more than anything else. Although the police were completely under central government control, three-quarters of police salaries and other costs were borne by the prefecture; the national treasury paid only the salary of the chief of police and a fraction of other constabulary expenses. Police expenditures rose in Ishikawa and over much of the nation in the early 1880s, as hot-blooded agitators in the inchoate political parties either actually fomented outbreaks of disorder and violence or seemed to the authorities to be threatening to kindle such incidents. In Ishikawa in 1882, the governor called for police reinforcements from Tokyo. Some of the cost in that case was paid by the national government. But in Ishikawa and around the rest of Japan, national funding for police expenditures dropped in 1884, and more of the burden fell on the localities. In some years the ratio of prefectural to national outlay for police in Ishikawa was five or six to one.

Probably the police and the various local officials whose support ate up nearly two-thirds of the subnational units' revenues did provide some services that local residents wanted. The teachers who were supported by local monies did teach local pupils. Residents of the prefecture and the towns and villages got some return for their local tax payments and their town and village rates, even though they had virtually no control over what police, local officials, and teachers did on the job. But the point so often made by historians critical of the patterns of Meiji governance remains: Most of the financial resources of subnational entities were exhausted in the performance of delegated tasks. After the biggest five categories of local expenditure were taken care of, less than a third of local revenues was left to be spent on public works or projects of local residents' own devising.

GOVERNORS IN THE THREE NEW LAWS SYSTEM

LEGAL FEATURES. A new set of regulations on bureaucratic organization went along with the Three New Laws.[89] The government strengthened the hierarchy of superintendence over local affairs. According to the 1875 regulations on prefectural officials and their duties, the home minister had had an indirect power to oversee the actions of governors.[90] The 1878 rules contained several articles that made that power of superintendence direct: The home minister should oversee governors' actions in those areas of business that were the purview of the home ministry, and the other ministers of the central government should supervise in those areas in which they had legal competence.[91] Governors were to accept the direction of the appropriate ministers in the various spheres of authority of those senior officials, and when governors took actions to implement national laws and national government orders, they were to report to the appropriate ministers. The chief minister of the Council of State could cancel a governor's edicts; a minister with responsibility for the area affected by a governor's edict could do likewise.

These 1878 rules on bureaucratic organization also strengthened the position of governors within their jurisdictions. The power of governors to establish and promulgate regulations for the purpose of carrying out central government policy was made legally explicit. Governors kept the power to appoint, promote, demote, and dismiss officials of middle rank *(hanninkan)*, and to assign these men to sections within the prefectural office. The appointive powers of governors were expanded by these 1878 regulations to include some new officials outside the prefectural office, as well. Governors were empowered to appoint, promote, demote, and dismiss chiefs and other middle-rank officials of the counties, and the law specified that governors were to "direct and supervise" county business.

In creating prefectural assemblies, Japan had opened the door to political participation for many men, if not for everyone, who had previously been excluded from the process of governing. But the way was not cleared for assemblymen to seize the initiative in prefectural affairs. The law on prefectural bureaucratic organization stipulated that it was up to the governor to summon the assembly; the body could not come into session without his action. The governor was vested with the power to prorogue the assembly. He alone had the power to originate bills in the assembly, and after that deliberative body had reached a decision, to approve or disapprove of its action. When he exercised his power over the assembly, the governor was obliged to report to the home minister. As the legal historian Ōshima Mitsuko has remarked, the restrictions on the power and initiative of the prefectural assembly made it little more than a consultative organ, without much decision-making competence; the governor had "overwhelmingly preponderant power".[92]

Vis-à-vis the towns and villages established by the Three New Laws, too, the prefectural governor had broad powers. Once again, the 1878 reforms of the local government system were double-edged: While towns and villages were recognized as self-governing bodies by the law, they were placed more firmly under the supervision and control of the governor.[93] Towns and villages were permitted, until 1884, to choose their own chiefs, but administrative law expressly provided that those chiefs stood at the bottom of a bureaucratic ladder on which all the higher rungs were occupied by appointees of the central government or the prefectural governor (see Figure 2). As already noted, an 1884 revision of the law abolished the election of town and village chiefs and made those positions appointive. In Ishikawa, the number of town and village chiefs was cut from 408 to 160 that year, and the governor probably made sure that the chiefs were men of his liking.

FIGURE 2   *The Hierarchy of Local Governance under the Three New Laws*

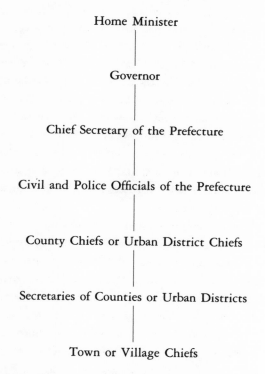

Home Minister

Governor

Chief Secretary of the Prefecture

Civil and Police Officials of the Prefecture

County Chiefs or Urban District Chiefs

Secretaries of Counties or Urban Districts

Town or Village Chiefs

Source: Cf. Yamanaka, p. 26

GOVERNORS OF ISHIKAWA PREFECTURE UNDER THE THREE NEW LAWS. Two men occupied the top spot in Kanazawa during most of the decade of the Three New Laws. The third governor of Ishikawa was a man who had led troops against the imperial forces in 1868 in the war waged

by Tokugawa loyalists in Northeastern Japan.[94] Chisaka Takamasa, born
into one of the highest ranking samurai families of the Yonezawa domain
in 1841, had entered official service in 1863, and early in 1868 had been
put in command of the *han* military forces. After the combined might of
Satsuma, Chōshū, and their allies under the imperial banner had defeated
his side, Chisaka managed to remain in a high post in the Yonezawa bureaucracy. He had the title *daisanji,* chief councilor, when his former lord,
Uesugi Mochinori, decided to go abroad in 1870. Chisaka resigned his
councilorship and accompanied Uesugi on a grand tour of Europe. In England and France, Chisaka imbibed the draughts of liberal thought, seeing
at first hand what other Japanese of his generation received only indirectly
from the translations of such "civilization and enlightenment" movement
luminaries as Fukuzawa Yukichi, Mori Arinori, Nishi Amane, and Katō
Hiroyuki, and from other liberal thinkers and translators like Nakae
Chōmin and Ueki Emori. Chisaka acquired a taste for European fashion as
well as liberal thought during his stay in the West—a portrait photograph
taken while he was governor of Ishikawa shows him in a cutaway, brocaded
and bemedalled in a manner condign with the dignity of his high office,
with moustache, full side-whiskers, and Ben Franklin spectacles. The contrast with the appearance of his predecessors, who had themselves photo-
graphed in kimono, is striking.[95]

Back home from his European sojourn, Chisaka was taken into the home
ministry in 1875. What his relations with Ōkubo Toshimichi might have
been, we do not know, but evidently Chisaka won someone's recognition as
a man fit to deal with crises, for in 1876, he was sent to restore order after
an uprising in Ibaraki Prefecture, and in July 1877, during the Satsuma
Rebellion, he was named a first lieutenant in the army and appointed a
middle-ranking secretary in the army ministry. His efforts in this last post
earned him a decoration and a pension. After the rebellion was crushed, he
went back to the home ministry to be a secretary again. Although he had
no close *han*-clique connections, Chisaka ingratiated himself with a powerful patron in the central government when he served Minister of the Right
Iwakura Tomomi, the old court noble, as an aide and secretary in 1878.[96]

Named to succeed Kiriyama Junkō in Kanazawa in March 1879, Chisaka
almost immediately proved himself both a persuasive speaker and an astute
political maneuverer. Upon learning that the high-born former chief coun-

cilor of Yonezawa was to be their new governor, several Ishikawa men who had immersed themselves in public affairs resolved to confront Chisaka before he even set foot in the big prefecture, and to take his measure. "If his views differ from ours," they agreed, "we must use our entire strength to drive him away." Endō Hidekage, Tomita Rentarō, Ishikawa Kurō, and Kanaiwa Torakichi met the incoming governor in the vicinity of Lake Biwa and put their questions to him. Chisaka swept them off their feet. Endō's party reported to their friends with a cryptic metaphor, "The scenery as far as we can see is remarkable."[97]

Once in Kanazawa, Chisaka dealt with the problems of succession by cultivating good relations with the several political groups in the city, including members of the Chūkokusha, with whom Kiriyama had had such poisonous relations. In an effort to build up a staff that would be responsive to his lead, Chisaka favored Endō Hidekage and his associates with jobs in the prefectural office. He named some members of the new prefectural assembly to fill important offices, most notably Katō Kō, the first speaker of the assembly, who became Nomi County Chief in 1880 and then Kanazawa Urban District Chief in 1881. In his early days in the governor's mansion, Chisaka welcomed all who might have something to say to him, even inexperienced young students.[98] He demonstrated in his early dealings with the new prefectural assembly that he had a positive attitude toward Western-type representative institutions and thus toward allowing more people to participate in politics. His openness to suggestions, his liberal ideals expressed in public statements, and his willingness to work with local men all won wide popularity for him in his first year as governor.

The glitter faded from the reputation of the man from Yonezawa after he had been in office for a couple of years. In part, this was because anyone in the governor's chair would have been nearly certain to draw heavy criticism during this time of economic difficulty, when inflation was followed by deflation. In part, it was because Chisaka could not translate talk into accomplishment when it came to developing the economy of his prefecture. In part, it was because his Westernized attitudes and his approachability made him seem undignified to conservative elements of the populace. By changing his strategy on appointments to the bureaucracy, Chisaka quickened his own decline in popular esteem. He went outside the pool of local talent for a new police chief for Ishikawa at the beginning of 1882, picking another Yonezawa man. Ishikawa natives in the prefectural office reacted by suspecting that Chisaka might be intending to force them out and to pack the bureaucracy with outsiders. In the same year, Chisaka had a falling out with the prefectural assembly. These conflicts are treated in more detail in the next chapter, but here it should be observed that when local bureaucratic and political opposition to him coalesced, Chisaka took advantage of the "overwhelmingly preponderant powers" of the governorship and called in help from Tokyo. Police reinforcements and a few new key officials were brought in, and the home minister stood behind the Ishikawa governor as he battled back against the threat to his authority.[99] By the time Chisaka left Kanazawa in January 1883, things had settled down considerably. Chisaka Takamasa, still regarded as a capable administrator by his superiors, put in a short stint in the home ministry, then served as governor of Okayama Prefecture for ten years. The Meiji Emperor capped his career by appointing him to the House of Peers.

The fourth governor, Iwamura Takatoshi, exchanged places with Chisaka, coming to Kanazawa from a home ministry position roughly equivalent to bureau chief *(dai shokikan)*.[100] Iwamura came from one of the *han* that had led in the Restoration, and he had been an activist in the imperial cause. Born in Tosa in 1845, he had joined the military forces of the new government immediately after the proclamation of the restoration of imperial rule. In the third month of 1868, Iwamura was granted a reward for meritorious service over "many years" on behalf of the restoration movement, and he was rewarded twice more in the next year for his efforts during the war against Tokugawa bitter-enders in the Northeast. He worked briefly as a steward in the household of Prince Arisugawa, who had commanded Meiji forces in the 1868 campaign. From 1873, Iwamura built a reputation as a good crisis manager, dealing with difficult situations while serving as governor of Saga (the former Hizen domain, one of the few places that had, at first, been given a local man as governor as a special concession by the Meiji authorities), as an aide to Ōkubo during the 1874 negotiations in China, as governor of Ehime Prefecture, and as a home ministry official.

His record made Iwamura Takatoshi a logical choice as the man to deal with the touchy situation that had arisen in Ishikawa under Chisaka. As a subordinate official, he was well known to, and enjoyed the confidence of, the home minister. Iwamura stayed longer in the Kanazawa post than in any other job in his career. His seven years and four months as governor of Ishikawa was twice as long as the tenure of any of his predecessors. Iwamura, like Chisaka, gained greater distinction after leaving the Ishikawa governor's office, later becoming a cabinet minister and a member of the House of Peers.

Coming to Kanazawa in the wake of a local political crisis and in the midst of an economic depression so bad that former samurai wearing crested silk kimono could be seen wandering the streets begging door to door, Iwamura was paid fifty yen a month over the usual governor's salary of ¥250.[101] Ishikawa was considered a problem area again. Quickly the new governor addressed the economic situation, obtaining government loans to avert a bank collapse. In 1884, he called on the Maeda family for assistance, asking them to contribute ¥80,000 to support a foundering bank.[102] This was a daring step for a representative of the central government. The last time Tokyo had asked for Maeda help, at the time of the Satsuma Rebellion, it had been so effective, and the response of former Maeda retainers so warm, that the government became uncomfortable and called it off. In the political arena, Iwamura let there be no doubt about who was boss. By the end of his first year in Kanazawa, he had made nine appointments among the top fifty-five positions that he had power to fill. Only one of the nine appointees was a man from Ishikawa.[103] It was Governor Iwamura, the reader will recall, who called his subordinates before him and made them bark like dogs, rewarding them with morsels of meat that he held out with his chopsticks.[104] A party of Ishikawa prefectural officials had formed to stand up for the interests of local men under Chisaka. It lost its vigor under Iwamura, as its members lost their posts.

Among prefectural assemblymen, the governor found a faction, led by Kawase Kan'ichirō of Kanazawa, willing to follow his lead. Iwamura found the leaders of the Chūkokusha, by this time a defunct organization, ready to help him, and he appointed such former officers of that society as Sugimura Hiromasa, Inagaki Yoshikata, and Ogawa Seita as chiefs of counties or the urban district of Kanazawa.[105] The Three New Laws system facilitated Iwamura's expansion of the governor's powers. He was abetted also by the bad economic conditions that prevailed during his years in Ishikawa Prefecture. Many public-spirited men directed their energies to schemes to improve the local economy. The attention of the recognized leaders of the prefecture was not on politics or on preserving local prerogatives against central authorities' encroachments. Politics was in the doldrums. The governor exploited that fact to govern without difficulty.

The territory that Iwamura Takatoshi governed had the same boundaries as Ishikawa Prefecture has today. In bureaucratic organization, in relations between the prefecture and subprefectural units of government, and in relations between the governor and the prefectural assembly, the process of prefecture-building, which was a very important part of nation-building, was completed during Iwamura's time in office. Basic patterns had been established, and they would endure in practice, even through the changes of 1888 and 1890 when the "local autonomy system" was introduced, until the eve of the Pacific War.

Through the first two decades of the Meiji era, whenever push had come to shove, governors had used their allotted powers to broaden or reinforce central authority. Their strategy in making appointments to office reveals this and can be taken as an index of their power. At times, as under Uchida Masakaze or at first under Chisaka Takamasa, appointments were used to involve locals; the governors intended to elicit sympathetic support for the regime. At other times, as under Kiriyama Junkō and Iwamura Takatoshi, appointments were made without particular regard for the feelings of the local populace; the governors were satisfied to be able to win through intimidation. Bureaucratic appointment could be used as either a carrot or a stick. When they cooperated nicely with the centrally appointed governors, local men were rewarded with official positions that lent them a certain amount of influence and prestige. When they crossed the men sent out by Tokyo, local men found their access to roles in policy-making and policy implementation to be blocked. No one could ever forget that it was in the governor's power to hire, fire, promote, and demote local officials.

In the former big *han* of Kanazawa, enough men sought prefectural, county, or urban district positions that the governor could have as many locals on his staff as he wanted. Many, that is to say, wanted to cooperate. Those who actually were appointed to the new bureaucracy did their jobs competently enough that Ishikawa Prefecture fit snugly into the young Meiji state by the end of the Three New Laws period. No sustained serious challenge to the state system ever emerged.

SIX

The Primacy of Economic Concerns: Ishikawa Activists in the Second Meiji Decade

The decade of the Three New Laws was a time when many of Ishikawa Prefecture's most popular and capable men redirected their energies from national political issues to matters of economic development and their own well-being. Some politically minded men continued to play roles in subnational government, particularly in the prefectural assembly. A few used the new deliberative body as a base for doing battle with higher authorities, and in 1882 the home minister reacted by ordering the Ishikawa Prefectural Assembly dissolved, making it one of the first popularly elected houses in the nation to gain this dubious distinction. The confrontation between high-level officials and the members of the Ishikawa assembly revolved around prefectural fiscal policy, but participants in the fracas brought questions of style and personal morality close to the hub. The system favored the officials in this conflict, and the assemblymen did not find the unifying issue or philosophy, or any other lever of power, that might have evened the balance. When a tough new governor took charge in 1883, the opposition folded. By the mid-1880s, no political resistance worthy of the name was to be found in Ishikawa. It was economic affairs that occupied the ablest men of the region. The politics of the prefecture became insipid.

It was not quite the case that all was completely calm in the onetime million-*koku* domain during the late seventies and eighties. On several occasions, arguments came to blows. But in the middle and later part of the decade, local men squabbled with each other more than with the governor and higher officialdom. Local autonomy hardly seems to have entered the minds of Ishikawa men. Certainly it never became a political principle around which they rallied. Those men who paid attention to public affairs did not object to the structure of subnational government that had been put in place by Tokyo leaders. And so far as the design and implementation of policies within the prefecture were concerned, Ishikawa activists cooperated with or deferred to their governors as often as they opposed them. The men who gained prominence in Ishikawa in the eighties tacitly abjured national power or fame, and therein they differed from their local forerunners of the early and middle 1870s. Former samurai, especially, devoted themselves to business ventures after 1882.

When local notables assigned primacy to economic matters, management of the prefecture and subprefectural units became easier for the governor and his bureaucratic appointees. Governor Iwamura described the job of ruling Ishikawa in the mid-1880s with a disdainful simile. It was, he said, "like kneading dumplings." [1]

This chapter examines the politics of Ishikawa in the decade of the Three New Laws, and also some of the nonpolitical activities of that time. The story of Ishikawa Prefecture provides little support for Ōishi Kaichirōs' thesis that there was strong popular desire for local self-government in these years. Ishikawa yields evidence of men's efforts to succeed in the new Japan through a mixture of new occupations and old dependency relationships, rather than a record of struggle for self-rule.

PREFECTURAL POLITICS

Ōmori Shōichi, a long-time associate of Yamagata Aritomo who became a senior home ministry official and a governor of note, once suggested that the period of the Three New Laws had three phases, which were defined by conditions in the prefectural assemblies:

1. From the first opening of prefectural assemblies in 1879 until around 1880 or 1881 was the period of infancy; legislative meetings were

generally quiet and for the most part ended without incident in the ratification of governor's proposals.

2. From around 1880 or 1881 to around 1884 or 1885, assemblies were dominated by young activists who opposed the government on virtually all issues and who frequently resorted to violent actions.

3. From around 1884 or 1885 until the implementation of the local autonomy system after 1888, prefectural assemblies were mature; members began to "understand the nature of legislatures" and to become accustomed to their proceedings; assemblymen perceived that the best way to promote the public weal was to plan affairs in cooperation with the authorities.[2]

Political activity in Ishikawa Prefecture followed a course similar to that described by Ōmori, although the timing of the phases is a little different. If it were represented graphically, with the years marked at intervals along the axis of abscissas and the level of controversy generated and energy spent marked by points along the axis of ordinates, the line of Ishikawa activity would curve gradually upward from 1879 to 1882; it would spike up and then plummet abruptly during 1882; and from 1883 it would become almost a straight line parallel to the axis of abscissas, with ordinates not far above zero. The figure is suggestive. When the line on the graph becomes almost horizontal, the process of national integration is, effectively, complete.

The prefectural assembly was the institution where the interests of the state, represented by the governor, and the people, represented by the assemblymen, rubbed against each other. When the friction was great, there was conflict. That there was not always much friction reflected both administrators' skill and local men's cooperative spirit.

THE EARLIEST PREFECTURAL ASSEMBLY SESSIONS. The Ishikawa Prefectural Assembly convened for the first time on May 25, 1879. The session should have opened in March, according to the regulations, but the maiden meeting of the assembly was later, setting a precedent that was followed the next year as well. The formal opening ceremony of the Ishikawa Prefectural Assembly took place in the hall of what had been the Kaga *han* school of Confucian studies, the Meirindō. Governor Chisaka addressed the delegates briefly, concluding, "I hope that you will realize the aims that the government had in decentralizing power, and that you will fulfill the great responsibility with which the people have entrusted you." Speaker Katō Kō responded on behalf of the assemblymen that they appreciated the gravity of their responsibility and would work assiduously to discharge it.[3]

Deliberation of the governor's tax bills was the primary business of the assembly. The body remained in session until the end of July, then met again for another month during September and October. A disastrous cholera epidemic, which claimed over 20,000 lives in Kanazawa before it was suppressed, forced the assembly to recess between July 29 and September 13. When the assembly concluded, it had approved ¥387,332 in prefectural spending out of local taxes. The governor had submitted a budget for ¥428,256.[4] The delegates proceeded very carefully, questioning the governor's proposal line by line and offering many amendments. In the end they assented to 90.4 percent of what Chisaka had proposed. The people's representatives made their deepest cuts in outlays for schools and for the prefectural assembly itself—they approved just 43 percent and 61 percent of the amounts the governor had put forward. There was no animosity between assembly and governor in this year, and Chisaka had Kumano report to the home minister that the deliberative body had met and concluded satisfactorily.[5] On the last day that the house convened, Chisaka complimented the members on their hard work and success in meeting their responsibilities.[6]

To the regular session of the second prefectural assembly, which met in May 1880, the governor presented a bill that would have reduced the number of assemblymen from sixty-nine to forty-six. The members turned it down. They "amended" the bill so that seats again totaled sixty-nine, explaining that the area within Ishikawa Prefecture was broader than other prefectures, and that having fewer representatives would give rise to unfair and incorrect decisions.[7] Chisaka's budget bill for fiscal year 1880 was larger than that of the year before, and after making minor modifications, the assembly approved prefectural spending of ¥567,208, an amount 46.8 percent greater than what the first assembly had finally approved. Most of the added expenditure was to go toward police, schools, and encouragement of business; these categories were up by 52 percent, 211 percent, and 64 percent, respectively, over the previous year. To balance the budget, of course, revenues also had to be increased from the 1879 level. Again the spirit of the assembly was cooperative. The elected representatives of the people went along with the authorities' arguments about the need for higher taxes, and raised all three types of local taxes, the land-based levy *(chisowari),* the household tax *(kosūwari),* and the business and other miscellaneous taxes.[8]

In accordance with Article XXI of the Prefectural Assembly Regulations, half of the seats of the assembly had to be put before the electorate in 1880. In July, the Ishikawa members drew lots to determine whose terms should end immediately. On July 20, at the final meeting before the assembly recessed for the election, Kumano Kurō expressed his satisfaction to the delegates. The speaker for this session was Yoneyama Michio of Kanazawa, and he reciprocated Kumano's praise with kind words for Chisaka and Kumano.[9]

Voters chose thirty-four representatives in the summer of 1880. The incumbent won reelection in twenty-two cases. An extraordinary session of the Ishikawa Prefectural Assembly met in the fall. The record of proceedings has been lost, but the session seems to have been uneventful. Kawase Kan'ichirō of Kanazawa was elected speaker, a position he would retain until 1887. Kawase was an officer of the Eishinsha, a society made up mostly of ex-samurai, but his political influence had little connection with that association—most of the Eishinsha's members were unconcerned with prefectural politics just then, being caught up instead in trying to make money. His election was a sign of the continuing dominance of former Kaga samurai in Ishikawa politics, even in years when commoners, especially men of farming and land-owning background, were taking the lead in many other prefectures. Not until 1890 did a former Kaga *han* commoner preside over the Ishikawa Prefectural Assembly.[10] Commoners made up a majority of the assembly, but for a long time they exhibited the traditional deference to their status "betters" when voting for assembly officers. They may simply have been manifesting a deeply ingrained habit in doing so. They may have been recognizing the superior education and experience in governmental affairs of the ex-samurai. Then again, commoner assemblymen who voted for former samurai as speakers may have calculated that as long as the governor and his top assistants in the prefectural bureaucracy were former samurai, the assembly would be most effectively represented in its dealings with officialdom by a speaker whose background was similar to that of the governor and bureaucrats.

Before the assembly met next, in February of 1881, seven counties were taken from Ishikawa and placed in the jurisdiction of the newly created Fukui Prefecture. The number of seats in the Ishikawa Prefectural Assembly was reduced to forty-nine.[11]

CONFLICT BETWEEN ELECTED REPRESENTATIVES AND THE GOVERNOR. When the regular session of the assembly convened in May 1881, Governor Chisaka appeared in the chamber and reminded the delegates of some institutional changes that the Tokyo government had legislated during the past year—changes that were to lead to repercussions in many parts of the nation. Most importantly, pursuant to Council of State Decree Number 48 of 1880, funds would be longer be disbursed from the national exchequer for construction and repair of prefectural office buildings, for prisons, or for public works.[12] The prefecture would have to bear the costs of these out of local taxes. In addition, Chisaka remarked, a sharp rise in prices had occurred. (This was several months before Matsukata became minister of finance and began to enforce deflationary policies.) It was therefore necessary to increase the prefectural budget. The governor asked the assemblymen to deliberate carefully and to approve his proposals. Then he presented a budget for ¥1,311,157. For a smaller territory, he proposed to more than double the amount spent by Ishikawa Prefecture in the previous year.[13] The governor wanted to increase revenues by imposing ¥455,117 in local land tax, nearly twice as much as in fiscal 1881. He did not explicitly remind delegates of a change of which they were keenly aware, that the local levy on property (*chisowari*) had been raised from one-fifth of the national land tax to one-third.

How the assembly reacted to these bills in its deliberations, and what amendments were put before the house, cannot be known in detail, because the proceedings of this 1881 regular session have been scattered. Surviving documents show that the prefecture actually spent ¥683,900 in fiscal 1881, only 52 percent as much as the governor had asked. Clearly the assembly was no longer so accommodating of the governor as it had been a year before.

In this regular session of 1881, several representatives argued that chiefs of counties and urban districts should be chosen by the people, rather than appointed by the government. Led by Iwama Kakuhei of Imizu County, a group of seventeen assemblymen signed a petition dated June 18, 1881, setting forth a principled discussion of the value of having local officials who knew the feelings and customs of their jurisdictions and who could satisfy the people. This was not an expression of sentiment of a single region. The signers were from all over the prefecture, including Kanazawa. They put their petition before the assembly as a motion, seeking formal endorsement. A proposal to submit a similar petition had been put forward and defeated in the assembly of 1879. In the session of June 27, 1881, however, with 78 spectators looking on, the motion for this memorial on the popular election of county and urban district chiefs passed.[14]

Whether the governor or the home minister or any other government figure responded to the Ishikawa petition, we unfortunately cannot tell. Ariizumi Sadao examined thirty-four prefectural assembly histories and found that similar motions were adopted in fourteen assemblies other than Ishikawa's.[15] These motions, which directly advert to the constitution of local government, are good evidence to support Ōishi's contention that there were widespread demands for local autonomy at this time, although it must be recognized that the Iwama petition was exceptional for Ishikawa Prefecture. The effect of these petitions was negligible—the local officials in question continued to be appointed through the rest of the Three New Laws period. Worth remarking, and characteristic of Ishikawa, is that the advocates of popular election did not go on to amplify on principles of local self-government or to sustain a campaign for local voting for county and urban district officers, a fact that weakens Ōishi's argument.[16]

During the 1881 assembly, a split in the membership developed. Assemblymen from Kaga and Noto provinces generally favored spending prefectural funds on office and road construction. Etchū representatives argued that resources should instead be allocated to flood control and irrigation systems. In several other prefectures the same division arose, with members favoring roads or water control according to the geographic characteristics of their home territory.[17] In Ishikawa, where catastrophic floods had hit in the late spring of 1881, the expenses of cleaning up combined with rising commodity prices and the demands of Governor Chisaka for more prefectural spending to produce an inflammable vapor in the political atmosphere.[18]

Chisaka Takamasa understood the hardship imposed on taxpayers by the decision to terminate central government grants to prefectures for public works spending. In January 1882, he submitted a memorial to the home minister asking that national grants be restored.[19] This demonstration of sympathy for the governed neither persuaded Chisaka's superior in Tokyo nor increased his popularity with the people's representatives in Kanazawa.

With his spending plans for the next fiscal year, the governor struck the spark that ignited Ishikawa Prefecture. He proposed to the 1882 assembly that funds be budgeted for a school for specialized legal studies. The assembly rejected the idea, on the grounds that expenditures for public building should be reduced, not raised.[20] Chisaka, not in a compromising mood, resubmitted the school construction proposal without change. Again the assembly voted no. This time they sliced a large sum off the whole public works section of the budget. On May 3, five weeks after the 1882 regular session convened, Assemblyman Minami Hyōkichi of Imizu County rose and introduced a motion for the governor's dismissal.[21] Ōgaki Hyōgi of Ishikawa County spoke in support of Minami's motion, and set the tone for what quickly evolved into an offensive against the top prefectural officer:

> Some time ago, Governor Chisaka had some trees from in front of the prefectural office building transplanted to the garden of his own residence. This is evidence that he has muddled very badly the distinction between public and private property. Moreover the governor has brought from his hometown of Yonezawa in Yamagata Prefecture a woman known as Miss Usami, and has made her his "lady in waiting." Recently he has appointed her as a teacher in the normal school, and she has been commuting to work from his residence. This is, in actuality, using local taxes to keep a mistress. We cannot but demand by all means that such an irresponsible governor be dismissed from office.[22]

The point of attack shifted from excessive spending on public construction to the governor's moral standards. Ōgaki and not a few other assemblymen believed that Chisaka had abused the perquisites of his position. Miss Usami was an easily exploitable issue. Few citizens, Ōgaki must have reckoned, would wittingly tolerate having at the head of a classroom a woman recruited for her extracurricular talents, rather than her educational attainments. The problem of the distinction between public and private was another readily usable bit of ammunition for a Meiji politician. It had become a commonplace analysis of the lately overthrown feudal system that one of its principal evils was that feudal rulers had regarded everything as their own private property. Thus to accuse Chisaka of taking public property for his own was to tar him with the brush of a society that the Japanese had rejected.

Whether because they were upset by Chisaka's behavior or because they abhorred his budget proposal and his insistence on the law school, more than half the assembly members voted for Minami's motion. Speaker Kawase, in accordance with a procedure stipulated in the Prefectural Assembly Regulations, appointed a three-man committee to draft a memorial to the home minister. By this time Governor Chisaka learned what the assembly had done. He promptly prorogued the body and reported to his superiors in Tokyo. Citing the Prefectural Assembly Regulations, he stated that the Ishikawa deliberative chamber had violated Article XXIX:

> Members shall have the right to give free expression of their views in debate; provided that this freedom shall not be deemed to make it permissible for a member to advert to the character of individuals whether in praise or blame.[23]

Not easily stilled, the assembly members countered by demanding an explanation of Chisaka's action from one of his highest-ranking aides. The aide stonewalled and said nothing. Chisaka's attackers repeated their charge of irresponsibility and added illegality to it.[24] The police intervened, jailing Ōgaki on suspicion of contempt of a government officer (*kanri bujoku*, not a trivial offense). The police chief, however, not wanting the outspoken assemblyman to become a symbol of the authorities' oppressiveness, dismissed the charge and released Ōgaki.

Home Minister Yamada Akiyoshi reacted to the turmoil by ordering the Ishikawa Prefectural Assembly dissolved on May 16, 1882. In its fourth year of existence, after harmonious beginnings, the Ishikawa deliberative chamber had suddenly become a trouble spot. Central government leaders were particularly sensitive about the goings-on in prefectural assemblies at this time, and Yamada and his fellow ministers were aware that in Fukushima in this same month of May, matters were coming to a head between Governor Mishima Michitsune and the prefectural assembly.[25] Those troubles turned out to be the prelude to the "Fukushima incident," which ended with the imprisonment of some of the most prominent people's rights activists and the evisceration of the Liberal Party in November. Minister of the Right Iwakura Tomomi, one of the most powerful men in Tokyo, began to have serious misgivings about the very existence of prefectural assemblies. By the end of 1882, in fact, Iwakura was writing that the assemblies should be prorogued and replaced by people's advisory councils.[26] And he was not alone in feeling critical of the prefectural assemblies. Fukuzawa Yukichi, the champion of "enlightenment" thought in early Meiji Japan, in 1882 wrote scornfully of the prefectural deliberative bodies that they cost too much to maintain and that the only thing they were good at was slowing down administration.[27]

Such criticisms of the prefectural assemblies might have somewhat diminished these bodies' prestige, but they did not change the law. Article XXXV of the Prefectural Assembly Regulations was still in force, requiring that after the dissolution of an assembly, an election for members of a new assembly must be held within ninety days.[28] In conformity with this, an election was held in Ishikawa Prefecture in June 1882.

The new assembly met for the first time on July 27, and it soon became obvious that opinions were almost unchanged from twelve weeks earlier.[29] This assembly was no more willing to approve the governor's budget requests than the previous one had been, and innuendoes about Chisaka's private affairs continued to circulate. The session had to be prolonged four times before it completed its business, and did not conclude until late December. Precisely how much Chisaka asked to spend out of local taxes is not known. The figures on actual spending in the fiscal year begun in July 1882 total ¥738,600, up by 8 percent over the year earlier. Probably the governor had asked for more.

When the question of expenditures for the girls' normal school was before the house, Inagaki Shimesu, another delegate from Imizu, who had been pounding away at Chisaka in the pages of a Liberal Party journal that he published in Kanazawa, seized the opportunity to reintroduce the morality issue. He scored the governor for paying a high salary to "someone's beloved mistress" and for demanding excessive funds for the school because of this salary. Speaker Kawase admonished Inagaki to retract this statement, but the assemblyman refused to do so. The night of September 8, Inagaki was arrested. The next day, Kawase asked prefectural officials for an explanation of what had happened. He was informed in writing that Inagaki had been arrested "in the incident of his having insulted the office of the governor of Ishikawa Prefecture." Assembly members upon hearing this sent an inquiry to the home minister, and seven representatives protested to the prefecture that Inagaki's speech, having been made within the assembly chamber, was privileged. Prefectural authorities rejected the protest, contending that Inagaki's speech had not been "within the limits of question and answer" (that is, it had not been strictly on point in the discussion of girls' normal school spending, and it had not been within the boundaries of debate permitted by the regulations). Inagaki never returned to the Ishikawa Prefectural Assembly. In October a Kanazawa criminal court found him guilty of insulting the office of the governor and sentenced him to five months in prison and a fine of ¥30. An appeal failed.[30]

The assembly went on without Inagaki, concluding finally on December 22. Members submitted a very long petition to the government requesting that the expense of controlling the Tedori, Jōganji, Shō, and Kurobe rivers be returned to the national budget.[31] Central government and imperial household grants had been given to the prefecture, in fact, after floods had done enormous damage in 1881. It does not appear that this 1882 memorial received any response. Successful or not, the entreaty illustrates the concerns of the representatives from the Etchū districts, concerns not shared so strongly by their counterparts from Kaga and Noto. Outside the assembly, Chisaka called in police reinforcements in the latter part of 1882, and order prevailed in the final months before he left Kanazawa in January 1883.

What might have developed into a politics of anti-authoritarianism in Ishikawa in 1882 divaricated into a futile ad hominem attack on the governor. No one raised questions about the fundamental forms of local governance, about the System of the Three New Laws. Why this was so had to do with the degree of sophistication—or lack of it—in the arts of political maneuver of the actors in this drama, and also with the backgrounds and present concerns of those actors. A closer look at some Ishikawa activists of the second Meiji decade will give us a better sense of the dynamics of the Three New Laws system in operation.

EX-SAMURAI IN POLITICS AND IN NON-POLITICAL VENTURES

THE SEIGISHA. The Chūkokusha and the Sankōji faction, which had dominated the Ishikawa political scene in the years from 1874 to 1878, were in eclipse by the time Governor Kiriyama Junkō retired, at his own request, in February 1879. Experienced Kanazawa leaders like Sugimura Hiromasa, Hasegawa Jun'ya, and Ōtsuka Shirō did not disappear forever, but they retired from center stage for a while, leaving the way clear for different men to make an impression on local affairs. These new men lacked experience, but they were in a position to benefit from the need of a new governor to build support for himself. Chisaka Takamasa had traveled to Europe, and English and French ideals had impressed him. In the early part of his tenure, at least, he tried to get to know the people by opening up the governor's office and making it known that he would be happy to talk to just about anybody. Only later did he run afoul of local men's moral sensibilities and sense of priority about policy.

Kyushu was the source of inspiration for former samurai of Kanazawa in the late seventies, as it had been earlier in the decade. This time it was Fukuoka, rather than Satsuma, and the object of admiration was a political society, not an individual hero. A young Kanazawa man named Seki Tokinobu took a trip during which he stopped in Fukuoka and was deeply struck by the ideals of the Kōyōsha, or Facing the Sun Society.[32] Upon his return home, Seki spoke ardently of the need for reform in Japan, and early in 1879, he gathered together some of his friends and formed a group which later historians have characterized as "closely resembling a pure political party,"[33] though it would never sponsor candidates for elective office. Like the Chūkokusha, this group turned to the Chinese classics for a name, adopting a phrase from the *Book of Changes;* they called themselves the Essential Righteousness Society (Seigisha).[34]

Seigisha members transcended traditional status-group boundaries by inviting some of the rising local leaders from the provinces of Etchū and Echizen to meet with them in Kanazawa to discuss affairs of state. Men of commoner birth such as Inagaki Shimesu of Etchū and Sugita Teiichi of Echizen shared with Seigisha members an enthusiasm for the doctrines of the emergent movement for liberty and people's rights. The Seigisha became the first group in the big prefecture to espouse the cause of a national assembly. The Chūkokusha had never gone so far, nor had Shimada Ichirō's band of hotheads.[35] One of the founders of the Seigisha, Kanaiwa Torakichi, had been on hand in Osaka in September 1878 when Itagaki Taisuke convened a national meeting to revive the Aikokusha, and in April 1880, when 104 representatives of political groups in twenty-four prefectures met in Osaka to decide how to present to the throne a petition requesting the opening of a national assembly, Seigisha members Takashima Shinjirō and Yoshida Kizashi were among the delegates.[36]

Endorsement of people's rights and the cause of a national legislature failed to bring success to the Seigisha, however. Its membership remained small. Possibly its identity was not clearly established in the eyes of contemporaries, for it did not take a stance wholly for or wholly against the central government or the prefectural appointees of that central government. Leaders such as Inagaki and Sugita were more consistent in their opposition, and they enjoyed greater popularity than the Seigisha leaders. Kanaiwa left the Seigisha to become an official not long after he returned from the Aikokusha gathering in Osaka. He found Governor Chisaka congenial and cooperated with him. Other Seigisha members followed Kanaiwa's example.[37]

The Seigisha advocated opening a national assembly, but did little in the way of collecting signatures on petitions, as was done elsewhere in the country.[38] Rather Seigisha members took a tack that brought repression down upon themselves, and probably damaged the welfare of the movement for a national assembly in Ishikawa. After they came home from the 1880 Osaka meeting, Yoshida Kizashi and Takashima Shinjirō decided to call weekly assemblies where the speakers would discuss political affairs. On several Sundays, orators used these meetings to call for representation at the national level. Inevitably, the police took an interest in these gatherings, and constables were dispatched to determine whether violations of the 1875 regulations on speech (*zanbōritsu*) might be occurring. Inevitably, there were words that the police found harmful to peace and order. Takashima's speeches were perceived to be especially threatening.[39]

The Kanazawa chief of police attended one of the Sunday meetings in June and ordered that the speeches cease. Speakers Furuya Jiromatsu and Susaki Ren refused, and the audience began to raise a hubbub. The chief drew his sword to impress his authority upon the assembly, but this merely excited wilder emotions. A bystander was unfortunate enough to get in the way of the blade and suffer a cut, whereupon a melee broke out. Several people were injured, both policemen and onlookers, and the chief himself was badly beaten up. Afterwards, Furuya and Susaki were jailed for inciting a riot.

Although more political speech meetings were held, they did not result in a significant increase in the numbers of Kanazawa men who supported establishment of a national diet. Conflicts among the leaders of the Seigisha eventuated in its breakup late in 1881, with some members thereafter devoting themselves to education, some to business affairs, and one, Furuya Toratarō, joining the household service of Marquis Maeda in Tokyo.[40] Efforts by former Seigisha members to found a school came to naught in 1882, and a reunion of several leaders of the society in 1885 ended in their being incarcerated for beating up a police spy.[41] The Seigisha faded away without making a lasting mark on local or national politics.

THE EISHINSHA. Another political society born about the same time as the Seigisha enjoyed a more vigorous life and left a deeper imprint in the history of Ishikawa Prefecture. Early in 1880, several discussion groups coalesced into an association that the members named, in a learned reference to the book of Mencius, the Society of Filling and Advancing (Eishinsha).[42] Although the phrase *eishin* derived from the Confucian Canon, and thereby reveals that Kanazawa men continued to look to the Great Tradition for inspiration, the name connoted forward movement and progress.[43]

The Eishinsha published a prospectus of its views in April 1880.[44] This document began with a statement of concern about the readiness of Japan to deal with an emergency that concluded, "National preparedness consists in the harmonious cooperation of all the people of the nation," and it was characteristic of the Eishinsha to make the nation, not localities or the family or the individual, the transcendent object of value. This sentiment and this language might have been inherited unadulterated from the Chūkokusha. But where the Chūkokusha had spoken generally about challenges that Japan faced, the Eishinsha identified an enemy, and did so in pugnacious and xenophobic tones. "Look at those insatiable jackals, the blue-eyed, red-haired dogs polishing their sharp teeth and stretching their hideous lips," the Eishinsha prospectus inveighed, spreading out the inventory of stock unflattering images for Westerners. "Have they not always desired to seize and gobble up weak and small nations?" In a world dominated by such people, might is all that matters: "Small and weak countries, even if they cultivate wisdom and store up their strengths, cannot escape the plunder and invasion of big countries." Lamentably,

> when we reflect upon the present situation of our imperial nation, [we see that] people's minds are scattered and do not come together, and their spirits have decayed and do not flourish. Although there are some men who deplore this, they found parties (*tō*) and fight among themselves. The first party excludes the second and calls its members strong-armed wild boars. The second party casts an eye at the first and calls its members glib purveyors of empty theories. Thus they prattle and they prate, until they end up placing their own personal desires and hopes for fame ahead of the interests of our Empire of Great Japan.

No man of spirit (*shishi*) could stand silent and idle in this situation, of course, and Eishinsha members saw themselves as men of spirit. "Desiring to unite the minds of the people of the Empire of Great Japan, we will take the first steps in Ishikawa Prefecture," they pledged, "and gradually we will reach into all the provinces of the Hokuriku region, and then, going on, we will reach all provinces of the nation."

Devotion to the emperor went along with nationalism in the thinking of the Eishinsha, just as it had for the Chūkokusha and the men around Shimada Ichirō. The 1880 manifesto proclaimed, "Our aim is to assist our august and sage emperor, to expand the power of our nation, to give rise to national prosperity, and to increase the welfare of the people."

Along with dedication to the emperor and a desire to make their country powerful and rich, the Eishinsha espoused the notion that all men were equal. Almost surely this idea had been learned when members of the society, like other Japanese intellectuals, were eagerly studying liberal Western political thought in the 1870s; the idea of social equality had hardly been widespread in the Confucian literature or in the social system to which Japanese had been accustomed for centuries. At the birth of their organization, the founders endorsed the ideal of a society in which status distinctions counted for nothing. The Eishinsha, they wrote, was for all like-minded men of spirit, "without question as to whether they be samurai or peasant, artisan or merchant." In the event, as we shall see, this ideal was less important than past identifications, and the association evolved into another of the many organizations of ex-samurai in Meiji Japan. It became, indeed, an organization for which ties of mutual obligation between former lord and former vassal were enduringly powerful.

Three of the four Kanazawa delegates in the first prefectural assembly were prominent in this association: Endō Hidekage, Kawase Kan'ichirō, and Yasuda Kōsha.[45] As an organization, however, the Eishinsha was not energized by concern for local politics. To the extent the society engaged in political matters, the focus was on the nation. Rather quickly after its formation, the Eishinsha turned to economic matters, and became a vehicle for coordinating business ventures to benefit former retainers of the Maeda. By the end of 1880, Endō and Yasuda had resigned from the prefectural assembly and been replaced by men who were not affiliated with the Eishinsha.[46] A few men who held bureaucratic office in Ishikawa Prefecture or in the urban district of Kanazawa were secret members of the Eishinsha, and were accorded the dignity of being designated "nonmember councilors" (*ingai hyōgiin*). As officials, they were constrained from open membership in what was at least ostensibly a political society, but the fact that they could simultaneously be bureaucrats and honored members of the society illustrates that Eishinsha men saw no contradiction between serving the system of The Three New Laws and participating in an organization that criticized the drift of national policy.

NON-SAMURAI IN THE POLITICAL AFFAIRS OF ISHIKAWA PREFECTURE

During the first years of the Three New Laws period, men of non-samurai background began to rise to prominence and influence. They offered an alternative vision and a different style from the Kanazawa-based groups made up of former Maeda vassals. Two of these non-samurai built strong local organizations and eventually won greater national recognition than any of the leaders of the Seigisha or Eishinsha.

SUGITA TEIICHI OF SAKAI. Sugita Teiichi was born into one of the wealthiest peasant families of Sakai County, in what was then part of the Matsudaira domain and is today part of Fukui Prefecture, in 1851.[47] His family could afford a good education for him, and he studied in Osaka, Yokohama, and Tokyo. After early training in Chinese studies, he took up English and German. In his mid-twenties, he put his literary skills to work as a staff member of a Tokyo journal called the *Hyōron Shinbun,* which specialized in severe criticism of the government and advocacy of people's rights. This paper first appeared in March 1875, and had been issued 109 times by July 1876, when government leaders decided they had seen too much of it. Invoking the Press Law and the Sedition Law of 1875, officials ordered the paper to stop publication. Sugita and some other writers resisted and were rewarded with jail sentences.

Six months in prison increased Sugita's resolve to work for liberal principles. Released by the time the Satsuma Rebellion broke out, he travelled around the country talking politics. Eventually he crossed the Inland Sea and spent some time in Kōchi, where he became acquainted with the leaders of the people's rights movement. When Itagaki Taisuke revived the Aikokusha in 1878, Sugita was present.

After the Aikokusha meeting in Osaka, Sugita returned to his home, which now was in Ishikawa Prefecture, and threw himself into the movement to reduce the land tax, in which his father was also active. To promote the progressive ideals he had learned in the big cities, he founded a school and a political society in Sakai. Undaunted by his experience in jail, he began to voice criticism of officials publicly. He was arrested and imprisoned again, but he had already made a name for himself as a local leader. His political organization, the Jigōsha, went on growing during his confinement, and when he was released in 1880, it had 113 members. Upon being freed, he took up where he had left off. He gained national prominence in the movement for the establishment of a national assembly, and he and his associates joined the Liberal Party when it was formed in 1881.

Sugita's society, renamed the Tenshinsha and then later the Nan'etsu Jiyūtō, was made up exclusively of commoners. Other leaders came from wealthy peasant backgrounds like his. With this composition, the organization was fairly typical of the second phase of the people's rights movement, "wealthy peasant people's rights," which followed a period in which ex-samurai groups such as the Risshisha in Kōchi and the Chūkokusha in Kanazawa had dominated.[48] Personally engaged in farming and land management, leaders of the second phase made land tax reduction one of their primary objectives. Sugita was closer, in origins and orientation, to the commoner Liberal Party leader Kōno Hironaka of Fukushima than he was to Itagaki.

The Sakai-based political society nettled Chisaka Takamasa at a time when the governor was under assault from several quarters. It seems credible that the creation of Fukui Prefecture in 1881 was in part an attempt to tighten the government's grip on that area, and to make sure that groups like Sugita's did not get too far out of line, as—in the eyes of officials such as Chisaka—they tended to when Ishikawa was the biggest prefecture and its governor had many other problems to worry about.

Sugita went on to have an illustrious career in and out of Fukui Prefecture after 1881. In the mid-eighties he traveled, staying for some time in China, the United States, and England. Back home in 1889 he was elected to the Fukui Prefectural Assembly, which chose him as speaker. The next year local voters sent him to Tokyo as a member of the first House of Representatives; in all he was elected to the Diet nine times.[49] He served as Governor of Hokkaidō, was instrumental in the formation of the great political party, the Seiyūkai, and topping off his public service, was directly appointed to the House of Peers by the emperor in 1911.

Politically prominent until his death in 1929, Sugita was probably without peer in the prefecture where he had begun as political organizer, Ishikawa. It may be natural to wonder why more people did not follow his lead before the 1881 partition of the prefecture, and why no organization similar to his made much headway in Kanazawa and the surrounding area. Plausibly, the explanation lies in social status and the traditionalism of the territory that had been Kaga *han*. Possibly no former peasant like Sugita could command a very big following in an area with such a large population of former samurai. If there had been no alternative in the Ishikawa political arena, if no ex-samurai had come forward with plans or with organized backing, some commoner might possibly have gained a following. But with the Eishinsha and other groups of quondam warrior-bureaucrats on the scene, the commoners of Ishikawa might have been too deferential to attempt to assert themselves in politics. When they did enter politics in such bodies as the prefectural assembly and town and village assemblies, Ishikawa commoners contented themselves—except in the instance of the governor and his female friend—with advocating modest goals by unflamboyant methods.[50]

INAGAKI SHIMESU OF IMIZU. The other leader of non-samurai background who particularly stood out in the prefectural politics of the early years of The Three New Laws had been born the eldest son of a wealthy peasant (*gōnō*) in Imizu County in 1849. For generations his family had been large landholders. Inagaki Shimesu received the kind of education in Chinese studies that was common for samurai during the Tokugawa era but rare for peasants, except the highest stratum of the peasant class. Also unusual for a peasant, he trained in the martial arts, and before the Restoration served as a military guard in a magistrate's office (*bugyōsho*). The lord of the domain recognized this service in a citation.[51]

Inagaki took up the cause of people's rights in the late seventies. In 1880 he founded a political society, the Society for Establishing the North (Hokuritsusha, "north" in this case referring to the region of Japan of which Ishikawa Prefecture is part). Later that year he collected 505 signatures on one of the many petitions for the opening of a national assembly that people's rights activists presented to the government.[52] At the end of November 1880, his was the first of four names on a memorial to the throne entreating the emperor to establish a national assembly; the four identified themselves as "general representatives of 4,079 people of the province of Etchū."[53] When the Liberal Party was organized in 1881, Inagaki joined. He built a base of support in his home district and was elected to the prefectural assembly in 1881 and reelected in 1882. In May 1882, he was selected as a member of the permanent council (*jōchi iin*) of the prefectural assembly. In 1882 and 1883 he employed the literary talents that he had honed in his youthful Chinese studies as one of the principal writers for the Kanazawa journal of the Liberal Party, the *Jiyū Shinshi,* of which he also served as publisher.

It was in the conflict with Governor Chisaka in 1882 that Inagaki gained fame as a fiery opponent of high-handed authoritarianism. As we have seen, so heatedly did the delegate from Imizu argue the case against the governor that the police finally charged him with the crime of insulting an official (*kanri bujoku*) and put him in jail. As it turned out, this clash resulted in his retirement from elective politics for some years. When Toyama was separated from Ishikawa in 1883, Inagaki's home was in the new prefecture, but he did not stand for election to its assembly. He turned his attention instead to Japan's external situation and became one of the contrivers of a scheme to force change in Korea.

With radicals in the Liberal Party like Ōi Kentarō, Inagaki planned in 1885 to go to Korea, raise troops, establish a constitutional form of government, and set up Korea as an independent state, free from its old subordination to China. Word of this wildly ambitious plot leaked to Japanese government authorities, who were not pleased. Police were detailed to round up the conspirators before any of them succeeded in crossing over to the continent. Inagaki was one of 139 men arrested in Osaka and Nagasaki, and, identified as a ringleader, he was one of thirty-one sentenced to prison terms. He remained behind bars until the general amnesty of 1890, proclaimed at the time the Meiji constitution took effect.

Inagaki made a comeback in elective politics in the 1890s. He was sent to the Diet three times by the voters of the third district of Toyama, and like Sugita, he became a member of the Seiyūkai when it was founded.[54] He died in 1902, on the eve of the general election, shortly after delivering a campaign speech for another candidate. Though he had accumulated fewer honors than the longer-lived Sugita Teiichi, Inagaki had probably been more effective than most of the ex-samurai leaders of Ishikawa in gaining recognition and support for the causes in which he believed. He made his name by adopting the organizing tactics and the stance of aggressive opposition to the government that characterized the people's rights movement in the early 1880s. Those tactics and that radical stance might have been uncomfortable for former Kaga samurai. Inagaki became neither a leader whom they would follow nor a model for their political activism.

In one important way, however, Inagaki was like the Kanazawa area activists who came from samurai families. For most of his career, Inagaki's focus was on national affairs. He did believe in broadening popular participation, and he did take a prominent part in the movement to get county

officials elected in the early 1880s, but he does not appear to have been
deeply and consistently concerned with principles of local self-government.
When he rose to oppose authority during the 1882 confrontation with Chisaka, he personalized the issues. More important than their opposition to
individual governors and those governors' views, the fact of participation by
men like Inagaki as assemblymen working within the system of the Three
New Laws effectively facilitated the establishment of a firmer centralized
control over all Japan. As a delegate and as a member of the permanent
council in the Ishikawa Prefectural Assembly, Inagaki Shimesu became a
part of the structure. He willingly complied with the new local government system.

DISREGARD OF THE STRICTLY POLITICAL AND DISAGREEMENT OVER ECONOMIC ISSUES

The desire for well-being was for many people a more powerful spur to
action than concern about the welfare of the nation or about the form being
taken by new institutions. Intramural conflicts over economic development
plans occupied Ishikawa men most of the time for the next several years.
This diversion of energies to economic matters surely had an impact on
politics within the prefecture, making it easier for appointees of the central
government to do what they wanted. That no local autonomy movement
sprouted up in the prefecture may be connected to the primacy of economic
concerns, though there is no certainty that very many residents of Ishikawa
would have cared deeply about local autonomy anyway.

Eishinsha members wanted to stimulate the regional economy. The first
inclination of men like Endō Hidekage was to start up and manage enterprises located in Ishikawa. They seem not to have considered that they
might have improved their chances of quick success if they invested some-
where with more favorable communications and transportation and better
access to other markets inside and outside Japan. They wanted to put local
people—especially ex-samurai—to work.

One of their ideas was to reclaim lands in the Ōsawano area along the
Jōganji River, directly south of Toyama, and at the same time to undertake
coal-mining operations in the mountains of Niikawa County. These plans
were ambitious beyond the means of the society. Eishinsha leaders realized

that they required external financing. They decided to look for a patron. Perhaps Endō and his associates had been discouraged by the dismal record of the Kaigyōsha, the economic arm of the Chūkokusha, which had been created as a joint-stock company. They did not even attempt to raise capital by issuing stock. Before a backer for the reclamation and mining scheme could be found, in any event, a divisive struggle broke out, for it happened that the Eishinsha's choice of a project was opposed by other leaders in the prefecture.

TURNING TO THE FORMER LORD OF THE DOMAIN. Right after the formation of the Eishinsha, Endō appointed a nine-man delegation to go to Tokyo to appeal to the Maeda family for funding for the Ōsawano-Niikawa plan. The Eishinsha asked the former lord of Kaga for ¥300,000. The Maeda household administration took the request under advisement, neither rejecting it out of hand nor handing over the money.

For the Maeda establishment, the heart of the matter was the sad condition of their erstwhile band of retainers. The Maeda determined to do something to promote employment of former samurai (shizoku jusan), and one of the most interesting stories of the succeeding decade is that of the relationship between onetime lords and retainers.[55] Of course the Maeda and other former daimyo were under no legal obligation at all to the ex-samurai, and conversely the former samurai owed nothing legally to the old lords. In their appeal to their old liege, the Eishinsha of Kanazawa showed its true colors. Despite the claims of its prospectus that it intended to unite all like-minded men regardless of social status, the Eishinsha was an organization of former samurai, for former samurai. All of the economic ventures promoted by the society in succeeding years had the express purpose of aiding former Kaga samurai.

Rivals to the Eishinsha appeared within the Kanazawa samurai class just as Endō and his associates hit upon the Ōsawano development plan. With the advice of Katō Kō, who had vacated his seat in the prefectural assembly in 1880 to accept Chisaka Takamasa's appointment as Nomi County Chief, Hikida Naoichi and others advocated linking the fate of Kanazawa ex-samurai with the building of a railroad, rather than land development and mining. Hikida's group also hit upon the idea of appealing for a grant from their old lord and in fact placed a proposal before the Maeda household in

Tokyo a few days before the Eishinsha group was able to lay out its plans for spending Maeda money.

The railroad-construction proposal looked attractive to the managers of the Maeda fortune, much as railways had appealed greatly to wealthy investors in England during the "railway manias" of the 1830s and 1840s. The Maeda were millionaires several times over. How rich they were in 1880, we do not know exactly, but almost certainly they were among the handful of richest families in Japan, a position they maintained throughout—and beyond—the Meiji era.[56] Fortunately for their heirs and for their former vassals, the members of the Maeda family in 1880 were not disposed to squander their patrimony in luxurious living. They lived fairly modestly, and husbanded their money. Railways probably looked good to them for two reasons. Almost nothing could have stood more plainly as a symbol of modern economic activity than a railroad, and the Maeda were as anxious as anyone else to promote economic modernization in the region that their ancestors had ruled for almost three centuries. The second reason why a railway might have interested the Maeda was that the returns on investment in a successful railroad business tended to be high—at least they had been in Europe.[57] Railway construction was costly, but the dividends might be handsome.

Presented with conflicting proposals by their former vassals, the Maeda preferred to initiate a process of mediation, rather than to make a decision that would favor one faction over the other. Kitagawa Inosaku, once a top-echelon *han* official and in 1880 a steward in his old lord's household, came down to Kanazawa from Tokyo in August of that year. He carried with him a message from the next-to-last daimyo, Maeda Nariyasu, and his grandson Toshitsugu. (Yoshiyasu, the last daimyo, had succumbed in 1874 to the consumption that had ailed him since the late 1860s, and Toshitsugu was now the head of the family.) Kitagawa brought together a council of thirty men, including some who had risen to prominence in the Chūkokusha, some from the Seigisha, some from the Eishinsha, and some, such as Hikida, who had recently emerged as proponents of railroad construction. In what may have been a demonstration of the assimilation of Western political ideas, the thirty members of this council were chosen in an election, with every 300 ex-samurai households selecting one delegate.[58] In a demonstration that the Maeda were still the patrons in this situation, the council was called into session in a residence belonging to the former lords, and the message from Nariyasu and Toshitsugu, addressed to all the former samurai of Kaga *han,* was presented to the delegates. The document makes obvious that the bonds of centuries had not melted away in the few years since the abolition of feudalism. Very much in the style of wise Confucian rulers, Nariyasu and Toshitsugu lectured the men of Kanazawa. But the content of the message was not entirely traditional:

We regret deeply to hear that the livelihood of our old retainers is daily growing more restricted, and that [some] families have been ruined. [Here] we offer our humble opinions [on the situation]. It is the way of the world that each man should carry on his own occupation and manage his own affairs. Thereby each aids the nation in its economic affairs. Thus those who have learning take up professions in which their learning is useful, those who have skills practice occupations in which their skills are useful, the peasants till the fields and the artisans manufacture their wares, merchants deal in the goods that people want, and those who have neither skills nor capital offer their labor for hire. Though each might differ in his means, none is unable to provide for himself. This is the way men have always dealt with [the problem of] human existence, and it also expresses the duty which men have to serve their state. Now the former samurai are the upper class of our society; they possess government certificates granted to them by the emperor in commutation of their old stipends. There is no disputing that they are in charge of their own financial affairs. It is because of their backgrounds that the former samurai will serve the state, and herein they properly differ from the common people. Yet generally [former samurai] have continued to practice traditional usages, and have hesitated to make sudden changes in their occupations. They spend their time idly, they do little more than sit and eat, and they find nothing at all strange [about their inactivity]. Is this not something to be ashamed of? Although our sympathy goes out to those of our former retainers who have not been able to find employment, still it is difficult to maintain that there are not some who are not merely steeped in bad old habits. Fortunately, today there is yet some capital remaining from the imperial grants [made in commutation of stipends]. If you combine these remaining funds and put them to use, we believe that you will be able to rescue yourselves from dire straits. At present the imports and exports of our nation are in imbalance, and we believe the national power is declining day by day. At such a time, what Japanese does not lament this and seek to redress it? What we hope for is that before all the money from the imperial grants is used up, every man will arouse his spirit and bestir himself, and immediately get started on the way to independence. Those who have funds should put them forward. Those who have no funds should contribute their labor. Together in a cooperative spirit you should start enterprises and settle upon how you want them to operate. In a large sense you will hope to double the population of every family. If you do so, you will be exerting yourselves both in the way men have always dealt with human existence and in the duty that you owe to the nation.[59]

Nariyasu and Toshitsugu favored their old dependents with a bit more moral exhortation in this message before they made known what everyone wanted to hear: that they intended to "contribute a little money to assist you in small part with the funds for starting new enterprises."

Kitagawa left it to the council to determine to what use the Maeda contribution—and such local capital as might be raised—should be put. Council members were in a paradoxical position. Encouraged by their old lord to become independent, they were still dependent on the Maeda purse if they wished to raise enough funds to have a good chance of getting a sustainable enterprise underway. Formally constituted as the Association for Starting Enterprise (Kigyōkai), the council was given bylaws by the Maeda house. The first of these defined the council's function: "It shall choose enterprises and establish responsible management of them for the sake of all the former samurai of the old Kanazawa domain, using the money [given] in aid [by the Maeda family] and other funds. The council shall determine all matters pertaining to the founding of new enterprises, such as the scope of business and regulations for the receipt and disbursement of funds."[60] Another article provided for cooperation with prefectural authorities in cases that might require official sanction for some action of the Association. And the Maeda household retained a veto power: "If the patron (*shikin hojosha*) does not approve of a decision of the council, it will not be implemented."

Internecine strife among the onetime Maeda retainers ceased for a time while the Kigyōkai deliberated. Opposing factions channeled their efforts into winning the support of the Association council. Finally the railway supporters persuaded some council members and Chūkokusha leaders Sugimura Hiromasa and Obata Zōji, who still pulled considerable weight in Kanazawa circles, that their way was the most promising. Over a year after Kitagawa had set the Maeda mediation effort in motion, in September

1881, the Maeda house announced the creation of the Northeast Railway (Tōhoku Tetsudō) and the simultaneous dissolution of the Kigyōkai.

The losers refused to accept defeat gracefully. Endō and his Eishinsha associates claimed that the decision in favor of a railway was the work of the Maeda household establishment alone, acting "oppressively and despotically." After setting up the Kigyōkai and fixing rules for decision making, they charged, the Maeda house had ignored the due process of the formal Kigyōkai meetings. Tempers flared in Kanazawa just as Marquis Maeda Toshitsugu and the former daimyo of Daishōji, Count Maeda Toshika, arrived in town to solicit investments to add to their own contribution of capital for the new railway company.[61] Despite the willingness of their former retainers to turn to the Maeda for assistance in time of need, the presence of Toshitsugu and Toshika did not have the same restraining effect on behavior in the old castle town as it might have some years earlier. The controversy continued.

Moving ahead regardless of the lack of unanimity among their old vassals, the Maeda sought stock investors among ex-samurai, and they also used their upper-class connections to raise funds from other rich families. The railroad they planned was to run from Yanagase, near Lake Biwa, to Toyama, and it was to have a branch line connecting Nagahama with Yokkaichi. These lines, they expected, would boost the economies of several areas besides Kanazawa, and this prospect drew the interest of some well-born men with long-time involvement in those areas. The heads of the former daimyo families of Fukui, Daishōji, Ōno, Fuchū, Katsuyama, Maruoka, and Sabae, all contributed, as did the chief abbot of the Ōtani sect of the Temple of the Original Vow. Maeda Toshitsugu's investment of ¥222,000 made him the biggest single stakeholder. Families that had been among the highest-ranking in the Maeda retinue before the Restoration— quite wealthy in their own right—bought shares also, and within a year, other investors had injected an amount greater than Toshitsugu's.[62]

Even as buyers were being sought for the railway stock, Endō's party continued their attack on the Maeda household administration, and at length, to placate the dissidents, one of the Maeda household stewards, Teranishi Seiki, took responsibility for the way the decision process had been conducted and resigned his post. Two other ex-retainers joined the

Maeda family administration after Teranishi left; one of them was Katō Kō, who had urged trains on Hikida Naoichi in the first place. The Eishinsha gained little by Teranishi's ouster.

Most of the former samurai of Kanazawa stood behind the decision of their old lord to build a railroad, even if they did not agree with how it had been arrived at. Endō, Hirose Senma, and other Eishinsha activists experienced an erosion of popularity, and Sugimura Hiromasa and a few other onetime Chūkokusha notables regained some of their prominence. The plan to develop the Ōsawano area was abandoned.

It is a sad irony that the Northeast Railway was never built. Sundry delays followed two years of planning, and eventually the other old lords pulled out. The whole venture had to be written off as a loss.[63] Meanwhile strife between the more volatile members of the Eishinsha—poor losers still—and the group led by Hikida and Sugimura broke out once more, culminating in a violent incident in which Hikida's front teeth were knocked out with an iron pipe. Order was restored only when the Maeda intervened again, bringing together neutral officials from the prefectural office, the police, and the Kanazawa Urban District Office to arbitrate between the railway advocates and the Eishinsha. Finally, a settlement satisfactory to both sides was reached. The railway construction operation and the business of aiding former samurai would henceforth be completely separate. Eishinsha members would sit on the Kigyōkai council and operate enterprises to benefit samurai, and the railway faction would work toward its goal outside the Kigyōkai. The two sides would leave each other alone. To the new Kigyōkai, the Maeda family gave a grant of ¥100,000.[64]

In all this debate about how best to promote economic progress along the coast of the Japan Sea, both the Eishinsha and its rivals turned away from politics. They ignored the national and local political issues that captured the imagination of activists in other prefectures at this time. In places like Fukushima or Chichibu, the authoritarianism and repressiveness of a governor or the high rate of taxation sparked large-scale conflicts and even uprisings at this time. In Kanazawa, leaders were more worried about how to aid former samurai. It was up to other men in Ishikawa Prefecture to deal with questions such as the size of the land tax and the allocation of the prefectural budget. Even the imperial announcement of October 1881, that a national assembly would be opened in 1890, evoked almost no response from Kanazawa men.[65]

OTHER DISAGREEMENTS, OTHER VENTURES. Accord about what to do had not been reached, although the combatants had agreed to the arbitrated settlement. Endō conceived a plan for a new private school in Kanazawa which would combine letters with the military arts in a nonstandard curriculum. With training in liberal arts, students would be able to contribute to the material and spiritual welfare of Japan, and with military training they would be prepared to "fend off the Russian curs who press southward, and strike the English barbarians who dominate Western Europe."[66] The Eishinsha publicized its plans for this school in January 1882. No sooner had they done so than another school proposal backed by Hikida, Sugimura, and several key figures from the Seigisha, including Susaki Ren and Takashima Shinjirō, was announced. Both schools opened. Neither developed into what its founders had hoped for. These new institutes were little more than study groups for young men affiliated with one or the other party.

Perplexed at having no gains to show for their earlier exertions and wanting expert advice about where best to start a business and what kind of endeavor might yield the highest returns, Endō and the other members of the reconstituted Kigyōkai looked to the central government. They sought the counsel of officials of the Ministry of Agriculture and Commerce at the very time that other Ishikawa men, mostly commoners, were doing battle in the prefectural assembly against the bureaucracy as represented by Governor Chisaka and the Home Ministry. For Endō and his associates, rehabilitation of the impoverished former samurai was more pressing than the fray between the assemblymen and the governor. How local taxes were spent meant little to ex-samurai families, most of whom had little or no land and paid almost nothing when the prefecture and towns and villages collected their levies. Local determination of local government policy was not a cause that could engage the former retainers of the Maeda.

The Ministry of Agriculture and Commerce guided the Kigyōkai toward Hokkaidō. The Meiji government itself was spending heavily on development of the northern island. With Itaga Yoshitoshi and Seki Tokinobu, Endō traveled north to reconnoiter. The idea of recovering and cultivating land that had been wild was still greatly appealing to Endō's party, and now that they had the encouragement of the central government it was not surprising that the Kigyōkai decided to invest in land in Hokkaidō. They enlisted several dozen poor ex-samurai families and set them up as farmers in a village in Shirubeshi Province, about seventy kilometers due west of Sapporo.[67] Endō, Itaga, and Seki saw possibilities in fishing and whaling, also, and with the encouragement of two men from Ishikawa who had become officials of the Ministry of Agriculture and Commerce, they picked Etorofu (Iturup) in the Kurile Islands as the base for Kigyōkai-backed marine activities.

In January 1885, the Kigyōkai held an election in which Kanazawa samurai were asked to choose a twenty-man board to manage new enterprises. All the successful candidates had been endorsed by the Eishinsha, though some were not members of that society. By prior agreement, Hikida and his followers took no stands. The board held its first meeting the next month. Once again the sponsorship of the Maeda family was symbolized by the meeting place: The board convened in the Seisonkaku, the stately retirement residence bordering the Kenroku Garden that Nariyasu had built for his mother in 1863.

At this meeting, the board voted to augment the ¥100,000 in capital that had been contributed by the Maeda by selling stock in their company. They offered shares with a par value totalling ¥150,000. Perhaps the timing was wrong, or it may be that the offering was poorly publicized. Virtually no buyers came forward. The Kigyōkai managers remained wholly dependent on their original patrons. For their part, the Maeda asserted control over the companies by appointing the top managers. Hori Kakuma was named president and Endō Hidekage vice-president. Hakodate was the site of the head office, and branch offices were opened in the Shirubeshi settlement that came to be called Maeda Village and in Etorofu.[68]

Like the overwhelming majority of samurai-initiated businesses of the first half of the Meiji era, the Hokkaidō enterprises of the Kigyōkai failed. Almost from the beginning, the managers of the Kigyōkai companies found themselves paring back the scale of their operations and cutting their losses. Then in 1886 Ōta Shōichirō, a close friend of Endō's who had become head of the fishing business a year earlier, despaired and committed suicide. The fishing and whaling unit was bankrupt, and it was beyond the capabilities of the Kigyōkai to reorganize and revive it. The agricultural operation held out for a few years longer, on the strength of the last ¥20,000 of the Maeda grant and some lands that it had purchased and others that it had been given by the Hokkaidō prefectural office. But this unit of the Kigyōkai also generated a steady succession of losses, and it was finally liquidated on the order of the government when the new commercial code was implemented in 1893.[69]

In retrospect, the business efforts of the former samurai of Kaga seem almost fated to failure. No doubt their inexperience in management was a bigger handicap than they realized, in an ever more competitive economy. Probably they had underestimated the importance of manual skills, as well, and it turned out that ex-samurai could not fish or farm as well as people who were born and raised as peasants and fishermen. Perhaps the disunity among Kanazawa leaders had harmed the chances of the Kigyōkai also. Had the rather generous Maeda grants all gone toward one enterprise, instead of being split among a railway company and various schemes to employ former vassals, and had Kanazawa men combined their own capital and invested in a single undertaking that they all supported, the outcome might have been different. To be sure, the economic environment in which they tried to launch their businesses was extremely inhospitable. The Matsukata deflation was having a depressing effect on ventures all over the nation, regardless of the status background of the managers and workers. Looking at how they approached the task, however, we are left wondering whether the sons of Kaga warriors had the determination to change themselves into businessmen by dint of their own efforts, even had the times been propitious.[70]

CIVIL DISORDER AND THE STRENGTHENING OF STATE CONTROL

Home Minister Yamada Akiyoshi had moved with dispatch to back Governor Chisaka in May and again in September 1882. His actions, along with some moves that Chisaka himself made, illustrate how the early Meiji local government system was not at all the balance between center and periphery that Ōkubo Toshimichi had idealized in 1878. The system was tilted in favor of the central government. Repressive features of the system could be used to shore up mechanisms of central control. No doubt, as Yamada and

Chisaka saw it, they were merely maintaining order. As critical historians have seen it, the bureaucrats were squelching local initiatives.

It is important to be clear about the point that local initiatives in Ishikawa in 1882 had a restricted vision. The events of that year had offered prefectural assembly members a chance to rally against the authorities. They considered demanding that their governor be replaced, and they tried to cut the prefecture's spending. What they did not do is significant. They did not persist in their demand for Chisaka's dismissal. They did not present a united front when one of their number was jailed for comments made in the assembly chamber. They obscured their desire for a reduction in local taxes and prefectural spending by concentrating on Chisaka's personal diversions. They did not make an issue of the form of local government or the balance of power between the central government and local citizens. What they did do was to continue to take part—to work with, and within, the system.

In addition to conflicts over taxes and over the governor's morality, there was a movement among some assemblymen and their constituents to separate Etchū from Kaga and Noto. This movement got underway as the conflict between governor and assembly reached its peak. Even this Toyama-based partition movement had limited aims, however, which were not really directed at winning self-government. The main objective was to gain independence from Kaga and Noto in order to be able to set different priorities in prefectural spending. Sentiment for creating Toyama Prefecture was defined in terms of relationships with Kaga, rather than with the central government.[71] The absence of any clearly articulated desire for local autonomy made it easier for the state to tighten its control.

An attack on the chief of police provided the central government with an occasion to reinforce state control of Ishikawa.[72] Early in 1882, Chisaka had selected a landsman of his from Yonezawa named Ogura Nobuchika as the new police chief. At least a few Kanazawa natives took offense at what they interpreted as a move in a conspiracy to hire and elevate outsiders over themselves. In February, shortly after Ogura arrived in the Ishikawa capital, a group of local ruffians caught him off his guard after a dinner party and beat him up. The attackers escaped unidentified, leaving him lying severely hurt.

Suspicion focused on two groups, with similar motives. One was made up of Eishinsha radicals, the other of a number of prefectural officials, all Ishikawa men, who had been accustomed to having a fair amount of influence over what went on in the prefectural office but had recently been ignored by Chisaka. Both groups were animated by a simple localism, a desire to keep jobs in the hands of local men.

To the central government and its chief representative in Kanazawa, it was immaterial that the vision behind the attack was apparently limited. An assault on a high-ranking official could be seen as a threat to authority or more broadly to the public order. Home Minister Yamada deplored the "threatening attitude toward government officials" that he observed in Ishikawa Prefecture, and he advised Chisaka to hold steadfastly to the line he had been following in his policies and not give in one iota to the demands of local troublemakers. When by April no arrests had been made and the rift between the governor and Ishikawa-born bureaucrats and the prefectural office had widened, Yamada decided the time had come for a show of force. The home minister sent 200 special policemen to Kanazawa from police headquarters in Tokyo, and he replaced the ailing Ogura with a home ministry official, Sonoda Anken, a Satsuma man.[73] The arrival of the police reinforcements helped to quiet things in Kanazawa, and when the controversy in the prefectural assembly over Chisaka's policies and morals grew heated, the extra police took positions outside the chamber to maintain order. At a couple of points, the police harassed assemblymen who were critics of the governor. Although it was nearly a year before the attackers of Police Chief Ogura were finally identified and apprehended—they were Eishinsha hotheads[74]—the government managed by mid-1882 to establish in the minds of most citizens that its power was potent and swiftly deployed.

Chisaka Takamasa limped through the last half of 1882 with the support of the home ministry and the special police. Among Ishikawa men he lost most of the overwhelming backing he had enjoyed at the beginning of his term. Violence no longer loomed as a present danger—the atmosphere and the mentality in Ishikawa was quite unlike that in Fukushima, or Kabasan, or Chichibu[75]—but Chisaka continued to face stiff opposition in the prefectural assembly. Upon the creation of Fukui, Ishikawa had ceased to be the biggest prefecture, yet it was still regarded as difficult to govern. The government recognized this when it appointed Iwamura Takatoshi as Chisaka's successor and set his salary at fifty yen a month more than other governors were paid.

Iwamura's mission was to make Ishikawa submit. He did so with almost incredible ease. His job was facilitated by the second partition of the prefecture in two years, by which such critics of the previous governor as Inagaki and Minami were defined out of his jurisdiction. Iwamura benefited from the presence for a while longer of the 200 extra policemen. He was helped also by his own reputation as a home ministry troubleshooter with the confidence of Iwakura Tomomi, Yamada Akiyoshi, and other powerful central government figures. He had already done stints as governor in two other prefectures, Saga and Ehime. And he was somewhat lucky as well. Many of the abler men of Kanazawa were inattentive to politics, especially local politics, at the time of his arrival. Finally, Iwamura was aided by men, more than just a few, led by Prefectural Assembly Speaker Kawase Kan'ichirō and his faction, who regarded cooperation with the new state and its representatives in subnational governance as the best strategy for achieving well-being in their home territory.[76]

Far from being merely the passive beneficiary of these factors that acted in his favor, Iwamura arrived in Kanazawa a seasoned bureaucratic and political maneuverer. He forced prefectural and subprefectural officials to affirm their submission to him in face-to-face encounters. With the elected representatives in the prefectural assembly, Iwamura proved adept at compromise, accepting cuts in his budget proposals but for the most part getting what he really wanted. From his first appearance in Kanazawa in January 1883 until 1888, he did not have to face any serious resistance to his policies—and in the latter year, opposition to him was the outcome of competition between Liberal and Progressive Party politicians as much as it was an expression of dissatisfaction with his actions.

In 1883, the Ishikawa Prefectural Assembly entered a quiescent phase that some historians have dubbed a "Yao-Shun period," that is, a Golden Age of little conflict.[77] The membership was reduced to thirty-six when the five counties of the ancient province of Etchū were split off into the new prefecture of Toyama. For several years, none of the members of the Ishikawa assembly were close to the two major national political parties, which were themselves in disarray after upheavals elsewhere in Japan in 1884.

Inagaki Shimesu and Sugita Teiichi joined in December 1883 to promote a
regional convention of men interested in the party movement, and their
meeting drew participants from societies in Shikoku and Kyushu as well as
from several regions of Honshu, along with men from Kaga, Noto,
Echizen, and Etchū. The convention hardly affected Ishikawa at all. The
only active Ishikawa prefectural assemblyman to attend was Koma Shuku of
Noto, at the time a perennial loser in assembly debates. No one from Kawase Kan'ichirō's dominant assembly faction took part.[78] As it turned out,
neither of Japan's national political parties put together an organization in
Ishikawa before 1887. People's rights movement luminaries Kataoka Kenkichi and Ueki Emori—famous Tosa-born leaders of the Liberal Party—
visited Kanazawa in 1884, but failed to drum up much interest in the cause
of party politics. On their return to Tokyo, it was with disappointed sar-
casm that they reported, "There is nothing to do in Kanazawa except see
Kenroku Garden."[79]

Prefectural assembly debates revealed most members to be interested in
curbing spending and holding down the level of prefectural taxes. Once
Chisaka left town, assemblymen seem to have had no appetite for confrontation with the governor or other high officials. In the first session to meet
after the creation of Toyama, Governor Iwamura put forward a budget proposal calling for ¥409,759 in spending. The assembly made a few changes,
but approved 95 percent of Iwamura's request.[80] Speaker Kawase Kan'ichirō
and his supporters settled into a working relationship with the governor
that facilitated the latter's accomplishing his aims.

Local politics in Ishikawa remained passive until 1887. In that year, a
quickening occurred, possibly owing to anticipation of the election of members of a national assembly, which was scheduled for 1890. In other parts
of Japan, also, interest in politics was picking up. Endō Hidekage, back
from Hokkaido, reemerged as a force in Kanazawa politics and joined a
group opposed to his one-time ally Kawase. Within the year, the Eishinsha
had affiliated with and merged into the Liberal Party, and Endō had won a
seat in the prefectural assembly. Kawase joined the rival Progressive
Party.[81] For the first time since the establishment of the prefectural assembly, enough men were interested in becoming delegates to make elections
hotly contested.[82] Endō and his followers attacked Kawase and his, and
unavoidably Governor Iwamura was pulled into the line of fire. A new phase

in the political history of the prefecture commenced with a sudden burst of energy at the beginning of the third Meiji decade. Ishikawa activists entered a new era, with more formal connection to national political organizations and more competition among themselves than they had been accustomed to. Finally, in 1888, a Liberal majority in the prefectural assembly turned against Iwamura and the Progressive minority that supported him, and in 1889, the governor prorogued, and Home Minister Yamagata Aritomo dissolved, the Ishikawa Prefectural Assembly.[83]

The dawning of a new phase provides a breaking point for our account of the early Meiji experiences of one region of Japan. As remarked earlier, however, the process of national unification had already reached its effective conclusion. By the middle 1880s, it was power within the system that was at stake. The combatants were groups of local men who saw each other, not the governor or the home ministry, as the principal foes. They had in mind local interests, and frequently sought to use the mechanism of the prefectural assembly to reduce the cost of government for their taxpayer constituents. But they did not fight for local control per se. In the early 1880s, there had been petitions to make county chiefs into elected, rather than appointed, officials, but from the time Governor Iwamura arrived, Ishikawa men did not fight for revision of the laws on subnational organization. Instead, they accepted the prefectural system and the subprefectural system, and the limits on their roles and their power within those systems. The prevailing ethos in the prefecture was what James McClain, writing of the city of Kanazawa, has called "the ethic of community responsibility."[84] Such opposition as there was, was expressed legally. In the political process and in the working of bureaucratic institutions, Ishikawa Prefecture had been successfully integrated into the centralized Meiji state.

Conclusion

With pomp and punctilio, the Emperor of Japan presented his subjects with a constitution on February 11, 1889, the supposed anniversary of the accession of his ancestor Jinmu to the throne 2,549 years earlier. The ceremony of promulgation in the expensively refurbished imperial palace in Tokyo was attended by some 270 personages, including ministers and high officials of the government, members of the diplomatic corps, and members of the titled aristocracy. In the last group were both the last shogun, Tokugawa Yoshinobu, and the last daimyo of Satsuma, Shimazu Tadayoshi.[1] When the document took effect, Japan became a constitutional monarchy in form as well as in practice.[2] The ceremony culminated the eight-year process of drafting, ratification, and proclamation that had been carefully planned and supervised by Itō Hirobumi. Essentially, the constitution made the Meiji state complete.

Even before the new constitution went into effect in 1890, separate legislation on the nature and functions of subnational entities was enacted. As he rushed the new "system of local autonomy" to ratification, Yamagata Aritomo had persuaded his fellow decision makers in the government that these codes on subnational institutions were as important in the construction of a strong modern state as the constitution. Four codes made up the legal foundation of the modified system of local government: the Regulations Governing Organization of Cities (1888), the Regulations Governing Organization of Towns and Villages (1888), the Regulations Governing Prefectural Organization (1890), and the Regulations Governing County Organization (1890).

More comprehensive than the local and prefectural organization laws that they replaced, the new codes drew heavily on German administrative jurisprudence in order to define what we can term the mature Meiji subnational system. That system functioned, with modifications, but without major structural overhaul, until World War II.[3] If historical turning points must be pinned to particular events, the issue in 1888 and 1890 of laws on the "system of local autonomy"—no less than the promulgation of the Meiji constitution in 1889—might be said to mark the completion of national unification in modern Japan.

Government leaders had thoroughly solidified their control over the various parts of Japan. Militarily they had consolidated their domestic dominance by creating a single national military and using it to put down several samurai rebellions, the last and greatest in 1877. Politically the abolition of *han* and creation of prefectures in 1871 had been the single biggest event before the adoption of the new constitution and local autonomy system, but institutional change and the routinization of central control had come about more incrementally than in the military sphere. Centralization, as Marius Jansen and Gilbert Rozman have put it, was "the essence of the transition" from Tokugawa to Meiji, and "administrative centralization was perhaps the most visible and important consequence of the Meiji Restoration."[4] Unification and national political integration, as we have seen, were completed for all practical purposes not in 1888 or 1890, but earlier, during the years when the Three New Laws were in force.

It was in the 1880s that central control over areas like Ishikawa was so firmly established as to become unchallengeable. The relationship that evolved between the national government and what had been the biggest *han* by the mid-eighties is perfectly compatible with Etzioni's model of an integrated political community, mentioned in the introduction to this book. Certainly the national government controlled the means of violence, through the new military and the centralized police. The central government could allocate resources and rewards quite effectively, through the bureaucratic hierarchy in which national authorities in Tokyo supervised prefectural officials, who in turn oversaw subprefectural officials. And old local political identifications had been superseded by new national ones, even though the ties that bound old lords and retainers socially and emotionally had not all been severed.

The mature system of local self-government was not a radical break with the early Meiji experience. It was as much an outgrowth of that experience as it was an adaptation of the best available European models. Many of the features of the new system had been anticipated in the administrative and consultative arrangements worked out in the 1870s and the early 1880s. Other scholars have treated the laws of 1888 and 1890, and the rationale underlying them; in English, George O. Totten, Ishii Ryōsuke, Kurt Steiner, and Richard Staubitz have given detailed analyses, and there is no need to try to recapitulate them here.[5] The examination in the preceding chapters of the formation of the local government system in the first two decades of Meiji reveals that the "system of local autonomy" continued or changed only slightly the arrangements of the Three New Laws. The 1888–1890 system provided for the election of city and town mayors and village chiefs, as well as assembly members, for example, but it retained the restrictive qualifications for participation in elections that had been adopted in 1878. The laws of 1888 and 1890 clarified the legal status of subnational units of government as "locally autonomous bodies" *(chihō jichi dantai)* possessed of a legal personality *(hōjinkaku)*,[6] but in practice the new laws did not significantly alter the imbalance of power. The scales tilted in favor of the Tokyo authorities and the governors whom they appointed, and against local citizens and their representatives, both before and after enactment of the "system of local autonomy." Before and after 1888–1890, the range of issues over which local bodies could exercise self-government and make independent decisions was narrow, and the supervisory hierarchy of officialdom was strong. Before and after, the amount of business delegated to subnational entities by the central government was large, and this delegated business was so costly that prefectures and local communities found their resources strained. Neither before nor after the establishment of the mature system could local entities afford to spend more than a pittance for projects that they initiated on their own.

Noting these continuities, we cannot adhere to the common view that the "system of local autonomy" brought something entirely different into being. A little further reflection might lead us to wonder whether a reevaluation of other views of the development of the Meiji local government system could also be due. At the very least, it seems appropriate to identify (or to reidentify, in most cases, as a look at the notes to the foregoing text should reveal) some of the previous research on local government and politics in nineteenth-century Japan, and to try to place the present study.

Many have seen Meiji local government as a generator of the undemocratic strains in Japanese life that welled up with evil force to overwhelm the democratic strains in the 1930s. Those who have seen excessive authoritarianism or, as some termed it, "absolutism" in the Meiji system have been negative and have generally argued that the repressiveness of the system was clear both before and after the laws of 1888 and 1890. Others have seen the Meiji forms of local rule as vessels that offered citizens a proper measure of responsibility and an education in politics valuable in national, as in local, affairs. Much of the early scholarship on both sides of this debate drew most of its evidence from the laws and the reasoning behind them, and kept the focus on national leaders and lawmakers. More recent work, including the present study, has attempted to rethink the meaning of national unification by concentrating on events in the process, and the actions and motivations of people away from the national center of power, rather than on the abstractions of legislation or the deeds and minds of the men at the top.

Let us begin this quick survey of some of the more prominent interpretations of Meiji local government and nation-building with unfavorable views. The earliest critics of the centralized Meiji system saw its creation as an act of the "despotism of the office-holders" (*yūshi sensei*) calculated to deprive all but a privileged few of their rights. From early in the Meiji era, opponents of the government insisted that representative bodies should be set up so that people like themselves might have a voice in policy formation. These advocates of people's rights, however, seldom articulated the case for changes in the local government system in very clear terms.

Liberalist historians have excoriated the "despotism of the office-holders" and the "clique government" (*hanbatsu seifu*) dominated by men like Ōkubo from Satsuma and Yamagata from Chōshū, and have done so more eloquently than the activists who battled with the central authorities in the early Meiji period. Fujita Takeo, one of the most prominent students of government finance and administration, for example, has characterized the Meiji local government system as "bureaucratic centralism" and has said that while the Meiji laws provided a facade of self-government by locals, in fact those laws reinforced the "absolutist regime of the Satsuma and Chōshū cliques."[7]

Another liberalist critic of institutional development whose views have been influential is political scientist Tsuji Kiyoaki. Comparing the Meiji local government system with that which emerged in England with the Municipal Reform Act of 1835, Tsuji takes the English example as definitive of the "modern type" and finds the Japanese system representative of a unique but inferior model best labelled simply the "Japanese type." Characteristic features of the Japanese type are the extremely heavy weight of the bureaucracy compared to local residents, the pervasiveness of the bureaucracy from the highest to the lowest levels of the system, and, as a natural concomitant of the nearly omnipresent bureaucracy, the hierarchical character of decision making. The modern type is not so burdened with the weight of officials, but allows for greater participation of local citizens who do not belong to the bureaucracy. The modern type is better than the Japanese type.[8]

Strongest among those expressing negative views of the Meiji local government system are Marxist historians who inherited the tradition of the Lectures Faction (Kōzaha) of the 1920s and 1930s. They have seen local government as part and parcel of the "emperor-system absolutism" *(tennō sei zettaishugi)* that characterized the Japanese state from the late nineteenth century through World War II.

A refinement of the Marxist approach appears in seminal works by Ōishi Kaichirō published in the 1960s, which are grounded in a deep knowledge of the society, economy, and politics of a locality, Fukushima Prefecture, as well as a thorough understanding of the institutional and political history of the central government.[9] While continuing to speak of the absolutist character of the Meiji state, and while retaining Marxian analytical terms like "parasitic landlords" and "the semi-feudal structure of local autonomy," Ōishi offers a more complex and nuanced interpretation than the reductionist view that marched under the flag of "emperor-system absolutism." Ōishi's position on the formation of the Meiji local government system is highly critical. The various subnational units of government were deprived of decision-making rights that they were competent to exercise and which, moreover, the people demanded. Contradictions inherent in the structure of the system at the end of the Meiji period gave rise to new problems later, he believes. His emphasis on the demands of citizens for a greater voice in local government distinguishes Ōishi from Fujita, who minimizes the desires of local residents for self-government and describes the system as essentially granted from above *(amakudariteki)*.

Views consonant with Ōishi's have been advanced by other progressive historians. Two deserving of mention here because their works have been very widely admired since the late 1950s are Gotō Yasushi and Irokawa Daikichi. Gotō in his studies of the "movement for liberty and people's rights" of the 1870s and 1880s, and Irokawa in his anti-elitist histories of the development of popular political consciousness in Meiji Japan, agree that the limited degree of autonomy that accrued to the localities was wrung from the government by threat.[10] When the people's rights movement grew in strength, the government perceived a danger to itself and attempted to appease the movement and coopt its membership by making local government posts available and by introducing some formal changes that appeared to expand the people's role in decision making. Gotō and Irokawa argue that men of influence in the community who became local officials were being made the tips *(mattan)* of the central government bureaucracy and that other changes in the system of subnational governance were in reality further steps on the road to "emperor-system absolutism." Gotō adheres to the "emperor-system absolutism" interpretation, holding that the changes of the 1880s and particularly the constitution of 1889 incarnated absolutist authority centered in the sovereign.[11] The protagonists in Gotō's works are the political activists of the people's rights movement, and his methodology is the analysis of economic class. Details of subnational administration do not concern him, except insofar as he identifies policies as repressive or absolutist. Men who worked within the system as local bureaucrats do not figure in Gotō's account. The opponents of the state do.

Among non-Japanese writers, Robert A. Scalapino's work on the prewar party movement still stands, four decades after its publication, as the outstanding exposition of the thesis that Meiji central government leaders were absolutist.[12] He can be grouped with the critics like Fujita, Ōishi, Gotō, and Irokawa on this point. When he turns to the opposition to the government, that is, the participants in the early party movement, however, Scalapino differs from these Japanese scholars. Where the Japanese scholars find men outside the government, often on the local stage, who might have represented truly popular democratic interests, the American political scientist emphasizes the fecklessness of the party leaders at the national level. Paring Scalapino's argument to its barest essentials, the Meiji system was undemocratic and therefore bad, but the people who might have and should have done something to correct the problem were not much better than the oligarchs whom they opposed; leaders of the party movement were all too ready to compromise with the undemocratic elements who controlled state power.

Roger Bowen's *Rebellion and Democracy* is reminiscent of Scalapino's book as well as of the postwar Japanese writing that influenced him, and certainly it fits into the line of negative views of the operation of the Meiji state at the prefectural and local levels. His account turns around opposition to the state and puts the story of protesters and violent activists into magnified perspective, as I noted in the introduction to this book. Bowen does what Tetsuo Najita and J. Victor Koschmann and their collaborators in *Conflict in Modern Japanese History* advocate: he "grapple[s] with the dimension of conflict as a central or core experience."[13]

Opposed to the above critical views are two types of analysis that evaluate the Meiji local government system favorably. The first of these stresses the positive aspects of the codes on subnational government organization. Kikegawa Hiroshi represents this line of interpretation in a number of studies, written both before and after World War II, premised on the notion that wide latitude for self-government by localities is desirable.[14] Kikegawa has recognized some of the undemocratic qualities and the frequent antilocal bias of the institutions of local government both prior to and following the adoption of the "system of local autonomy." But it is his contention that the system as it developed was what Japan required at the time; the foundations of central government had to be established in order to meet national exigencies. Some measure of citizens' participation in the determination of policies affecting their communities was, after all, part of the Meiji system. The most urgent needs of the early Meiji period, however, were national, as Kikegawa sees it. He argues that the impetus for change in the subnational system came from the Meiji leaders' long-cherished hope to win revision of the unequal treaties that Japan had been forced to sign with Western powers in the late 1850s and early 1860s. To win acceptance as an equal by Western governments, Japan had practically no choice but to adopt a European-type local government structure as well as a constitution and other Western-style institutions. Local demands for self-government play a negligible role in Kikegawa's presentation of the story of Meiji local government. National lawmakers worked out a modern subnational system despite the absence of irresistible pressure from below.

Much like Kikegawa, the eminent legal historian Ishii Ryōsuke has found development in the direction of greater local autonomy in the early Meiji years.[15] Looking at the prefectural level, for example, he notes that while prefectures shortly after the Restoration were no more than administrative zones of the central government *(kanchi no gyōsei kuiki)*, later, with the Prefectural Assembly Regulations and Local Tax Regulations of 1878 and the Regulations Governing Prefectural Organization of 1890, they were given the status of autonomous bodies. Professor Ishii focuses largely on the letter of the law, and he is a proponent of the belief that the modernization of law means a change from arbitrary rule by status or rule by law to an equitable rule of law in which, among other things, the governed have both rights and the possibility of juridical recourse against government actions.[16] Ishii's discussion of laws on local government is informed throughout by the assumption that it is undesirable for the central government to be too strong and local units too weak, and he does point out many limitations on the scope of local government actions and on the rights of residents. By his accounting, though, the liabilities of the system are balanced by the assets.

A second type of analysis that yielded a basically favorable assessment of Meiji institutions of local government is that which applied "modernization theory" to the study of nineteenth- and twentieth-century Japan. Modernization scholars have identified the real problem as the transformation of traditional structures and processes, which are inapplicable and cannot survive in a rapidly changing, international, and increasingly interdependent world, into new forms and ways which can adapt and survive. These students have tended to view the Meiji experience in a different light from the critics mentioned above. One particularly important point of difference between those oriented toward modernization theory and the mainstream of postwar Japanese historians is the use of the level of democracy in a political institution as a criterion for judging its modernity. Users of modernization theory have held that it is an oversimplification, at best, to define the modern (and by extension, the advanced and indeed the good) in terms of degree of democracy. At worst, say the modernization theorists, because of confusion and disagreement over the concept of democracy itself, trying to assess modernization by democratization threatens to ensnarl a potentially fruitful analytical construct in debilitating ideological controversy before we have discovered how much this construct might enable us to learn.[17]

Applied to the evaluation of the system of local government, analysis grounded on modernization theory, notably that of Kurt Steiner, emphasizes the success of that system in quickly bringing about a remarkable degree of national integration. The new organization of subnational governance permitted national policy objectives to be transmitted to and carried out at the local level, and it contributed to a reorientation of people's attitudes toward politics.[18] As to whether local autonomy is in principle more desirable than centralization of policy making, Steiner formulates a somewhat elusive position for the modernization theorists, a sort of political agnosticism: the answer "will always depend to a large extent on political value judgments," and must look beyond the political system to the social system and to the history of the particular place being considered.[19] There is no absolute standard. Thus, by the lights of modernization theory, the evaluation of local government and politics in the Meiji period could be either negative or positive. Steiner himself comes down on the positive side.

The latest English-language scholarship on matters of center and periphery in Meiji Japan is harder to fit neatly into the "negative" and "positive" categories than earlier writing. Both Andrew Fraser and Michio Umegaki contributed to a 1986 volume of essays that draw inspiration from the modernization hypothesis at the same time as they back away from using "modernization" as an analytical construct.[20] The chapters by Fraser and Umegaki do not praise the system and cannot easily be called "positive" about the changes. Neither are they negative. Casting change in terms of "transition" from the old to new, both scholars seem fairly neutral, but certainly they do not fit in with the critics like Gotō or Ōishi. Fraser states an important, though unstartling, conclusion at the outset: "The transformation of local administration between 1860 and 1890 was one of the major achievements of modern Japan."[21] I agree. The critics would gainsay that the Meiji system of subnational governance was an achievement.

Neil Waters has an interesting angle on the process of local government

and local economic development, different from other studies. He does not
consider whether the Meiji system for subnational rule was oppressive or
absolutist, instead stressing horizontal social and economic structures and
continuity in those from the period before the Restoration through the early
Meiji years. Treating local leaders whom historians with negative views
might see as coopted by an authoritarian system, he describes these men as
responsible and acting in the interest of their communities. Their adaptation to central government control preserved stability and at the same time
made further economic and political development possible. Waters is pow-
erfully persuasive that it is a mistake to overlook places where "nothing
happened" if one wants to understand how Japan made the change from the
Tokugawa system to the Meiji system.

James McClain takes as his point of departure a sensitivity to the limitations of conceptualizing local history chiefly in terms of the imposition of
institutional reforms from above, and of local "contentious reaction to . . .
centralization." Expressly setting out not "to continue to write the story of
the periphery from the point of view of the center," he views local actors in
Fukui Prefecture and in Kanazawa—people at the same level and in the
same region as those treated in this book—and finds them to have been
responsible citizens. He observes that "many persons in local towns and
villages . . . welcomed the coming of the new order, and many aspects of
the new order took on a meaning and an import in those towns and villages
that was very different from what the oligarchs in Tokyo had expected."
More interested in the role played by prominent local leaders in mediating
between the interests of the community and the demands of the outside
world than he is in the development of the institutions of local governance,
Professor McClain does not offer a judgment of whether the influence of the
system itself was positive or negative. But he shows superior perceptiveness
in his observation that the tradition of community responsibility exempli-
fied in Kanazawa in the early Meiji years meshed nicely into the system of
local autonomy defined by the laws of 1888 and 1890. "The energy of
local elites," he writes, "would serve both to advance the interests of local
communities and to integrate them into the national polity."[22] In a variety
of ways, we have seen that this was true in the first two Meiji decades,
as well.

M. William Steele and Michael Lewis, deliberately giving priority to the periphery over the center, have recently directed their attention to regional politics in the 1880s in articles on Yoshino Taizō of Kanagawa Prefecture and Inagaki Shimesu of Toyama Prefecture.[23] Both of these scholars arrive at views that differ from Scalapino and Bowen. Steele finds that local leaders had a desire for self-government and opposed central government policy on subnational finance from 1880 on. Although he does not dwell on the point, the opposition that he notes took place largely within the prefectural assembly, that is, within the system. Some 102 local political societies were formed in Kanagawa Prefecture between 1878 and 1886, many of which took the advancement of local community interests as their goal. Lewis comes to see Inagaki as a pragmatic practitioner of the art of the possible. The party movement in Toyama, in which Inagaki was a commanding figure, might best be understood as "a struggle, not only against political centralization per se, but one waged in opposition to the Tokyo government's settling of taxation and budgetary priorities." Parties became "mediating groups, . . . agencies that could facilitate or frustrate central reforms and make central resources available for local uses."[24] Opposition to the centralized interests of the state there was, in Kanagawa and Toyama, but it was neither ineffectual—Scalapino's verdict on the people's rights activists—nor radical—Bowen's judgment of which participants most deserve our attention.

Ariizumi Sadao and Mikuriya Takashi might be taken as outstanding exemplars of recent Japanese research into the dynamics of center and periphery in the Meiji period.[25] Like Fraser, Waters, McClain, Steele, and Lewis, neither can be readily grouped with either the critics of the Meiji system or the writers who accentuate the positive aspects of that system.

Ariizumi is the nonpareil master of the documentary evidence on Yamanashi Prefecture in the Meiji period, in addition to having an extremely deep familiarity, amplified in thirteen years on the staff of the National Diet Library, with the collections of papers of the central government leaders who were involved in making policy affecting subnational units of government. In his *Meiji seijishi no kiso katei* he analyzes the politics of the 1880s, especially local fiscal policy and the process by which it was made, by delving into the politics of the Yamanashi prefectural assembly. Although he adopts one of the socioeconomic categories of which Marxist historians have made much, namely "the stratum of wealthy farmers" (*gō-*

nōsō), and although he writes that the Meiji government was "nothing but a plunderer" of localities in the years 1871–1878, Professor Ariizumi is not in the thrall of earlier Marxist terminology or interpretations, and his book is a model of how a careful observer can use the single case to reveal the way things work in general.[26] Avoiding also the language of the modernizationists, he shows how local men and central government figures struggled to deal with the needs of the countryside while satisfying the growing needs of the state.

Mikuriya showcases an extraordinary intimacy with the primary sources on government leaders in his dissection of the internal policy conflicts among key Meiji officials in the 1880s over questions of subnational finance and central government aid. The vocabulary of Marxists and modernization theorists is nowhere to be found in his study, which is a painstaking, close analysis of policy making at the center. What is new and different about this work is not the approach or the focus on factions and interest groups within the government, but the depth and the quality of execution. Mikuriya, dealing with the 1880s, can be compared to Umegaki, who reweighs the first Meiji decade, in that both writers identify processes and disagreements that earlier historians had not observed, and in so doing, reveal that the making of the Meiji state was more fluid and less predictable than most of us had long imagined.[27]

What I hope is a healthy respect for the complexity of the evidence and for the achievements of these previous studies, and not merely indecisiveness about settling upon a single approach as the most promising avenue to truth, has made me eclectic. In this work I have tried to look at several dimensions of the process of unification and national integration during the first two Meiji decades—legal, institutional, political, factional, administrative and financial, and personal—in a single local setting. The story of Kaga and Ishikawa shows that it was not easy to build local government institutions that would serve the nation and the people both, nor was it easy to choose how to act when one's career was on a stage far from the theater of national events. The systemic changes of the early Meiji period brought both gains and losses for local residents. Some people opposed, and some cooperated with the authorities, and some alternately helped and struggled against the subnational bureaucracy. The thought and actions of more than a few men were inconsistent, even though they may have constantly wanted to do their best for their fellows, for the community, and for the nation.

Kaga in 1871 had seemed to be difficult to control and to submerge in the Meiji state. Its traditions and its initial unruliness after the abolition of *han* and the creation of prefectures had not augured a smooth transition from near-autonomy to rule by outsiders dispatched to Kanazawa by the central government. Yet within fifteen years or so, the area was woven into the durable fabric of the new Japan. Routines of administration and finance, and of the workings of the political process, had been established. Kaga *han,* which had stood out as special in the pre-Meiji polity, was liquidated, and Ishikawa Prefecture had been erected in its place. By the mid-1880s Ishikawa was no longer treated by the central government as something special, but as just another prefecture. This was a sign that unification with the rest of the nation had been successfully completed.

Administratively, the integration of Ishikawa had been accomplished under the leadership of four governors. Each of these men had his distinctive strong points, conferred by background, personality, or management skill, and each of them enjoyed the full support of the central government while in office in Kanazawa. Each contributed to the emerging subnational political order. The central regime gave these early Ishikawa governors time to get acquainted with their jurisdiction and to make a mark on it—all four served in the prefecture for at least three-and-a-half years, and one served over seven years, in a period when such lengthy stays in the governor's chair were uncommon. In the late nineteenth century, three-fourths of Japan's prefectural governors remained at their posts for less than three years.[28] None of the first four Ishikawa governors had been a bureaucratic greenhorn when he took up his charge. All four had been officials for at least seven years, and all had held at least five offices before being named governor. By experience, the men who shepherded the once-great domain of Kaga through the formative years of Meiji state centralism were in the top quartile of pre-1900 prefectural governors.[29]

In their public pronouncements, the early governors often struck the chords of the reformistic spirit of their day, proclaiming the need to serve the people, to educate the people, and to harmonize policy and public opinion. At the same time, these men made clear their dedication to the emperor and their commitment to creating a strong nation that would be able to stand up to foreign powers. Sentiments like these tempered the governors' reformism. Endorsements of constitutionalism and statements about serving the people aside, Kiriyama was probably typical in believing that the times called for discipline and for a slow, gradual approach to constitutionalism on the part of the Japanese people. The first four Ishikawa governors, like their Tokyo superiors, were willing to involve the people in public affairs by appointing some men to administrative posts and by creating consultative assemblies, but the leaders had no intention of letting the initiative in policy making and execution pass to non-elite persons or groups.

Building a bureaucracy that would take care of prefectural and subprefectural business had been one of the most important tasks facing the early Meiji state. In Ishikawa, Governors Uchida, Kiriyama, Chisaka, and Iwamura rose in turn to the challenge. None of them relied on holdovers from the inherited bureaucratic apparatus. All made personnel changes that ensured that the officials below them would be responsive to their direction. For the most part, the early chief executives drew on the pool of local talent in filling staff positions in this prefecture. This practice benefited the governors by linking their regimes with the personal networks of family and friendship to which the prefectural and subprefectural officials belonged, thereby eliciting local support for the governors' policies and organizational moves. For local men, service in the new state brought some social recognition and, perhaps as importantly, some personal satisfaction that they were contributing to the making of a new Japan.

The most remarkable feature of the subnational bureaucracy that came into being in the Meiji period was that it worked. This point may have been implicit in previous chapters, but it ought to be made explicit. The census was taken, land deeds issued and recorded, taxes assessed and collected, military conscription implemented, schools built, bridges erected, roads laid or maintained, and water conservancy systems installed. New facilities were kept in working condition, and a variety of other services were provided at the local level. Public order was established and maintained. "Breakdown" did not occur in the critical years of nation-building. When we consider the range of institutional changes that the Meiji state made, we must conclude that both national and subnational officials had to have functioned reasonably competently. Probably the relative absence of antibureaucratic activity on the part of the common people of Ishikawa in the early Meiji years reflects a fair measure of satisfaction with the performance of prefectural and local officials. If one accepts the standards of modern nation-building, that is, if one thinks that it is desirable to have a cohesive and strong state, then one must count Japan luckier than most late-developing nations in possessing the ability quickly to create an effective subnational bureaucracy. Nearly all politically conscious Japanese of the late nineteenth century did accept these standards, either because they wished their country to be able to stand up to other nations, especially Western nations, or because they wanted to have a system that promoted greater material well-being.

The subnational institutional structure of Japan underwent many changes in the first two decades of the Meiji era. In general, these increased the power of the central government, especially that of the higher levels of officialdom. In order to direct the development of "a rich nation and a strong military," central government lawmakers delegated a good deal of business to local entities. This left communities with little means, and little leeway, to set their own priorities. National leaders altered the tax structure in such a way that they nearly emptied the reservoir of funds on which communities might have drawn for locally initiated projects. But in the case of Ishikawa, the timing of changes in the laws and the way in which new institutions were operated do not support the charge that Meiji leaders were rolling out "emperor-system absolutism" according to a premeditated plan. Rather, many of the changes seem to have been attempts by men in the countryside to improve the functionality of the prefectural and subprefectural organizations. The standard was effectiveness. When making procedural or structural adjustments, Uchida and his successors appear to have been as interested in eliminating confusion, corruption, and waste as in any abstract notion of centralized absolute rule. Central government directives did not always precede changes in the prefecture. Several reforms in Ishikawa anticipated national changes of policy on local government organization. A reading of the record of Ishikawa does not suggest that the end product of the early Meiji changes was anything other than a greatly strengthened system of centralized authority over the localities. It does imply, however, that the motives behind the changes might not have been monolithic, as past interpretations stressing absolutism have held.

Moreover, the systemic changes of the early Meiji years were not one-sided. New deliberative assemblies were opened at the prefectural level in 1879 and at the town and village level in 1880. Elections for these bodies were introduced. Participation in the political system was limited by restrictions on eligibility to vote and to hold office, but even so, by far more men were allowed to participate in public affairs in 1888 than had been at the time of the Restoration. In the biggest prefecture of the late 1870s and early 1880s, there had not been any sustained demand for local deliberative bodies, although district chiefs on one occasion in 1875 had voiced a hope for such assemblies.

Politically conscious men of Kaga accepted the rule of the Meiji state and the governorships of Uchida Masakaze and his successors with an alacrity that could not have been predicted by an observer of Kaga in the 1860s. Although the highest-ranking retainers of the Maeda all retired from official service, enough local men of both samurai and commoner status were eager to join their fates to that of the new state that the early governors could employ as many Ishikawa men as they wanted in subnational administrative posts. The sporadic violence that marred the public order at the time of the changeover from *han* to prefecture never developed into a movement of political resistance to the Meiji authorities. Nor did any other locally oriented, anti-central-government activity excite significant numbers of Ishikawa men. When local men did resist higher authority, as when district chiefs fought Governor Kiriyama in 1875 and when prefectural assemblymen attacked Governor Chisaka in 1882, they did not spell out a vision of local control over local affairs. Political activism usually found expression in established channels, as Ishikawa men became bureaucrats or participants in assemblies or political discussions. The kind of radicalism that proposes the overthrow of the whole system never emerged. Even the most extreme elements in the region, Shimada Ichirō and his group, catalogued their grievances against several individual central government leaders, rather than against the new nation-state or its structure.

From the beginning of prefectural rule, Ishikawa men evinced a strong desire to serve the emperor and the nation. In part they seemed to have been motivated by feelings of shame at not having participated in the great event of their lifetimes, the restoration of imperial rule. They wanted to make up for past failings. Their pride had been wounded by the fact that their domain of Kaga, which had been special for many generations and therefore presumably should have had a leading role in the upheaval of 1867–1868, had played no part in the Restoration. But local identity and pride did not lead men of Kaga to reject the new nation and to try to hold onto domanial autonomy. Local identity was compatible with nationalism in their minds. The orientation of Ishikawa men toward national service and national policy issues was reinforced by their perception of a foreign threat to Japan, which, whether real or imaginary, stirred thousands of Kanazawa men to volunteer their services as troops to invade Korea and China in the early 1870s, and stimulated activists of the early 1880s to pledge to serve the emperor and the nation lest Japan be gobbled up by the "blue-eyed, red-haired dogs" from the West.

The new nationalism that moved many Ishikawa samurai in the years after the Meiji Restoration coexisted in their hearts with a strong residue of respect for the Maeda family, whom these samurai and their forebears had served for hundreds of years. No one seems to have found this anomalous. For their part, even after being displaced from power, removed to Tokyo, and relieved of any legal obligation toward their old retainers, the Maeda did not completely abjure responsibility for the welfare of their one-time vassals. In the first two Meiji decades, the relations between lord and retainer were transmuted—we might say that they changed from primary political relations, with lord and vassal bound together within the frame of the domain, to secondary political relations, with both sides oriented primarily toward the national polity. What continued was an informal paternalistic association with each other. In the 1880s this association took the form of economic patronage by the former daimyo. The Maeda counselled their old liegemen to become independent and to work for the development of national wealth and strength, but at the same time as they offered this advice, the old lords extended generous aid to schemes for employing their former samurai. Probably unintentionally, the Maeda encouraged a prolongation of dependency. After a decade in which the most visible former Kaga samurai had spent their energies in politics, in the second Meiji decade many of them directed their efforts to economic affairs.

On first examination, it might seem that the former Kaga samurai were inconsistent or unprincipled, in maintaining simultaneously an orientation to the new nation and a warm, quasi-familial relationship with the supplanted local lord. Things were not so simple. One strand ran through nearly all these men's actions: they were seriously trying to adapt themselves to the changing circumstances of the new nation, and to do so responsibly. They may not have been consistent, but they were not feckless.

In the first two decades of Meiji rule, government organization changed considerably. As institutions changed, so did the politically conscious people who interacted with those institutions. Sometimes this was a matter of a change of mind on the part of an official, an assembly delegate, or a political movement participant. At other times it was a matter of new people entering the world of affairs in response to opportunities that had not previously existed. Many commoners became members of prefectural and subprefectural assemblies, for example. Men like Sugita Teiichi and Inagaki Shimesu could rise to a prominence unimagined for men of their status in the old Japan. More and more commoners were appointed as officials as time went on, also. In Ishikawa, by 1884 21 percent of prefectural bureaucrats were of commoner origin, up from less than 8 percent between 1871 and 1875.[30] Men of samurai background likewise entered areas such as private enterprise and the lower levels of local administration that would not have been open to them in the closed status system before the Restoration. Uchida, Kiriyama, Chisaka, and Iwamura constituted the core of their bureaucratic organizations with such men, locally born men from both samurai and commoner families. Perhaps the system of subnational administration of early Meiji Japan was essentially authoritarian, even tending toward "absolutist," but it cannot be denied that it made way for participation by many "new" men who desired to serve, men whose attitudes and intentions probably had more in common with the would-be prudent officials of pre-Restoration Kaga and the civil servants of post-World War II Japan than they did with the citizens' movement protesters of recent years.

As people tried to adapt themselves to circumstances in the first twenty years after the Restoration, and to help meet the needs of nation and locality, there was a lot of turnover. Some switched fields of concentration, from bureaucratic appointive service to elective politics, for instance, or from politics to business. Others sandwiched careers of political activism around periods in which they devoted themselves to economic matters. Men joined to form associations for political or economic ends, to help themselves, to develop their region, to serve the nation. Political and economic societies came into being and faded away in patterns much like the careers of the individuals whose activities we have followed. The world of early Meiji was multifarious and unpredictable. Plans and best efforts did not always yield the results that had been hoped for.

In the sphere of government, however, by the mid-1880s, the nation was stable, and a system that assured the implementation of national policy objectives at all levels down to the towns and villages was in place. The forms of this network of local government organs were the creation of central government leaders such as Home Ministers Ōkubo Toshimichi, Yamada Akiyoshi, and Yamagata Aritomo. But this system could not have been assembled, and would not have worked at all, without the active cooperation of many men of various backgrounds and career experiences who became the nerves and sinews of the new organism, in Ishikawa and all around the nation.

Appendixes

Abbreviations Used in the Notes

Notes

Bibliography

Index

APPENDIX 1 *Stratification of the Maeda Retainer Corps in the Late Tokugawa Period*

	Stipend in koku						
	10,000[+]	5,000–9,999	1,000–4,999	700–999	300–699	100–299	1–99
No. of samurai	12	11	114	51	377	1,072	205
% of samurai	0.6	0.6	6.2	2.8	20.5	58.2	11.1
Samurai class[a]	Upper	Upper	Upper	Middle	Middle	Middle	Lower

Source: Tabata Tsutomu, "Bunkyū-Keiōki ni okeru Kaga han no sanbutsukata seisaku ni tsuite," p. 79, constructed from data in the register of samurai *(Samurai chō),* Appendix 2 of *Ishikawa ken shi,* vol. 2.

Note:[a] Tabata's classification. Cf. the domain's own classification system for those of *heishi (hirazamurai)* rank and above, viz., in descending order, *toshiyori, hitomochi, yoriai,* and *heishi.* The *heishi* category included members of the *onmamawarigumi* and the *okoshōgumi.*

APPENDIX 2 Administration and Population of Kanazawa Prefecture, 1871, and Ishikawa Prefecture, 1872–1884

	1871	1872	1873	1874	1875	1876	1877	1878	1879	1880	1881	1882	1883	1884
Administration														
Provinces	3	1	2	2	2	4	4	4	4	4	3	3	2	2
Counties	10	4	8	8	8	—	—	—	—	—	—	—	—	—
Administrative districts	—	44	44	43	—	—	—	—	—	—	—	—	—	—
Towns/Wards	515	606	641	548	—	—	—	—	—	—	—	—	—	—
Villages	2,860	970	1,830	1,873	—	—	—	—	—	—	—	—	—	—
Households	240,053	94,949	159,370	137,049	136,608	374,496	373,555	373,553	362,278	375,338	282,253	280,370	145,117	145,857
Shrines	N/A	1,166	2,510	2,646	2,672	8,592	8,456	8,463	8,316	9,740	7,050	6,735	3,184	3,184
Temples	2,045	558	1,171	1,133	1,124	3,449	3,371	3,371	3,649	3,961	2,808	2,730	1,263	1,263
Schools	—	—	190	329	—	—	—	—	—	—	—	—	—	—
Private academies	—	—	70	—	—	—	—	—	—	—	—	—	—	—
Hospitals	—	—	1	1	—	—	—	—	—	—	—	—	—	—
Population Total	1,083,691	403,357	686,249	691,735	696,429	1,811,146	1,826,927	1,826,927	1,852,811	1,856,395	1,412,802	1,428,062	743,676	752,085
Males	543,312	202,093	343,186	345,898	348,277	914,663	920,642	920,642	936,675	934,332	712,070	720,545	—	—
Females	540,379	201,264	343,063	345,837	348,152	896,483	906,285	906,285	916,136	922,063	700,732	707,517	—	—
Births	—	—	16,270	19,062	17,946	56,587	53,826	49,618	50,847	48,681	40,360	37,417	22,451	21,472
Deaths	—	—	15,598	17,442	13,098	36,568	34,828	30,274	59,738	35,516	27,077	25,318	13,656	12,861
Shizoku	7,077	7,452	14,627	14,298	14,285	23,070	22,888	22,819	86,712	90,694	68,621	68,605	53,262	53,997
Shizoku family members	18,955	19,730	37,485	37,437	37,611	66,463	—	—	—	—	—	—	—	—
Sotsu	9,474	9,986	—	—	—	—	—	—	—	—	—	—	—	—
Sotsu family members	17,486	19,128	—	—	—	—	—	—	—	—	—	—	—	—
Commoners	219,142	81,204	137,503	141,050	142,463	376,504	380,635	380,671	1,766,099	1,765,701	1,344,181	1,359,457	690,414	698,988
Commoners' family members	790,310	262,418	473,939	493,646	502,070	1,345,133	—	—	—	—	—	—	—	—

Family members of shizoku and commoners												
—	—	—	—	—	1,423,474	1,423,737	—	—	—	—	—	—
Monks[a] 2,045	815	1,248	1,595	1,041	—	—	3,251	3,613	2,531	2,543	1,156	1,133
Monks' family members 7,094	1,494	4,251	3,762	—	—	—	—	—	—	—	—	—
Shinto priests[b] 434	84	242	—	211	—	—	404	451	375	377	213	212
Shinto priests' family members 1,487	224	749	—	—	—	—	—	—	—	—	—	—
Former eta 1,881	—	—	—	—	—	—	—	—	—	—	—	—
Former eta family members 10,579	—	—	—	—	—	—	—	—	—	—	—	—
Geisha —	—	—	—	—	—	—	1,386	1,411	974	899	435	349
Licensed prostitutes —	—	—	—	—	—	—	367	427	328	260	188	233

Source: Compiled from *Ishikawa ken shiryō*, kan 20, kokō, Meiji 4–17 nen, *IKSR*, vol. 2, pp. 119–169.

Notes: [a] From 1879, identified as chief priests of temples (*jushoku*). [b] Identified as former Shinto priests (*moto shinshoku*) in 1872–1873; from 1879, identified as shrine officials (*shinkan*).

APPENDIX 3   Budget of Ishikawa Prefecture, 1871/10–1872/9

Amounts in the original document from which the following table is drawn are expressed in *koku* (ca. 5.12 bushels) of rice and in ryō. Here those have been translated into yen. In the case of ryō, the conversion rate was one to one at the time that Japan adopted the yen as the standard unit of currency (1872/2). In the case of *koku*, I have converted at the average price of one *koku* of rice in the markets of Kanazawa, Kanaiwa, Tsurugi, Mattō, and Mikawa during the five years 1870–1874. That average price was ¥4. (Rice prices are in *Fuken chiso kaisei kiyō*, Ishikawa ken, p. 7, in *Meiji zenki sangyō shi shiryō*, bekkan 9, vol. 2.)

The document was signed by Kiriyama and Uchida in 1872/5 and addressed to the Ministry of Finance.

The assessed product of the prefecture measured in *koku* was 468,698. Expressed in yen, it was ¥1,874,792.

Expenditures in Ishikawa Prefecture, 1871/10–1872/9

Method of actual payment and budgetary item	Value in yen	Percent of total
Expenditures paid in rice		
1. Fixed stipend of the former governor of Daishōji Prefecture	11,492	0.7
2. Fixed stipend of the former samurai of Kanazawa Prefecture (14,958 persons)	334,000	19.2
3. Fixed stipend of the former samurai of Daishōji Prefecture (1,178 persons)	70,513	4.0
4. Child-care expenditures for orphans (5 persons)	14	0.0
5. Expenditures within the prefectural office of the former Kanazawa Prefecture	22	0.0
6. Expenditures within the prefectural office of the former Daishōji Prefecture	720	0.0
7. Expenditures on schools for the same prefectures	1,820	0.1
8. Old age allowances (to 1871/12)	418	0.0
9. Rations for inmates of penal institutions (270 persons)	2,740	0.2

Method of actual payment and budgetary item	Value in yen	Percent of total
11. Rations for relief	2,200	0.1
12. Miscellaneous expenditures for collection of taxes in kind	12,002	0.7
13. Compensation for damage to agricultural land and rice given for moving	15,022	0.9
14–16. Expenditures associated with ruined lands	3,061	0.2
17. Grants upon the collection of taxes to former post stations which had been tax-exempt	2,103	0.1
18. Grants toward funeral expenses and compensation of artillerymen killed or wounded	25	0.0
19. Expenditures of the military of the former Daishōji Prefecture	2,360	0.1
20. Expenditures on postal service for the former Daishōji Prefecture	40	0.0
Expenditures paid in money		
21. Primary regular expenses	2,548	0.1
22. Secondary regular expenses	7,425	0.4
23. Officials' salaries	20,229	1.2
24. Expenditures for moving the capital, and per diem and moving expenditures for officials	1,250	0.1
25. District police expenditures	2,508	0.1
26. Hereditary stipend of the former governor of Kanazawa Prefecture [Maeda]	230,475	13.2
27. Stipends and other payments to former samurai of Kanazawa Prefecture (14,958 persons)	675,440	38.7
28. Traditional salaries in money to the above, in addition to payments in rice (3,730 persons)	6,468	0.4
29. Salaries in money to former samurai of Daishōji Prefecture (4 persons)	18	0.0
30. Money gifts in congratulation of longevity (1 person 100 years old, 45 persons 88 years old)	235	0.0
31. Monthly salaries of ex-officials of the former Kanazawa Prefecture (270 persons)	10,800	0.6
32. Monthly salaries of ex-officials of the former Daishōji Prefecture (120 persons)	797	0.0
33. Office expenses and guards' salaries for the Prefectural Office of the former Kanazawa Prefecture and its branch offices	52,980	3.0
34. Office expenses of the Prefectural Office of the former Daishōji Prefecture and its branch offices	7,648	0.4
35. Money expenditures on the believers in the heterodox religion [Christianity] interned in Kanazawa (195 persons)	4,930	0.3
36. Expenditures on orphans	3,150	0.2

Expenditures in Ishikawa Prefecture, (continued)

Method of actual payment and budgetary item	Value in yen	Percent of total
37. Expenditures on inmates of penal institutions (270 persons) and salaries of prison officials, etc.	9,520	0.5
38. Expenditures on military units (up to 1872/3 when the military units were dissolved)	94,800	5.4
39. Expenditures for sending soldiers to the various corps area headquarters	74,950	4.3
40. Schools expenditures	37,860	2.2
41. Aid to postal service and former supervisors' salaries	1,140	0.1
42. Mining expenditures	12,180	0.7
43. Grants upon the collection of taxes to former post stations which had been tax-exempt	3	0.0
44. Loans and grants to families whose houses had burned and to poor villages for the purpose of carrying on	3,189	0.2
45. Expenditure for the operation of and improvements on dikes and dams	20,190	1.2
46. Aid to the Ukita house (over 70 persons, formerly employed by Kanazawa han)	1,500	0.1
TOTAL	1,743,745	100.0

Source: IKSR (kan 54, seido bu, kaikei, 1872), vol. 4, pp. 264–266.

APPENDIX 4 *Expenditures of Ishikawa Prefecture, 1873–1874*

The assessed product for Ishikawa Prefecture in both 1873 and 1874 was 755,825 *koku* or ¥ 3,023,300.

Expenditures	1873 (in yen)	% of Total	1874 (in yen)	% of Total	Change in Relative Weight (%)
Salaries	31,758	3.3	32,658	53.6	1,500
Primary regular expenditures	3,650	0.4	3,650	6.0	1,456
Secondary regular expenditures	11,000	1.2	11,000	18.1	1,456
Constabulary expenditures	4,025	0.4	4,025	6.6	1,456
Hereditary stipends [a]	869,212	91.7	—	—	− 100
Money gifts in congratulation of longevity [b]	770	0.1	—	—	− 100
Expenditures on the internees [c]	6,902	0.7	—	—	− 100
Provisions for inmates of penal institutions [d]	4,552	0.5	6,648	10.9	2,173
Expenditures on the homeless [e]	528	0.1	907	1.5	2,573
Provisions for inmates of the poorhouse	408	0.0	360	0.6	1,273
Pensions for artillerymen (injured in the fire of 1871/9)	11	0.0	11	0.0	1,456
Reward stipend paid to the former governor of Kanazawa han	13,750	1.5	—	—	− 100
Salaries of Shinto priests	1,686	0.2	1,572	2.6	1,351
Pay of a prison medic	—	—	100	0.2	NM [f]
Expenditures for orphans	—	—	3	0.0	NM
TOTAL	948,252	100.0	60,934	100.0	0

Sources: IKGS, vol. 1, pp. 134–136 (Tables 3, 4, 5); *IKSR* (kan 54, seido bu, kaikei, 1871–1874), vol. 4, pp. 264–292.

Notes: [a] 16,386 persons in 1872/10–1873/9; 16,214 persons in 1873. [b] 89 persons 87 years old; 4 persons 99 years old. [c] 458 persons, believers in a heterodox religion (Christianity). [d] 200–300 persons. [e] 40–70 persons. [f] NM indicates not meaningful.

APPENDIX 5 *Subprefectural Districts in Ishikawa Prefecture, November 1, 1876*

Daiku number	Kōri encompassed by the daiku	Number of shōku in this daiku	Households	Population
1	Enuma	10	10,714	55,960
2	Nomi	17	17,834	91,622
3	Ishikawa, except part of the town of Kanazawa	18	18,909	99,998
4	Kanazawa	23	23,995	108,758
5	Kahoku, except part of the town of Kanazawa	12	12,164	68,271
6	Hakui	14	14,346	72,879
7	Kashima	14	14,493	71,667
8	Fugeshi and Suzu	23	24,153	127,274
9	Tonami	22	39,561	174,588
10	Imizu	30	32,848	142,381
11	Nei and the town of Toyama	20	24,625	105,863
12	Niikawa west of the Hayatsuki River	24	26,598	128,532
13	Niikawa east of the Hayatsuki River	18	20,975	98,094
	TOTALS	245	281,215	1,345,887

Source: IKSR (*kan* 2, *seiji bu, kenchi,* Meiji 9-nen), vol. 1, pp. 3–6.

Notes: There were one *kuchō* and one *fuku kuchō* in each *daiku,* and one *kochō* in each *shōku.* The number of *fuku kochō* is not recorded, nor are numbers of other staff personnel. Daiku 1–5 were in Kaga Province; daiku 6–8 in Noto Province; and daiku 9–13, in Etchū Province. Data for Echizen are not recorded.

APPENDIX 6 *Counties in Ishikawa Prefecture, 1878*

County (gun)	Location of County Office	Number of Town or Village Offices	Number of Wards of Towns	Number of Villages
Echizen Province				
Nanjō	Takefu machi	102	29	86
Imadachi	Takefu machi	137	12	188
Nyū	Yoshie machi	79	1	229
Asuwa	Fukui machi	78	86	156
Yoshida	Fukui machi	44	4	146
Ōno	Ōno machi	136	29	246
Sakai	Sakai minato	257	12	244
Kaga Province				
Enuma	Daishōji machi	23	1	138
Nomi	Komatsu machi	35	86	359
Ishikawa	Mattō machi	73	4	322
Kahoku	Tsubata eki	72	16	265
Noto Province				
Hagui	Hagui mura	26	58	235
Kashima	Nanao machi	22	33	193
Fugeshi	Wajima machi	47	43	304
Suzu	Wajima machi	14	-	105
Etchū Province				
Tonami	Imaisurugi eki	64	0	700
Imizu	Takaoka machi	48	99	338
Nei	Toyama Atago machi	24	11	366
Kami Niikawa	Toyama Sōgawa	109	126	752
Shimo Niikawa	Uozu machi	31	30	313
TOTALS		1,421	680	5,685

Sources: IKS, vol. 4, p. 131; *Chihō enkaku ryakufu,* comp. Hoshina Tamotsu (Tokyo: Naimushō Toshokyoku, 1882), pp. 204, 208–209; *Ishikawa kenchi gairan,* 1878, *MNFTS,* reel 185.

Notes: Pronunciations of place names generally follow *Chimei sakuin,* comp. Naimushō Chiri Kyoku (Tokyo, 1885), hence Hagui gun rather than Hakui gun, and Imadachi rather than Imadate, as they are pronounced today. Some names do not appear in *Chimei sakuin,* e.g., Sōgawa; in such cases I have relied on *Nihon chimei hatsuon jiten,* comp. Nihon Hōsō Kyōkai (Tokyo, 1960). The number of wards given by *Ishikawa kenchi gairan* for Suzu, 532, is plainly an error and is omitted here.

APPENDIX 7 *Sources of Funds Expended by Ishikawa Prefecture, 1880–1890*

	1880	1881	1882	1883	1884	1885	1886	1887	1888	1889	1890
In thousands of yen											
Local tax	489.9	683.9	738.6	368.5	355.1	268.3	425.4	345.9	385.4	276.2	264.3
National exchequer	243.6	114.7	144.5	145.9	119.3	92.2	124.6	132.6	114.7	116.1	124.5
Prefectural excise tax	8.9	9.8	16.6	5.5	8.8	6.6	7.8	8.7	11.3	6.6	6.3
TOTAL	742.4	808.4	899.7	519.9	483.2	367.1	557.8	487.2	511.4	398.9	395.1
In percentages											
Local tax	66.0	84.6	82.1	70.9	73.5	73.1	76.3	71.0	75.4	69.2	66.9
National exchequer	32.8	14.2	16.1	28.1	24.7	25.1	22.3	27.2	22.4	29.1	31.5
Prefectural excise tax	1.2	1.2	1.8	1.1	1.8	1.8	1.4	1.8	2.2	1.7	1.6
TOTAL	100.0	100.0	100.0	100.0	100.0	100.0	100.0	100.0	100.0	100.0	100.0

Source: Dai Nihon Teikoku tōkei nenkan (1881, 1883, 1885, 1887, 1889, 1891).

APPENDIX 8   *Expenditures of Local Taxes in Ishikawa Prefecture, 1880–1890 (in ¥ thousands)*

	Miscel- laneous	Officials' salaries	Promoting enterprise	Education	Public Works	Police
1880	77.2	195.1	22.7	87.8	—	107.2
1881	124.3	174.5	16.7	80.3	194.1	94.0
1882	156.3	200.2	21.2	99.9	153.2	107.8
1883	66.0	109.0	8.8	59.2	62.1	63.4
1884	61.6	114.2	8.8	57.1	52.7	60.7
1885	49.2	91.0	5.7	47.7	23.9	50.8
1886	110.0	130.5	6.8	73.4	34.6	70.1
1887	48.2	130.0	6.2	56.3	39.7	65.5
1888	129.8	51.5	9.5	69.6	55.9	69.1
1889	49.2	63.5	6.1	42.0	47.6	67.8
1890	61.1	37.1	10.5	39.9	44.9	70.8

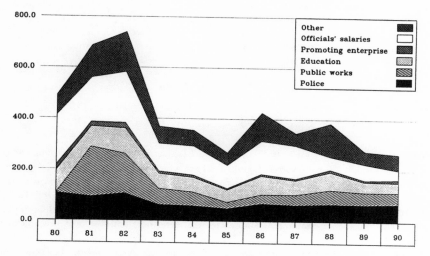

Sources: Ishikawa ken tōkei hyō, 1880, and *Ishikawa ken tōkeisho,* 1881, 1883–1891, all reproduced in *MNFTS,* reels 185–187; see also *IKGS,* vol. 1, pp. 250–251.

APPENDIX 9   *Representation in the First Ishikawa Prefectural Assembly, 1879*

Urban District or County	Population	Prefectural Assembly Seats	Population Per Seat	Ex-Samurai Assemblymen	Commoner Assemblymen	Assemblymen of Unclear Status
1. Kanazawa	108,328	4	27,082	4	0	1
2. Enuma	58,580	2	29,290	1	—	1
3. Nomi	97,000	3	32,333	1	2	—
4. Ishikawa	104,767	4	26,192	1	—	3
5. Kahoku	71,937	3	23,979	1	—	2
6. Hagui	77,298	3	25,766	0	3	—
7. Kashima	76,144	3	25,381	—	2	1
8. Fugeshi	88,550	3	29,517	1	—	2
9. Suzu	42,240	2	21,120	—	1	1
10. Tonami	182,749	5	36,550	—	—	5
11. Imizu	149,327	5	29,865	—	3	2
12. Nei	65,537	3	22,512	—	1	2
13. Kami Niikawa	177,783	5	35,557	—	—	5
14. Shimo Niikawa	99,583	4	24,896	—	4	—
15. Nanjo	93,128	2	18,626	—	2	—
16. Imadachi		3	18,626	—	3	—
17. Nyu	63,286	3	21,095	—	3	—
18. Asuwa	114,580	3	22,916	—	3	—
19. Yoshida		2	22,916	—	2	—
20. Ono	80,280	3	26,760	—	3	—
21. Sakai	97,061	4	24,265	—	3	1
TOTALS	1,848,158	69	26,785	9	32	28

Notes: Population figures for lines 1–14 are from *Ishikawa ken tōkei hyō,* 1880 (pub. 1882), *MNFTS,* reel 185 (Tokyo, 1963). Figures for lines 15–21 are from *Chihō enkaku ryakufu,* ed. Hoshina Tamotsu (Tokyo, 1882, reprinted 1963). Disaggregated population statistics for Nanjō-Imadachi and Asuwa-Yoshida are not available. Actual figures as of the date of the first election in April 1879 must have been slightly different from those in the columns for Population and Ex-Samurai Assemblymen; the difference, however, was probably not material.

Information on numbers of seats and the status of assemblymen appears in *IKGS,* vol. 1, pp. 584 and 1393–1657.

Population per seat in the counties of Nanjō-Imadachi and Asuwa-Yoshida is estimated by dividing the total population by the total number of seats; again the actual figure was probably somewhat different.

APPENDIX 10 *Eligibility to Participate in Prefectural Elections, 1881*

Urban District or County	Assembly Seats	Persons Eligible for Election	Eligible Voters	Population	Percentage of Population Eligible to be Elected	Percentage of Population Eligible to Vote	Number of Voters per Prefectural Assembly Seat
Kanazawa	4	150	346	107,624	0.14	0.32	86.5
Enuma	2	1,890	3,158	59,213	3.19	5.33	1,579.0
Nomi	3	2,809	7,466	98,349	2.86	7.59	2,488.7
Ishikawa	4	4,513	6,909	104,887	4.30	6.59	1,727.3
Kahoku	3	2,168	3,909	72,528	2.99	5.39	1,303.0
Hagui	3	2,061	3,377	77,417	2.66	4.36	1,125.7
Kashima	3	2,246	3,912	76,714	2.93	5.10	1,304.0
Fugeshi–Suzu	5	2,674	5,342	131,953	2.03	4.05	1,068.4
Tonami	5	5,166	8,040	185,469	2.79	4.33	1,608.0
Imizu	5	3,090	4,640	150,873	2.05	3.08	928.0
Nei	3	1,709	2,710	68,210	2.51	3.97	903.3
Kami Niikawa	5	3,762	6,342	178,834	2.10	3.55	1,268.4
Shimo Niikawa	4	1,600	2,905	100,731	1.59	2.88	726.3
TOTAL	49	33,838	59,056	1,412,802			
Mean					2.47	4.35	1,239.7
Median					2.66	4.33	1,268.4

Source: Data is from *Ishikawa ken tōkei byō*, 1881 (pub. 1884), MNFTS, reel 185.

Note: Population figures are for persons permanently registered (having a *bonseki*) in the urban district and counties. There is no table with a breakdown by age and sex in the 1881 Ishikawa statistics; but in 1880, there were 405,247 males twenty years of age and older in a total population of 1,400,824 in the territory included in this table. Males over twenty thus comprised 28.9% of the 1880 population. If we assume no change in the proportion of males over twenty, we can estimate the proportion of men in Ishikawa Prefecture who met the tax-paying requirement to participate. About 8.3% were eligible to be elected, and about 14.5% were eligible to vote.

Abbreviations Used in the Notes

FS	*Fuken shiryō*
FSS	*Fuken seido shiryō*
HSS, G	*Hakui shi shi, gendai hen*
IKGS	*Ishikawa kengikai shi*
IKS	*Ishikawa ken shi*
IKSR	*Ishikawa ken shiryō*
KHS	*Kaga han shiryō*
KKSS, G	*(Kōhon) Kanazawa shi shi, gakuji hen*
KKSS, S	*(Kōhon) Kanazawa shi shi, seiji hen*
KSS, G	*Kanazawa shi shi, gendai hen*
Kuranami, *KHKK*	Kuranami Seiji, *Kaga hansei kaikaku no kenkyū*
MNFTS	*Meiji nenkan fuken tōkeisho shūsei*
NSS	*Nanao shi shi*
PFEH	*Papers on Far Eastern History*
Wakabayashi, *KNSK*	Wakabayashi Kisaburō, *Kaga han nōsei shi no kenkyū*

Notes

INTRODUCTION

1. See Tokuda Toshiaki, "Ishin ni okeru Kaga han no seiji dōkō," *Hokuriku shigaku*, no. 18 (1970), pp. 1–13. For elaborated discussions of the rationales behind *kakkyo*, see H. D. Harootunian, "Sectionalism and National Unity: Yokoi Shōnan," in *Toward Restoration* (Berkeley: University of California Press, 1970), pp. 321–379, and Ōkubo Toshiaki, "Bakumatsu no Satsuma hanritsu Kaiseisho ni kansuru shinshiryō: Satsuma han no 'ippan kakkyo' shugi seisaku no ikkan," *Seiji keizaishigaku*, no. 150 (1978), pp. 21–35. The tendency of *han* to become independent is discussed in an important article by Ikeda Takamasa, "Bakumatsu seijishi no jiki kubun ni tsuite," *Nihonshi kenkyū*, no. 122 (1971), reprinted in *(Ronshū Nihon rekishi 8) Bakuhan taisei II* (Tokyo: Yūseidō, 1973). Cf. also Albert M. Craig, *Chōshū in the Meiji Restoration* (Cambridge: Harvard University Press, 1961), passim; W. G. Beasley, *The Meiji Restoration* (Stanford: Stanford University Press, 1972), pp. 117–139; Conrad Totman, *The Collapse of the Tokugawa Bakufu* (Honolulu: University Press of Hawaii, 1980), passim.

2. *Kōbu gattai taisei,* thus labelled by Ōkubo Toshiaki, "Bakumatsu seiji to seiken inin mondai," *Shien,* vol. 20, no. 1; cited by Tanaka Akira, *Meiji ishin (Nihon no rekishi 24)* (Tokyo: Shōgakkan, 1976), pp. 113–114.

3. *Kido Kōin monjo,* 3, quoted by Tanaka, pp. 115–116. Cf. Beasley paraphrasing and quoting Kido: "To allow each domain to go on being preoccupied solely with its own affairs would so weaken the government that Japan would become nothing more than a conglomeration of 'little Bakufus,' a situation as bad as the one that the Restoration had been designed to end." *The Meiji Restoration,* p. 330.

4. "A Monarch for Modern Japan," in Robert E. Ward, ed., *Political Develop-*

ment in Modern Japan (Princeton: Princeton University Press, 1968), p. 51. Cf. Ardath W. Burks' formulation of the alternatives in "Administrative Transition from *Han* to *Ken:* The Example of Okayama," *Far Eastern Quarterly,* vol. 15, no. 3 (1956), p. 372: "The alternatives facing the new government may be briefly stated: either feudalism would continue with a different clan or coalition of clans holding the power, or a centralized state embracing all parts of the country would be established." Hall's statement seems to me to convey the complexity of the new government's problems better than Burks'.

5. Tanaka, pp. 148–149, quoting *Kido Kōin nikki,* 1871/6/11.
6. Translation in W. W. McLaren, ed., "Japanese Government Documents," *Transactions of the Asiatic Society of Japan,* vol. 42, part I (1914), pp. 32–33. I have substituted "domains" and *"han"* for "clans" in the McLaren translation, "prefectures" for "domains (kens)," and *"han* governors" for "chiji."
7. G. B. Sansom, *The Western World and Japan* (New York: Knopf, 1950), p. 326.
8. The assertion of the central government's power in abolishing the *han* and replacing the former daimyo was so dramatic that Yamagata Aritomo called it "the second Restoration coup d'état." Invalidating at a single stroke the networks of personal connection that had tied families together into local power systems in the domains for hundreds of years, *haihan chiken* might have been expected to produce a reaction, maybe even a drastic one. It did not.

   The absence of any strong resistance to *haihan chiken* has struck historians as worthy of comment. Indeed most writers have seen the success of the abolition of *han* and establishment of prefectures as the key to explaining national unification in early Meiji Japan. Typically, the historian reflecting on the apparently smooth process of transforming *han* into prefectures observes a number of things that help explain. One, the government was able to sweeten the pill for the former daimyo by giving them a generous financial settlement. Two, many of the *han* had been swamped with fiscal difficulties, and when the central government abolished the *han,* it assumed responsibility for *han* debts. Most *han* administrators were happy to be relieved of the pressure. Three, the Tokyo government took on the burden of the stipend system for ex-samurai *(shizoku* and *sotsu),* and while the authorities reduced the amounts paid to the former feudal retainers, still, by continuing the stipend payments for a few more years, the government lessened the impact of the abolition of *han.* Another factor adduced to explain the lack of resistance to *haihan chiken* is the political mindset of the ex-samurai—the class most affected—in the early 1870s. Sensing a national crisis, a foreign threat to the independence of

Japan, the former warrior retainers were willing to subsume their particularistic interests in the existence of the *han* to the general need to build
a powerful nation. Premising this willingness, according to this line of
explanation, was the transfer of samurai loyalty from their daimyo and
han to the nation. The absence of a strong reaction to *haihan chiken* on
the part of the masses of people is usually attributed to the fact that the
basic conditions of their lives were little affected by it. For the time
being, taxes continued to be collected as before, and though they now
went into the national exchequer, that did not have an immediate impact
on the peasant.

Certainly, the financial arrangements that the Tokyo government made
for the ex-daimyo, the *han,* and the ex-samurai did contribute to the
success of the second stage of centralization. So, probably, did samurai
concern about foreign danger and peasant indifference. All these should
be taken into account in explaining why *haihan chiken* worked.

They are not, however, the only reasons that *haihan chiken* succeeded,
nor is the accomplishment of *haihan chiken* the only key to explaining
national unification. To appreciate the strong, centralized state structure
that was erected in Japan in the first two Meiji decades, we must give
attention to the development of the subnational system that replaced the
han and to the people who replaced the former daimyo and other local officials.

9. Cf. Kurt Steiner, "Popular Political Participation and Political Development in Japan: The Rural Level," in R. E. Ward, ed., *Political Development in Modern Japan* (Princeton: Princeton University Press, 1968), pp.
213–214, and Samuel P. Huntington, *Political Order in Changing Societies*
(New Haven: Yale University Press, 1968), pp. 32–39.

10. Cf. S. N. Eisenstadt, *Modernization: Protest and Change* (Englewood Cliffs,
N.J.: Prentice-Hall, 1966), esp. pp. 129–144.

11. *The Dynamics of Modernization* (New York: Harper and Row, 1966), p. 13.

12. Amitai Etzioni, *Political Unification* (New York: Holt, Rinehart and Winston, 1965), p. 4.

13. Among writers in English, two recent notable representatives of the criti-
cal line of thinking are Roger Bowen, *Rebellion and Democracy in Meiji
Japan: A Study of Commoners in the Popular Rights Movement* (Berkeley and
Los Angeles: University of California Press, 1980), and Mikiso Hane,
Peasants, Rebels, and Outcastes: The Underside of Modern Japan (New York:
Pantheon, 1982).

14. See especially Kikegawa's *Jichi 50-nen shi* (Tokyo: Tōkyō Shisei Chōsa
Kai, 1941) and *Meiji chihō seido no seiritsu katei* (Tokyo: Tōkyō Shisei
Chōsa Kai, 1957).

15. *Local Government in Japan* (Stanford: Stanford University Press, 1965), and

"Popular Political Participation and Political Development in Japan," cited above.

16. Harold S. Quigley, "Local Government," *Japanese Government and Politics* (New York: Century, 1932); S. Shimizu, "Local Government in Japan," in Shigenobu Okuma, comp., *Fifty Years of New Japan,* (London: Smith, Elder and Co., 1909), vol. 1; Oda Yorodzu, *Principes de droit administratif du Japon* (Paris: Société anonyme du Recueil Sirey, 1928); Ernest W. Clement, "Local Self-Government in Japan," *Political Science Quarterly,* vol. 7, no. 2 (1892); Burks, "Administrative Transition," cited above. See Chapter Seven, below, for more discussion of the writing on this problem.

17. *Rebellion and Democracy,* cited above.

18. See Carol Gluck, "The People in History: Recent Trends in Japanese Historiography," *Journal of Asian Studies,* vol. 38, no. 1 (November 1978), pp. 25–50, and also Neal L. Waters, *Japan's Local Pragmatists: The Transition from Bakumatsu to Meiji in the Kawasaki Region* (Cambridge: Council on East Asian Studies, Harvard University, 1983), pp. 3–30. Attention to the non-elite and especially to "the dimension of conflict, dissent, and, in general, the turbulence" of late Tokugawa and the modern period is the unifying theme of Tetsuo Najita and J. Victor Koschmann, eds., *Conflict in Modern Japanese History: The Neglected Tradition* (Princeton: Princeton University Press, 1982). On the approach taken by the contributors to this book, see Najita, "Introduction: A Synchronous Approach to the Study of Conflict in Modern Japanese History"; the focus, if not the methodology, is similar to Bowen's.

19. Cf. Aldous Huxley, "Tragedy and the Whole Truth," published in *Music at Night* (1931) and included in *Collected Essays* (New York: Harper and Brothers, 1959), pp. 96–103.

20. Waters, *Japan's Local Pragmatists.*

21. Michio Umegaki, *After the Restoration: The Beginning of Japan's Modern State* (New York: New York University Press, 1988).

22. Fraser's long articles are "From Domain to Prefecture: Political Development in Tokushima, 1871–1880," *Papers on Far Eastern History,* no. 12 (hereafter *PFEH,* Canberra, 1975); "Hachisuka Mochiaki (1846–1918): A Meiji Domain Lord and Statesman," *PFEH,* no. 2 (1970); "Komuro Shinobu (1839–1898): A Meiji Politician and Businessman," *PFEH,* no. 3 (1971); "Abe Okito (1845–1920): A Meiji Local Politician and Businessman," *PFEH,* no. 5 (1972); and *National Election Politics in Tokushima Prefecture, 1890–1902* (Canberra: Australian National University Faculty of East Asian Studies, 1972). The shorter article that I called a gem is "Local Administration: The Example of Awa-Tokushima," in Marius B. Jansen and Gilbert Rozman, eds., *Japan in Transition from Tokugawa to Meiji* (Princeton: Princeton University Press, 1986).

23. Ōishi, *Nihon chihō zaigyōseishi josetsu* (Tokyo: Ochanomizu Shobō, 1961), uses evidence from Fukushima Prefecture; Haraguchi, *Meiji zenki chihō seiji shi kenkyū*, 2 vols. (Tokyo: Hanawa Shobō, 1972, 1974) draws largely on Shizuoka Prefecture; and Ariizumi, *Meiji seijishi no kiso katei* (Tokyo: Yoshikawa Kōbunkan, 1980) takes the bulk of his material from Yamanashi Prefecture.

24. In English, the best discussion is Margaret McKean's, in her *Environmental Protest and Citizen Politics in Japan* (Berkeley: University of California Press, 1981). A brief, thoughtful discussion of the *jūmin undō* phenomenon is Kano Tsutomu's "Peasant Uprisings and Citizens' Revolts," *Japan Interpreter*, vol. 8, no. 3 (1973), pp. 279–283. See also Kurt Steiner, Ellis S. Krauss, and Scott C. Flanagan, eds., *Political Opposition and Local Politics in Japan* (Princeton: Princeton University Press, 1980), and J. Victor Koschmann, *Authority and the Individual in Japan* (Tokyo: University of Tokyo Press, 1978). In the 1990s, the attempt to address quality of life issues has led to a sharp increase in the scale of spending on infrastructure improvements (e.g., roads and sewers) decided upon and funded by local government entities. Total outlays for this kind of work, called *chihō tandoku jigyō*, grew at between 5 percent and 12 percent a year from 1988 through 1992, and they are projected to grow by 20 percent in 1993. See "Chihō tandoku jigyō saikō no 18-chō en," *Nihon Keizai Shinbun* (American Edition), November 28, 1992, p. 1.

25. *Koku* is a grain measure; one *koku* equals 5.12 U.S. bushels. The Kaga figure given here (1,022,700 *koku*) is from *Taisei bukan*, 1853, cited by Toshio G. Tsukahira, *Feudal Control in Tokugawa Japan: The Sankin Kōtai System* (Cambridge: Harvard University Press, 1966), p. 152. In 1869 or 1870, Kanazawa *han* reported its actual product *(kusadaka)* as 1,353,353 *koku* (*Hansei ichiran*, ed. Ōtsuka Takematsu, vol. 1, p. 149 [Tokyo: Nihon Shiseki Kyōkai, 1928]). Cf. the 969,594 *koku* reported by Kagoshima (Satsuma) *han* at the same time (ibid., p. 151), and the 988,004 *koku* reported by Yamaguchi (Chōshū) (ibid., p. 360).

26. This figure is reported by Albert M. Craig as the assessed product of *bakufu* lands on the eve of the Restoration. *Chōshū in the Meiji Restoration*, p. 15.

27. Tsukahira, p. 153.

28. For the vital statistics, court ranks, and career highlights of the Maeda of Kanazawa, see *Keizu san'yō*, comp. Iida Tadahiko, ed. Hōgetsu Keigo (Tokyo: Meicho Shuppan, 1972–1974), vol. 8, pp. 97–112. Heads of the clan seem routinely to have held high court titles such as *chūnagon* and *chūjō*.

29. See Appendix 2.

30. Cf. Kozo Yamamura, *A Study of Samurai Income and Entrepreneurship* (Cam-

bridge: Harvard University Press, 1974), p. 102; Craig, *Chōshū in the Meiji Restoration*, pp. 14–15, and "The Restoration Movement in Chōshū," in John W. Hall and Marius B. Jansen, eds., *Studies in the Institutional History of Early Modern Japan* (Princeton: Princeton University Press, 1968); and Ivan P. Hall, *Mori Arinori* (Cambridge: Harvard University Press, 1973), pp. 24–25.

31. See *Kaetsunō ishin kinnō shiryaku*, ed. Nakada Takayoshi (Tokyo: Kaetsunō Ishin Kinnōka Hyōshō Kai, 1930), *passim*.

32. This summary discussion of Kaga in the 1860's draws on *IKS*, vol. 2; *Ishikawa ken no rekishi*, ed. Wakabayashi Kisaburō (Kanazawa: Hokkoku Shuppan Sha, 1970); Wakabayashi Kisaburō, *Kaga han nōseishi no kenkyū*, vol. 2 (Tokyo: Yoshikawa Kōbunkan, 1972); and Shimode Sekiyo, *Ishikawa ken no rekishi* (Tokyo: Yamakawa Shuppan Sha, 1970).

33. Gotō Yasushi has tabulated statistics on the finances of twenty-five *han* at the time of the Restoration, and by the most important of his measures, the ratio of *han* debt plus *han* currency issue to current receipts, Kaga was in the third-best position. Kaga's debt plus currency issue came to 161 percent of current receipts. It is interesting to note that Chōshū was deeper in red ink—the same indicator for Chōshū stood at 361 percent. Kaga samurai received a larger share of their recorded stipends than did samurai of most other *han*, also in the two years immediately following the proclamation of the Restoration of imperial rule. Gotō, "Karoku seiri to shizoku no dōkō," in Furushima Toshio, et al., eds., *Meiji zenki kyōdoshi kenkyū hō*, (Tokyo: Asakura Shoten, 1970), pp. 102–103. Kaga could afford to invest a large sum in the Kanazawa Kawase Gaisha when that was founded in 1869 (see Tokuda Toshiaki, "Kanazawa Kawase Gaisha no kenkyū," *Nihon rekishi*, no. 307 [1973]).

34. Sir Ernest Satow, *A Diplomat in Japan: The Inner History of the Critical Years in the Evolution of Japan When the Ports Were Opened and the Monarchy Restored* (London: Seeley, Service, 1921), pp. 236–237. On Kaga's fence-sitting, self-preserving attitudes in the Restoration period, see Tokuda, "Ishin ni okeru Kaga han no seiji dōkō," *Hokuriku shigaku*, no. 18 (1970), and Lord Redesdale, *Memories* (New York: E. P. Dutton, n.d.) vol. 2, pp. 397–405.

35. Waters also suspects that this is the case. He concludes his book by saying: "Whether or not the response of the Kawasaki region is typical of the Meiji period cannot be known until Japan scholars investigate other regions where 'nothing happened.'" *Japan's Local Pragmatists*, p. 131.

1. THE PERILS OF PRUDENCE: KAGA UNDER MAEDA NARIYASU AND MAEDA YOSHIYASU

1. *IKS,* vol. 2, pp. 828, 829, 1425, 1491–1492; *(Shinsen) Dai jinmei jiten,* comp. Shimonaka Yasaburō (Tokyo: Heibonsha, 1937), vol. 5, p. 561; *Kanō kyōdo jii.*

2. *IKS,* vol. 2, pp. 801–805; Kuranami Seiji, *Kaga hansei kaikaku no kenkyū* (Tokyo: Sekai Shoin, 1969, hereafter cited as Kuranami, *KHKK*), p. 166–172, and Kuranami, *Hyakumangoku daimyō: Kaga han no seiritsu to tenkai* (Tokyo: Tōgensha, 1965), pp. 125–131; *KHS,* vol. 13.

3. *Kanō kyōdo jii; IKS,* vol. 2, p. 816; Kuranami, *KHKK,* p. 181–183; *KHS,* vol. 13.

4. *Kanazawa jō: sono shizen to rekishi,* ed. Kanazawa Daigaku Kanazawa Jō Gakujutsu Chōsa Iinkai Nai *Kanazawa jō* Henshū Iin (Kanazawa: Kanazawa Daigaku Seikatsu Kyōdō Kumiai Shuppan Bu, 1967), pp. 12–13; Shinbo Chiyoko and Matsubara Shigeru, *Kenrokuen* (Kanazawa: Hokkoku Shuppan Sha, 1972), esp. pp. 109–112.

5. Wakabayashi Kisaburō, *Kaga han nōsei shi no kenkyū* (Tokyo: Yoshikawa Kōbunkan, 1970, 1972, hereafter cited as Wakabayashi, *KNSK*), vol. 2, pp. 236–323; Kuranami, *KHKK,* pp. 181–248; *IKS,* vol. 2, pp. 901–950.

6. Tabata Tsutomu, "Tenpō-Kōkaki ni okeru Kaga han zaisei to hansai hensai shihō no kōzō," *Shien,* vol. 34, no. 1 (1974).

7. Kuranami, *KHKK,* pp. 205–206; Kobayashi Yasutoshi, "Kaga han Tenpōki hansei no dōkō ni tsuite," *Hokuriku shigaku,* no. 9 (1960), pp. 27–29.

8. Kuranami, *KHKK,* pp. 206–208; Kobayashi, pp. 29–32; Tabata, "Tenpō-Kōkaki," passim.

9. Tabata, "Tenpō-Kōkaki."

10. Cf. Thomas C. Smith, "Pre-modern Economic Growth: Japan and the West," *Past and Present,* no. 60 (1973); idem, "Ōkura Nagatsune and the Technologists," in Albert M. Craig and Donald H. Shively, eds., *Personality in Japanese History* (Berkeley: University of California Press, 1970); idem, *The Agrarian Origins of Modern Japan* (Stanford: Stanford University Press, 1959); and Susan B. Hanley and Kozo Yamamura, *Economic and Demographic Change in Preindustrial Japan, 1600–1868* (Princeton: Princeton University Press, 1977).

11. Wakabayashi, *KNSK,* vol. 2, pp. 292–298; *KHS,* vol. 14.

12. Wakabayashi, ed., *Kaga Noto no rekishi* (Tokyo: Kōdansha, 1978), pp. 300–302.

13. Tabata, "Tenpō-Kōkaki"; *IKS,* vol. 2, pp. 927–928.

14. Wakabayashi, ed., *Kaga Noto no rekishi*, pp. 303–304; Kobayashi, pp. 34–37.

15. Tabata, "Tenpō-Kōkaki"; Kuranami, *KHKK*, p. 220 ff.; Wakabayashi, *KNSK*, vol. 2, pp. 236–243.

16. *KHS*, vol. 14; *IKS*, vol. 2; Wakabayashi, ed., *Kaga Noto no rekishi;* Okumura Satoshi, "Hansei no suii," *Ishikawa ken no rekishi*, ed. Wakabayashi, pp. 136–137.

17. On Zeniya Gohei and on the relations between Kaga officials and merchants in the last decades of *han* rule, see Takase Tamotsu, "Zeniya Gohei kō," *Nihon rekishi*, no. 252 (1969); Wakabayashi, *Zeniya Gohei* (Tokyo: Sōgensha, 1957); *IKS*, vol. 2, pp. 986–1063.

18. Kuranami, *KHKK*, pp. 189, 218. Kuranami cites a memorandum on Okumura's views, "Okumura Hidezane iiagegaki," vol. 1, a document preserved in the Kaetsunō Bunko of the Kanazawa City Library.

19. Tabata, "Tenpō-Kōkaki"; see also Mizushima Shigeru, "Kaga han Kaeiki no hansei kaikaku," *Chihōshi kenkyū*, 66 (vol. 13, no. 6) (1963).

20. In Japanese periodization, these years were the Kōka and Kaei eras, 1844–1848 and 1848–1854, respectively.

21. Wakabayashi, *KNSK*, vol. 2, pp. 160, 329–346; cf. Kuranami, *KHKK*, pp. 244–245; *IKS*, vol. 2, pp. 948–986; Tabata, "Ueda Sakunojō no Kaga han Tenpō kaikaku kōsō ni tsuite: Han zaisei kaikaku ron o chūshin ni," in Hayashi Hideo and Yamada Shōji, eds., *Bakuhansei kara kindai e* (Tokyo: Kashiwa Shobō, 1979); *Bakumatsu ishin jinmei jiten*, ed. Naramoto Tatsuya (Tokyo: Gakugei Shorin, 1978).

22. The explanation that the party's name came from their black *haori* is not universally accepted. Another theory holds that the name of this clique came from a dialect word for blowfish (*fugu*, called, because of its appearance, *kurohaori*). As a carelessly selected bite of the flesh of this fish could poison one, so could the barbs of the black coat party members' utterances. *IKS*, vol. 2, p. 951; *Kaga Noto no rekishi*, pp. 310–311; Wakabayashi, *KNSK*, vol. 2, p. 244.

23. Wakabayashi, *KNSK*, vol. 2, p. 349.

24. Ibid.

25. *KHS, H*, vol. 1; *IKS*, vol. 2; Wakabayashi, *KNSK*, vol. 2, pp. 391–400; Sakai Seiichi, "Kaga han no kaibō to shomin no dōin," *Etchū shidan*, 20; Mizushima, p. 21.

26. *IKS*, vol. 2; *KHS, H*, vol. 1.

27. Mizushima, "Kaga han Kaeiki no hansei kaikaku," p. 25; *KHS, H*, vol. 1, p. 528.

28. Mizushima, pp. 21–22.

29. The name of the new office was *nushitsuke sekoyaku*. Ibid., p. 23.

30. Ibid., pp. 25–26; Wakabayashi, *KNSK*, vol. 2, pp. 258–360, passim.

31. *IKS*, vol. 2.
32. Ibid.
33. *Kanō kyōdo jii.*
34. Wakabayashi, *KNSK*, vol. 2, p. 370; *Kaga Noto no rekishi.*
35. *IKS*, vol. 2.
36. *Kaga Noto no rekishi.*
37. *IKS*, vol. 2.
38. This time the offices to promote economic development were called *sanbutsu kaisho.* Wakabayashi, *KNSK*, vol. 2, pp. 382–390.
39. *Kaga Noto no rekishi.*
40. Tagawa Shōichi, "Hōkaiki no hansei to sesō," *Ishikawa ken no rekishi,* ed. Wakabayashi, p. 200.
41. Tabata, "Bunkyū-Keiōki ni okeru Kaga han no sanbutsukata seisaku ni tsuite," *Nihon rekishi,* no. 299 (1973); Wakabayashi, *KNSK*, vol. 2.
42. Craig, *Chōshū in the Meiji Restoration.*
43. This discussion of the economic policies of 1863–1864 draws heavily on Tabata, "Bunkyū-Keiōki," the most detailed account and analysis.
44. *IKS*, vol. 2, pp. 1063–1162, contains the most detailed account of the events of 1864 and their background and consequences. Much of this section draws on the *IKS* version. Cf. also *Kaetsunō ishin kinnō shiryaku,* ed. Nakada Takayoshi (Tokyo: Kaetsunō Ishin Kinnō Hyōshō Kai, 1930).
45. *IKS*, vol. 2.
46. Ibid.
47. The best analysis of Ogawa's thought and actions is Miyazawa Seiichi, "Kaga han sonnō undō to Ansei no komesōdō: ichi 'sōmō' no kōdō no bunseki o tsūjite," in Kano Masanao and Takagi Shunsuke, eds., *Ishin henkaku ni okeru zaisonteki shochōryū,* (Tokyo: San'ichi Shobō, 1972).
48. See Conrad Totman, *The Collapse of the Tokugawa Bakufu,* esp. pp. 49–54. For an account in English of how another domain and its lord acted in these circumstances, see Andrew Fraser, "Hachisuka Mochiaki (1846–1918)"; see also Craig, *Chōshū,* and Marius B. Jansen, *Sakamoto Ryoma and the Meiji Restoration.*
49. *IKS*, vol. 2, p. 1074.
50. Ibid., pp. 1079–1080.
51. Ibid., pp. 1089–1090; *KHS, H,* vol. 2.
52. A lengthy excerpt of Sagawa's diary is printed in *IKS*, vol. 2, pp. 1128–1133.
53. Ibid., pp. 1126–1128.
54. Ibid., p. 1221.
55. Ibid., pp. 1220–1221.
56. Ibid., p. 1222; *KHS, H,* vol. 2; Tokuda Toshiaki, "Han taisei kaitai no

katei: zaisei tōitsusaku ni taisuru Kaga han no taisho kara kōsatsu shite," *Hokuriku shigaku,* no. 16 (1968), pp. 28–29.

57. Tokuda, "Han taisei kaitai no katei," p. 28; for details, see *KHS, H,* vol. 2, pp. 552–720.

58. *IKS,* vol. 2, p. 1229; *KHS, H,* vol. 2.

59. Satow, *A Diplomat in Japan,* pp. 236–237.

60. Tokuda, "Han taisei kaitai no katei," p. 29.

61. Tokuda, "Ishin ni okeru Kaga han no seiji dōkō," *Hokuriku shigaku,* no. 18 (1970); *Kaga Noto no rekishi.*

62. Tokuda, "Ishin ni okeru Kaga han no seiji dōkō."

63. Ibid.

64. Ibid.

65. *IKS,* vol. 2, pp. 1240–1241.

66. Tokuda, "Ishin ni okeru Kaga han no seiji dōkō"; *KHS, H,* vol. 2.

67. *IKS,* vol. 2, p. 1244; *KHS, H,* vol. 2.

68. *IKS,* vol. 2, p. 1253.

69. Ibid., p. 1267.

70. Ibid., p. 1269.

71. Tokuda, "Han taisei no kaitai no katei," p. 30; *KHS, H,* vol. 2; Inoue Ichiji, "Meiji ishin ni okeru Kaga hyakumangoku," *Rekishi kōron,* vol. 3, no. 6 (1934), p. 85.

72. *FSS.* The government order was called *hanchi shokusei* (Regulations Governing Domain Administration); it was issued by the Gyōseikan. For the text, see also *Hōrei zensho* Meiji gan boshin no toshi (1868), p. 37 (number 902).

73. Tokuda, "Han taisei kaitai no katei," pp. 34–35.

74. Inoue, "Meiji ishin ni okeru Kaga hyakumangoku."

75. *IKS,* vol. 2, p. 1382; *KHS, H,* vol. 2.

76. *IKS,* vol. 2, pp. 1385–1386; Tokuda, "Han taisei kaitai no katei," p. 35.

77. Ibid., pp. 30–31.

78. *IKS,* vol. 2, p. 1414.

79. Ibid., p. 1404.

80. Haraguchi Kiyoshi, "Han taisei no kaitai," *(Iwanami kōza) Nihon rekishi* 15 *kindai* 2 (Tokyo: Iwanami Shoten, 1962). On the debate, see also Umegaki, *After the Restoration,* pp. 48–49. On the intellectual background of the debate about *hōken* and *gunken,* see Kawahara Hiroshi, " 'Gunken' no kannen to kindai 'chūō' kan no keisei," *Kindai Nihon seiji ni okeru chūō to chihō (Nenpō seijigaku)* 1984 (Tokyo: Iwanami Shoten, 1985), pp. 61–77.

81. McLaren, ed., "Japanese Government Documents," *Transactions of the Asiatic Society of Japan,* cited in the Introduction.

2. A Han Is Made a Prefecture: Administration in Ishikawa Prefecture, 1871–1878

1. One of the earliest accounts of the history of the local government system in modern Japan can be taken as representative of this view: Ōmori Shōichi, *Jichi sei seitei no tenmatsu* (Tokyo: Zenkoku Chōsonchō Kai, 1928). This book is drawn from lectures that Ōmori gave to the National Conference of Town and Village Chiefs (Zenkoku Chōsonchō Kai) when he was governor of Kyoto. Ōmori (1856–1927) had begun his bureaucratic rise in the 1880s as an aide to Yamagata Aritomo, working on the establishment of the local government system.

2. Richard L. Staubitz, "The Establishment of the System of Local Self-Government (1888–1890) in Meiji Japan: Yamagata Aritomo and the Meaning of *'Jichi'* (Self-Government)," unpublished Ph.D. dissertation, Yale University, 1973, p. ix. Staubitz cites Ōmori's periodization.

3. See Ōishi, "Chichō jichi," *(Iwanami kōza) Nihon rekishi 16, kindai 3* (Tokyo: Iwanami Shoten, 1967), p. 233; Ōishi, *Nihon chihō zaigyōseishi josetsu* (Tokyo: Ochanomizu Shobō, 1961); Ōshima Tarō, *Nihon chihō gyōzaiseishi josetsu* (Tokyo: Miraisha, 1968).

4. Ariizumi, *Meiji seijishi no kiso katei: Chihō seiji jōkyō shiron* (Tokyo: Yoshikawa Kōbunkan, 1980), p. 13.

5. Ōishi can again be taken as representative; see "Chihō jichi," p. 238.

6. Cf. Fujita Takeo, "Meiji shi ni okeru chihō jichi sei seitei no igi," *(Kaikoku 100-nen kinen) Meiji bunka shi ronshū* (Tokyo: Kangensha, 1952), especially pp. 714–717.

7. *Kido Kōin nikki*, April 18, 1877, vol. 3, p. 563. Part of this passage is cited by Kikegawa Hiroshi (see note following), p. 18.

8. Tōkyō Shisei Chōsa Kai, *Jichi 50-nen shi, seido hen* (Tokyo: Tōkyō Shisei Chōsa Kai, 1940), pp. 18–19. The author of this study was Kikegawa. A reprint of this work was issued by Bunsei Shoin of Tokyo in 1977, with Kikegawa's authorship recognized on the title page.

9. "Chief councilor" here is used to translate *daisanji*.

10. *IKS*, vol. 4, p. 2. Hayashi, who went on to serve as governor of Myōtō Prefecture and Hamamatsu Prefecture, was an official in the Ministry of Finance in 1871/8 when he was designated for duty in Kanazawa. Ōshima Mitsuko has identified him as one of the men whom MOF sent to trouble spots, arming them with powers superior even to the prefectural governor, to ensure that the central government's policies were enforced as intended. Other men were posted to Hiroshima and Saga prefectures at the same time as Hayashi was named to go to Kanazawa. Ōshima, "Ōkubo shihai taisei ka no fuken tōchi," *Kindai Nihon seiji ni okeru chūō to chihō (Nenpō Seijigaku)* 1984, p. 38. I have found no evidence that Hayashi

ever actually reached Kanazawa or played the role that Ōshima describes. Moreover I think it questionable whether Minister of Finance Ōkubo, one of the preeminent leaders of Satsuma, would have felt that Hayashi, born an Awa samurai, would be more responsive to his direction than the other man appointed to go to Kanazawa, Uchida Masakaze of Satsuma.

11. Most of this material on Uchida comes from his short autobiographical note, *Zen Ishikawa kenrei jū goi ge Uchida Masakaze shi seiden,* included in *Shūjin zatsuroku,* MS in the Kaetsunō Bunko, Kanazawa City Library. Uchida's autobiography is addressed to Morita Heiji, a local historian; it is dated August 1887, and stamped with the seal "Masakaze." Neither this account nor any other that I have found contains any information about Uchida's upbringing, education, or early career. Of his life before 1863, Uchida tells only that he had been adopted by his childless brother. He does mention his wife, two sons, and two daughters (one of the latter born of a concubine), and from his age and the fact that he writes of his family before treating his career after 1863, we might guess that the children were born before that year.

12. Sengoku Yoshihisa, *Ishikawa ken rekidai chōkan monogatari* (Kanazawa: Kanazawa Shinpō Sha, 1928). Sengoku represents the Kaga samurai as saying, "Satsuma shōbushi no Uchida ga nan da!" (p. 9).

13. The Uchida family was of the *koban* rank, according to Masakaze. This was the seventh highest rank of Satsuma samurai, and was composed of some 760 families in the last years of *han* rule. About 120 families were in the six ranks above *koban.* See Ivan P. Hall, *Mori Arinori* (Cambridge, Mass.: Harvard University Press, 1973), pp. 24–25, on Satsuma samurai ranks. On the problem of defining "upper" and "lower" samurai, see Albert M. Craig, "The Restoration Movement in Chōshū," in John W. Hall and Marius B. Jansen, eds., *Studies in the Institutional History of Early Modern Japan* (Princeton: Princeton University Press, 1968), pp. 363–367. Professor Craig estimates the Satsuma samurai population at nearly 28,000 (*Chōshū in the Meiji Restoration,* p. 14), and using this figure and the numbers of families given by Ivan Hall, we can infer that the Uchida family's rank placed it within the top 10 percent of Satsuma samurai.

14. Modestly, Uchida omits mention of this incident from his autobiographical note. The story is included in the entries on Uchida in *(Shinsen) Dai jinmei jiten,* vol. 1, p. 428, and *Nihon rekishi daijiten* (Encyclopedia of Japanese History), comp. Kawade Takao (Tokyo: Kawade Shobō, 1964), vol. 2, p. 220.

15. For accounts of the Kyoto discussions and the political context, see W. G. Beasley, *The Meiji Restoration* pp. 184–196: Craig; *Chōshū,* pp. 192–207; and Totman, *Collapse,* pp. 32–99.

16. The Satsuma office in Osaka was called *Ōzaka-zume kinkata;* Uchida's title

was *mono bugyō*. On Satsuma bureaucratic organization, see the chart "Han no shokusei hyō," *(Kadokawa) Nihonshi jiten,* ed. Takayanagi Mitsutoshi and Takeuchi Rizō (Tokyo: Kadokawa Shoten, 1966), pp. 1087–1088.

17. The government order was *hanchi shokusei* (Regulations Governing Domain Administration), issued by the Gyōseikan on 1868/10/28. For the text, see *Hōrei zensho, Meiji gan boshin no toshi (1868),* p. 337 (number 902). Uchida was named sansei on 1869/3/7.

18. William J. Chambliss translates *sansei* as Assistant Chief Administrator, *shissei* as Chief Administrator. Ishii Ryosuke, ed., *Japanese Legislation in the Meiji Era,* tr. Chambliss (Tokyo: Obunsha, 1958), p. 85. The entry on Uchida in *Bakumatsu ishin jinmei jiten,* ed. Naramoto Tatsuya (Tokyo: Gakugei Shorin, 1978), tells us that he won favor in governmental circles at this time by helping the imperial forces learn of revenues and supplies that could be confiscated from the domains that were resisting the new imperial regime.

19. Uchida's position in the *dajōkan* was *shōben*. In the rank system he was *jū goi ge*.

20. In his autobiographical note, Uchida wrote that on 1871/8/15, he was named Kanazawa *han daisanji*. "Han" would seem to be a mistake. It apparently took government officials a while to get used to their own new terminology.

21. *Dai jinmei jiten,* loc. cit.

22. Relations between Kanazawa and Kagoshima are detailed in *KKSS, S,* vol. 1, pp. 77–81, and *IKS,* vol. 4, pp. 229–231.

23. *KKSS, S* puts the voyage to Nagasaki in 1869, *IKS* in 1870/1. The former account notes that Kuga and Yoneyama entered the Kōdōkan, the Hizen *han* school, where they associated with other young, politically aware men.

24. *IKS,* vol. 4, p. 230. Kuga is quoted talking about his feelings of that time in *KKSS, S,* vol. 1, pp. 78–79.

25. *KKSS, S,* vol. 1, p. 79.

26. The Satsuma friend was named Nakai Hiroshi. Ibid.

27. Sengoku (*Chōkan monogatari,* p. 2) does not completely accept this story, but writes, "According to one account, men from Kaga who were in Tokyo, concerned with political arrangements in Ishikawa [*sic*] Prefecture, lobbied with Count Itagaki and got Uchida appointed."

28. In 1874, for example, the highest-ranking official who gave Ishikawa Prefecture as his place of registry was a *shōgaishi* of the Sei-in in the Council of State, a position that carried the designation fifth or sixth rank (*tō*). Just one other man from Ishikawa was in the Sei-in, and he had a lower post, *daishuki*, with the seventh or eighth rank. In the Home Ministry, the most powerful ministry in the government at the time, in

1874, there were no men from Ishikawa. In the Ministry of Finance there were only two men from Ishikawa, neither among the top officials of the ministry. Whether or not one subscribes to the "*han* clique" (*hanbatsu*) interpretation of the structure of the Meiji government, it must be admitted that several prefectures were much better represented by men in high positions in these key parts of the government. See Masumi Junnosuke, *Nihon seitō shi ron* (Tokyo: Tōkyō Daigaku Shuppan Kai, 1966–1968), vol. 1, pp. 100–105.

29. There were unusually large numbers of governors from Kagoshima and Kōchi, nine and six, respectively, among the seventy-two men serving in that post at the end of 1871. Three governors gave Saga, and only one gave Yamaguchi, as their place of registry at that time. Fifty-three governors had other places of registry. Three of the Kagoshima-born governors were placed in Kagoshima and adjacent prefectures, and thus there were six men from Satsuma serving as governors in other parts of Japan. There is no apparent pattern in the placement of these Satsuma-born governors. See ibid., pp. 107–108. Masumi cites *Kindai Nihon seiji shi hikkei*, ed. Tōyama Shigeki et al. (Tokyo, 1960), p. 67, and Kurihara Teiichi, *Chihō-kan kai no hensen* (1930), appendix. Ōshima Mitsuko, noting the large number of early governors with their family registries in Satsuma, Chōshū, and Tosa, and the large number who had been active in the Restoration movement, argues that it was *shishi*—"men of spirit"—whom the central government appointed most gladly to governorships. Ōshima, "Meiji shoki no chihōkan," *Nihon hō to Ajia* (vol. 3 of the Festschrift in honor of Niida Noboru) (Tokyo: Keisō Shobō, 1970), p. 198. On *shishi*, see Marius B. Jansen, *Sakamoto Ryōma and the Meiji Restoration* (Princeton: Princeton University Press, 1961); and Albert M. Craig, "Introduction: Perspectives on Personality in Japanese History," *Personality in Japanese History*, ed. Albert M. Craig and Donald H. Shively (Berkeley and Los Angeles: University of California Press, 1970). Uchida Masakaze seems not to have had a *shishi*-type personality.

30. *IKSR, kan* 57, *kan'in rireki, Meiji* 1–7 *nen*, in the series *Fuken shiryō*. The original of this document is in the Naikaku Bunko of the Kōbunsho Kan. *Fuken shiryō* has been copied on microfilm; hereafter, notes will cite it as *FS* followed by the reel number. The career records of officials (*kan'in rireki*) of Ishikawa Prefecture appear in *FS* reels 113–116. *IKSR* was set in type and issued in 5 vols. by the Ishikawa Prefectural Library between 1971 and 1975; some later citations refer to this printed version.

31. *KKSS, S*, vol. 1, p. 80. Sugimura's title was *gon daisanji*, Yoneyama's was *daizoku*.

32. Shimode Sekiyo, *Ishikawa ken no rekishi*, pp. 201–202. *IKS*, vol. 4, p. 2. The Chō was one of the *hakka*, as observed in the preceding chapter; it

was the family of Tsurahiro, one of the leaders of the council of elders in the latter part of the era of Maeda rule.

33. See Kida Sadakichi, "Meiji ishin go fuken setchi no tenmatsu oyobi sono go no bungō ni tsuite," *Rekishi chiri,* vol. 11, no. 3 (1908). Following Chambliss (see note 18 above), *fu* is translated "urban prefecture," and *ken* is translated "rural prefecture" here. But because some *ken* like Ishikawa contained towns or cities with large populations, the designation "rural" is not always apt, and it will be used only when it seems necessary to distinguish between *fu* and *ken*.

34. A chart tracing the amalgamations and divisions is printed in *IKGS,* vol. 1, p. 385.

35. Changes in administrative boundaries are summarized by Shimode, pp. 200–205.

36. Memorial to the emperor from the Risshisha, June 1877, in *Meiji Japan Through Contemporary Sources,* comp. Centre for East Asian Cultural Studies (Tokyo: Centre for East Asian Cultural Studies, 1970), vol. 2, p. 195.

37. *Shizoku* and *sotsu* were early Meiji classifications applied to men who had been samurai *(bushi)* vassals of the daimyo, or sub-vassals of other samurai. Craig ("The Restoration Movement in Chōshū") and Beasley *(The Meiji Restoration,* pp. 24–32) provide good brief discussions of samurai ranks in the Tokugawa period. In 1869 all *bushi* above the *hirazamurai* rank were relabeled *shizoku,* and lesser samurai were lumped together under the designation *sotsu.* In 1872 all ex-samurai whose stipends were hereditary were classified simply as *shizoku,* and the remainder of ex-samurai were redesignated *heimin,* "commoners." It is imprecise to speak of "samurai" after 1869, for *shizoku* and *sotsu* were not feudal retainers. Properly, one should speak only of "ex-samurai" or "former *bushi*" or the like.

38. "Province" is used here to translate *kuni;* "county" renders *kōri;* "administrative district," *ku;* "town" or "ward," *chō* (sometimes pronounced *machi*); and "village," *mura.*

39. *Kenchi jōrei,* January 6, 1872. Translation in McLaren, "Japanese Government Documents," pp. 254–255. Bernard S. Silberman published an excellent analysis of the difficulties that faced officials like Uchida: "Bureacratization of the Meiji State: The Problem of Succession in the Meiji Restoration, 1868–1900," *Journal of Asian Studies,* vol. 35, no. 3 (1976), pp. 421–430.

40. *IKGS,* vol. 1, p. 483.

41. Cf. *IKSR, kan* 57, *kan'in rireki, Meiji* 1–7 *nen,* FS reel 113, and *IKSR, kan* 68, *(Kyū Kanazawa ken) kan'in rireki,* FS reel 116. The entries for officials who stayed on in the transition period (see reel 116) seem incomplete, as they give only the dates of formal dismissal or retirement; these entries probably should not be relied on for the dates when men actually

left office. From other sources, e.g., the report of Tsutsui Ei cited below, we know that some men were still in office months after the *kan'in rireki* date for their dismissal or retirement. Still, judging from the appointment dates of men in Ishikawa prefectural service (see reel 113) and the numbers of men in office, I think it probable that high *han* officials were replaced fairly quickly.

42. The number 504 is so large that it may be the case that some of these men had been in and out of office during the last days of *han* rule. See *IKSR, kan 42, seido bu, shokusei, FS* reel 112; ibid., *kan 68–69, (Kyū Kanazawa ken) kan'in rireki 1, 2, FS* reel 116.

43. Ōshima Mitsuko, "Meiji shoki no chihōkan," p. 197.

44. As noted above, the Council of State at first ordered *han* officials from *dai sanji* on down to stay on the job. Then on 1872/2/8, the Council of State ordered that no regard be paid to past customs in naming personnel or setting up administrative district boundaries. Ōshima Mitsuko, "Meiji shoki no chihōkan," pp. 197–198.

45. Obata had been *daizoku* of Kanazawa *han*, then, from 1871/6, chief councilor of Toyama *han* (which had, of course, been a branch *han* of Kaga before 1869). *IKSR, kan 68–69, furoku, (Kyū Kanazawa ken) kan'in rireki, FS* reel 116; *IKS*, vol. 4, p. 231; *IKSR, kan 57, kan'in rireki, FS* reel 113.

46. The retired councilors included Maeda Naonobu, Yokoyama Masakazu, and Okada Masatada. The group of other senior administrators who left office included Yasui Akichika, Kugawara Yuikō, Naitō Sei, and Kitagawa Inosaku. *IKS*, vol. 4, pp. 227, 231.

47. On Yasui's service as a *chōshi* (an official recommended to the central government by the *han*) and on his relationship with Sanjō, Kido, and Hirosawa Saneomi, see *KKSS, S*, vol. 1, p. 75.

48. See Ishibayashi Bunkichi, *Ishikawa 100-nen shi* (Kanazawa, 1972), p. 39.

49. See *IKSR, kan 57, kan'in rireki, FS* reel 113 and *IKSR*, vol. 4, pp. 431–494.

50. Ibid.

51. Ōshima, "Ōkubo shihai taisei ka no fuken tōchi," pp. 36–37; Haraguchi, *Meiji zenki chihō seiji shi kenkyū*, vol. 1, p. 227. Cf. Masumi, vol. 1, 109–110, and also Ardath W. Burks, "Administrative Transition from *Han* to *Ken:* The Example of Okayama," *Far Eastern Quarterly*, vol. 15, no. 3 (1956), p. 380. Burks notes a housecleaning of "some fifty officials" in Okayama, but offers no explanation of this, nor does he note where the "equal number of new ones" came from, or what their career backgrounds were.

52. Ōshima tabulated the percentages of locally born men in all the prefectural offices that reported in a survey by the Council of State dated 1872/5/20. Of the fifty-eight offices for which there is data, three (Sakata,

Asuwa, and Kumamoto) had staffs entirely comprised of local men; three (Saga, Kōchi, and Okayama) had over 90 percent locals; and five (Nagasaki, Fukuoka, Hiroshima, Ishikawa, and Shizuoka) had over 80 percent locals. Yamaguchi is one of twelve prefectures for which data is not available in this survey, but it reported 80 percent locals in August 1873. Even counting Yamaguchi, fewer than one-fifth of all prefectures had as many as 80 percent local men in office, and about three-fifths of the prefectures had fewer than 50 percent locals as staff members. It is not surprising that areas that had opposed the new government in the Restoration war tended to have very few locals; among those with fewer than 30 percent were Fukushima, Niibari, Inba, Wakamatsu, Iwasaki, and Iruma. When Ōshima counted the relatively high-ranking locals in the new prefectural offices (those who headed one of the four working departments into which prefectural offices were organized in 1872), the reliance by governors on outsiders is even more evident. In just over one-sixth of the prefectures were half of the department chiefs, or more than half, locally born. Ishikawa was one of those where half were locals. "Ōkubo shihai taisei ka no fuken tōchi," loc. cit.

53. Uchida to Shikan, *IKSR, kan 1, seiji bu, kenchi FS* reel 109.
54. *IKGS*, vol. 1, p. 106. Subprefectural government is treated in the next chapter.
55. *IKSR, kan 47, kan'in rireki, FS* reel 113.
56. On the vendetta, see *IKSR, kan 10, seiji bu, keishō, FS* reel 109, and *IKS*, vol. 4, pp. 1066–1097. On Honda's assassination, see *IKS*, vol. 2, pp. 1338–1370, and *KHS, bakumatsu hen ge kan*, pp. 1092–1093, 1110, 1112–1119. The third victim of Honda's followers was Sugano Hokichi, who had been sentenced to domiciliary confinement after Honda's assassination, and who operated a school in his home.
57. *IKSR, kan 10, seiji bu, keishō, FS* reel 109.
58. *IKS*, vol. 4, p. 1089; Ishibayashi, p. 27.
59. On this "uprising of the straw raincoats" *(minomushi sōdō)*, see the report of Daishōji prefectural authorities, *IKSR, kan 38, seiji bu, sōyō jihen, IKSR*, vol. 3, pp. 299–300. See also Wakabayashi, *KNSK*, vol. 2, pp. 416–423, and Sonozaki Zen'ichi, "Seitō no seisui to kensei," *Ishikawa ken no rekishi*, ed. Wakabayashi, p. 214. According to Wakabayashi, *minomushi* is local dialect for "short straw raincoat"; in standard Japanese, it means "bagworm." Presumably the wearing of this kind of rain garment was popularly identified with the peasants of the area of this disturbance. Daishōji prefectural chief councilor (i.e., governor) Aochi, it is interesting to note, was a local samurai; the central government did not send an outsider to govern the former Daishōji *han*. See also Ishibayashi, *Ishikawa 100-nen shi*, p. 273.

60. Sonozaki, p. 214; Wakabayashi, *KNSK*, vol. 2, p. 423. Tanaka Akira has given us a good, clear discussion of early Meiji peasant disturbances in "Ishin seiken ron," *(Kōza Nihon shi 5) Meiji ishin*, ed. Shigaku Kenkyū Kai and Nihonshi Kenkyū Kai (Tokyo: Tōkyō Daigaku Shuppan Kai, 1970), pp. 150–156.

61. For historians' views of the reasons for moving the prefectural office, see, for example, Shimode, p. 203; Saguchi Tōru, "Gendaishi," *Ishikawa ken no rekishi*, ed. Miyashita Yokichi (Kanazawa: Hokkoku Shinbun Sha, 1950), p. 227; *IKS*, vol. 4, p. 235; and *KKSS, S*, vol. 1, p. 81.

62. Uchida to Shikan, *IKSR, kan 1, seiji bu, kenchi, FS* reel 109.

63. *IKS*, vol. 4, pp. 4–5.

64. *KKSS, S*, vol. 1, pp. 81–82. Uchida's house was in Kanazawa; as it turned out, he never got around to moving to Mikawa.

65. *IKS*, vol. 4, pp. 7–8; *IKGS*, vol. 1, pp. 483–484; Sengoku, *Chōkan monogatari*, pp. 5–6.

66. *IKSR, kan 42, seido bu, shokusei, FS* reel 112.

67. The text of Uchida's appeal *(gekibun)* is reproduced in *IKS*, vol. 4, pp. 235–237, and Sengoku, *Chōkan monogatari*, pp. 6–7.

68. "Kokoroekata kajō," *KKSS, S*, vol. 1, p. 83. Cf. *IKSR, kan 33, seiji bu, keiho, Meiji 5-nen, FS* reel 111, where it is noted that "more than a hundred men" applied to serve as police auxiliaries. Both *IKS and KKSS* say that more than five hundred men joined to form the force.

69. *IKSR, kan 33, seiji bu, keiho, Meiji 5-nen, FS* reel 111. One of the men who paid for the police auxiliary was surnamed Taga. I have been unable to ascertain whether he was related to the assassinated official Taga Kenzaburō.

70. *IKS*, vol. 4, p. 9.

71. *IKSR, kan 20, seiji bu, kokō, Meiji 5-nen, FS* reel 110, and Ishibayashi, *Ishikawa 100-nen shi*, p. 44.

72. *IKSR, kan 1, seiji bu, kenchi, FS* reel 109. On the date: as is well known, Japan switched from the lunar calendar *(taiinreki)* to the solar calendar *(taiyōreki*, i.e., Gregorian calendar) on January 1, 1873. This change was ordered by Imperial Rescript and a Notification of the Council of State dated 1872/11/9. It may be of interest to note how the change was effected within the prefecture. Pursuant to an order transmitted to "all district chiefs *(kaku kukochō)* in Kaga Province and all district chiefs in Noto Province," signed by Uchida Masakaze and dated 1872/11/20, these subprefectural officials informed all the people *(shimin ippan)* of the change. By the old calendar, January 1, 1873, was the third day of the twelfth month of the fifth year of the Meiji era. The text of Uchida's order is given in *IKS*, vol. 4, pp. 8–9. In the present work, dates prior

to the change in the calendar are given in the form year/month/day (e.g., 1872/11/9).

73. Shimode (pp. 225–227) reports that Kanazawa used to be known as a "town of mistresses" *(mekake no machi)*. Not surprisingly, prefectural officials made no mention of this when they requested permission to move their office back to Kanazawa, but reported progress in "rinsing away old practices," and put the stress on the administrative convenience of that city's location. Kiriyama and Uchida to Shikan, 1872/10, *IKSR, kan 1, seiji bu, kenchi,* FS reel 109.

74. *IKS,* vol. 4, pp. 233–234. Tsutsui does not appear in *kan'in rireki,* but his report is quoted in *IKS* and cited in other sources. Tsutsui mentions *(IKS,* vol. 4, p. 234) that from the beginning of 1872/3 he is going abroad for study. From this we can guess that his service in Kanazawa was abbreviated.

75. Ibid.

76. *KKSS, S,* vol. 1, pp. 72–77; *IKSR, kan 68–69, furoku, (Kyū Kanazawa ken) kan'in rireki 1, 2,* FS reel 116. We can imagine that there might have been other issues dividing Kanazawa men, and other factions, but the Chōshū-Satsuma split is the only one that historians have recorded for the years 1868–1872.

77. See *IKSR, kan 38, seiji bu, sōyō jihen,* FS reel 112.

78. We do not have a precise measurement of the gross prefectural product in the early Meiji period. The best measurement is in the famous Ministry of Finance report of 1874, *Meiji 7-nen fuken bussan hyō* (reprinted in *Meiji zenki sangyō hattatsushi shiryō,* vol. 1 [Tokyo: Ryūkei Shosha, 1966]), which recorded the value of all production in Ishikawa Prefecture (Kaga and Noto Provinces) as ¥6,647,458.961. This figure double-counts some things (e.g., rice used in brewing *sake*) and leaves out others (e.g., services). It cannot be interpreted in the same way as later statistics on total output.

79. Refer to Appendixes 3 and 2. The samurai class is usually estimated to have composed about 6 percent of the population of Japan as a whole at the end of the Tokugawa period. It is an irony that although payments to them were an unsustainable burden on prefectural finances, many former samurai received less than was necessary to maintain a comfortable standard of living. Expressed in monetary terms, the per capita stipend income of this class in Ishikawa in the early 1870s, excluding former daimyo, was around ¥20. This estimate was arrived at by calculating the value of one *koku* of rice to be ¥4 and rounding off both population and stipend payment totals. (On Kanazawa rice prices, see the note to Appendix 3.) In actuality most former warriors received less than ¥20, because

a few former high-ranking families still drew relatively large stipends. Theoretically the stipend payments should have been enough to feed the more than 35,000 members of the Ishikawa samurai class, if one *koku* of rice is enough for one person for a year, and leave some money over for other purposes. Whether in fact this was common is open to question. The data are poor. Certainly Ishikawa samurai were only modest investors, and that might suggest a lack of surplus in their personal finances.

80. Kumano Kurō to Ōkuma Shigenobu, October 29, 1874, *IKSR, kan 47, seido bu, rokusei, FS* reel 113.

81. See W. G. Beasley, *Meiji Restoration*, pp. 381–382; Beasley cites Seki Jun'ya, *Meiji ishin to chiso kaisei* (Kyoto, 1967), tables, pp. 21, 51.

82. The other prefectures in University District Three were Nanao, Niikawa, Asuwa, Tsuruga, and Chikuma. The main office of the district was to be in Ishikawa. See Chapter 3 of *gakusei*, the complete text of which is reprinted in *(Meiji ikō) Kyōiku seido hattatsu shi*, comp. Monbushō Kyōikushi Hensan Kai (Tokyo: Ryūginsha, 1938), vol. 1, pp. 277–299.

83. *KKSS, G*, vol. 3, p. 588. This time the other prefectures were Aichi, Hamamatsu, Gifu, Mie, Watarai, Chikuma, Tsuruga, and Shizuoka, and the main office was placed in Aichi. This alteration of the regulations may have affected Kanazawa more than any other city, as it lost its place as a university seat.

84. *IKSR, kan 22, seiji bu, gakkō, FS* reel 110.

85. *IKS*, vol. 4, p. 640; *KKSS, G*, vol. 3, p. 588.

86. Cf. *IKSR, kan 22, seiji bu, gakkō*, May 1875, *FS* reel 110. Educational matters falling within the authority of the General Affairs Section *(shomuka)* of the prefecture are enumerated here. They include issuing regulations, supervision of the establishment of schools, employment of foreign teachers, inspection of schools, administering the aid to schools given by the Ministry of Education, establishing rules for collecting other funds for schools, determining amounts to be spent for the maintenance of public schools, and supervision of various kinds of private schools.

87. See the *tadashigaki* (proviso) to Chapter 89 of the regulations, *Kyōiku seido hattatsu shi*, vol. 1, p. 294.

88. *KKSS, G*, vol. 3, p. 564.

89. *IKSR, kan 22, seiji bu, gakkō*, May 10, 1873, *FS* reel 110. On the local exactions *(minpi)*, see below. The absence of figures on national aid to education from the prefectural budgets of 1873 and 1874 suggests that there was some mechanism for funneling aid directly to the primary schools and other educational institutions.

90. *IKSR, kan 22, seiji bu, gakkō furoku, gakushi kenkin, FS* reel 110. It appears that *shizoku* contributions were used for schools in all districts in the prefecture, while commoners' gifts went to specific schools.

91. *KKSS, G*, vol. 3, p. 564.
92. Chapters 8 and 9 of the Regulations for Education, *Kyōiku seido hattatsu shi*, vol. 1, p. 281.
93. *IKSR, kan 22, seiji bu, gakkō*, February 1873, June 3, 1873, and June 5, 1873, *FS* reel 110.
94. See below, Chapter Four.
95. As noted above, however, stipend payments are omitted from the budget figures for 1874.
96. *IKSR, kan 54, seiji bu, kaikei*, June 12, 1874, *FS* reel 113. Regular expenditures were classified primary and secondary; I have found itemization of only the primary category.
97. On the renewal of the ban, see Ishii, *Japanese Legislation in the Meiji Era*, p. 44.
98. The letter of transmission of this group of Christians, from the governor of Nagasaki Prefecture to the governor of Kanazawa *han*, is reprinted in *KHS, bakumatsu hen, gekan*, pp. 1150–1151, and *IKS*, vol. 4, p. 708. The Catholic prisoners were from the village of Uragami, near Nagasaki.
99. A brief account of the Kanazawa internment of these Christians, and of the unsuccessful effort to get them to apostatize, is in *IKS*, vol. 4, pp. 707–709.
100. See Appendix 4.
101. The figure for 1871 includes relief payments, loans, grants, and aid. See Appendix 3, lines 11, 44, and 46. The 1873 budget omits this category of spending, but other records reveal the amount ¥650, which went entirely for loans, as no grants were made in that year. *IKSR, kan 17, seiji bu, shinjutsu, FS* reel 110.
102. Ibid.
103. Kiriyama to Uchida, June 8, 1873, *IKGS*, vol. 1, p. 108.
104. *Fuken jimu shōtei*, November 30, 1875; translated in McLaren, "Japanese Government Documents," pp. 260–264.
105. See Uchida's autobiographical sketch, cited above.
106. Biographical information on Kiriyama is drawn from *IKSR, kan 57, furoku, kan'in rireki, Meiji 1–7 nen, FS* reel 113; *Hyakukan rireki*, comp. Nihon Shiseki Kyōkai (Tokyo: Nihon Shiseki Kyōkai, 1928, reprinted 1973), vol. 2; and Sengoku, *Chōkan monogatari*. Sengoku calls Kiriyama a *jimuka shusshin no hito*—a born administrator (p. 19).
107. On Kumano's career, see *IKSR, kan 57*. Sengoku asserts that Kumano exploited his *han*-clique connections and acted despotically in office in Ishikawa, earning a bad reputation as a result; Sengoku provides no evidence to support this claim about Kumano's connections, however. *Chōkan monogatari*, p. 19.

108. Dajōkan fukoku dai 140 gō, September 8, 1875; revision, October 1875. Both quoted in *IKGS*, vol. 1, p. 147.
109. *IKSR, kan 41, seido bu, sohō, Meiji 9-nen, FS* reel 112.
110. The Assessed Product was reported as 755,825 *koku* in the budget-like documents for 1873 and 1874 (*IKSR*, IV, 275–292). Using the average price of rice in several markets in and around Kanazawa, that figure was equivalent to ¥3,023,300. (See the note to Appendix 3.)
111. Exact figures on the land tax are not available. My estimate of more than 35 percent is based on the figures for the land tax for Kaga and Noto and the assessed product of the same area in 1874. (The 1881 figure comes from *Fuken chiso kaisei kiyō*, vol. 2, Ishikawa ken, p. 1, as reprinted in *Meiji zenki sangyō hattatsu shi shiryō, bekkan* [9] vol. 2 [Tokyo: Ryūkei Shosha, 1965]). The rate for land tax collections was supposed to be 3 percent of the land value from 1873 through 1876; in January 1877, it was reduced to 2.5 percent. In making this estimate, I took the 1881 land tax figure for Kaga and Noto provinces, ¥933,222.7, and multiplied it by 1.2 (because 3 percent equals 1.2 times 2.5 percent), to yield the approximate land tax amount before January 1877. This rough calculation suggests that the land tax in Ishikawa was about ¥1,119,867 per year through 1876. That is just over 37 percent of the assessed product of the prefecture in 1874 (see the previous note). The old formula "four to the lord and six to the people" apparently still applied.
112. *IKGS*, vol. 1, p. 150.
113. Estimated in the way described in the note above, the land tax was about 30.9 percent of the assessed product.
114. *IKGS*, vol. 1, p. 150. Statistics on spending out of prefectural tax and excise tax in 1878 are not available; probably they were not much higher than in 1877. Routine expenditures came to ¥122,060 in 1878.
115. *Ishikawa kenchi gaihyō*, figures for fiscal year 1878, *MNFTS*, reel 185.
116. *Jōhi*, routine or regular expenditures, were classified into two categories, *teigaku jōhi* ("fixed amount routine expenditures") and *gakugai jōhi* (variable routine expenditures). Salaries of officials and office maintenance costs mostly fell into the first category; samurai stipends fell into the second. The estimate that prefectural taxes covered 30 percent of routine expenditures assumes that those taxes were the same in 1878 as in 1877; figures on taxes are not available for 1878.
117. Sengoku, *Chōkan monogatari*, p. 19.
118. Ibid., pp. 27–28.
119. Saitō Yoshio, *Meiji Taishō kenka seikai hishi*, cited by Ōshima Mitsuko, "Meiji shoki no chihōkan," p. 191.
120. *IKS*, vol. 4, p. 34.
121. Ibid., p. 1149.

122. *Meiji Tennō ki,* vol. 4, p. 414.
123. See ibid., vol. 2, pp. 689–731, vol. 3, pp. 614–683; see also *Meiji bunka zenshū,* vol. 17, *Kōshitsu hen* (Tokyo, 1928, reprinted 1967).
124. *Meiji Tennō ki,* vol. 2, pp. 674–675.
125. See Tanaka Akira's brief but good discussion of the 1876 Tōhoku tour and emperor-worship in his *Meiji ishin* (Tokyo: Shōgakkan, 1976), pp. 171–176. On the imperial institution of the Meiji period, see John Whitney Hall, "A Monarch for Modern Japan," in Robert E. Ward, ed., *Political Development in Modern Japan,* (Princeton, 1968), and Marius B. Jansen, "Monarchy and Modernization in Japan," *Journal of Asian Studies,* vol. 36, no. 4 (1977), pp. 611–622.
126. On the Meiji leaders' motives, see Irokawa Daikichi's interpretation in his *Kindai kokka no shuppatsu* (Tokyo: Chūō Kōron Sha, 1971), pp. 17–28, 210. A more fully elaborated statement of Irokawa's views on the emperor system is in his "Tennōsei no shisō," in *(Sōgō kōza) Nihon no shakai bunka shi, 6, kindai kokka no shisō,* ed. Joseph Pittau (Tokyo: Kōdansha, 1974).
127. The best single source on all six of the Meiji Emperor's tours is the quasi-official record of his reign, *Meiji Tennō ki.* On the Hokuriku tour, cf. Irokawa, *Kindai kokka no shuppatsu,* pp. 2–30; Tōyama Shigeki treats the four major tours between 1876 and 1881, and the attempt by the government to change the popular image of the emperor, in *Meiji ishin to tennō* (Tokyo: Iwanami Shoten, 1991), pp. 117–134.
128. See Sengoku, *Chōkan monogatari,* p. 25.
129. *Meiji Tennō ki,* vol. 4, pp. 507–512.
130. Ibid., pp. 519–520.
131. See Chapter Four, below, on the assassination of Ōkubo and the document prepared by the conspirators.
132. *Meiji Tennō ki,* vol. 4, pp. 520, 523.
133. Ibid., pp. 519–523; Irokawa, pp. 29–30.
134. *Meiji Tennō ki,* vol. 4, p. 526.
135. Ibid., p. 527.
136. *Kindai kokka no shuppatsu,* pp. 23–30.
137. See, e.g., the account of the emperor's 1872 stay in Kagoshima, in *Meiji Tennō ki,* vol. 2, pp. 716–725. The quote about soil-gathering is from William Elliot Griffis, *The Mikado: Institution and Person* (Princeton: Princeton University Press, 1915), p. 261; it is paraphrased by Tanaka, *Meiji ishin,* p. 173. Tōyama cites several contemporary sources critical of the tours, including the major newspapers *Chōya Shinbun,* which emphasized that localities were spending a great deal on superficial things like clothing and decorations to impress the emperor, and *Tōkyō Yokohama Mainichi Shinbun,* which suggested that if one (if Tōyama's paraphrase accurately reflects the original, the writer did not say the emperor) wished

to know what people's feelings were, it would be sufficient to read the papers, which reported the news from all over Japan, and to have governors pass the opinions of the people on up to the authorities in the capital. A thorough and scrupulous searcher of archives for evidence of popular feeling about the tours, Tōyama notes that there are almost no materials that tell the thought of "people of the middle and lower strata themselves" *(chūkasō minshū mizukara)*, and he includes no citations of reactions to the 1878 Hokuriku trip. As a source of insight into popular feeling about the 1880 trip, Tōyama ends up quoting a reminiscence written years later (in 1906) by the novelist Kinoshita Naoe of the day the emperor passed by his school in Matsumoto. Crowds who had come miles and waited in the rain to see their ruler were ordered to bow when his carriage approached, and thus were prevented from actually glimpsing him. But after the procession had passed, many of them scrambled to pick up pieces of gravel that had been run over by the carriage wheels, exclaiming that if they took it home, it would bring protection and prosperity. *Meiji ishin to tennō*, pp. 122–123.

138. *Meiji Tennō ki*, vol. 2, p. 716. The city was Kagoshima, the date, 1872/6/22.

139. *After the Restoration*, cited in the introduction.

3. SUBPREFECTURAL GOVERNMENT IN THE NEW PREFECTURE, *1871–1878*

1. See John W. Hall, "The Castle Town and Japan's Modern Urbanization," in John W. Hall and Marius B. Jansen, eds., *Studies in the Institutional History of Early Modern Japan*, (Princeton: Princeton University Press, 1968), p. 181.

2. *Kanazawa: A Seventeenth-Century Japanese Castle Town* (New Haven: Yale University Press, 1982), esp. pp. 85–101; and James L. McClain, "Local Elites and the Meiji Transition in Kanazawa," *Asian Cultural Studies*, no. 18 (February 1992), esp. pp. 108–113.

3. Nakada Kaoru, "Tokugawa jidai ni okeru mura no jinkaku," *Hōseishi ronsō*, vol. 2 (Tokyo: Iwanami Shoten, 1938). I am grateful to Professor Hiramatsu Yoshirō for this reference and for his explanation of the concept of *realler Gesamtperson*. For another, briefer explanation of this view of the Tokugawa village, see Ishii Ryosuke, ed., *Japanese Legislation in the Meiji Era*, pp. 205–206. A modern corporation—for example, a company incorporated under the laws of the State of Delaware—is recognized as having a legal existence apart from the individuals who are its directors, officers, and employees.

4. The fullest treatment of agricultural administration in Kaga *han,* and of the various organizations and units of government within the *han,* is in Wakabayashi Kisaburō, *Kaga han nōseishi no kenkyū,* 2 vols. A capsulized treatment appears in *Ishikawa ken no rekishi,* ed. Wakabayashi, pp. 146–152.

5. Cf. Asakawa Kan'ichi, "Notes on Village Government in Japan after 1600," *Journal of the American Oriental Society,* vol. 30 (1909–1910) and vol. 31 (1911); Harumi Befu, "Village Autonomy and Articulation with the State," *Studies in the Institutional History of Early Modern Japan;* Befu, "Duty, Reward, Sanction and Power: Four-Cornered Office of the Tokugawa Village Headman," in Bernard S. Silberman and Harry D. Harootunian, eds., *Modern Japanese Leadership,* (Tucson: University of Arizona Press, 1966); and William Jones Chambliss, *Chiaraijima Village* (Tucson: University of Arizona Press for the Association for Asian Studies, 1965). Asakawa, incidentally, speculates on the etymology of the title *kimoiri* used for headmen, noting the Chinese expression "to break one's liver and bile," meaning to be diligent (p. 166).

6. Kaga villages did not have the third type of official who rounded out the cast of village officials in most parts of Japan, the "peasants' deputy" or "peasants' representative" *(hyakushō dai).*

7. This description of the *tomura* omits many complexities. There were, for example, three classes of village-group headmen, and these were further subdivided into three grades each, yielding nine levels of peasant officials called *tomura.* See Wakabayashi, *KNSK;* Yonezawa Mototake, *Kaga han no tomura seido* (Toyama: Toyama Ken Kyōdōshi Kai, 1956); Oda Kichinojō, *Kaga han nōsei shi kō* (Tokyo: Tōkō Shoin, 1929), and *(Kaga han tomura yaku) Ishiguro ke monjo,* comp. Ishikawa Ken Toshokan Kyōkai (Kanazawa: Ishikawa Ken Toshokan, 1974), 3 vols.

8. Over 1,400 houses in Kaga were of *heishi* status, with stipends between 50 *koku* and 2,050 *koku* per year. See the mid-nineteenth-century *Samurai chō* in *IKS,* vol. 2, pp. 1521–1572. The characters pronounced *heishi* in Kaga were often read *hirazamurai* elsewhere.

9. Kuranami, *Kaga hansei kaikaku shi no kenkyū.*

10. Kaga samurai were in effect disenfeoffed by Toshitsune's action, although they continued to have putative fiefs. The policies implemented from 1651 are known as the *kaisakuhō;* see Philip C. Brown, "Practical Constraints on Early Tokugawa Land Taxation: Annual Versus Fixed Assessments in Kaga Domain," *Journal of Japanese Studies,* vol. 14, no. 2 (1988). pp. 369–401.

11. There were no agricultural affairs magistrates from 1656 to 1661 and again from 1821 to 1839. On the latter period, see Chapter One.

12. This discussion of the Household Registration Law and its sources and implications draws on a 1975 lecture at Harvard University by Professor Tanaka Akira, and on his *Meiji ishin*, pp. 271–272.

13. *KSS, G*, vol. 1, p. 2. See also McClain, "Local Elites and the Meiji Transition in Kanazawa," pp. 115–117.

14. *IKS*, vol. 4, p. 98.

15. These were not the only changes; the minute details do not bear going into. Some of those details can be found in *IKSR, kan 1, seiji bu, kenchi, FS* reel 109; *KSS, G*, vol. 1; *KKSS, S*, vol. 1; and *IKS*, vol. 4, pp. 100–119.

16. *IKSR, kan 20, kokō, 1871–1877, FS* reel 110.

17. 1873 *Ishikawa ken kenchi gaihyō*, in *Meiji nenkan fuken tōkeisho shūsei* (microfilm, Tokyo, 1963, hereafter cited as *MNFTS*) reel 185.

18. Ibid., and *Hakui shi shi, gendai hen*, comp. Hakui Shi Shi Hensan Iinkai (Hakui: Hakui Shi, 1972, hereafter cited as *HSS, G*), p. 30. The tax officer *(sozei shirabeyaku)* was dropped, and the other local officials took over his duties, at this time.

19. McLaren, "Japanese Government Documents," p. 255; *Chihō kōmuin seido shiryō*, comp. Jichichō (Tokyo: Jichichō, 1955), vol. 2, p. 42.

20. *Chihō kōmuin seido shiryō*, vol. 2, p. 45.

21. "The Bureaucracy as a Political Force, 1920–45," in J. W. Morley, ed., *Dilemmas of Growth in Prewar Japan* (Princeton: Princeton University Press, 1971), p. 35.

22. *HSS, G*, p. 29.

23. Waters, "The Early Meiji Period: Local Response to Modern Administration," *Japan's Local Pragmatists*, pp. 57–82; the quote is from p. 58. In the prefectural office of Kanagawa Prefecture, in which Kawasaki is located, the personnel complement symbolized discontinuity, not continuity. Ōshima Mitsuko found that a sizable majority of the officials were men from other parts of Japan; between 30 and 39 percent were locals ("Okubo shihai taisei ka no fuken tōchi," p. 37).

24. Ōishi, *Nihon chihō zaigyōseishi josetsu*, pp. 55, 56–57; Ariizumi, *Meiji seijishi no kiso katei*, p. 10; Allinson, *Japanese Urbanism* (Berkeley and Los Angeles: University of California Press, 1975), p. 31.

25. Yonezawa, *Kaga han no tomura seido*, p. 331.

26. *Fugeshi gun shi*, comp. Fugeshi Gunyakusho (Fugeshi, 1924, reprinted Tokyo: Meicho Shuppan, 1973). Conceivably the other two large district chiefs were also from *tomura* families.

27. *(Kaga han tomura yaku) Ishiguro ke monjo*, vol. 3, p. 826.

28. *IKSR*, printed version, vol. 4 (Kanazawa, 1974), *1884 kan'in rireki*.

29. Yonezawa estimates that 80 to 90 percent of old *tomura* families were registered as commoners *(heimin)*. Yonezawa, *Kaga han no tomura seido*, p.

332. If he is correct, 10 to 20 percent of the village-group headman families were classified *shizoku* after 1872.

30. Cf. *KKSS, S*, vol. 1, pp. 14–15; *IKS*, vol. 4, pp. 119, 237, 242–255; *KSS, G*, vol. 1, p. 2. The *shizoku* status of Yoshida, Hayashi, Nagao, and Tsuda is confirmed by *IKSR, kan 58–59, furoku kan'in rireki, 1871–1875, FS* reel 114 (*IKSR*, printed version, vol. 4, pp. 557, 535, 508.

31. *KKSS, S*, vol. 1, pp. 16–19. The writers of the city history report that the date of this redistricting is unclear, but that it was "at the beginning of 1875." It is my guess that this reform and the list of names antedate the controversy between the governor and the district chiefs of mid-1875.

32. Cf. *KKSS, S*, vol. 1, and *IKSR, furoku, kan'in rireki.*

33. The phrase is Ishii's. See *Japanese Legislation*, p. 209.

34. Ishii, *Meiji bunka shi*, vol. 2, *hōsei hen*, p. 160. The notice was Dajōkan *tatsu* 28, March 8, 1874.

35. *KSS, G*, vol. 1, p. 3. The Provisional Regulations on Districts, *Kukata kari jōrei*, are reprinted in ibid., pp. 3–7.

36. *NSS*, p. 574. Nationwide at this time, there was much diversity in the method of selection of subprefectural officials; cf. *Jichi 50-nen shi*, pp. 38–39. The web of high officials' control was spun tighter in Ishikawa than in many other areas.

37. *Kukata kari jōrei, IKSR, kan 43, seido bu, shokusei, FS* reel 112 (see *KSS, G*, vol. 1, pp. 3–7 also). McClain has an interesting commentary on these rules in "Local Elites and the Meiji Transition in Kanazawa," pp. 125–127.

38. See *KKSS, S*, vol. 1, p. 129, and Chapter Four, below.

39. *Kokoroe, IKSR, kan 43, seido bu, shokusei, FS* reel 112.

40. This request was submitted in September 1876; it is summarized in *IKSR, kan 2, seiji bu, kenchi, 1876, FS* reel 109.

41. Ibid.

42. Cf. ibid., and 1874 *Ishikawa kenchi ichiran gaihyō, MNFTS* reel 185.

43. Cf. 1873 *Ishikawa kenchi gaihyō* and 1874 *Ishikawa kenchi gaihyō, MNFTS* reel 185. The exact numbers of *kochō* were 586 (in 1873) and 581 (in 1874), and of *fuku kochō*, 1,647 (1873) and 1,680 (1874).

44. *IKSR, kan 2, seiji bu, kenchi, FS* reel 109.

45. The new regulations were called *Kakkuchōson kinkoku kōshaku kyōyūbutsu toriatsukai doboku kikō kisoku.*

46. Ōkubo Toshiaki, in *Naimushō shi*, comp. Daika Kai Naimushō Shi Hensan Iinkai (Tokyo: Daika Kai, 1970–1971), vol. 1, p. 127.

47. *NSS*, p. 575; Kobayashi cites *IKSR*, printed version, vol. 3, *seido bu. Minpi* denoted in fact local taxes of various kinds. The word has given rise to confusion, and it is mistranslated as "private expense" in McLaren, "Japanese Government Documents," p. 263. Kikegawa Hiroshi notes the

difficulty of the term and quotes the Journal of the Prefectural Governors Conference of 1878 (*Meiji 11-nen chihō kan kaigi nisshi*, XI, pp. 13–15), which attempted to clarify the distinction between prefectural taxes and local taxes: "Prefectural taxes (*fukenzei*) are those that have until now been collected within the prefecture, to apply toward expenditures of the prefecture only. In fact these collections are not enough to cover all expenses within the prefecture. Thus the so-called *minpi* are used both for expenses of the prefecture and expenses of the districts. *Minpi* are, that is to say, a type of local taxes (*chihōzei*)." Kikegawa Hiroshi, *Meiji chihō jichi seido no seiritsu katei*, pp. 33–34.

48. The levy on households was called *kosūwari*. *IKGS*, vol. 1, pp. 140–143. For the text of the plan, *minpi fuka hōhō*, see *IKSR*, printed version, vol. 3, pp. 485–487. Some revisions were made in the plan two months later on the recommendation of a *kuchō*. Ibid., pp. 489–490.

49. Fujita Takeo, *Nihon chihō zaisei seido no seiritsu* (Tokyo: Iwanami Shoten, 1941), p. 51.

50. See Chapter Two for my estimates of the burden of the land tax and prefectural taxes.

51. *IKSR, kan 42, seido bu, shokusei furoku, Meiji 7-nen*, vol. 3, pp. 487–489; *IKGS*, vol. 1, pp. 144–145.

52. *IKGS*, vol. 1, pp. 143–146.

53. Ōkurashō, *Fuken chiso kaisei kiyō* (1881), reprinted in *Meiji zenki sangyō hattatsushi shiryō, bekkan* (9) 3 vols. (Tokyo: Ryūkei Shosha, 1965).

54. Ibid., vol. 2, *Ishikawa ken Kaga Noto ryōkoku*, p. 26.

55. Fujita Takeo, *Nihon chihō zaisei seido no seiritsu*, pp. 42–48.

56. Miyamoto Ken'ichi in *IKGS*, vol. 1, pp. 143, 146; Kobayashi Akira in *NSS*, p. 579.

57. 1876 *Ishikawa kenchi ichiran hyō*, MNFTS reel 185. These figures are for the enlarged prefecture that included Etchū and seven counties of Echizen as well as Kaga and Noto.

58. *Ishikawa kenchi ichiran hyō*, MNFTS reel 185. The format of the 1878 figures on *minpi* differs from that used in 1874. The 1878 table shows that ¥107,323 went to pay *kuri kyūryō* (district officials' salaries) and ¥21,821 went to pay *gunri hōkyū* (county officials' salaries). In that year prefectural taxes came to ¥61,717, and prefectural expenditures to ¥324,842.

59. Uchida Masakaze to Mutsu Munemitsu, head of the central tax office, May 1873, *IKSR, kan 39, seido bu, sohō*, FS reel 112; quoted by Miyamoto, in *IKGS*, vol. 1, p. 129. The land tax reform had not yet been implemented when Uchida wrote.

60. *HSS, G*, pp. 32–33.

61. *NSS*, p. 580.

4. HOPES FOR NATIONAL INFLUENCE AND THEIR FRUSTRATION: POLITICS IN ISHIKAWA PREFECTURE, 1872–1878

1. E.g., Fujita Takeo, "Meiji shi ni okeru chihō jichi sei seitei no igi," (*Kaikoku 100-nen kinen*) *Meiji bunka shi ronshū* (Tokyo: Kangensha, 1952); Kikegawa Hiroshi, *Meiji chihō jichi seido no seiritsu katei.*

2. E.g., Ōishi Kaichirō, *Nihon chihō zaigyōseishi josetsu;* Ōshima Tarō, *Nihon chihō gyōzaiseishi josetsu;* Kajinishi Mitsuhaya, "Josetsu," *Chiso kaisei to chihō jichi,* ed. Meiji Shiryō Kenkyū Renraku Kai (Tokyo: Ochanomizu Shobō, 1956, reprinted 1968).

3. *KKSS, S,* vol. 1, p. 85.

4. Ibid., pp. 85–86. The Kawase Gaisha was a financial institution that had been founded in 1869 by Kitani Tōemon, a wealthy merchant. The company encouraged samurai to put their savings in its care, and Kanazawa *han* made a substantial investment in the company, as well. Of over 4,000 depositors in the Kawase Gaisha, over two-thirds were samurai. Eventually the company was transformed into the biggest bank in the region, and by 1883 it had split into two parts known as The Hokuriku Bank and The Kanazawa Bank. In the hard times of the early 1880s, the successors of the Kawase Gaisha suffered, and in 1886 they were liquidated, paying ¥20 for every ¥100 they had in liabilities. Kanazawa Shōkō Kaigisho 70-nen shi, ed. Maki Hisao (Kanazawa: Kanazawa Shōkō Kaigisho Henshū Iinkai, 1960), pp. 9–10; Tokuda Toshiaki, "Kanazawa Kawase Gaisha no kenkyū," *Nihon rekishi,* no. 307 (1973), pp. 99–120.

5. Saigō's thinking is detailed in a letter to Itagaki Taisuke, included in *Genyōsha shi* (Tokyo: Genyōsha, 1917), pp. 50–51, and in *Tōin sendan,* cited by Oka Yoshitake, *Kindai Nihon seiji shi I* (Tokyo: Sōbunsha, 1962), pp. 167–168. See below for more on *Tōin sendan.*

6. See Marlene J. Mayo, "The Korean Crisis of 1873 and Early Meiji Foreign Policy," *Journal of Asian Studies,* vol. 31, no. 4 (1972).

7. The text of the petition is reprinted in *KKSS, S,* vol. 1, p. 86. See also *Tōin sendan.*

8. The text of this petition of April 5, 1873, is reprinted in *KKSS, S,* vol. 1, pp. 88–89.

9. Oka, pp. 174–180, summarizes the views and events relating to the expedition to Taiwan and the settlement with the Ch'ing government. As is well known, Kido Takayoshi opposed sending troops to Taiwan or China, and resigned from his position as Councilor of State when he was defeated on this issue.

10. The text of this petition is included in *KKSS, S,* vol. 1, pp. 89–92; the quoted passage is on pp. 90–91. The Left Chamber (Sain) was the body that received and acted on petitions and memorials at this time.

11. *Meiji bunka zenshū,* ed. Yoshino Sakuzō, et al. (Tokyo: Nihon Hyōron Sha, 1927–1930, reprinted 1967–1970), vol. 2, pp. 212–214; Oka, p. 170.

12. *IKSR, kan 57, furoku, kan'in rireki, FS* reel 114. Kuga had been *daizoku* until August 17, 1873, then had been dropped in rank to *chūzoku.*

13. *KKSS, S,* vol. 1, p. 108, reports that Sugimura did not get along with Kiriyama. Sugimura was the only fairly high-ranking prefectural official besides Uchida and Kiriyama whose title was not downgraded in the summer of 1873.

14. *IKSR, kan 42, seido bu, shokusei 1873, FS* reel 112.

15. *IKSR, kan 57* (see note 12 above). The demotions apparently were entirely a local decision. In the collection of documents pertaining to local officials compiled by the Autonomy Agency, *Chihō kōmuin seido shiryō* (Tokyo: Jichichō, 1955), only one document is included for 1873. That document (Council of State Decree Number 216, June 19, 1873) applies to dates of appointment to and dismissal from office and has no relation to prefectural office demotions or a reorganization of titles.

16. *KKSS, S,* vol. 1, pp. 93–94.

17. The derivation of the Risshisha's name is explained in J. K. Fairbank, E. O. Reischauer, and A. M. Craig, *East Asia: The Modern Transformation* (Boston: Houghton Mifflin, 1965), p. 281.

18. My rendition of the relevant phrases of *Analects* XII, 23. Cf., for the entire passage, James Legge, *The Chinese Classics* (Oxford: Oxford University Press, 1893), vol. 1, pp. 261–262: "Tsze-kung asked about friendship. The master said, "Faithfully admonish your friend, and skillfully lead him on. If you find him impracticable, stop. Do not disgrace yourself." Cf. also *The Analects of Confucius,* tr. Arthur Waley (London: Allen & Unwin, 1938), p. 170: "Tzu-kung asked about friends. The Master said, inform them loyally and guide them discreetly. If that fails, then desist. Do not court humiliation."

19. This first meeting was held in a branch temple of the Ōtani sect of True Pure Land Buddhism (Eastern Honganji). This sect had for centuries been extremely powerful in the Kaga and Noto regions; its adherents had carried out the famous "Single-minded sect uprisings" *(ikkō ikki)* in the late 1400s and had exercised control over the area for a century thereafter. The choice of this branch temple for the opening ceremonies of the Chūkokusha may have been entirely coincidental, determined by the size and impressiveness of the meeting hall or the religious affiliation of some members of the new society. Nevertheless, the temple's historical associations with local power and local pride could hardly have been lost on the participants in the meeting, and this makes it almost ironic that the objectives of the Chūkokusha had so little to do with concrete local needs or issues.

20. Cf. *IKS*, vol. 4, p. 242; Shimode, p. 209; Sonozaki, p. 214. A comparison of the list of Chūkokusha leaders in *KKSS, S*, vol. 1, with the career records of officials under Uchida *(IKSR, kan 57–58)* reveals that all eighteen men whose names appear in both places were of *shizoku* status.

21. The phrase "upper class people's rights" was coined by Torio Koyata in his *Kokusei inga ron*. Torio is cited in *(Shinkō) Nihonshi gairon*, ed. Hōgetsu Keigo and Kodama Kōta (Tokyo: Yoshikawa Kōbunkan, 1969), pp. 272, 280 n., and in Nobutaka Ike, *The Beginnings of Political Democracy in Japan* (Baltimore: The Johns Hopkins Press, 1950), p. 59. Cf. also Tōyama Shigeki, "Jiyūminkenundō ni okeru shizokuteki yōso," *Jiyūminken*, ed. Sakane Yoshihisa (*Ronshū Nihon rekishi*, 10, Tokyo: Yūseidō, 1973).

22. *KKSS, S*, vol. 1, pp. 113–114.

23. Uno Shun'ichi, "Tennōsei shihai taisei no kakuritsu katei," in Ōkubo Toshiaki, ed., *(Taikei Nihonshi sōsho 3) Seijishi III*, (Tokyo: Yamakawa Shuppan Sha, 1967), p. 151.

24. On the Risshisha prospectus, see, for example, Tōyama, "Jiyūminkenundō ni hokeru shizokuteki yōso," pp. 1–2. As for the appearance of Kanazawa men's hopes, it may seem obvious in retrospect that the defeat of the *seikanron* and the ascendancy of Ōkubo Toshimichi had precluded the possibility of Kanazawa outsiders making any impact on national policy. But historical situations look clearer in hindsight than they did to those who lived through them.

25. The text of the Chūkokusha prospectus can be found in *IKS*, vol. 4, pp. 242–245; *IKGS*, vol. 1, pp. 578–580; and *KKSS, S*, vol. 1. The phrase here translated "the people of Imperial Japan" is *kōkoku okuchō no jinmin*, and "certain rights" is *ittei no kenri*.

26. "Jiyūminkenundō ni okeru shizokuteki yōso," pp. 1–2. Tōyama finds phrases in the Risshisha foundation document that proclaim that there are no distinctions between status groups, but he argues that such phrases are empty, and that they are belied by passages identifying *shizoku* as an elite with a special role. The ambiguous phrase in the Chūkokusha prospectus was, *"Dōshi no shoyū no gotoki wa saiwai ni jūrai shirin ni ari."*

27. "Destitute people who have not yet achieved their due" (*kyūmin no imada sono tokoro ezaru mono*) might also be understood as "destitute people who still have no income."

28. *KKSS, S*, vol. 1, p. 113.

29. For the text of this document, *kigyō yotei gaiyō*, see ibid., pp. 114–115.

30. *Kanazawa Shōkō Kaigisho 70-nen shi*, ed. Maki Hisao, cited above.

31. Curiously, none of the histories of Ishikawa or Kanazawa attempt to account for the failure of the Kaigyōsha. It may have suffered from some of the weakness that later plagued another ex-samurai venture of Kanazawa men, the Kigyōkai, treated in Chapter Six.

32. On the Aikokusha, see *Jiyūtō shi*, comp. Itagaki Taisuke (Tokyo: Gosharō, 1910), vol. 1, pp. 178–181. On the Chūkokusha's participation, see *KKSS, S,* vol. 1 p. 116, and *IKS*, vol. 4, p. 246.

33. The quotations are from the Aikokusha foundation document, *Jiyūtō shi*, vol. 1, pp. 179–181.

34. *KKSS, S,* vol. 1, p. 116; *Jiyūtō shi*, vol. 1, p. 180. The delegates from Kanazawa were Kuga, Ishikawa Kurō, Tomita Rentarō, Iwata Hidemasa, Tsuji Akimichi, Togashi Heitarō, and Wazuno Fugyo. Cf. *Hasegawa Jun'ya kun*, ed. Wada Bunjirō (Kanazawa: published by the editor, 1921).

35. Itagaki and Kido resumed their positions as Councilors of State as one of the results of their famous meeting with Ōkubo Toshimichi in Osaka in February 1875. Cf. R. A. Scalapino, *Democracy and the Party Movement in Pre-war Japan* (Berkeley: University of California Press, 1953, reissued 1967), pp. 59–60.

36. Sengoku likens the resignations to a strike against Kiriyama. But the journalistic historian goes on to place the resignations of Sugimura and Kuga, among others, after Kiriyama's appointment as provisional governor in 1875. This is a mistake. *Chōkan monogatari*, p. 20.

37. Ishibayashi, *Ishikawa 100-nen shi*, p. 53.

38. Texts of the original announcement of the meeting, the announcement of its postponement, and the notice of its rescheduling are printed together in *Fuken seido shiryō*, comp. Jichi Shinkō Chūō Kai (Tokyo: Jichi Shinkō Chūō Kai, 1941), *gyōsei hen, zenpen*, p. 89.

39. Kikegawa Hiroshi (*Jichi 50-nen shi*, pp. 42–43) gives primary credit for the idea of a conference of governors to Kido Takayoshi, who had since early in the Meiji period hoped to promote subnational popular assemblies as preparation for the opening of a national assembly later on. Kido had discussed this matter with Itō Hirobumi, Ōkubo Toshimichi, and Itagaki Taisuke before their famous meeting of February 1875 in Osaka, and the decision to call a Prefectural Governors Conference was one of the important outcomes of the Osaka meeting. Kido's role in convening the assembly of governors was acknowledged in his appointment as chairman of the meeting.

40. Council of State Notification Number 71, May 19, 1875, *Fuken seido shiryō, gyōsei hen, zenpen*, pp. 87–88.

41. Council of State Notification Number 84, May 19, 1875, ibid., p. 88.

42. *IKS*, vol. 4, p. 247; Ishibayashi, *Ishikawa 100-nen shi*, pp. 53–54.

43. Kumano's announcement of a prefectural assembly (May 15, 1875), and his addendum (May 26, 1875) are reprinted in *KKSS, S,* vol. 1, pp. 118–119.

44. The report is abstracted in ibid., p. 120 ff., and *IKS*, vol. 4, pp. 247–248.

45. *KKSS, S,* p. 120. Precisely what those views were, I have been unable to ascertain. The district chiefs' petition to the Genrōin, cited below, states that their positions are recorded in a separate volume *(bessatsu),* but I have not been able to locate that. For our consideration here, however, perhaps the most important part of the district chiefs' position is their opposition to the type of prefectural assembly that Kiriyama and Kumano wanted to call. Cf. ibid., pp. 122–123, and *IKS,* vol. 4, p. 247.
46. *KKSS, S,* vol. 1, pp. 120–121.
47. The text of the Nakamura group's petition appears in ibid., p. 122 ff. Quotations are from this source.
48. Again *KKSS, S,* vol. 1, has the most detailed account, with key documents (pp. 125–128). Other leaders of the group opposed to the district chiefs were Katō Kanji, Mizuno Narikiyo, Kubo Kakichirō, and Narita Yasujirō. It has been speculated that the behind-the-scenes prime mover of this group was Inagaki Yoshikata, an officer of the Chūkokusha who often disagreed with Sugimura's tactics (ibid., p. 153). Inagaki, later elected the first mayor of Kanazawa, was the only prominent Chūkokusha member to remain in prefectural office beyond the first year of Kiriyama's term as governor of Ishikawa Prefecture.
49. For the anti-district-chiefs group's statement, see ibid., pp. 125–127. "Not what the people want": *jinmin no kibō ni arazu.*
50. Katō Kō, Mizuno Narikiyo, Kubo Kakichirō, Narita Yasujirō, and Shimada Ichirō to the District Chiefs of the District of Kanazawa, June 15, 1875, reprinted in ibid.

    For Shimada, at least, this expression of willingness to go along with government policy seems to be inconsistent with other views he held at the same time, for which see below.
51. See *Chihōkan kaigi nisshi,* in *Meiji bunka zenshū,* vol. 4, p. 313. There were sixty-two prefectures at the time the conference took place, and Kido's count took in only forty-two or forty-nine; he did not make clear whether some of the seven with prefectural assemblies were counted again in his figure for prefectures with assemblies of district chiefs.
52. Kiriyama's statement, "minken o ronzuru seishin to gaikei to nirui aru setsu," appears in *IKS,* vol. 4, pp. 250–253.
53. For the rescript, see *Meiji Tennō ki,* comp. Kunaichō Rinji Teishitsu Henshūkyoku (Tokyo: Yoshikawa Kōbunkan, 1969–1977), vol. 3, pp. 425–426.
54. See Joseph Pittau, *Political Thought in Early Meiji Japan* (Cambridge: Harvard University Press, 1967), pp. 43–50.
55. Some Meiji statesmen endorsed constitutionalism, it is often argued, out of desire to win the approbation of the Western powers and a revision of the unequal treaties, rather than out of conviction that constitutional

principles of government were right, or better than other forms of government. Kiriyama was silent on the treaty revision issue. We do not know where he stood, or how that might have influenced what he wrote on people's rights.

56. Cf. Richard Hofstadter, *The American Political Tradition* (New York: Alfred A. Knopf, 1948), pp. 3–17.
57. George Akita, *Foundations of Constitutional Government in Modern Japan, 1868–1900* (Cambridge: Harvard University Press, 1967), p. 164.
58. The text of this memorial is in *KKSS, S,* vol. 1, pp. 128–130. Emphasis in the quotation has been added. This belief that district chiefs should be elected by the public was shared by many Tokyo leaders and some governors. Under the Three New Laws system of 1878, the chiefs of local governmental units (i.e., towns and villages, which replaced the small districts as the lowest level of administration) were elected.
59. When Shimada Ichirō and Chō Tsurahide first approached Kuga requesting that he write a justification of an act of terror for them (see the section "Discontent among Former Samurai," below), Kuga refused, citing his membership in the Chūkokusha, an organization that was opposed to violent tactics. Kuga's oral deposition, quoted by Odanaka Toshiki, "Ōkubo Toshimichi ansatsu jiken," in Wagatsuma Sakae, et al., eds., *Nihon seiji saiban shiroku (Meiji zen)* (Tokyo: Daiichi Hōki, 1968), p. 442.
60. See the photograph of Shimada in a Western-style military uniform in *IKS,* vol. 4, following p. 1150, and the writing specimen, ibid., following p. 1154.
61. Recollection of Kuga Yoshinao, quoted in *KKSS, S,* vol. 1, p. 148.
62. Shimada's oral deposition at his trial for the assassination of Ōkubo Toshimichi, quoted by Odanaka Toshiki, p. 438.
63. *KKSS, S,* vol. 1, pp. 108–109.
64. This broadside of Shimada's group, dated November 21, 1874, is quoted in ibid.
65. *Sakamoto Ryōma and the Meiji Restoration,* p. 98.
66. *IKS,* vol. 4, pp. 234–235.
67. *KKSS, S,* vol. 1, pp. 140–141.
68. The record of the conversation among Kirino Toshiaki, Nakamura Shunjirō, and Ishikawa Kurō is known as *Tōin sendan.* The MS is in the Kaetsunō Bunko, Kanazawa City Library; substantial excerpts are printed in *Seinan kiden,* comp. Kokuryū Kai, vol. 1 (Tokyo: Hara Shobō, 1969 reprint of 1911 original).
69. "*Ō-A kakkoku ni shinnyū suru no motoi o tatsu beshi,*" quoted by Oka, *Kindai Nihon seiji shi,* vol. 1, p. 166.
70. *Seinan kiden,* vol. 1, part 1, appendix, pp. 3–5. Kirino frequently represented himself as quoting Saigō; e.g., on pp. 5–6, Saigō is said to have

stated, "We plan to spread our national prestige abroad, and to stand as equals with all nations. We must soon adopt a policy of sending troops abroad, and first we should gain control of Korea and Manchuria."

71. Kirino's diction here (p. 4)—"*toan taida mi o kaerimi kuni o wasururu jushi tomogara*"—may be slightly more scornful than his choice of words to describe the Tokyo leaders later on in the conversation (pp. 18–20), when he referred to them as "*zaitei no joji tomogara*" ("the little girls at court"). At any rate it is clear that he had a gift for invective.

72. Ibid., pp. 17–18.

73. Ibid.

74. Ibid., pp. 18–19.

75. By "last question," I mean the last question printed in *Seinan kiden*, vol. 1.

76. Ibid., p. 19. Paraphrased by Ishibayashi, *Ishikawa 100-nen shi*, p. 42.

77. *Seinan kiden*, vol. 1, part 1, appendix, p. 20.

78. Ibid., pp. 20–21; *KKSS, S*, vol. 1, pp. 145–147.

79. *KKSS, S*, vol. 1, pp. 157–158.

80. See *IKS*, vol. 4, p. 259, and *KKSS, S*, vol. 1, pp. 141–142.

81. On Inagaki, see note 48, above.

82. *KKSS, S*, vol. 1, p. 154. Shimada called Inagaki "a tricky, untrustworthy, small man." Inagaki retorted by tagging Shimada "a violent, shallow-minded coolie."

83. Shimada Ichirō to Chūkokusha *kakui*, August 8, 1874, reprinted in *IKS*, vol. 4, pp. 260–263, and *KKSS, S*, vol. 1, pp. 150–152.

84. *KKSS, S*, vol. 1, p. 152.

85. Ibid., p. 149; *IKS*, vol. 4, p. 263.

86. *IKS*, vol. 4, pp. 1120–1121.

87. Ibid., pp. 270–271.

88. *Seinan kiden*, vol. 2, part 1, pp. 420–421.

89. Ibid., p. 420. The scheme was mentioned by Judge Tamano in his report to the Ministry of Justice, September 12, 1878, with his recommendation that Shioya be imprisoned for three years, Murai and Sawada for two years, and Itaga and Kakida for eighteen months, and that all be stripped of *shizoku* status. The sentence was approved by the ministry and handed down by the Special Court on Spetember 26. See Odanaka, pp. 462–464, where Tamano's report is reprinted.

90. *IKS*, vol. 4, p. 272.

91. Deposition of Ishikawa Kurō in the Kanazawa Prison, 1878, ibid., p. 273.

92. Kiriyama had appointed Hasegawa Jun'ya and Ōtsuka Shirō to do the recruiting in Kanazawa. Ibid., p. 280. It is worth noting that none of the contributors of reminiscences to Hasegawa's biography mentions

that episode in Hasegawa's career. See *Hasegawa Jun'ya kun,* ed. Wada
Bunjirō.

93. The text of the letter signed by Maeda Toshitsugu and Maeda Nariyasu—
of which the recipient is unclear, though the text twice mentions "your
request," using the word *kyō* (lord; sir; minister of state) for "you"—dated
June 3, 1877, is reprinted in *KKSS, S,* vol. 1, p. 171. A brief account
of the Maeda role in recruiting that does not mention this document or
its results is in *IKS,* vol. 4, pp. 280–282.

94. See Chō's statement on this plot in his oral deposition, quoted by Odanaka, p. 440.

95. *KKSS, S,* vol. 1, pp. 162–163.

96. Tomita Rentarō is quoted in a clear statement of why he refused to go
along with Shimada in *IKS,* vol. 4, p. 281; see also Tomita's biography,
Tomita Kishō sensei den, comp. Tomita Kishō Sensei Kinenzō Kensetsu Kai
(Kanazawa: Tomita Kishō Sensei Kinenzō Kensetsu Kai, 1928), pp. 6–7.

97. Cf. Kuga Yoshinao's statement to the police, quoted in *IKS,* vol. 4, p.
1122. *Taigi meibun* is a concept applying especially to the relations between lord or sovereign and subject. Whether the Kanazawa men meant
taigi meibun vis-à-vis the Meiji Emperor or vis-à-vis the Maeda family is
not clear.

98. Oral deposition, quoted by Odanaka, pp. 440–441.

99. *IKS,* vol. 4, p. 281.

100. *Seinan kiden,* vol. 2, part 1, p. 422; see also Odanaka, p. 441.

101. For one thing, Ōkubo's removal from the scene made possible the ascendancy of the so-called Chōshū faction led by Itō Hirobumi and Yamagata Aritomo.

102. Kuga Yoshinao's oral deposition, quoted by Odanaka, pp. 442–443. For
the date, April 20 or 21, another statement of Kuga's to the police who
were investigating the assassination is the source (*IKS,* vol. 4, pp.
1121–1122).

103. Kuga's deposition, Odanaka, p. 443; *IKS,* vol. 4, p. 1122.

104. Kuga's oral deposition, quoted in *IKS,* vol. 4, p. 1124.

105. Ibid., p. 1123. Matsuda was not present. Pleading that he had spent all
his money, he had gone home to Kanazawa in March, leaving the others
worried that he would leak the plot. Kuga, in line with his statement of
a year earlier, did not take part in this meeting or in the rough business
that followed; he was away from Tokyo at the time.

106. Odanaka, p. 445.

107. *IKS,* vol. 4, p. 1125.

108. The full text of the Kinji Hyōron Sha copy of the *zankanjō* is reprinted in
IKS, vol. 4, pp. 1125–1144, and *KKSS, S,* vol. 1, pp. 178–190. The
Chōya Shinbun copy is reprinted in *KKSS, S,* vol. 1, pp. 191–203. Both

zankanjō were written in *kanamajiri*, but if the orthography of *KKSS* is correct, the one addressed to the Kinji Hyōron Sha employed *hiragana*, while the Chōya Shinbun copy used *katakana*, along with the Chinese characters. The *zankanjō* is also reprinted in *Seinan kiden*, vol. 2, part 1, pp. 436–454. According to *Seinan kiden* (p. 454), copies were also to be transmitted to the Yomiuri and Akebono newspapers.

109. Tōkyō Nichinichi Shinbun, May 15, 1878, repirnted in *(Shiryō) Kindai Nihon shi,* ed. Kawae Suiho (Takamatsu: Kagawa Shinpō Sha, 1933), ch. 11, "Meiji 11-nen shi," pp. 3–4. This article is quoted at length by Odanaka, pp. 445–447. On Ōkubo's last moments as recalled by Shimada, see *Seinan kiden,* vol. 2, part 1, p. 432. The Tōkyō Nichinichi Shinbun (May 27, 1878) reported that one of the assassins (unnamed) had, during interrogation, quoted the home minister's last word as "Wait!" *(matte!) (Shinbun shūsei) Meiji hennen shi,* comp. Meiji Hennen Shi Hensan Kai (Tokyo: Zaisei Keizai Gakkai, 1936–1941), vol. 3, p. 397.

110. Nichinichi Shinbun, May 15, 1878, cited above.

111. Chōya Shinbun, May 15, 1878, *(Shinbun shūsei) Meiji hennen shi,* vol. 3, p. 391. Incautiously, the Chōya praised the style of the document: *"Bunshō mo nakanaka fude no tachitaru kakikata nari."*

112. Tōkyō Nichinichi Shinbun, May 16, 1878, ibid., p. 393.

113. Akebono, May 24, 1878, ibid., p. 395. The suspension of the Chōya was lifted ten days later. Akebono, May 25, 1878, ibid., p. 396. In connection with the government's reaction to the *zankanjō,* it is worth mentioning that Kimura, for having posted two letters at the request of his boyhood chum, was sentenced to five years in prison and deprived of his status as a *shizoku* in the registry of households.

114. See Odanaka, pp. 464–468, for the sentences handed down by the special court. Cf. *Seinan kiden,* vol. 2, part 1, pp. 459–463, and Tōkyō Nichinichi Shinbun, July 29, 1878, extract in *(Shinbun shūsei) Meiji hennen shi,* vol. 3, pp. 425–426. Odanaka notes that the sentences in the Ōkubo assassination case were not reprinted in *Dajō ruiten.*

115. Asai, who came into the plot late, and had not participated in the early planning, was from Shimane Prefecture. All the others were from Ishikawa.

116. *Seinan kiden,* vol. 2, part 1, p. 436. Sidney DeVere Brown discusses the *zankanjō* along with the personalities involved in the event in "Political Assassination in Early Meiji Japan: The Plot Against Ōkubo Toshimichi," in David Wurfel, ed., *Meiji Japan's Centennial: Aspects of Political Thought and Action* (Lawrence, Kansas: University Press of Kansas, 1971). Almost certainly Brown is mistaken in identifying Ōkubo alone as the subject of the five charges made against government officials in the *zankanjō* (pp. 29–30, where he says he quotes the "exact words" of the document). The

subject of the charges is unexpressed in the Japanese original, and there are over two pages of these charges before Ōkubo's name is even mentioned. The charges are enumerated in a context in which "important officials" and their failings are under discussion, with no individuals singled out. These officials are referred to as "the gang of bad officials" *(kanri yakara)*. When Ōkubo's name first appears, it is in a list of evil ministers, in company with the deceased Kido, Iwakura Tomomi, Ōkuma Shigenobu, Itō Hirobumi, Kuroda Kiyotaka, Kawaji Toshiyoshi, and Sanjō Sanetomi. Only later is Ōkubo identified as the principal target of Shimada and his fellow conspirators.

117. *Seinan kiden,* vol. 2, part 1, p. 436.

118. Ibid., p. 438.

119. Ibid., p. 439.

120. Ibid. The word here translated as "vigor," *ryūsei* in the phrase *koto no ryūsei,* can be pronounced Takamori as a personal name; the characters are those of Saigō Takamori's name. Surely Kuga's choice of words was no coincidence.

121. Ibid., p. 440. This rendering of the promise is taken from The Charter Oath, in Ryusaku Tsunoda et al., eds., *Sources of Japanese Tradition* (New York: Columbia University Press, 1958), vol. 2, pp. 136–137.

122. *Seinan kiden,* vol. 2, part 1, p. 442.

123. Ibid., p. 447.

124. Ibid., pp. 445–446.

125. Odanaka, p. 455; *Shihō enkaku shi,* comp. Shihōshō (Tokyo: Hōsōkai, 1939), p. 45. Tamano was named Daishin'in *chō* for the first time on September 13, 1878 (ibid, p. 47), and served until October 1879; his second term was from July 1881 to August 1886 (ibid., p. 576).

126. Judge Tamano to the Ministry of Justice, Inquiry, July 5, 1878, quoted in Odanaka, pp. 456–462.

127. For the sentences, see Odanaka, pp. 464–468; Odanaka writes that twenty-six were sentenced, but he omits the sentences of Sugimura Bun'ichi and one other person among the twenty-six. *Seinan kiden,* vol. 2, part 1, pp. 462–463, gives names and punishments of twenty-three men, several of whom Odanaka reported sentenced in September 1878. Tōkyō Nichinichi Shinbun, July 29, 1878, reported twenty-eight sentences. *(Shinbun shūsei) Meiji hennen shi,* vol. 3, pp. 425–426. Matsuda Hidehiko, sentenced to ten years as an accomplice, was from Shimane, like Asai Hisaatsu. Wakida was identified in trial records as a commoner *(heimin),* but he had voluntarily changed his status from *shizoku* to commoner not long before. See Brown, "Political Assassination," p. 32, n.

128. Shimada and the five others who were executed for Ōkubo's murder actually are buried in a municipal cemetery in Taito-ku, Tokyo; at the time

of their interment it was part of the Tennō Temple's burial ground. Gravestones there were erected only in 1899, by relatives of the deceased. "Shimada Ichirō ra no haka mitsukaru," *Hokkoku Shinbun,* July 15, 1973, p. 17.

5. NATIONAL INTEGRATION COMPLETED: ISHIKAWA PREFECTURE IN THE DECADE OF THE THREE NEW LAWS

1. Ōkubo did not live to see the reforms through the final stages of consideration by the government. The proposals had passed the Second Prefectural Governors Conference in April, and were being deliberated in the Genrōin at the time of his assassination. Amended, the bill passed the Genrōin on June 13; the bill was reported to the emperor, then further revisions were introduced and the bill resubmitted to the Genrōin on July 9. See *Fuken seido shiryō, gyōsei hen,* p. 108. In the early stages of drafting these regulations, Ōkubo was assisted by Matsuda Michiyuki and Inoue Kowashi. Kobayakawa Kingo, *Meiji hōsei shi ron,* vol. 2, pp. 674, 724.
2. Ōkubo Toshiaki, "Tsūshi," in *Naimushō shi* (cited in Chapter Four), vol. 1, p. 125. This view is not idiosyncratic, and it is not necessarily the case that Ōkubo Toshiaki has let his relationship to Ōkubo Toshimichi affect his historical judgment. In fairness to the complexity of Ōkubo Toshiaki's view, it should be noted that he said also: "The characteristic that can be seen running through the Three New Laws is the penetration of strong, unitary administrative controlling power into local politics, in all areas of local administration. In this sense the establishment of the Three New Laws fixed the course of Home Ministry domestic policy." Ibid., p. 127.
3. Ōishi, "Chihō jichi," *(Iwanami kōza) Nihon rekishi 16 kindai 3* (Tokyo: Iwanami Shoten, 1967), p. 246. For support of his contention that Ōkubo Toshimichi was motivated by the desire to counter agrarian unrest and the people's rights movement, Ōishi refers to Ōshima Mitsuko, "Meiji zenki chihō seido no kōsatsu, 1," *Tōyō bunka,* no. 22, p. 89 ff.; Tokuda Ryōji, "Meiji shonen no chōsonkai no hattatsu," in Meiji Shiryō Kenkyū Renraku Kai, comp., *Meiji kenryoku no hōteki kōzō* (Tokyo: Ocha-nomizu Shobō, 1958); and Kikegawa Hiroshi, *Meiji chihō jichi seido no seiritsu katei,* p. 36 ff. In his contribution to the history of the Ishikawa Prefectural Assembly, the scholar of administration and finance Miyamoto Ken'ichi takes a position close to Ōishi's: "Local powers granted under the Three New Laws were no more than a policy of compromise with the parasitic landlords, but within the framework of these laws, popular local self-government made rapid advances." *IKGS,* vol. 1, p. 153.
4. Yamanaka Einosuke, *Nihon kindai kokka no keisei to kanryōsei* (Tokyo: Kō-

bundō, 1974), pp. 22–24. Yamanaka's view is echoed by Watanabe Takaki in "Meiji kokka to chihō jichi," *(Taikei) Nihon kokka shi,* vol. 4.
Kindai (Tokyo: Tōkyō Daigaku Shuppan Kai, 1975), vol. 1, p. 227.

5. See Ishii Ryōsuke, ed., *Meiji bunka shi,* vol. 2, *Hōseishi* (Tokyo: Yōyōsha, 1954), p. 163.

6. Ōishi, Yamanaka, and a great many other recent historians have concentrated their research on the opposition to government policy, and on conflict. Among non-Japanese writers sharing this focus are Bowen, in *Rebellion and Democracy* (cited in the introduction), Stephen Vlastos, in his
chapter "Opposition Movements in Early Meiji, 1868–1885," in Marius
B. Jansen, ed., *The Cambridge History of Japan, Vol 5: The Nineteenth Century* (Cambridge: Cambridge University Press, 1989), and Tetsuo Najita
and J. Victor Koschmann and their collaborators in *Conflict in Modern
Japanese History: The Neglected Tradition* (cited in the introduction). Opposition and conflict were abundant in this period. The intent here is not
to deny that or to try to refute the evidence that these studies have
brought forward. The point I wish to make is that we should not overlook
the fact that many local citizens complied with the new system and cooperated with the new authorities. Recognition of that seems to require
modification of the interpretation that the system of this era was essentially an absolutism imposed unilaterally from above.

7. Ōkubo Toshimichi's view, cited by Ishii, *Japanese Legislation,* p. 214.

8. Translations for the most part follow Chambliss, except that *ku* in Decree
17 is translated "urban districts" instead of "city wards." See *Japanese
Legislation,* p. 215 ff. For texts of the laws, see *Fuken seido shiryō, gyōsei
hen,* pp. 108–111, for the first law (*gunku chōson hensei hō, Dajōkan fukoku
17*), pp. 116–130 for the second law *(fukenkai kisoku, Dajōkan fukoku
18*), and idem, *zaisei hen,* pp. 31–33, for the third law (*chihōzei kisoku,
Dajōkan fukoku 19*). Translations of the first two of the Three New Laws
appear in McLaren, "Japanese Government Documents," pp. 270–276.
These decrees were sometimes called the Three Great New Laws *(sandai-
shinpō)*.

9. Kikegawa draws on Ōmori Shōichi, *Chihō seido enkaku,* MS in the Tokyo
Institute for Municipal Research, for this periodization; see Kikegawa,
Meiji chihō jichi seido no seiritsu katei, p. 63.

10. Cf. Council of State Decree 48, November 5, 1880. The items shifted
from the national exchequer to localities included construction and repairs
of prefectural office buildings, prefectural prison expenditures, and construction and repairs of prefectural prisons. Ibid., pp. 61–62. Moreover,
in order to facilitate the delegation and implementation of national policy, the government strengthened the financial base of the prefectures and

the new administrative units, counties, by drawing on what had been the tax reservoir of the towns and villages. *NSS*, p. 581.

11. *Fuken kanshoku sei, Dajōkan tatsu* 32, July 25, 1878, *Fuken seido shiryō, kansei hen*, pp. 72–79. See also McLaren, "Japanese Government Documents," pp. 276–285.
12. *IKSR, kan 2, seiji bu, kenchi, FS* reel 109.
13. *IKSR, kan 44, seido bu, shokusei, Meiji 11-nen, FS* reel 112.
14. See the charts on *gunchō, kuchō*, and *shichō*, in *IKS*, vol. 4, pp. 168–178. The compilers of *IKS* did not see fit to provide charts for counties that later became part of Fukui and Toyama Prefectures.
15. Yamanaka, p. 30, citing Sanjiin, "Gunkuchōson hensei hō riyūsho."
16. On Ōnogi, see *IKS*, vol. 4, pp. 1212–1213, and *Kanō kyōdo jii*, comp. Heki Ken (Kanazawa, 1956), p. 140. Ōnogi's family was of *hitomochigumi* rank in Kaga, placing it just below the *hakka*, eight houses. Seventy Kaga families in the late Tokugawa period had *hitomochigumi* status; their stipends ranged from 1,000 to 14,000 *koku* per annum. Ibid., p. 744.
17. Nakagawa had been *shōsanji* (minor councilor, or junior councilor) at the time of *haihan chiken*. *IKSR, kan 68, (Kyū Kanazawa ken) kan'in rireki, FS* reel 116.
18. Data drawn from ibid., and *IKSR, kan 57, 58, furoku, kan'in rireki, FS* reels 113, 114.
19. Cf. *Ishikawa ken tōkei hyō*, 1880, 1881, *MNFTS* reel 185.
20. Cf. *Fuken kanshoku sei*, cited above.
21. Ibid.
22. See *Ishikawa ken tōkei hyō*, 1880, and *Fuken kanshoku sei*.
23. Cf. *IKSR, kan 44, seido bu, shokusei, Meiji 11-nen, FS* reel 112; *Ishikawa ken tōkei hyō*, 1880.
24. *FSS, gyōsei hen*, p. 111.
25. Ishii, *Japanese Legislation*, pp. 217–218. Cf. Kikegawa, *Meiji chihō jichi seido no seiritsu katei*, p. 64.
26. Ishii, *Japanese Legislation*, p. 218.
27. *KKSS, S*, vol. 1, p. 30.
28. Ibid., pp. 34–35.
29. In 1880, there were 14,659 female heads of households in Ishikawa. *Ishikawa ken tōkei hyō*, 1880, *MNFTS* reel 185. Certainly some of those women met the taxpaying qualification to vote, and were disqualified on the grounds of gender.
30. *IKSR*, printed version (Kanazawa, 1973), vol. 3, p. 571. This set of rules pertained to the election of town and village representatives under an 1876 law which was superseded by the Three New Laws.

31. *KKSS, S,* vol. 1, pp. 34–35.

32. *IKSR, kan 44, seido bu, shokusei, Meiji 11-nen, FS* reel 112; *Hakui shi shi, gendai hen,* comp. Hakui Shi Shi Hensan Iinkai (Hakui: Hakui Shi, 1972), p. 33.

33. *Ishikawa kenchi gairan,* 1878, *MNFTS* reel 185. Cf. *Chihō enkaku ryakufu,* pp. 204, 208–209. The 537 *machi* (city wards) of Kanazawa *ku* are included in the figure 1,028.

34. Ibid.; *Ishikawa kenchi gairan,* 1878, *Ishikawa ken tōkei hyō,* 1880, *MNFTS* reel 185.

35. Idem.

36. *IKGS,* vol. 1, pp. 405–406.

37. See Kobayashi Akira, "Kingendai gyōzaisei," in *Nanao shi shi,* comp. Nanao Shi Shi Hensan Senmu Iinkai (Nanao: Nanao Shiyakusho, 1974), pp. 582–583.

38. *Fuken kanshoku sei,* cited above.

39. *IKSR, kan 44, seido bu, shokusei, FS* reel 112.

40. *(Kaga han tomura yaku) Ishiguro ke monjo,* vol. 2, p. 826.

41. Yonezawa, *Kaga han no tomura seido,* p. 332.

42. Cf. Thomas C. Smith, *The Agrarian Origins of Modern Japan* (Stanford: Stanford University Press, 1959), pp. 180–200.

43. Cf. Andrew Fraser, *A Political Profile of Tokushima Prefecture in the Early and Middle Meiji Period, 1868–1902* (Canberra: Australian National University Faculty of Asian Studies, 1971), esp. pp. 12–27.

44. Ishii, *Japanese Legislation,* p. 409.

45. *Ishikawa ken tōkeisho 1885, MNFTS* reel 185.

46. Kikegawa, *Meiji chihō jichi seido no seiritsu katei,* p. 77.

47. *NSS,* pp. 586–587.

48. *KKSS, S,* vol. 1.

49. *IKS,* vol. 4, p. 48 ff.

50. See the biographical sketches in *IKGS,* vol. 1: Katagiri Sakuhei, pp. 1448–1449; Tachimoto Naoyuki, p. 1509; Nitta Jinzaemon, pp. 1548–1550; Murata Yaemon, p. 1618; Yoshimoto Shōzō, pp. 1649–1650.

51. Enforcement Regulations for the Three New Laws (*gunku chōson hensei hō fukenkai kisoku chihōzei kisoku shikō junjo, Dajōkan tatsu,* July 22, 1878), *FSS, gyōsei hen,* pp. 106–108.

52. For the text of the regulations, *chōson junsoku,* see *KKSS, S,* vol. 1, pp. 29–30. See also Kobayashi Akira, "Kingendai gyōzaisei," in *NSS,* p. 583. Heads of households registered in a town or village who possessed real property and whose finances were solvent had the qualification (*shikaku*) to participate. In cases where one town or village assembly served as the deliberative body for several towns or villages, the Ishikawa regulation

provided for the election of representatives to the assembly in the ratio of approximately one delegate per twenty households.

53. Kiriyama's phrase was, *"Ippan jinmin no zenji shinpo o kibō seraru"*; see *KKSS, S,* vol. 1, p. 29.

54. Ibid.

55. *NSS,* p. 584; *IKS,* vol. 4, p. 179.

56. *KKSS, S,* vol. 1, p. 38. Evidence of the election has disappeared, and the record of implementation of the March 1879 regulations is almost a blank.

57. Ibid., p. 39.

58. Ibid. At least seven of the twenty-four men can be positively identified as former samurai *(shizoku),* and from their surnames it seems possible that the number of *shizoku* was even higher, though available records do not permit confirmation of this.

59. See the roster of Kaga samurai in the *bakumatsu* period, appendix to *IKS,* vol. 2.

60. *IKGS,* vol. 1, pp. 1654–1655.

61. *KKSS, S,* vol. 1, p. 40.

62. Kikegawa, *Jichi 50-nen shi,* p. 61.

63. "Some Observations on Local Government at the Village Level in Present-Day Japan," *Far Eastern Quarterly,* vol. 12, no. 2 (1953), p. 192. Cf. also Kurt Steiner, "The Japanese Village and Its Government," *Far Eastern Quarterly,* vol. 15, no. 2, (1956), pp. 189–190.

64. *KKSS, S,* vol. 1, pp. 45–46. Cf. the translation of the national law in McLaren, "Japanese Government Documents," p. 296.

65. *KKSS, S,* vol. 1, pp. 45–46.

66. Ishii, *Japanese Legislation,* p. 408.

67. That is, expenditures out of funds raised by local levies *(kyōgihi),* rather than by the local tax set by the prefecture *(chihōzei).* On the May 7, 1884, revisions and Yamagata's commentary, see Kikegawa, *Jichi 50-nen shi,* pp. 60–67, and Ishii, *Japanese Legislation,* pp. 408–409.

68. See McLaren, "Japanese Government Documents," pp. 272–276, and *Fukenkai kisoku,* in *FSS, gyōsei hen,* pp. 116–120.

69. *Dai Nihon Teikoku tōkei nenkan,* comp. Naikaku Tōkei Kyoku (Tokyo: Naikaku Tōkei Kyoku, 1882), vol. 1, pp. 651–653.

70. Kikegawa, "Meiji chihō jichi seido no seiritsu katei," *Toshi mondai,* vol. 45, no. 1 (1954), p. 123.

71. This incident is discussed in the next chapter. See *IKGS,* vol. 1, pp. 765–767, and *KKSS, S,* vol. 1, pp. 277–283.

72. Kawa Yoshio has found what he believes to be a list of the names of the first Ishikawa Prefectural Assembly members, and presents it in *IKGS,*

vol. 1, pp. 584–585. *IKS,* vol. 4, p. 40 ff., lists members, but omits the names of all assemblymen elected between 1879 and 1882 and excludes assemblymen from Etchū and Echizen, which later became Toyama and Fukui prefectures.

73. *Dai Nihon Teikoku tōkei nenkan,* vol. 1, pp. 651–653. Figures for 1879, the year of the first prefectural assembly election, are not available.

74. *IKS,* vol. 4, p. 288; *KKSS, S,* vol. 1, p. 237.

75. See Appendixes 9 and 10. Similar disparities continue to exist in Japan today. James Sterngold of *The New York Times* reported on the 1992 election of members of the House of Councilors: "There are nearly two million residents per seat in crowded Kanagawa Prefecture, an industrial area adjacent to Tokyo, while in Tottori Prefecture, a rural region several hundred miles to the west, there are 308,000 residents per seat. That means each vote in Tottori carries nearly 6.5 times as much weight as a vote in Kanagawa." The reporter went on to note that "the ratio between the strongest and weakest votes in the lower house, which has 512 members, is 3.34 to 1." Although Japan's Supreme Court has ruled such disparities unconstitutional, it has refused to invalidate election results, "arguing that a nullification would create chaos." *The New York Times,* July 26, 1992, Section 1, p. 10.

76. Cf. the data in the two tables in the appendix, cited immediately above, with that in *Dai Nihon Teikoku tōkei nenkan,* vol. 2 (1883, reprinted Tokyo, 1962), pp. 717–719.

77. Nobutaka Ike's pioneering study in English, *The Beginnings of Political Democracy in Japan,* tends to accept this interpretation, which has continued to enjoy popularity among Japanese writers.

78. *Chihōkan kaigi ni okeru dai-3-gō gian (chihōzei kisoku) setsumeisho, FSS, zaisei hen,* pp. 36–37.

79. Ibid.

80. For the text, see ibid., pp. 31–33. For explications, see *Jichi 50-nen shi,* pp. 58–60, and Kikegawa, "Meiji chihō jichi seido no seiritsu katei," in *Toshi mondai,* vol. 45, no. 1 (1954), pp. 124–125.

81. See Chapter Three, above.

82. "Discussion of the people" in this article might also be translated "conference of the people"; the Japanese is *jinmin no kyōgi.*

83. Enforcement Regulations *(gunkuchōson hensei hō fukenkai kisoku chihōzei kisoku shikō junjo),* July 22, 1878, *FSS, zaisei hen,* pp. 37–38.

84. *Kanazawa ku kakuchō kosūwari kafu kata,* September 6, 1879. This document is preserved in the Kanazawa City Library.

85. *Dajōkan fukoku* 48, November 5, 1880, *FSS, zaisei hen,* p. 85.

86. *Chihōzei chū eigyōzei zasshuzei no shurui oyobi seigen,* December 20, 1878, ibid., pp. 40–53; cf. *IKGS,* vol. 1, p. 231.

87. Cf. Haraguchi, *Meiji zenki chihō seiji shi kenkyū*, vol. 2, p. 103, although his main point here is that the local tax on land was increasing.

88. The appendix, *Hitsuyōhi zuiihi sabetsu no koto* (The Distinction between Required Expenditures and Discretionary Expenditures), was attached to *Chihōzei chū eigyōzei zasshuzei no shurui oyobi seigen,* cited above. *FSS, zaisei hen,* pp. 54–55. See also *IKGS,* vol. 1, p. 232. The seven areas of required expenditure were police; construction and maintenance of riparian works, bridges, and roads; prefectural assembly; construction and maintenance of county or urban district office buildings; salaries, travel expenses, and office expenses of county or urban district officals; port officials and shipwrecks; and dissemination of proclamations or regulations pertaining only to the prefecture.

89. *Fuken kanshoku sei, FSS, kansei hen.*

90. *Fuken shokusei narabini jimu shōtei,* ibid.

91. This discussion draws on Yamanaka, p. 28.

92. "Meiji shoki no chihōkan," p. 208. The phrase "overwhelmingly preponderant power" renders *zetsadai na kengen.*

93. Cf. Yamanaka, p. 29.

94. Sengoku, pp. 31–45; *Hyakukan rireki; Dai jinmei jiten.*

95. See the photographs in *IKS,* vol. 4, following pp. 240, 246, and 286.

96. Chisaka's position under Iwakura is mentioned by Irokawa, who refers to a memo written by Chisaka during Meiji leaders' discussions of how to handle Kuroda Kiyotaka after Kuroda, then Minister of Colonial Development, killed his wife in a drunken rage. *Kindai kokka no shuppatsu,* pp. 13–14.

97. *IKS,* vol. 4, pp. 285–286.

98. Sengoku, p. 32.

99. *IKS,* vol. 4, pp. 316–321; *KKSS, S,* vol. 1, p. 280 ff.

100. *IKS,* vol. 4, p. 34; *IKSR, kan 60, furoku, kan'in rireki, 1876–1884, FS* reel 114; *Rekidai kenkan roku,* ed. Ijiri Tsunekichi (Tokyo, 1967 reprint of Naikaku Insatsu Kokunai Choyo Kai ed., 1928); *Hyakukan rireki,* vol. 2, p. 100 f.

101. Sengoku, pp. 46, 52–53.

102. Ibid.

103. *IKSR* (printed version), vol. 4, pp. 601–698.

104. Sonozaki Zen'ichi, "Seitō no seisui to kensei," in *Ishikawa ken no rekishi,* ed. Wakabayashi, p. 217.

105. *IKS,* vol. 4, pp. 169–177. James L. McClain found a "culture of community responsibility" borne by men such as these in Kanazawa. See McClain, "Local Elites and the Meiji Transition in Kanazawa," *Asian Cultural Studies,* no. 18 (February 1992), pp. 107–136, esp. pp. 123–128. See Chapter Six below for more on the question of whether cooperating

with Iwamura was a pragmatic response to conditions under the system of the Three New Laws, and could have been seen as a way of promoting local self-interest.

6. THE PRIMACY OF ECONOMIC CONCERNS: ISHIKAWA'S ACTIVISTS IN THE SECOND MEIJI DECADE

1. Sengoku, p. 47; *IKS*, vol. 4, p. 327.
2. *Chihō seido enkaku*, MS in the Tokyo Institute for Municipal Research, summarized by Kikegawa, *Meiji chihō jichi seido no seiritsu katei*, p. 63.
3. *IKGS*, vol. 1, p. 706.
4. Ibid., pp. 708–751.
5. Kumano was still the number two man in the prefectural office. His message to the home minister appears in *IKS*, vol. 4, pp. 287–288.
6. *IKGS*, vol. 1, p. 752. In their close attention to detail, and their careful deliberation, the delegates to the first Ishikawa assembly behaved as did the Fukui assemblymen treated by James L. McClain in "Local Politics and National Integration: The Fukui Prefectural Assembly in the 1880s," *Monumenta Nipponica*, vol. 31, no. 1 (Spring 1976), pp. 51–75; see esp. pp. 62–63. McClain emphasizes the delegates' seriousness of purpose and sober approach to their duties.
7. *IKGS*, vol. 1, pp. 755–756.
8. Cf. data in ibid., pp. 751, 754–755. It appears that there is a misprint on p. 755; the total for revenues is printed as ¥567,207.741 (matching expenditures), but the three local tax items (*chisowari, kosūwari,* and *eigyō-zei zasshuzei gyogyōsaisōzei*) add up only to ¥519,863.298.
9. Ibid., pp. 759–760.
10. A man whose father had been a village chief in a fief belonging directly to the Tokugawa followed Kawase as speaker for a year, then Endō Hide-kage, another Kanazawa ex-samurai, was elected and served for two years. See ibid., pp. 701–926, passim, plus ibid., *giin ichiran*, passim. The first Ishikawa Prefectural Assembly speaker to have been born in Kaga domain of a commoner (in his case, wealthy peasant) family was Muramoto Shōzō of Ishikawa County. The members of the assembly, if not the leaders, were from the earliest sessions predominantly from commoner back-grounds. In the 1880 election, for example, all but three of the twenty-two reelected incumbents were commoners.
11. Ibid., pp. 760–763. See again McClain, "Local Politics and National Integration: The Fukui Prefectural Assembly in the 1880s." McClain found that the assembly of the new prefecture was an important arena for the settlement of local political disputes and mechanism for the integra-

tion of the locality into the national polity. In his conclusion he observed—as is consistent with our findings in Ishikawa—that though the participants in the Fukui Assembly "did not always agree with the policies and programs of the national government . . . they accepted the system and strove to make it effective" (p. 74), and that "new insights into the peaceful character of the Meiji transition can be gained by examining the role played by local deliberative bodies. The Fukui Prefectural Assembly, like those in Japan's other prefectures, helped to open the doors to participation in the Meiji government system to scores of individuals and interest groups. By smoothing the entry of these men and groups into the new political community and by giving them a defined participatory role in the political process, the prefectural assembly system contributed to the relatively harmonious transformation of Japanese society during the early Meiji period" (p. 75). Early prefectural assemblies in Fukui included several members who had served in the Ishikawa Prefectural Assembly and several who had served in the Shiga Prefectural Assembly in 1879–1880.

12. See Chapter Five, above, on this change. Ariizumi Sadao has an excellent chapter on the significance of Council of State Decree Number 48 in *Meiji seijishi no kiso katei*, pp. 35–65. It was this policy of passing along construction and public works costs to the prefectures that made the road-building program of Governor Mishima Toshitsune so onerous to citizens of Fukushima Prefecture, who could no longer look to the central government for fiscal assistance in this expensive undertaking. Cf. Kobayashi Seiji and Yamada Akira, *Fukushima ken no rekishi* (Tokyo: Yamakawa Shuppan Sha, 1970), esp. pp. 188–189.

13. *IKGS*, vol. 1, pp. 764–765.

14. The text of the memorial, "Gunkuchō wa yoroshiku minsen ni shitagaubeki no kengi," and notes on the assembly discussion and voting that followed the reading of this memorial on June 27, 1881, are contained in an excerpt of *Ishikawa kenkai nisshi* reproduced in *Toyama kenshi, shiryō hen VI, kindai jō*, comp. Toyama Prefecture (Toyama: Toyama Ken, 1978).

15. *Meiji seijishi no kiso katei*, pp. 40–41.

16. Professor Ōishi put the point thus: "The crux of the demands of the wealthy peasant people's rights advocates in the prefectural assemblies was the establishment of local self-government." "Chihō jichi," in *Iwanami kōza Nihon rekishi 16 kindai 3*, p. 250; this essay was reprinted, with supplementary notes, as "Chihō jichisei no seiritsu" in Ōishi, *Kindai Nihon no chihō jichi* (Tokyo: Tōkyō Daigaku Shuppan Kai, 1990). Ōishi wrote in detail of "demands for local self rule" (*chihō jichi no yōkyū*) by the people's rights movement participants in *Nihon chihō zaigyōseishi josetsu*,

esp. pp. 324–372. He notes that the "demands" made in the assemblies were rooted in the demand to reduce the burden of land tax on local citizens, and he identifies the demands as including elimination of localities' financial liability for business delegated by the national government; establishment and expansion of local assemblies' fiscal powers; establishment of precedence of local assemblies' legislative authority over administrative authority; abolition of authoritarian central control over localities; and democratization of the internal workings of local self-governing bodies ("Chihō jichi," pp. 250–251). Basically he seems to equate prefectural assemblies' moves to cut governors' budget proposals with demands for self-government. While the one seems to presume the other—assertions of the right to reduce prefectural spending might be taken to imply that the makers of those assertions presume also that they have a right to self-government—I think a distinction can, and should, be made. When we try to account for the development of political institutions and politics at the subnational level in Meiji Japan, we might conclude that local politicians' lack of an articulated position on the form and content of local autonomy influenced their behavior in relations with central government appointees and in the way they organized their own support bases. What Ōishi has observed is local politicians demanding that their input be recognized within the system of the Three New Laws. What he has not convinced me of is that the local politicians of the 1880s had more than an episodic commitment to principles of local self-government—a feeling for local autonomy that transcended the present realities of the Three New Laws. Ariizumi, tallying the various motions of dozens of prefectural assemblies, comes closer to being persuasive. Yet we are left to explain why direct demands for local self-government were not persistently and repeatedly put forward after 1881.

17. Ariizumi, p. 43. McClain identified three factions in the Fukui Prefectural Assembly in the late 1880s: the *dobokuha,* which advocated increased expenditures for public works; the *kangyōha,* which wanted prefectural spending to promote agriculture and industry; and the *nōminha,* which wanted to reduce all expenditures because it was primarily the farmers (*nōmin*) whose tax-bearing capacity was being tested whenever a prefectural spending program was passed. McClain, "Local Politics and National Integration," p. 71. Michael Lewis paraphrases a historian of Toyama Prefecture as saying that the history of the Etchū region "is largely the history of struggling against the waters," and observes that "Inagaki and other Toyama politicians recognized the importance of river conservation and devoted much of their time and energy to securing influence within local, prefectural, and central government institutions to procure funds for various construction projects." Lewis, "Interest and Ideology in

Meiji Politics: Inagaki Shimesu and the Toyama Jiyūtō," *Asian Cultural Studies*, no. 18 (February 1992), p. 167.

18. The heavy flooding of 1881 is reported in *IKGS*, vol. 1, p. 765. Oddly there is little on these floods in *IKSR, kan 73, seiji bu, sōyō jihen 1881, FS* reel 116 (printed version: *IKSR*, vol. 3, p. 309); there was a more extensive report on the floods of February 1877 (ibid., pp. 307–308).

19. The governor of Kanagawa Prefecture had memorialized Sanjō Sanetomi in September 1881, arguing that the burden of public works spending was too large to be managed out of prefectural taxes without central government fiscal assistance and expressing an opinion much like Chisaka's. Ariizumi, pp. 38–39, citing *Inoue Kowashi kankei monjo*, comp. Kokuritsu Kokkai Toshokan, 659–19, for the memorial by Governor Nomura Kiyoshi, and *Kōmon ruiju*, comp. Kokuritsu Kōbunsho Kan, dai 6-hen, 47 kan (2 A 11 rui 47), for the memorial by Chisaka. Ariizumi interprets these documents as showing that first-rank governors recognized that the government's abolition of grants to prefectures for public works spending was "wholly unfair" in light of the changes that had just been made in the land tax system.

20. *IKS*, vol. 4, p. 314.

21. Minami, born into a wealthy peasant family and for a time in the early 1870s a small district chief, later became speaker of the Toyama Prefectural Assembly. *IKGS*, vol. 1, p. 1606.

22. Ibid., p. 766; *KKSS, S*, vol. 1, pp. 280–281.

23. McLaren, "Japanese Government Documents," p. 294.

24. *KKSS, S*, vol. 1, p. 281.

25. Kikegawa, *Jichi 50-nen shi*, pp. 71–72, provides several instances to show how the government was watching closely over prefectural assembly actions at this time. On Fukushima, in English, see Bowen, *Rebellion and Democracy in Meiji Japan*, and Stephen Vlastos, "Opposition Movements in Early Meiji, 1868–1885," in Marius B. Jansen, ed., *The Cambridge History of Japan*, vol. 5: *The Nineteenth Century*, (Cambridge: Cambridge University Press, 1989). Vlastos first wrote about Fukushima while in graduate school at the University of California at Berkeley, in "The Aizu Road Construction Controversy: A Political Movement in Rural Japan 1882," unpublished (1971).

26. Kikegawa, *Meiji chihō jichi seido no seiritsu katei*, p. 82.

27. Ibid., p. 83.

28. McLaren, "Japanese Government Documents," p. 295.

29. Once again the record of assembly proceedings is missing. I draw on *IKGS*, vol. 1, pp. 767–772, and *KKSS, S*, vol. 1, pp. 281–282.

30. This summary of the Inagaki affair follows *IKGS*, vol. 1, p. 767.

31. Ibid., pp. 768–771.

32. The Kōyōsha was a forerunner of the Genyōsha, or Dark Ocean Society, which was formed in 1881. The Genyōsha later (in 1901) spawned the Kokuryūkai, or Amur Society. Patriotic and expansionist, these groups contributed to the rise of ultranationalism in prewar Japan. In English, see E. H. Norman, "The Genyōsha: A Study in the Origins of Japanese Imperialism," *Pacific Affairs*, vol. 42, no. 3 (1944), pp. 261–284.

33. *IKS*, vol. 4, p. 284.

34. The passage that they selected from the Great Treatise *(Ta chuan)* of the *I-ching* is rendered by Richard Wilhelm as follows: "Thus the penetration of a germinal thought into the mind promotes the working of the mind. When this working furthers and brings peace of life it elevates a man's nature." *The I-Ching or Book of Changes*, tr. Richard Wilhelm, tr. into English by Cary F. Baynes (Princeton: Princeton University Press, 1950, reprinted 1970), p. 338. I am grateful to Paul W. Kroll for help in pinning down this reference. The word *seigi (ching-i)*, which Wilhelm and Baynes translate as "germinal thought," more literally means something like "essential righteousness"; hence my translation of the name of the Kanazawa political society.

35. *IKS*, vol. 4, p. 284; *KKSS, S*, vol. 1, pp. 235–236.

36. *KKSS, S*, vol. 1, pp. 239–240.

37. Ibid., pp. 236, 238.

38. Yoshida Kizashi did carry a petition with seventy names to the 1880 meeting of the League to Establish a National Assembly (Kokkai Kisei Dōmei Kai). *Jiyūtō shi*, ed. Itagaki Taisuke, with corrections by Tōyama Shigeki and Satō Shigerō (Tokyo: Iwanami Shoten, 1957), vol. 1, pp. 294–295.

39. *IKS*, vol. 4, p. 290.

40. *KKSS, S*, vol. 1, p. 243; *IKS*, vol. 4, p. 291. Maeda Toshitsugu received the title marquis in July 1879, by the way, in a special sign of imperial favor. Most of the titles of nobility conferred by the Meiji Emperor were bestowed in 1884 and thereafter. See ibid., p. 1231, and *Meiji Tennō ki*, vol. 6, p. 227. Seigisha member Furuya Toratarō became steward, *kajū*, in the Maeda household.

41. *IKS*, vol. 4, p. 292.

42. The phrase *eishin* derived from a passage in which Mencius explicated a story about Confucius' admiration for water: " 'Water from an ample source,' said Mencius, 'comes tumbling down, day and night without ceasing, *going forward* [Japanese: *shin*] only after all the hollows are *filled* [Japanese: *ei*], and then draining into the sea. Anything that has an ample source is like this. What Confucius saw in water is just this and nothing more. If a thing has no source, it is like the rain water that collects after a downpour in the seventh and eighth months. It may fill all the gutters,

but we can stand and wait for it to dry up. Thus a gentleman is ashamed of an exaggerated reputation.' " *Mencius,* tr. D. C. Lau (Baltimore: Penguin, 1970), pp. 130–131 (emphasis added). The reference was traced from a fragmentary quotation in *IKS,* vol. 4, p. 292, through Morohashi Tetsuji's *Dai Kan-Wa jiten,* to Book vol. 4, Part B (Li Lou, II) of *Mencius.*

43. A bit of speculation about the name may be permissible. The quotation from *Mencius* suggests that progress could only be expected once the hollows had been filled, or, to change the image, a man's reputation might be enhanced only after he had repaired the defects in his character. Almost surely the men who chose this phrase saw in Mencius' words a metaphor for their own condition. "The hollows" could be compared with the failure of Kaga to produce Restoration leaders and the unimpressive record of the regional economy, and probably the members of the new Eishinsha shared with the Ishikawa activists of the previous decade a sense of shame about their failure to accomplish any great deeds. If these men of the Society of Filling and Advancing could imbue themselves with sufficient virtue, however, they would have a "source" from which their actions could go forward, and they might make up for past shortcomings.

44. This document is reprinted in *KKSS, S,* vol. 1, pp. 247–248, and *IKS,* vol. 4, pp. 293–294. The writers were Endō Hidekage and Iguchi Mukashi. The latter was a journalist for the Kaetsunō Shinbun at the time, and was renowned for his fluent brush—admirers styled him "the Han Yü of the Hokuriku."

45. *IKGS,* vol. 1, p. 584.

46. Ibid., p. 586. Yasuda's replacement was Yoneyama Michio, known to us as a pro-Satsuma activist before the abolition of the *han,* and as a Chūkokusha leader and sometime bureaucrat in the 1870s.

Endō Hidekage went on to figure prominently in Kanazawa affairs for many years, and was the individual whose personal career was most intimately involved with the collective activities of the Eishinsha. Born the year Perry first visited Japan, in 1853, as the son of a rear-vassal who served as barber to the upper-samurai Fuwa family of Kanazawa, Endō was able to cap his career by being elected to the first Diet in 1890. The path to eminence for Endō was in working with—and promoting the welfare of—fellow former samurai. His father Ryū had parlayed a small stipend into enough capital that when occupational freedom was granted to former samurai in 1871, he could set himself up as a pawnbroker. As a boy, Hidekage lent a hand in his father's business and conceived a precocious interest in plans to promote industry in Japan *(shokusan kōgyō).* Too many uncreditworthy borrowers defaulted on Endō loans, unfortunately, and the family's small wealth was quickly dissipated. By the time Hidekage was in his twenties, however, he had begun to win a reputation as a leader in non-mercantile endeavors. When martial arts experienced a renaissance in popularity at the time of Saigō's rebellion in Kyushu, he opened a fencing school in his yard in Kanazawa, enrolling some youths and hiring an expert teacher to prepare them to defend their nation. Next he planned to invest in a land reclamation project in Northeastern Japan, but he and his fellow principals were dissuaded from this scheme before they had gotten very far. In 1879, he became one of a group of ex-samurai who founded a paper manufacturing firm in his home town. The venture soon went bankrupt. Fortunately for Endō, he was elected to the prefectural assembly in that same year, and soon thereafter became a founding officer of the Eishinsha. In and out of elective posts, he continued through the 1880s to busy himself on behalf of schemes to promote economic development and at the same time to aid former samurai in their transition to the new circumstances of the Meiji state. On Endō, see *KKSS, S,* vol. 1, passim, esp. pp. 244–246, and *IKGS,* vol. 1, pp. 1427–1428.

47. Masumi Junnosuke writes about Sugita in *Nihon seitō shi ron,* vol. 1, pp. 285–287, but the leading authority on the Sakai political leader is Ōtsuki Hiromu, a professor at the Osaka University of Economics, which houses the Sugita Library (Sugita Bunko). See Ōtsuki, *Echizen jiyūminken undō no kenkyū* (Kyoto: Hōritsu Bunkasha, 1980).

48. Cf. Horie Eiichi, "Jiyūminkenundō no tenbō," in Rekishigaku Kenkyū Kai, ed., *Rekishi to minshū* (Tokyo: Iwanami Shoten, 1955). Horie outlines the history of the people's rights movement as falling into three phases, defined by who the leaders were: (1) former samurai people's rights, (2) wealthy peasants' people's rights, and (3) peasants' peoples rights.

49. *Gikai seido 70-nen shi,* comp. Shūgiin and Sangiin, XI, *Shūgiin giin meikan* (Tokyo: Ōkurashō Insatsu Kyoku, 1962).

50. Status-consciousness remained strong in Kanazawa. I once asked several descendants of old merchant families in that city about how their forebears related to the political changes of Meiji, and whether any of them had become politically active. Andō Haruo, fifth-generation head of an apothecary firm begun early in the Meiji period, gave a typical answer: to merchants of the Meiji era, politics was not their business. (Conversation, 1973.)

51. Biographical information on Inagaki can be found in *Toyama kensei shi,* vol. 4 (Toyama, 1941). Masumi Junnosuke has a short account of Inagaki's activities in his *Nihon seitō shi ron,* vol. 1, p. 284. Inagaki Gōichi, a historian and secondary school principal in Toyama Prefecture, who is not descended from the Meiji politician with the same surname, has written about the career of Inagaki Shimesu: "Inagaki Shimesu to Shimada

Takayuki," (place, publisher, and date unknown; the author provided me with a photocopy); "Etchū jiyū minken undō no ayumi," *Kyōdo bunka kōza yōshi,* 62nd meeting (Toyama, n.d.); and "Jiyū minken undō to Toyama ken no seiritsu," chapter 3 of *Toyama kenshi, tsūshi hen,* vol. 5, *kindai* 1 (Toyama: Toyama Ken, 1981). Then a high school history teacher in Shin Minato, Inagaki Gōichi kindly spent much of December 18, 1973, talking with me about Inagaki Shimesu, and he took me to see the memorial stone erected near the village of the Meiji political leader's birth. Mr. Inagaki also gave me a photocopy of a useful brief chronology of Inagaki Shimesu's life ("Ko Inagaki Shimesu kun jiseki gaiyō," comp. anon. [n.p., n.d., a brush-written MS on the manuscript paper of the Toyama Chamber of Commerce (Toyama Shōgyō Kaigi Sho)]). Michael Lewis, in his insightful article on Inagaki, "Interest and Ideology in Meiji Politics: Inagaki Shimesu and the Toyama Jiyūtō" (cited above), stresses Inagaki's pragmatism in promoting local interests, particularly in his later career as a Diet member after 1892.

52. *Jiyūtō shi,* vol. 1, p. 299. Sugita Teiichi also submitted such a petition as "general representative of the people of Echizen in Ishikawa Prefecture who desire a national assembly," but how many others had signed that petition is unclear. Ibid.

53. "Kokkai kaisetsu aigan hyō," dated November 30, 1880, addressed to the emperor and actually presented to Sanjō Sanetomi, reproduced in *Meiji kenpakusho shūsei,* vol. 6, supervising editors Irokawa Daikichi and Gabe Masao, edited by Tsurumaki Takao (Tokyo: Chikuma Shobō, 1987), pp. 280–281.

54. *Gikai seido 70-nen shi,* vol. 9, *Shūgiin giin meikan,* p. 57. Lewis tells how Inagaki reached an accommodation with Home Minister Shinagawa Yajirō in 1892, during Shinagawa's notorious heavy-handed interference in the election of members of the lower house of the Diet, and helped to prevent the election of Kaishintō candidates in return for assistance with his own candidacy and the candidacies of Inagaki allies in four other electoral districts. In Lewis' view, Inagaki was not thereby betraying his liberal principles, but simply being practical about getting power and seeing that things in the interest of his constituency got accomplished. He continued to practice compromise rather than confrontation, but he certainly did not always adhere to the line laid down by the government or by his party in the period 1892–1902 ("Interest and Ideology," esp. pp. 160–162).

55. This tale is told best in *KKSS, S,* vol. 1, pp. 249–301.

56. In 1916, according to the newspaper *Jiji Shinpō,* Marquis Maeda had a fortune exceeding ¥15 million, putting him among the top fourteen wealthiest men in the land. See the table constructed by Ishii Kanji, "Nihon shihonshugi no kakuritsu," in Rekishigaku Kenkyū Kai and Ni-

honshi Kenkyū Kai, eds., *(Kōza Nihonshi 6) Nihon teikokushugi no keisei*
(Tokyo: Tōkyō Daigaku Shuppan Kai, 1970), vol. 6, p. 204. The same
newspaper had published a list for which one qualified by having more
than ¥5 million. The head of the Maeda family was on it. Jiji Shinpō,
"Nihon zenkoku chōja banzuke," *(Shinbun shūsei) Meiji hennen shi*, comp.
Meiji Hennen Shi Hensan Kai (Tokyo: Zaisei Keizai Gakkai, 1936), pp.
314–317.

57. Railways were less profitable to average or small investors than to those
who were able put up large sums of capital. See E. J. Hobsbawm, *The Age
of Revolution 1789–1848* (New York: Mentor Books, 1962), pp. 64–65.

58. *KKSS, S*, vol. 1, p. 252.

59. Ibid., pp. 253–254. I have translated slightly more than half of the
message, enough to show the Maedas' tone and also their social and economic attitudes. In the passage that states that former samurai differ from
the common people, the latter are designated by the offhandedly disparag-
ing phrase *jinjō shūmin*. Nariyasu and Toshitsugu wished to make their
former vassals feel special at a time when old status distinctions were
losing their meaning.

60. Ibid., p. 255. The preamble and the first three chapters of the Kigyōkai
regulations are reproduced on pp. 254–258.

61. Again *KKSS, S*, vol. 1, is the best source, giving us another document
signed by Maeda Nariyasu and Maeda Toshitsugu (pp. 259–261).

62. Several families that had been retainers of the Maeda were also millionaires. Among the 441 richest men in Japan in 1901, we find Honda
Masazane, Yokoyama Takahira, and Yokoyama Takaoki, descendants of
two of the eight highest-ranking samurai families of Kaga. "Nihon zenkoku chōja banzuke," cited in note 56.

63. *IKS*, vol. 4, p. 311. The collapse occurred in 1883.

64. Ibid., pp. 302–308; *KKSS, S*, vol. 1, pp. 263–265; Ishibayashi, *Ishikawa 100-nen shi*, pp. 258–260.

65. *IKS*, vol. 4, pp. 301–302.

66. Prospectus for the Establishment of a Private Non-Standard Middle
School *(shiritsu hensoku chūgakkō setsuritsu no shui), IKS*, vol. 4, pp. 306–
308.

67. The village was called Maeda-mura, after the Kigyōkai patron. Today,
after amalgamation, it is part of Kyōwa-mura. Ishibayashi, p. 263.

68. *IKS*, vol. 4, pp. 309–310.

69. The decline of the Kigyōkai is treated in *KKSS, S*, vol. 1, pp. 268–275.

70. It is tempting to speculate about the character of the would-be railway
builders, land developers, and maritime capitalists of Kanazawa. Might
Kaga ex-samurai have been psychologically unsuited for entrepreneurial
roles? Leaving aside the political implications of their seeking the assis-

tance of their old feudal lord, the dependency relations established by Hikida and Endō and their followers do not seem to be the product of the kind of independent, "inner-directed," risk-taking spirit that students have found characteristic of successful entrepreneurs. We lack materials such as correspondence, diaries, memoirs, and biographies on Hikida and Endō and the other actors in this play; we know only about their public careers.

External circumstances might have reinforced the psychology of dependency in this case. As we have noted, the former samurai population of Kanazawa was huge, some 37,000 people. Aiding so many no doubt seemed an enormous task, one that hardly could be accomplished without help, preferably help from someone with deep pockets. And on their side, the former lords encouraged dependency, feeling something closely akin to maternal affection and responsibility for their old vassals and being quite willing to spend some of their own money to help those "children." Though they lectured their "children" on the importance of becoming independent, the Maeda played the "parent" role in their Meiji-period relationship with Kanazawa men, and the affection and support proffered by the parent were not conditional. The former retainers did not have to measure up to established standards of behavior or performance. Cf. Ruth Benedict, *The Chrysanthemum and the Sword* (Boston: Houghton Mifflin, 1946), esp. pp. 101–105 and 114–118; and Albert M. Craig's suggestive comment about the similarity of daimyo and father figures in "Kido Kōin and Ōkubo Toshimichi: A Psychohistorical Analysis," *Personality in Japanese History*, p. 285.

In addition to the constellation of dependent characteristics, it may be that Meiji-era Kanazawa men had inherited from pre-Restoration Kaga men habits of caution. There might have been a reluctance to plunge boldly into the unknown, particularly in the realms of agriculture, commerce, and manufacture.

Stimulating analyses of the entrepreneurial spirit can be found in David C. McClelland, *The Achieving Society* (Princeton: Princeton University Press, 1961), and M. W. Flinn, *Origins of the Industrial Revolution* (London: Longmans, 1966), pp. 69–90. Johannes Hirschmaier discusses entrepreneurial efforts of samurai in Meiji Japan in *The Origins of Enterprise in Meiji Japan* (Cambridge: Harvard University Press, 1964), pp. 44–68; he deals with the failure of most samurai banking ventures on pp. 66–67. Kozo Yamamura, in *A Study of Samurai Income and Entrepreneurship*, does not give extensive treatment to the failure of samurai enterprises in Meiji Japan, concentrating instead on the role of non-samurai in the formation of the modern Japanese economy.

On the question of psychological dependency, the outstanding authority is Takeo Doi, *The Anatomy of Dependence,* tr. John Bester (Tokyo, 1973).

71. See Inagaki, "Toyama ken bunritsu no rekishiteki haikei," *Kita Nihon Shinbun,* May 11, 1973.

72. This attack and its aftermath are described in *IKS,* vol. 4, pp. 316–318; *KKSS, S,* vol. 1, pp. 290–295; and Ishibayashi, pp. 283–284.

73. Sonoda was named chief secretary of Ishikawa, i.e., the top-ranking official after the governor, at the same time he was appointed as police chief. *IKSR,* vol. 4; *KKSS, S,* vol. 1, p. 292. Satsuma-born policemen had already become famous for their toughness, and they continued to set the tone for the Japanese police down through the end of the Pacific War.

74. There were four culprits, whose identities were revealed by one of their number, Toshikura Moriyuki, who was tricked by a police spy into getting inebriated and spilling the story. The four were sentenced to prison terms of three-and-a-half to four months, and two of them, Toshikura and Iida Hidekai, lost government jobs. *KKSS, S,* vol. 1, pp. 293, 297.

75. Again, see Bowen, *Rebellion and Democracy in Meiji Japan.*

76. On Kawase's relationship with Iwamura and the power it brought him, see *KKSS, S,* vol. 1, pp. 308–310. One writer (*IKS,* vol. 4, pp. 223, 224) described Kawase and his followers as "pumpkin assemblymen" (*kabocha giin*). But from a different perspective, Kawase might be seen as merely pragmatic about getting things done for his constituents, comparable in many ways to a Kanagawa Prefecture politician who has been analyzed by M. William Steele, in "Political Localism in Meiji Japan: The Case of Yoshino Taizō," *Asian Cultural Studies,* no. 18 (1992), pp. 137–155.

77. *KKSS, S,* vol. 1, p. 298.

78. *IKS,* vol. 4, pp. 319–320; *KKSS, S,* vol. 1, pp. 295–296; I checked the list of participants in this conference against the biographies of prefectural assemblymen in *IKGS,* vol. 1, pp. 1393–1657.

79. *IKS,* vol. 4, p. 322. Kataoka and Ueki may have been discouraged also by the reversals suffered by the Liberal Party in the wake of its involvement in political disturbances in Gunma and Kabayama earlier in 1884. Itagaki Taisuke and other key leaders decided in October of that year to dissolve the Liberal Party. Although some members participated in the formation of an opposition party in 1887, it was not until 1890 that the Liberal Party reconstituted itself under that name.

80. *IKGS,* vol. 1, pp. 776–777.

81. Sengoku, p. 61.

82. *IKS,* vol. 4, p. 328.

83. *IKGS,* vol. 1, pp. 880–884.

84. "Local Elites and the Meiji Transition in Kanazawa," esp. p. 123 ff.

CONCLUSION

1. That evening, the imperial family hosted a banquet to commemorate the occasion. Guests were seated in several different rooms, according to their rank and importance. In the hall with the emperor and empress were 119 people, including the imperial couple's children, ministers of foreign states, the few officials who had been directly appointed to their posts by the emperor, princes and marquises, and governors of prefectures. See *(Shiryō) Kindai Nihon shi,* ed. Tsuchiya Giei (Tokyo: Shinbun Shiryō Kenkyū Kai, 1933), vol. 1, section on 1889 (Meiji 22), pp. 3–5. Presumably the governor of Ishikawa and Marquis Maeda were among those in this room. We can also guess that the attire for the evening was formal Western dress. All those invited to the morning ceremony had worn Western clothes. In the woodblock prints depicting the occasion (there were no photographs), the emperor and his entourage of chamberlains, Prime Minister Kuroda, and the other cabinet ministers all are shown in full-dress military uniforms. See, for example, *Nishikie bakumatsu Meiji no rekishi,* ed. Konishi Shirō (Tokyo: Kōdansha, 1976). Gotō Yasushi sees the emperor's sartorial choice as emblematic of the tenor of the constitution and of the Meiji state. Wearing the uniform of a grand field marshal *(daigensui),* Mutsuhito gave observers a visual reminder that he was "the absolute ruler grasping all political powers extending over domestic policy, diplomacy, and military matters." The uniform symbolized his possession of supreme command over the military forces. Gotō, *Jiyū minken* (Tokyo: Chūō Kōron Sha, 1972), pp. 206–207. Unrelated to the symbolism of the ceremony but perhaps of interest to those who know the story of Shimada Ichirō of Kanazawa and his co-conspirators in the assassination of Ōkubo Toshimichi, the person who received the constitution from the emperor's hand as the representative of the Japanese people was the prime minister. This was the same Kuroda Kiyotaka who had been the sixth man named on the "cut list" of evil officials in the *zankanjō* prepared by Shimada's group before they carried out their attack on Ōkubo; that Kuroda's homicide of his young wife had gone unpunished stood in the minds of Shimada and his fellows as an egregious example of the abuse of power by the top leaders of the Meiji state.
2. The constitution became effective on November 29, 1890.
3. The most comprehensive analysis of the Meiji local autonomy system is Kikegawa's, especially in his *Jichi 50-nen shi* and *Meiji chihō jichi seido no seiritsu katei.* For translations of the two codes of 1888, see McLaren, "Japanese Government Documents," pp. 331–403. Richard Louis Staubitz's "The Establishment of the System of Local Self-Government (1888–1890) in Meiji Japan: Yamagata Aritomo and the Meaning of '*Jichi*' (Self-

Government)" (Ph.D. dissertation, Yale University, 1973) is the most thorough treatment in English of the process of making the mature Meiji system. My own article under the heading "local government" in *Kodansha Encyclopedia of Japan* places the Meiji local autonomy system in the context of a longer period, from 1868 through 1945. *Kodansha Encyclopedia of Japan* (Tokyo: Kodansha, 1983), vol. 5, pp. 62–65.

4. "Overview," in Jansen and Rozman, eds., *Japan in Transition from Tokugawa to Meiji*, esp. pp. 16–22.

5. Totten, "Japanese Municipal Government under Meiji and Taishō," unpublished master's thesis, Columbia University, 1949; Ishii, *Japanese Legislation in the Meiji Era;* Steiner, *Local Government in Japan;* Staubitz, "The Establishment of the System of Local Self-Government."

6. Ishii, *Japanese Legislation,* pp. 416–417.

7. Fujita, "Meiji shi ni okeru chihō jichi sei seitei no igi."

8. Tsuji, "Chihō jichi no kindai kei to Nihon kei," *Nihon kanryōsei no kenkyū* (Tokyo: Kōbundō, 1952; reissued 1967).

9. Ōishi, *Nihon chihō zaigyōseishi josetsu,* and "Chihō jichi."

10. Representatative works by Gotō are *Jiyū minken undō* (Tokyo: Sōgensha, 1958); *Jiyū minken undō no tenkai* (Tokyo: Yūhikaku, 1966), and *Jiyū minken,* cited above; by Irokawa, *Kindai kokka no shuppatsu; Meiji seishin shi* (Tokyo: Chūō Kōron Sha, 1954, rev. ed. 1974); and *The Culture of the Meiji Period,* translations edited by Marius B. Jansen (Princeton: Princeton University Press, 1985). Umegaki discusses several important historians who have argued that the making of the Meiji state was a process of establishing absolutism: he treats E. H. Norman, Tōyama Shigeki, Tanaka Akira, Ōe Shinobu, Haraguchi Kiyoshi, Inoue Kiyoshi, and Shimoyama Saburō (*After the Restoration,* pp. 8–13).

11. See *Jiyū minken,* esp. pp. 134–170 and 205–213.

12. Scalapino, *Democracy and the Party Movement in Pre-war Japan.*

13. Najita and Koschmann, p. 9.

14. See the works cited in note 3 above, and also *Meiji chihō seido seiritsu shi* (Tokyo: Kashiwa Shobō, 1967) and *Chihō seido shōshi* (Tokyo: Keisō Shobō, 1962).

15. Ishii, ed., *Meiji bunka shi,* vol. 2, *hōsei hen;* translated as *Japanese Legislation in the Meiji Era,* cited above.

16. This view has been expounded also by Kenzo Takayanagi, "A Century of Innovation: The Development of Japanese Law, 1868–1961," in Arthur Taylor von Mehren, ed., *Law in Japan* (Cambridge: Harvard University Press, 1963), and Dan Fenno Henderson, "Law and Political Modernization in Japan," in Robert E. Ward, ed., *Political Development in Modern Japan.*

17. James William Morley, "Introduction: Choice and Consequence," in Mor-

ley, ed., *Dilemmas of Growth in Prewar Japan* (Princeton: Princeton University Press, 1971).

18. Steiner, "Popular Political Participation and Political Development," pp. 213–215.

19. Steiner, *Local Government in Japan,* p. 3.

20. Marius B. Jansen and Gilbert Rosman, eds., *Japan in Transition from Tokugawa to Meiji.*

21. "Local Administration: The Example of Awa-Tokushima," ibid., p. 111.

22. McClain, "Local Politics and National Integration," and "Local Elites and the Meiji Transition in Kanazawa," cited above. The quotations here are from "Local Elites," p. 107 and p. 132.

23. Steele, "Political Localism in Meiji Japan," and Lewis, "Interest and Ideology in Meiji Politics," both cited in Chapter Six. Professor Steele has also given us an amusing and insightful piece of scholarship on the reaction of ordinary folk in Edo to the Restoration, "Edo in 1868: The View from Below," *Monumenta Nipponica,* vol. 45, no. 2 (1990), pp. 127–155. While it does not deal with the system of local governance or the response of people to that system, this article nevertheless makes a point that is suggestive to students of the process of political unification and integration: the major concern of Edo townsmen in "a year filled with an extraordinary amount of hardship and trouble . . . was simply to make the best of a difficult situation" (p. 155). People were aware that the leadership had changed at the top of their society, but they were intent above all on just getting along. Just as Tōyama Shigeki found it hard to document ordinary people's reactions to the imperial tours of the late 1870s and early 1880s (see the notes to Chapter Two), Steele concedes that "in the final analysis, the search for commoner political consciousness and loyalties may be futile. Evidence . . . suggests that resignation was more common than indignation" (p. 153).

24. Lewis, pp. 171 and 172.

25. Ariizumi, *Meiji seijishi no kiso katei,* and Mikuriya, *Meiji kokka keisei to chihō keiei* (Tokyo: Tōkyō Daigaku Shuppan Kai, 1980).

26. As noted in an earlier reference, Ariizumi has read widely about other prefectures and cites many other cases besides Yamanashi's, but he is immersed in Yamanashi more deeply than anywhere else and uses its history the most. For instances of his use of the *gōnōsō* category, see, e.g., pp. 82 and 91; on p. 120 he writes of *gōnōshō,* "wealthy farmers and merchants." The phrase "nothing but a plunderer" (*hitasura no shūdatsusha*) appears on p. 35. Ariizumi's years in the National Diet Library, mentioned above, were from 1960 to 1973.

27. See again Umegaki, *After the Restoration,* passim, elaborating the point he states succinctly on p. 5: "From the very beginning, in fact, the progres-

sion toward the consolidation and expansion of Imperial rule was complex and haphazard. . . . [T]he whole process unveiled complex and unstable interactions among the various actors supporting or resisting the changes of the decade."

28. Bernard Silberman, *"Ringisei*—Traditional Values or Organizational Imperatives in the Japanese Upper Civil Service, 1868–1945," *Journal of Asian Studies,* vol. 32, no. 2 (1973), pp. 251–264.

29. Ibid., p. 259.

30. Data extracted from personnel histories in *IKSR,* vol. 4, pp. 429–698.

Bibliography

Akita, George. *Foundations of Constitutional Government in Modern Japan, 1868–1900.* Cambridge: Harvard University Press, 1967.

Allinson, Gary. *Japanese Urbanism.* Berkeley: University of California Press, 1975.

The Analects of Confucius, tr. Arthur Waley. London: Allen and Unwin, 1938.

Ariizumi Sadao. *Meiji seijishi no kiso katei.* Tokyo: Yoshikawa Kōbunkan, 1980.

Asakawa Kan'ichi. "Notes on Village Government in Japan after 1600," *Journal of the American Oriental Society,* vol. 30, pp. 259–300 (1909–1910), and vol. 31, pp. 151–216 (1911).

Bakumatsu ishin jinmei jiten, ed. Naramoto Tatsuya. Tokyo: Gakugei Shorin, 1978.

Beasley, W. G. *The Meiji Restoration.* Stanford: Stanford University Press, 1972.

Befu, Harumi. "Duty, Reward, Sanction and Power: Four-Cornered Office of the Tokugawa Village Headman," in Bernard S. Silberman and Harry D. Harootunian, eds., *Modern Japanese Leadership.* Tucson: University of Arizona Press, 1966.

————. "Village Autonomy and Articulation with the State," in John W. Hall and Marius B. Jansen, eds. *Studies in the Institutional History of Early Modern Japan.* Princeton: Princeton University Press, 1968.

Black, C. E. *The Dynamics of Modernization.* New York: Harper and Row, 1966.

Bowen, Roger. *Rebellion and Democracy in Meiji Japan: A Study of Commoners in the Popular Rights Movement.* Berkeley: University of California Press, 1980.

Brown, Philip C. "Practical Constraints on Early Tokugawa Land Taxation: Annual Versus Fixed Assessments in Kaga Domain," *Journal of Japanese Studies,* vol. 14, no. 2, pp. 369–401 (1988).

Brown, Sidney DeVere. "Political Assassination in Early Meiji Japan: The Plot Against Ōkubo Toshimichi," in David Wurfel, ed., *Meiji Japan's Centennial:*

Aspects of Political Thought and Action. Lawrence: University Press of Kansas, 1971.

Burks, Ardath. "Administrative Transition from *Han* to *Ken:* The Example of Okayama," *Far Eastern Quarterly,* vol. 14, no. 3, pp. 371–382 (1956).

Chambliss, William Jones. *Chiaraijima Village.* Tucson: University of Arizona Press for the Association for Asian Studies, 1965.

Chihō kōmuin seido shiryō, comp. Jichichō. Tokyo: Jichichō, 1955.

Chihō zaisei seido shiryō, comp. Jichishō. Tokyo: Jichishō, 1965.

Clement, Ernest W. "Local Self-Government in Japan," *Political Science Quarterly,* vol. 7, no. 2, pp. 294–306 (1892).

Craig, Albert M. *Chōshū in the Meiji Restoration.* Cambridge: Harvard University Press, 1961.

———. "Introduction: Perspectives on Personality in Japanese History," in Albert M. Craig and Donald H. Shively, eds., *Personality in Japanese History.* Berkeley: University of California Press, 1970.

———. "The Restoration Movement in Chōshū," in John W. Hall and Marius B. Jansen, eds., *Studies in the Institutional History of Early Modern Japan.* Princeton: Princeton University Press, 1968.

Dai Nihon Teikoku tōkei nenkan, comp. Naikaku Tōkei Kyoku. Tokyo: Naikaku Tōkei Kyoku, 1882–1940.

Eisenstadt, S. N. *Modernization: Protest and Change.* Englewood Cliffs, N.J.: Prentice-Hall, 1966.

Etzioni, Amitai. *Political Unification.* New York: Holt, Rinehart and Winston, 1965.

Fairbank, John K., Edwin O. Reischauer, and Albert M. Craig. *East Asia: The Modern Transformation.* Boston: Houghton Mifflin, 1965.

Fraser, Andrew. "Abe Okito (1845–1920): A Meiji Local Politician and Businessman," *Papers on Far Eastern History,* no. 5, pp. 109–134 (1972).

———. "From Domain to Prefecture: Political Development in Tokushima, 1871–1880," *Papers on Far Eastern History,* no. 12, pp. 87–147 (1975).

———. "Hachisuka Mochiaki (1846–1918): A Meiji Domain Lord and Statesman," *Papers on Far Eastern History,* no. 2, pp. 43–61 (1970).

———. "Komuro Shinobu (1839–1898): A Meiji Politician and Businessman," *Papers on Far Eastern History,* no. 3, pp. 61–83 (1971).

———. "Local Administration: The Example of Awa-Tokushima," in Marius B. Jansen and Gilbert Rozman, eds., *Japan in Transition from Tokugawa to Meiji.* Princeton: Princeton University Press, 1986.

————. *National Election Politics in Tokushima Prefecture, 1890–1902.* Canberra: Australian National University Faculty of Asian Studies, 1972.

————. *A Political Profile of Tokushima Prefecture in the Early and Middle Meiji Period, 1868–1902.* Canberra: Australian National University Faculty of Asian Studies, 1971.

Fugeshi gun shi, comp. Fugeshi Gunyakusho. Fugeshi, 1924; reprinted Tokyo: Meicho Shuppan, 1973.

Fujita Takeo. *Chihō jichi ron.* Tokyo: Kasumigaseki Shobō, 1947.

————. "Meiji shi ni okeru chihō jichi sei seitei no igi," *(Kaikoku 100-nen kinen) Meiji bunka shi ronshū.* Tokyo: Kangensha, 1952.

————. *Nihon chihō zaisei seido no seiritsu.* Tokyo: Iwanami Shoten, 1941.

Fuken chiso kaisei kiyō, comp. Ministry of Finance, 1881. Reprinted in *Meiji zenki sangyō hattatsu shi shiryō,* supplemental volumes *(bekkan)* no. 9. 3 vols. Tokyo: Ryūkei Shosha, 1965.

Fuken seido shiryō, comp. Jichi Shinkō Chūō Kai. Tokyo: Jichi Shinkō Chūō Kai, 1941.

Fuken shiryō, comp. Yūshōdō Microfilms. Tokyo: Yūshōdō Microfilms, 1962.

Genyōsha shi, ed. Genyōsha. Tokyo: Genyōsha, 1917.

Gikai seido 70-nen shi, comp. Shūgiin and Sangiin. 12 vols. Tokyo: Ōkurashō Insatu Kyoku, 1961–1963.

Gluck, Carol. "The People in History: Recent Trends in Japanese Historiography," *Journal of Asian Studies,* vol. 38, no. 1, pp. 25–50 (November 1978).

Gotō Yasushi. *Jiyū minken.* Tokyo: Chūō Kōron Sha, 1972.

————. *Jiyū minken undō.* Tokyo: Sōgensha, 1958.

————. *Jiyū minken undō no tenkai.* Tokyo: Yūhikaku, 1966.

————. "Karoku seiri to shizoku no dōkō," in Furushima Toshio et al., eds., *Meiji zenki kyōdoshi kenkyū hō,* vol. 6 of *Kyōdoshi kenkyū kōza.* Tokyo: Asakura Shoten, 1970.

Griffis, William Elliot. *The Mikado: Institution and Person.* Princeton: Princeton University Press, 1915.

Hakui shi shi, gendai hen, comp. Hakui Shi Shi Hensan Iinkai. Hakui: Hakui Shi, 1972.

Hall, Ivan P. *Mori Arinori.* Cambridge: Harvard University Press, 1973.

Hall, John W. "The Castle Town and Japan's Modern Urbanization," in John W. Hall and Marius B. Jansen, eds., *Studies in the Institutional History of Early Modern Japan.* Princeton: Princeton University Press, 1968.

————. "A Monarch for Modern Japan," in Robert E. Ward, ed., *Political Development in Modern Japan.* Princeton: Princeton University Press, 1968.

Hane, Mikiso. *Peasants, Rebels, and Outcastes: The Underside of Modern Japan.* New York: Pantheon, 1982.

Hanley, Susan B., and Kozo Yamamura. *Economic and Demographic Change in Preindustrial Japan, 1600–1868.* Princeton: Princeton University Press, 1977.

Hansei ichiran, ed. Ōtsuka Takematsu. 2 vols. Tokyo: Nihon Shiseki Kyōkai, 1928–1929.

Haraguchi Kiyoshi. "Han taisei no kaitai," *(Iwanami kōza) Nihon rekishi 15 kindai 2.* Tokyo: Iwanami Shoten, 1962.

————. *Meiji zenki chihō seiji shi kenkyū.* 2 vols. Tokyo: Hanawa Shobō, 1972, 1974.

Harootunian, H. D. *Toward Restoration.* Berkeley: University of California Press, 1970.

Hasegawa Jun'ya kun, ed. Wada Bunjirō. Kanazawa: n.p., 1921.

Henderson, Dan Fenno. "Law and Political Modernization in Japan," in Robert E. Ward, ed., *Political Development in Modern Japan.* Princeton: Princeton University Press, 1968.

Hobsbawm, E. J. *The Age of Revolution 1789–1848.* New York: New American Library, 1962.

Hōgetsu Keigo and Kodama Kōta, eds. *(Shinkō) Nihonshi gairon.* Tokyo: Yoshikawa Kōbunkan, 1969.

Hōrei zensho. Meiji gan boshin no toshi (1868). Tokyo: Naikaku Insatsu Kyoku, n.d.

Horie Eiichi. "Jiyūminkenundō no tenbō," in Rekishigaku Kenkyū Kai, ed., *Rekishi to minshū.* Tokyo: Iwanami Shoten, 1955.

Huntington, Samuel P. *Political Order in Changing Societies.* New Haven: Yale University Press, 1968.

Hyakukan rireki, comp. Nihon Shiseki Kyōkai. 2 vols. Tokyo: Nihon Shiseki Kyōkai, 1928, reprinted 1973.

The I-Ching or Book of Changes, tr. Richard Wilhelm, tr. into English by Cary F. Baynes. Princeton: Princeton University Press, 1950, 1970.

Ike, Nobutaka. *The Beginnings of Political Democracy in Japan.* Baltimore: The Johns Hopkins Press, 1950.

Ikeda Takamasa. "Bakumatsu seijishi no kubun ni tsuite," *Nihonshi kenkyū,* no. 122 (1971), reprinted in *(Ronshū Nihon rekishi 8) Bakuhan taisei II.* Tokyo: Yūseidō, 1973.

Inagaki Gōichi. "Etchū jiyū minken undō no ayumi," *Kyōdo bunka kōza yōshi,* 62nd meeting. Toyama, n.d.

————. "Inagaki Shimesu to Shimada Takayuki." Photocopy, n.p., n.d., pp. 63–72.

————. "Jiyū minken undō to Toyama ken no seiritsu," chapter 3 of *Toyama kenshi, tsūshi hen,* vol. 5, *kindai* 1. Toyama: Toyama Ken, 1981.

————. "Toyama ken bunritsu no rekishiteki haikei," *Kita Nihon Shinbun,* May 11, 1973.

Inoue Ichiji. "Meiji ishin ni okeru Kaga hyakumangoku," *Rekishi kōron,* vol. 3, no. 6, pp. 79–87 (1934).

Irokawa Daikichi. *The Culture of the Meiji Period,* translations edited by Marius B. Jansen. Princeton: Princeton University Press, 1985.

————. *Kindai kokka no shuppatsu.* Tokyo: Chūō Kōron Sha, 1971.

————. *Meiji seishin shi.* Rev. ed. Tokyo: Chūō Kōron Sha, 1974.

————. "Tennōsei no shisō," in Joseph Pittau, ed., *(Sōgō kōza) Nihon no shakai bunka shi, 6, kindai kokka no shisō.* Tokyo: Kōdansha, 1974.

Ishibayashi Bunkichi. *Ishikawa 100-nen shi.* Kanazawa: Ishikawa Ken Kōminkan Rengō Kai, 1972.

Ishii Kanji. "Nihon shihonshugi no kakuritsu," in Rekishigaku Kenkyū Kai and Nihonshi Kenkyū Kai, eds., *(Kōza Nihonshi 6) Nihon teikokushugi no keisei.* Tokyo: Tōkyō Daigaku Shuppan Kai, 1970.

Ishii Ryōsuke. *Meiji bunka shi,* vol. 2. *Hōsei hen.* Tokyo: Yōyōsha, 1954.

————, ed. *(Taikei Nihon shi sōsho 4) Hōsei shi.* Tokyo: Yamakawa Shuppan Sha, 1964.

————, ed. *Japanese Legislation in the Meiji Era,* tr. William J. Chambliss. Tokyo: Obunsha, 1958.

Ishikawa Kengikai shi, comp. Ishikawa Kengikai Shi Hensan Iinkai. 3 vols. Kanazawa: Ishikawa Kengikai Jimu Kyoku, 1967–1969.

Ishikawa ken no rekishi, ed. Miyashita Yokichi. Kanazawa: Hokkoku Shinbun Sha, 1950.

Ishikawa ken no rekishi, ed. Wakabayashi Kisaburō. Kanazawa: Hokkoku Shuppan Sha, 1970.

Ishikawa ken shi, ed. Heki Ken. 5 vols. Kanazawa: Ishikawa Ken, 1927–1933.

Ishikawa ken shiryō, comp. Ishikawa Kenritsu Toshokan. 5 vols. Kanazawa: Ishikawa Kenritsu Toshokan, 1971–1975.

Jansen, Marius B. "Monarchy and Modernization in Japan," *Journal of Asian Studies,* vol. 36, no. 4, pp. 611–622 (1977).

————. *Sakamoto Ryōma and the Meiji Restoration.* Princeton: Princeton University Press, 1961.

———— and Gilbert Rozman. "Overview," in Jansen and Rozman, eds., *Japan in Transition from Tokugawa to Meiji.* Princeton: Princeton University Press, 1985.

Jiyūtō shi, comp. Itagaki Taisuke. 2 vols. Tokyo: Gosharō, 1919.

(Kadokawa) Nihonshi jiten, ed. Takayanagi Mitsutoshi and Takeuchi Rizō. Tokyo: Kadokawa Shoten, 1966.

Kaetsunō ishin kinnō shiryaku, ed. Nakada Takayoshi. Tokyo: Kaetsunō Ishin Kinnōka Hyōshō Kai, 1930.

Kaga han shiryō, ed. Heki Ken et al. 16 vols. Kanazawa: Maeda Ke, 1929–1943.

Kaga han shiryō, hanmatsu hen, ed. Heki Ken. 2 vols. Kanazawa: Maeda Ikutoku Kai, 1958.

(Kaga han tomura yaku) Ishiguro ke monjo, comp. Ishikawa Ken Toshokan Kyōkai. 3 vols. Kanazawa: Ishikawa Kenritsu Toshokan, 1974.

Kajinishi Mitsuhaya. "Josetsu," in Meiji Shiryō Kenkyū Renraku Kai, ed., *Chiso kaisei to chihō jichisei.* Tokyo: Ochanomizu Shobō, 1968.

Kanazawa jō: sono shizen to rekishi, ed. Kanazawa Daigaku Kanazawa Jō Gakujutsu Chōsa Iinkai Nai *Kanazawa jō* Henshū Iin. Kanazawa: Kanazawa Daigaku Seikatsu Kyōdō Kumiai Shuppan Bu, 1967.

Kanazawa shi shi, gendai hen, comp. Kanazawa Shi. 2 vols. Kanazawa: Kanazawa Shi, 1969.

Kanazawa Shōkō Kaigisho 70-nen shi, ed. Maki Hisao. Kanazawa: Kanazawa Shōkō Kaigisho Henshū Iinkai, 1960.

Kanō kyōdo jii, comp. Heki Ken. Kanazawa: Hokkoku Shinbun Sha, 1956.

Kano Tsutomu. "Peasant Uprisings and Citizens' Revolts," *Japan Interpreter,* vol. 8, no. 3, pp. 279–283 (1973).

Kawahara Hiroshi. " 'Gunken' no kannen to kindai 'chūō' kan no keisei," in Nihon Seiji Gakkai, ed., *Kindai Nihon seiji ni okeru chūō to chihō (Nenpō Seijigaku 1984).* Tokyo: Iwanami Shoten, 1985.

Keizu san'yō, comp. Iida Tadahiko, ed. Hōgetsu Keigo. 18 vols. Tokyo: Meicho Shuppan, 1973–1974.

Kikegawa Hiroshi. *Chihō seido shōshi.* Tokyo: Keisō Shobō, 1962.

———. *Jichi 50-nen shi.* Tokyo: Tōkyō Shisei Chōsa Kai, 1941.

———. *Meiji chihō jichi seido no seiritsu katei.* Tokyo: Tōkyō Shisei Chōsa Kai, 1957.

———. *Meiji chihō seido seiritsu shi.* Tokyo: Kashiwa Shobō, 1967.

Kida Sadakichi. "Meiji ishin go fuken setchi no tenmatsu oyobi sono go no bungō ni tsuite," *Rekishi chiri,* vol. 11, no. 3, pp. 419–427 (1908).

"Ko Inagaki Shimesu kun jiseki gaiyō," comp. anon. Manuscript on stationery of Toyama Shōgyō Kaigi Sho. N.p., n.d.

Kobayakawa Kingo. *Meiji hōsei shi ron.* 2 vols. Tokyo, 1940.

Kobayashi Seiji and Yamada Akira. *Fukushima ken no rekishi.* Tokyo: Yamakawa Shuppan Sha, 1970.

Kobayashi Yasutoshi. "Kaga han Tenpōki hansei no dōkō ni tsuite," *Hokuriku shigaku,* no. 9, pp. 27–39 (1960).

(Kōhon) Kanazawa shi shi, ed. Wada Bunjirō. 14 vols. Kanazawa: Kanazawa Shiyakusho, 1916–1942, reprinted Tokyo, 1973.

Kuranami Seiji. *Hyakumangoku daimyō: Kaga han no seiritsu to tenkai.* Tokyo: Tōgensha, 1965.

———. *Kaga hansei kaikaku no kenkyū.* Tokyo: Sekai Shoin, 1969.

Legge, James. *The Chinese Classics.* 5 vols. Oxford: Oxford University Press, 1893.

Lewis, Michael. "Interest and Ideology in Meiji Politics: Inagaki Shimesu and the Toyama Jiyūtō," *Asian Cultural Studies,* no. 18, pp. 157–176 (February 1992).

Masumi Junnosuke. *Nihon seitō shi ron.* 4 vols. Tokyo: Tōkyō Daigaku Shuppan Kai, 1966–1968.

Mayo, Marlene J. "The Korean Crisis of 1873 and Early Meiji Foreign Policy," *Journal of Asian Studies,* vol. 31, no. 4, pp. 793–818 (1972).

McClain, James L. *Kanazawa: A Seventeenth-Century Japanese Castle Town.* New Haven: Yale University Press, 1982.

———. "Local Elites and the Meiji Transition in Kanazawa," *Asian Cultural Studies,* no. 18, pp. 107–136 (February 1992).

———. "Local Politics and National Integration: The Fukui Prefectural Assembly in the 1880s," *Monumenta Nipponica,* vol. 31, no. 1, pp. 51–75 (Spring 1976).

McKean, Margaret. *Environmental Protest and Citizen Politics in Japan.* Berkeley: University of California Press, 1981.

McLaren, W. W., ed. "Japanese Government Documents," *Transactions of the Asiatic Society of Japan,* vol. 42, part 1 (1914).

Meiji 7-nen fuken bussan hyō, comp. Ōkurashō. Reprinted in *Meiji zenki sangyō hattatsushi shiryō,* vol. 1. Tokyo: Ryūkei Shosha, 1966.

Meiji bunka zenshū, ed. Yoshino Sakuzō. 29 vols. 1927–1930; rpt. Tokyo: Nihon Hyōron Sha, 1967–1970.

(Meiji ikō) Kyōiku seido hattatsu shi, comp. Monbushō Nai Kyōikushi Hensan Kai. 12 vols. Tokyo: Ryūginsha, 1938–1939.

Meiji Japan through Contemporary Sources, comp. Centre for East Asian Cultural Studies. 3 vols. Tokyo: Centre for East Asian Cultural Studies, 1970.

Meiji kenpakusho shūsei, supervising editors Irokawa Daikichi and Gabe Masao, ed. Tsurumaki Takao. 6 vols. projected, 3 vols. published as of 1992. Tokyo: Chikuma Shobō, 1986–.

(Meiji nenkan) fuken tōkeisho shūsei, comp. Yūshōdō Microfilms. Tokyo: Yūshōdō Microfilms, 1963.

Meiji Tennō ki, comp. Kunaichō Rinji Teishitsu Henshūkyoku. 13 vols. Tokyo: Yoshikawa Kōbunkan, 1969–1977.

Mencius, tr. D. C. Lau. Baltimore: Penguin, 1970.

Mikuriya Takashi. *Meiji kokka keisei to chihō keiei.* Tokyo: Tōkyō Daigaku Shuppan Kai, 1980.

Miyazawa Seiichi. "Kaga han sonnō undō to Ansei no komesōdō: ichi 'sōmō' no kōdō no bunseki o tsūjite," in Kano Masanao and Takagi Shunsuke, eds., *Ishin henkaku ni okeru zaisonteki shochōryū.* Tokyo: San'ichi Shobō, 1972.

Mizushima Shigeru. "Kaga han Kaeiki no hansei kaikaku," *Chihōshi kenkyū,* 66 (vol. 13, no. 6), pp. 13–27 (1963).

Morley, James William. "Introduction: Choice and Consequence," in James W. Morley, ed., *Dilemmas of Growth in Prewar Japan.* Princeton: Princeton University Press, 1971.

Naimushō shi, comp. Daika Kai Naimushō Shi Hensan Iinkai. 4 vols. Tokyo: Daika Kai, 1970–1971.

Najita, Tetsuo, and J. Victor Koschmann, eds., *Conflict in Modern Japanese History: The Neglected Tradition.* Princeton: Princeton University Press, 1982.

Nakada Kaoru. "Tokugawa jidai ni okeru mura no jinkaku," *Hōseishi ronshū,* vol. 2. Tokyo: Iwanami Shoten, 1970 reprint of 1938 ed.

Nanao shi shi, comp. Nanao Shi Shi Hensan Senmon Iinkai. Nanao: Nanao Shiyakusho, 1974.

Nihon rekishi daijiten, comp. Kawade Takao. 20 vols. Tokyo: Kawade Shobō, 1964.

Nihon teikoku tōkei nenkan, comp. Naikaku Shokikan Shitsu Tōkei Ka. Tokyo: Naikaku Insatsu Kyoku, 1881–.

Nishikie bakumatsu Meiji no rekishi, ed. Konishi Shirō. 12 vols. Tokyo: Kōdansha, 1977–1978.

Norman, E. H. "The Genyōsha: A Study in the Origins of Japanese Imperialism, *Pacific Affairs,* vol. 17, no. 3, pp. 261–284 (1944).

Oda Kichinojō. *Kaga han nōsei shi kō.* Tokyo: Tōkō Shoin, 1929.

Oda Yorodzu. *Principes de droit administratif du Japon.* Paris: Société anonyme du Recueil Sirey, 1928.

Odanaka Toshiki. "Ōkubo Toshimichi ansatsu jiken," in Wagatsuma Sakae, et al., eds., *Nihon seiji saiban shiroku (Meiji zen).* Tokyo: Daiichi Hōki, 1968.

Ōishi Kaichirō. "Chihō jichi," *(Iwanami kōza) Nihon rekishi 16, kindai 3.* Tokyo: Iwanami Shoten, 1967.

———. *Kindai Nihon no chihō jichi.* Tokyo: Tōkyō Daigaku Shuppan Kai, 1990.

———. *Nihon chihō zaigyōseishi josetsu.* Tokyo: Ochanomizu Shobō, 1961.

Oka Yoshitake. *Kindai Nihon seiji shi,* vol. 1. Tokyo: Sōbunsha, 1962.

Ōkubo Toshiaki. "Bakumatsu no Satsuma hanritsu Kaiseisho ni kansuru shin-shiryō: Satsuma han no 'ippan kakkyo' shugi seisaku no ikkan," *Seiji keizai-shigaku,* no. 150, pp. 21–34 (1978).

Okumura Satoshi. "Hansei no suii," in Wakabayashi Kisaburō, ed., *Ishikawa ken no rekishi.* Kanazawa: Hokkoku Shuppan Sha, 1970.

Ōkurashō. *Fuken chiso kaisei kiyō* (1881), reprinted in *Meiji zenki sangyō hatta-tsushi shiryō,* supplemental volumes *(bekkan)* no. 9, 3 vols. Tokyo: Ryūkei Shosha, 1965.

Ōmori Shōichi. *Jichi sei seitei no tenmatsu.* Tokyo: Zenkoku Chōsonchō Kai, 1928.

Ōshima Mitsuko. "Meiji shoki no chihōkan," *Nihon hō to Ajia* (vol. 3 of the Festschrift in honor of Niida Noboru). Tokyo: Keisō Shobō, 1970.

————. "Meiji zenki chihō seido no kōsatsu," reprinted in Haraguchi Mune-hisa, ed., *Meiji ishin (Ronshū Nihon rekishi, 9).* Tokyo: Yūseidō, 1973.

————. "Ōkubo shihai taisei ka no fuken tōchi," in Nihon Seiji Gakkai, ed., *Kindai Nihon seiji ni okeru chūō to chihō (Nenpō Seijigaku 1984).* Tokyo: Iwa-nami Shoten, 1985.

Ōshima Tarō. *Nihon chihō gyōzaiseishi josetsu.* Tokyo: Miraisha, 1968.

Ōtsuki Hiromu. *Echizen jiyūminken undō no kenkyū.* Kyoto: Hōritsu Bunkasha, 1980.

Pittau, Joseph. *Political Thought in Early Meiji Japan.* Cambridge: Harvard University Press, 1967.

Quigley, Harold S. "Local Government," *Japanese Government and Politics.* New York: Century, 1932.

Redesdale, Lord [Algernon Mitford]. *Memories.* New York: E. P. Dutton, n.d.

Rekidai kenkan roku, ed. Ijiri Tsunekichi. Tokyo: Hara Shobō, 1967 reprint of 1928 Naikaku Insatsu Kokunai Choyo Kai, ed.

Saguchi Tōru. "Gendaishi," in Miyashita Yokichi, ed., *Ishikawa ken no rekishi.* Kanazawa: Hokkoku Shinbun Sha, 1950.

Sakai Seiichi. "Kaga han no kaibō to shomin no dōin," *Etchū shidan,* no. 20.

Sansom, G. B. *The Western World and Japan.* New York: Knopf, 1950.

Satow, Sir Ernest. *A Diplomat in Japan: The Inner History of the Critical Years in the Evolution of Japan When the Ports Were Opened and the Monarchy Restored.* London: Seeley, Service, 1921.

Scalapino, Robert A. *Democracy and the Party Movement in Pre-war Japan.* Berkeley: University of California Press, 1967.

Seinan kiden, comp. Kokuryū Kai. 3 vols. Tokyo: Hara Shobō, 1969 reprint of 1911 original.

Sengoku Yoshihisa. *Ishikawa ken rekidai chōkan monogatari.* Kanazawa: Kanazawa Shinpō Sha, 1928.

Shihō enkaku shi, comp. Shihōshō. Tokyo: Hōsōkai, 1939.

Shimizu, S. "Local Government in Japan," *Fifty Years of New Japan,* comp. Count Shigenobu Okuma, Eng. version ed. by Marcus B. Huish, vol. 1. London: Smith, Elder and Co., 1909.

Shimode Sekiyo. *Ishikawa ken no rekishi.* Tokyo: Yamakawa Shuppan Sha, 1970.

Shimomura Fujio. *Nihon zenshi 9 kindai II.* Tokyo: Tōkyō Daigaku Shuppan Kai, 1968.

Shinbo Chiyoko and Matsubara Shigeru. *Kenrokuen.* Kanazawa: Hokkoku Shuppan Sha, 1972.

(Shinbun shūsei) Meiji hennen shi, comp. Meiji Hennen Shi Hensan Kai. 15 vols. Tokyo: Zaisei Keizai Gakkai, 1936–1941.

(Shinkō) Nihonshi gairon, ed. Hōgetsu Keigo and Kodama Kōta. Tokyo: Yoshikawa Kōbunkan, 1969.

(Shinsen) Dai jinmei jiten, comp. Shimonaka Yasaburō. 9 vols. Tokyo: Heibonsha, 1937–1941.

(Shiryō) Kindai Nihon shi, ed. Kawae Suiho. Takamatsu: Kagawa Shinpō Sha, 1933.

(Shiryō) Kindai Nihon shi, ed. Tsuchiya Giei. Tokyo: Shinbun Shiryo Kenkyū Kai, 1933.

Silberman, Bernard. "Bureaucratic Development and the Structure of Decision-Making in Japan: 1868–1925," *Journal of Asian Studies,* vol. 29, no. 2, pp. 347–362 (1970).

————. "Bureaucratization of the Meiji State: The Problem of Succession in the Meiji Restoration, 1868–1900," *Journal of Asian Studies,* vol. 35, no. 3, pp. 421–430 (1976).

————. "*Ringisei*—Traditional Values or Organizational Imperatives in the Japanese Upper Civil Service, 1868–1945," *Journal of Asian Studies,* vol. 32, no. 2, pp. 251–264 (1973).

Smith, Thomas C. *The Agrarian Origins of Modern Japan.* Stanford: Stanford University Press, 1959.

————. "Ōkura Nagatsune and the Technologists," *Personality in Japanese History,* ed. Albert M. Craig and Donald H. Shively. Berkeley: University of California Press, 1970.

————. "Pre-modern Economic Growth: Japan and the West," *Past and Present,* no. 60, pp. 127–160 (1973).

Sonozaki Zen'ichi. "Seitō no seisui to kensei," in Wakabayashi Kisaburō, ed., *Ishikawa ken no rekishi.* Kanazawa: Hokkoku Shuppan Sha, 1970.

Spaulding, Robert. "The Bureaucracy as a Political Force, 1920–45," in J. W. Morley, ed., *Dilemmas of Growth in Prewar Japan.* Princeton: Princeton University Press, 1971.

Staubitz, Richard L. "The Establishment of the System of Local Self-Government (1888–1890) in Meiji Japan: Yamagata Aritomo and the Meaning of *'Jichi'* (Self-Government)." Ph.D. dissertation, Yale University, 1973.

Steele, M. William. "Edo in 1868: The View from Below," *Monumenta Nipponica*, vol. 45, no. 2, pp. 127–155 (1990).

———. "Political Localism in Meiji Japan: The Case of Yoshino Taizō," *Asian Cultural Studies*, no. 18, pp. 137–155 (February 1992).

Steiner, Kurt. "The Japanese Village and Its Government," *Far Eastern Quarterly*, vol. 15, no. 2, pp. 185–199 (1956).

———. *Local Government in Japan.* Stanford: Stanford University Press, 1965.

———. "Popular Political Participation and Political Development in Japan: The Rural Level," in R. E. Ward, ed., *Political Development in Modern Japan.* Princeton: Princeton University Press, 1968.

Tabata Tsutomu. "Bunkyū-Keiōki ni okeru Kaga han no sanbutsukata seisaku ni tsuite," *Nihon rekishi,* no. 299, pp. 65–92 (1973).

———. "Tenpō-Kōkaki ni okeru Kaga han zaisei to hansai hensai shihō no kōzō," *Shien,* vol. 34, no. 1, pp. 43–65 (1974).

———. "Ueda Sakunojō no Kaga han Tenpō kaikaku kōsō ni tsuite: Han zaisei kaikaku ron o chūshin ni," in Hayashi Hideo and Yamada Shōji, eds., *Bakuhansei kara kindai e.* Tokyo: Kashiwa Shobō, 1979.

Tagawa Shōichi. "Hōkaiki no hansei to sesō," in Wakabayashi Kisaburō, ed., *Ishikawa ken no rekishi.* Kanazawa: Hokkoku Shuppan Sha, 1970.

Takagi Shōsaku. "K. Steiner 'Nihon no fukensei'—Amerika Seiji Gakkai de no hōkoku," *Toshi mondai,* vol. 48, no. 4, pp. 107–116 (1957).

Takase Tamotsu. "Zeniya Gohei kō," *Nihon rekishi,* no. 252, pp. 44–66 (1969).

Takayanagi, Kenzo. "A Century of Innovation: The Development of Japanese Law, 1868–1961," in Arthur Taylor von Mehren, ed., *Law in Japan.* Cambridge: Harvard University Press, 1963.

Tanaka Akira. "Ishin seiken ron," in Shigaku Kenkyū Kai and Nihonshi Kenkyū Kai, eds., *(Kōza Nihon shi 5) Meiji ishin.* Tokyo: Tōkyō Daigaku Shuppan Kai, 1970.

———. *Meiji ishin (Nihon no rekishi 24).* Tokyo: Shōgakkan, 1976.

Tokuda Ryōji. "Meiji shonen no chōsonkai no hattatsu," in Meiji Shiryō Kenkyū Renraku Kai, comp., *Meiji kenryoku no hōteki kōzō.* Tokyo: Ochanomizu Shobō, 1958.

Tokuda Toshiaki. "Han taisei kaitai no katei: zaisei tōitsusaku ni taisuru Kaga han no taisho kara kōsatsu shite," *Hokuriku shigaku,* no. 16, pp. 26–38 (1968).

———. "Ishin ni okeru Kaga han no seiji dōkō, *Hokuriku shigaku,* no. 18, pp. 1–13 (1970).

————. "Kanazawa Kawase Gaisha no kenkyū," *Nihon rekishi,* no. 307, pp. 99–120 (1973).

Tomita Kishō sensei den, comp. Tomita Kishō Sensei Kinenzō Kensetsu Kai. Kanazawa: Tomita Kishō Sensei Kinenzō Kensetsu Kai, 1928.

Totman, Conrad. *The Collapse of the Tokugawa Bakufu.* Honolulu: University of Hawaii Press, 1980.

Totten, George O. "Adoption of the Prussian Model for Municipal Government in Meiji Japan: Principles and Compromises," *The Developing Economies,* vol. 15, no. 4, pp. 487–510 (1977).

————. "Japanese Municipal Government under Meiji and Taishō." Master's thesis, Columbia University, 1949.

Toyama kenshi, shiryō hen VI, kindai jō, comp. Toyama Prefecture. Toyama: Toyama Ken, 1978.

Tōyama Shigeki. "Jiyūminkenundō ni okeru shizokuteki yōso," in Sakane Yoshihisa, ed., *Jiyūminken. (Ronshū Nihon rekishi, 10.)* Tokyo: Yūseidō, 1973.

————. *Meiji ishin to tennō.* Tokyo: Iwanami Shoten, 1991.

Tsuji Kiyoaki. "Chihō jichi no kindai kei to Nihon kei," *Nihon kanryōsei no kenkyū.* Tokyo: Kōbundō, 1952, reissued 1967.

Tsukahira, Toshio G. *Feudal Control in Tokugawa Japan: The Sankin Kōtai System.* Cambridge: Harvard University Press, 1966.

Tsunoda, Ryusaku et al., eds. *Sources of Japanese Tradition.* 2 vols. New York: Columbia University Press, 1958.

Uchida Masakaze. "Zen Ishikawa kenrei jū goi ge Uchida Masakaze shi seiden," 1887. Included in *Shūjin zatsuroku,* manuscript in the Kaetsunō Bunko, Kanazawa City Library.

Umegaki, Michio. *After the Restoration: The Beginning of Japan's Modern State.* New York: New York University Press, 1988.

Uno Shun'ichi. "Tennōsei shihai taisei no kakuritsu katei," in Ōkubo Toshiaki, ed., *(Taikei Nihonshi sōsho 3) Seijishi III.* Tokyo: Yamakawa Shuppan Sha, 1967.

Vlastos, Stephen. "Opposition Movements in Early Meiji, 1868–1885," in Marius B. Jansen, ed., *The Cambridge History of Japan,* Vol 5: *The Nineteenth Century.* Cambridge: Cambridge University Press, 1989.

Wakabayashi Kisaburō. *Kaga han nōseishi no kenkyū.* 2 vols. Tokyo: Yoshikawa Kōbunkan, 1970, 1972.

————. *Zeniya Gohei.* Tokyo: Sōgensha, 1957.

————, ed. *Kaga Noto no rekishi.* Tokyo: Kōdansha, 1978.

Ward, Robert E. "Some Observations on Local Government at the Village Level in Present-Day Japan," *Far Eastern Quarterly,* vol. 12, no. 2, pp. 183–202 (1953).

Watanabe Takaki. "Meiji kokka to chihō jichi," *(Taikei) Nihon kokka shi,* vol. 4. *Kindai.* Tokyo: Tōkyō Daigaku Shuppan Kai, 1975.

Waters, Neal L. *Japan's Local Pragmatists: The Transition from Bakumatsu to Meiji in the Kawasaki Region.* Cambridge: Council on East Asian Studies, Harvard University, 1983.

Yamagata Aritomo. "Chōheisei oyobi chihō seido kakuritsu no enkaku," *Meiji kensei keizai shiron,* comp. Kokka Gakkai. Tokyo, n.d.

Yamamura, Kozo. *A Study of Samurai Income and Entrepreneurship: Quantitative Analyses of Economic and Social Aspects of the Samurai in Tokugawa and Meiji Japan.* Cambridge: Harvard University Press, 1974.

Yamanaka Einosuke. *Nihon kindai kokka no keisei to kanryōsei.* Tokyo: Kō-bundō, 1974.

Yonezawa Mototake. *Kaga han no tomura seido.* Toyama: Toyama Ken Kyōdoshi Kai, 1956.

Index

Chōshū: against shogunate, 40, 42; debt, 50; deficit finance in, 35; Maeda Yoshiyasu and, 40–42; peasant militia in, 34; politics in, 32; proposed alliance with Kaga, 49; role in Restoration, 46, 47; samurai population of, 16; uprising of ex-samurai in Hagi, 141, 149

Chūkokusha (Society for Loyal Advice), 73, 104, 168, 212, 218; and Aikokusha, 129–130; branches of, 127–128; ceremony commemorating foundation of, 146–147; and Chisaka Takamasa, 197; compared to other societies, 122–124, 127, 213, 215; and district chiefs, 131; factions of, 130, 146–147; formation of, 122; former activists and Maeda-sponsored economic council, 223, 225; and Iwamura Takatoshi, 199; and Kiriyama Junkō, 130; members elected to Kanazawa assembly, 178; opposes violent action, 153; principles and aims of, 124–127; and Shimada Ichirō, 142–143, 146–147, 148, 151, 160; unconcern about local autonomy, 124, 127, 128

Collective responsibility, 100, 102

Commercialized agriculture, 25

Common property and public works, regulations on, 108

Commoners: businesses in Kanazawa, 72; as commercial facilitators, 31, 35, 36; contributions for education, 78; in Kaga *han,* 25, 26; military training, 34–35; political activities contrasted with ex-samurai, 218, 219, 228; in politics, 174–176, 179, 185; in prefectural assembly, 205; protest movements, 33. *See also* Inagaki Shimesu; Sugita Teiichi

Confucius, 122

Conscription, 250

Constitution, 237, 238, 242, 244

Constitutional government: ideas of Ishikawa district chiefs, 133; rescript of April 14, 1875, 135–136

Council of elders. *See* Kaga *han*

Council of State, 164, 172, 189, 194; abolition of village headman office, 102; ban on vendettas, 67; Decree Number 48, 190, 206; decree on national and prefectural taxes, 84; directive moving prefectural capital, 68; notification on Prefectural Governors Conference, 131–132; notification simplifying

prefectural operations, 82; and report on *minpi,* 109; on status of subprefectural officials, 105

Counties, 61–62, 94, 101, 107, 162, 164–173 passim; in Kaga *han,* 99; prefectural spending for, 192; required expenditures, 190; restored as administrative districts, 165–166, 169; variation in composition of, 172

County chiefs, 166, 168, 173; appointment and supervision by governor, 168, 194–195; oversight of town and village actions, 178; oversight of town and village elections, 171; prefectural assembly petition for election of, 207, 220

County magistrates, 23, 25–26, 99

Court ranks, 15

Daimyo, 4, 6, 7, 15, 87; appointed governors, 5, 49–50; conference of eastern, 39; left alone in early Meiji, 48; and Matsudaira surname, 47. *See also* Maeda Narinaga; Maeda Nariyasu; Maeda Yoshiyasu

Daishōji *han,* 32–33, 46

Daishōji Prefecture, 61, 67–68

Dappan todoke (notification of withdrawal from rolls of samurai), 58–59

Deflation, 191, 197, 230

Delegated business, 14, 87, 102, 105, 108, 112, 164, 172–173, 190, 239, 251

Depression, 199

Diet, 174

Dikes, 111, 113, 131, 173

District assemblies: mandated by Council of State, 131

District chiefs, 66, 79, 94, 101–108 passim; attitudes toward prefectural authority and local autonomy, 139–141; and district assemblies, 132, 139–140, 252; meeting prior to Prefectural Governors Conference, 131–132; opposed by assistants et al., 134–140; petition to Genrōin, 132–134; and popular elections, 139–140; resignation of, 139–140

"Dual nature" of local government, 162, 169, 170, 173

Echizen Province, 61, 172

Education, 77–79, 86–87, 106, 177, 178, 192; funding of, 78, 110–113 passim, 204;

Harvard East Asian Monographs

69. Eric Widmer, *The Russian Ecclesiastical Mission in Peking during the Eighteenth Century*

70. Charlton M. Lewis, *Prologue to the Chinese Revolution: The Transformation of Ideas and Institutions in Hunan Province, 1891–1907*

71. Preston Torbert, *The Ch'ing Imperial Household Department: A Study of its Organization and Principal Functions, 1662–1796*

72. Paul A. Cohen and John E. Schrecker, eds., *Reform in Nineteenth-Century China*

73. Jon Sigurdson, *Rural Industrialism in China*

74. Kang Chao, *The Development of Cotton Textile Production in China*

75. Valentin Rabe, *The Home Base of American China Missions, 1880–1920*

76. Sarasin Viraphol, *Tribute and Profit: Sino-Siamese Trade, 1652–1853*

77. Ch'i-ch'ing Hsiao, *The Military Establishment of the Yuan Dynasty*

78. Meishi Tsai, *Contemporary Chinese Novels and Short Stories, 1949–1974: An Annotated Bibliography*

79. Wellington K. K. Chan, *Merchants, Mandarins and Modern Enterprise in Late Ch'ing China*

80. Endymion Wilkinson, *Landlord and Labor in Late Imperial China: Case Studies from Shandong by Jing Su and Luo Lun*

81. Barry Keenan, *The Dewey Experiment in China: Educational Reform and Political Power in the Early Republic*

82. George A. Hayden, *Crime and Punishment in Medieval Chinese Drama: Three Judge Pao Plays*

83. Sang-Chul Suh, *Growth and Structural Changes in the Korean Economy, 1910–1940*

84. J. W. Dower, *Empire and Aftermath: Yoshida Shigeru and the Japanese Experience, 1878–1954*

85. Martin Collcutt, *Five Mountains: The Rinzai Zen Monastic Institution in Medieval Japan*

86. Kwang Suk Kim and Michael Roemer, *Growth and Structural Transformation*

87. Anne O. Krueger, *The Developmental Role of the Foreign Sector and Aid*

88. Edwin S. Mills and Byung-Nak Song, *Urbanization and Urban Problems*

89. Sung Hwan Ban, Pal Yong Moon, and Dwight H. Perkins, *Rural Development*

90. Noel F. McGinn, Donald R. Snodgrass, Yung Bong Kim, Shin-Bok Kim, and Quee-Young Kim, *Education and Development in Korea*

91. Leroy P. Jones and Il SaKong, *Government, Business, and Entrepreneurship in Economic Development: The Korean Case*

92. Edward S. Mason, Dwight H. Perkins, Kwang Suk Kim, David C. Cole, Mahn Je Kim, et al., *The Economic and Social Modernization of the Republic of Korea*

115. Jeffrey C. Kinkley, ed., *After Mao: Chinese Literature and Society, 1978–1981*

116. C. Andrew Gerstle, *Circles of Fantasy: Convention in the Plays of Chikamatsu*

117. Andrew Gordon, *The Evolution of Labor Relations in Japan: Heavy Industry, 1853–1955*

118. Daniel K. Gardner, *Chu Hsi and the* Ta Hsueh: *Neo-Confucian Reflection on the Confucian Canon*

119. Christine Guth Kanda, *Shinzō: Hachiman Imagery and its Development*

120. Robert Borgen, *Sugawara no Michizane and the Early Heian Court*

121. Chang-tai Hung, *Going to the People: Chinese Intellectual and Folk Literature, 1918–1937*

122. Michael A. Cusumano, *The Japanese Automobile Industry: Technology and Management at Nissan and Toyota*

123. Richard von Glahn, *The Country of Streams and Grottoes: Expansion, Settlement, and the Civilizing of the Sichuan Frontier in Song Times*

124. Steven D. Carter, *The Road to Komatsubara: A Classical Reading of the Renga Hyakuin*

125. Katherine F. Bruner, John K. Fairbank, and Richard T. Smith, *Entering China's Service: Robert Hart's Journals, 1854–1863*

126. Bob Tadashi Wakabayashi, *Anti-Foreignism and Western Learning in Early-Modern Japan: The New Theses of 1825*

127. Atsuko Hirai, *Individualism and Socialism: The Life and Thought of Kawai Eijirō (1891–1944)*

128. Ellen Widmer, *The Margins of Utopia:* Shui-hu hou-chuan *and the Literature of Ming Loyalism*

129. R. Kent Guy, *The Emperor's Four Treasuries: Scholars and the State in the Late Ch'ien-lung Era*

130. Peter C. Perdue, *Exhausting the Earth: State and Peasant in Hunan, 1500–1850*

131. Susan Chan Egan, *A Latterday Confucian: Reminiscences of William Hung (1893–1980)*

132. James T. C. Liu, *China Turning Inward: Intellectual-Political Changes in the Early Twelfth Century*

133. Paul A. Cohen, *Between Tradition and Modernity: Wang T'ao and Reform in Late Ch'ing China*

134. Kate Wildman Nakai, *Shogunal Politics: Arai Hakuseki and the Premises of Tokugawa Rule*

135. Parks M. Coble, *Facing Japan: Chinese Politics and Japanese Imperialism, 1931–1937*

136. Jon L. Saari, *Legacies of Childhood: Growing Up Chinese in a Time of Crisis, 1890–1920*

137. Susan Downing Videen, *Tales of Heichū*

163. Constantine Nomikos Vaporis, *Breaking Barriers: Travel and the State in Early Modern Japan*

165. James C. Baxter, *The Meiji Unification through the Lens of Ishikawa Prefecture*

166. Thomas R. H. Havens, *Architects of Affluence: The Tsutsumi Family and the Seibu-Saison Enterprises in Twentieth-Century Japan*

167. Anthony Hood Chambers, *The Secret Window: Ideal Worlds in Tanizaki's Fiction*